To John Davi

a descendant wh

Basil Wilson Duke, CSA

Basil Wilson Duke, CSA

THE RIGHT MAN IN THE RIGHT PLACE

Gary Robert Matthews

With a Foreword by James A. Ramage

THE UNIVERSITY PRESS OF KENTUCKY

Publication of this volume was made possible in part by a grant from the National Endowment for the Humanities.

Scholarly publisher for the Commonwealth,
serving Bellarmine University, Berea College, Centre College of Kentucky, Eastern Kentucky University, The Filson Historical Society, Georgetown College, Kentucky Historical Society, Kentucky State University, Morehead State University, Murray State University, Northern Kentucky University, Transylvania University, University of Kentucky, University of Louisville, and Western Kentucky University.

Editorial and Sales Offices: The University Press of Kentucky
663 South Limestone Street, Lexington, Kentucky 40508-4008
www.kentuckypress.com

09 08 07 06 05   5 4 3 2 1

Library of Congress Cataloging-in-Publication Data

Matthews, Gary Robert, 1949-
Basil Wilson Duke, CSA : the right man in the right place / Gary Robert Matthews ; with a foreword by James A. Ramage.
p. cm.
Includes bibliographical references and index.
ISBN 0-8131-2375-5 (hardcover : alk. paper)
1. Duke, Basil Wilson, 1838–1916. 2. Generals—Confederate States of America—Biography. 3. Confederate States of America. Army—Biography. 4. Morgan, John Hunt, 1825–1864—Friends and associates. 5. United States—History—Civil War, 1861–1865—Cavalry operations. 6. Lawyers—Kentucky—Louisville—Biography. 7. Legislators—Kentucky—Biography. I. Title.
E467.1.D88M38 2005
973.7'42'092—dc22
2005018317

This book is printed on acid-free recycled paper meeting the requirements of the American National Standard for Permanence in Paper for Printed Library Materials.

Manufactured in the United States of America.

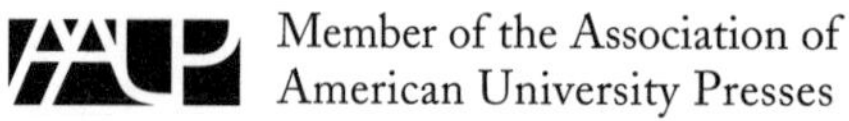

For Mike Courtney and Burl McCoy

Contents

Maps and Illustrations

Maps

Illustrations

Foreword

Gary Matthews contributes new information and significant insights in this first biography of famous Confederate general Basil W. Duke, General John Hunt Morgan's brother-in-law, closest friend, and second in command. Morgan kept no diary, and Duke's *A History of Morgan's Cavalry* is the most comprehensive and valuable primary source on Morgan's Civil War career. Duke focused on Morgan, however, and his narrative underrated his own role. With pathbreaking research in manuscripts and other primary materials, Matthews provides answers to long-held questions and reevaluates Duke's contribution to Morgan's career and to history. Morgan once reported that Duke was invaluable: "wise in counsel, gallant in the field," and always "the right man in the right place."[1] With commendable scholarly restraint and balance, Matthews demonstrates that Morgan was in charge but that Duke perfectly complemented him by developing his irregular hit-and-run raiding style and tactic of fighting dismounted. Matthews offers as one example of Duke's contributions his discovery that Duke wrote a pamphlet entitled *Tactics for Mounted Riflemen.* Duke handled discipline and enabled Morgan to become a folk hero of the Southern people and the primary model for the Confederate Partisan Ranger Act.

Duke's contribution to Morgan's career was so vital that he deserves a share of the credit for the strategic achievements of the command; he helped make Morgan a thorn in the side of Union commanders in the West. In his memoirs, General Ulysses S. Grant declared that, because of Morgan, "every foot of road had to be guarded by troops" and "places he did not attack had to be guarded as if threatened by him."[2] Duke and Morgan and other Confederate raiders diverted over twenty thousand troops from the fighting to protect lines of communication in the rear. The Christmas Raid diverted seventy-three hundred Union infantry from the Battle of Stones River. Morgan was the nemesis of the Union military telegraph in the West and the Louisville and Nashville (L&N) Railroad—he and Duke closed the L&N for a total of four and a half months. The August 12, 1862, raid on Gallatin, Tennessee, closed the L&N for ninety-eight days and gave General Braxton Bragg the initiative for the Kentucky invasion. Grant echoed Northern newspaper editorials during the war when he pointed out that Morgan's strategy was a force multiplier that enabled the raiders to wreak damage on the Union war effort several times beyond what was expected for such a small force.

When Morgan was killed, Duke took charge, restored the command to fighting trim, and led the men to victory over General Alvan C. Gillem, the Union commander of the force that killed Morgan. Duke reported to General John C. Breckinridge, and, in the battle near Russellville, Tennessee, in November 1864, the Confederates routed Gillem's men and sent them running away in panic. Throughout the book, Matthews analyzes Duke's personality and motives and explains why he entered each new passage in his life. For this reader, the characteristic of Duke that stands out is loyalty, which one observes running consistently throughout his life: he was loyal to his family and friends and remained loyal to the Confederate cause to the end of his life. After General Robert E. Lee's surrender, Duke led his men east, intending to continue fighting in North Carolina with General Joseph E. Johnston. He met President Jefferson Davis in Charlotte, North Carolina, and, after Johnston surrendered, escorted Davis in his attempted escape. At Abbeville, South Carolina, Duke participated in the last cabinet meeting, at which Davis proposed continuing the war with irregular tactics. Duke joined others in speaking against the idea. He said that he felt it was his duty to protect the president but that continuing the war would result in needless bloodshed. At the time, Duke was in command of over seven hundred veteran cavalry, and he was one of the most experienced guerrilla warriors alive. One can only imagine what might have happened had he agreed with Davis's suggestion. Fortunately, no one in the meeting agreed with the president, and Davis dropped the idea. In the withdrawal from Abbeville, Duke was placed in charge of the Confederate treasury and funds from several Richmond banks. He handled the gold with great care, avoided embarrassment, and, after the war, published an article denying false rumors and setting the record straight on these events.

Confederate defeat left men like Duke without a country, and many never adjusted to the changing times. On the other hand, Matthews describes how Duke adapted to changes in postwar America, even while remaining loyal to his Confederate heritage. He opened a law practice in Louisville with fellow Confederate hero Major Adolphus E. "Dolly" Richards, a key lieutenant of Morgan's counterpart in the East, Colonel John Singleton Mosby. He changed from a Bourbon Democrat in favor of the old prewar order to a New Departure Democrat in favor of reconciliation with the North and railroad development. When he was forty-five, in 1882, the institution that he and Morgan had damaged so effectively in the Civil War employed him—Duke became the chief lobbyist for the L&N. Writing position papers and applying his reputation as a Southern hero and highly talented raconteur, he defended the special interests of the L&N and opposed government regulation. In the Civil War, he had been in the center of some of the most exciting action, and, from 1890 to 1900, he found himself engaged in one of the great political feuds of the century.

President Theodore Roosevelt considered Duke a high-minded gentleman and appointed him commissioner of the Shiloh National Battlefield. But to William Goebel, president pro tem of the Kentucky Senate and candidate for governor, Duke was the embodiment of evil. Goebel advocated state regulation of the L&N, and he conducted a bitter personal attack on Duke as the railroad's symbol and lobbyist. Goebel and Duke were both extremely intelligent and shrewd, and it was black gum and thunder—played out in public and widely reported for all to see. Matthews brings alive this contest between two giants of public relations and describes how it ended with Governor Goebel's assassination.

As a historian and magazine editor, Duke faithfully adhered to the Lost Cause movement that defended the Confederacy and blamed defeat on superior Northern numbers and resources. Matthews makes it clear that Duke was a leader of the movement for sectional reconciliation that sought to ignore discrimination against African Americans and to sweep aside the goal of equality for black people. Today, we stand firmly on the other side, for equality of opportunity for African Americans and for all people. But there is value in our being acquainted with Duke—he was a spokesman for many in his day—and, knowing where he stood, we are encouraged by how far American society has come. Now we celebrate the progress our nation has made toward equality and individual dignity and rights.

Duke was modest about his own accomplishments and left unanswered several interesting questions about his own life. Matthews fully considers these matters. For example, it has always seemed unusual that Duke resigned from the Kentucky House of Representatives during his first term. Matthews explains that there was no demand for his resignation but that he had begun lobbying for the L&N and personally felt uncomfortable with the conflict of interest. Duke was slim and agile, and writers have described him as short. Matthews discovered a reliable eyewitness account that reported him at five feet, ten inches—about two inches above average in the Civil War. This is an example of many new details in the book. "Black care rarely sits behind a rider whose pace is fast enough," said Theodore Roosevelt;[3] and Duke and his family lived at a fast pace, constantly active in the community. Duke's wife, Henrietta, or "Tommie," was an officer in the United Daughters of the Confederacy, and Duke, with Reuben T. Durrett and others, helped create the Filson Club, today's Filson Historical Society. A newspaper editor asked Duke to write a report on a horse race at a new racetrack south of Louisville, and Duke wrote about the stakes race that became the first Kentucky Derby. Civil War veterans greatly admired him, and he was one of the most sought-after speakers for their reunions. When he stood on the bannered platform and brought to life scenes of camp life and courage in battle, eyes brightened, and shoulders straightened, as the audience of white-haired gentlemen relived their days of youth and vigor, adventure and sacrifice. Duke's presence touched their souls, and his compelling human story lights up these pages.

James A. Ramage
Northern Kentucky University

Preface

I first learned of Basil Wilson Duke in 1975 when a rare-book dealer offered me a copy of *A History of Morgan's Cavalry*. A few years later, I met an old gentleman in Lexington, Kentucky, who, as a child, knew Duke in his last years. He told me many stories about Duke, some of which were true, and all of which captivated my interest. In time, I began to study Duke and discovered that here was a man, a popular Civil War hero, the story of whose fascinating postwar life was virtually untold. No biography had ever appeared, only several short monographs. I found the lack of biography to be disappointing, for surely, I thought, this man deserved to be remembered.

My journey with Duke soon revealed to me a man who was very reticent about his own accomplishments. This, of course, was a major reason for the lack of an in-depth biography. I asked myself how a man who charged with Morgan on horseback and smoked cigars and talked about history with Theodore Roosevelt could be so modest. But, time and again, my research revealed to me that his contemporaries were also impressed with his modesty. Fortunately, Duke interacted with many historically significant people, who were not so reticent. This was particularly helpful when piecing together his elusive postwar career.

It is impossible to separate Duke's Civil War career from that of John Hunt Morgan without distorting the significance of his military accomplishments. The history of Morgan's cavalry is also Duke's war story, and the two must be told in tandem. A reader would not appreciate all that Duke was able to accomplish during the war without this background. Although the story of Morgan's exploits has been told many times before, it was my intention to ferret through the old glory stories and present an objective historical picture of Duke as a soldier and tactician.

Unlike his Civil War career, Duke's post-1865 career was far more elusive. Much of this elusiveness can be traced to Duke's twenty-year-plus affiliation with the Louisville and Nashville Railroad as its chief lobbyist. These were politically charged years when most of Duke's activities were tied directly to the nuances of state and federal legislation. In writing this part of Duke's life, I felt that it was imperative that the reader understand the complex issues facing Duke as he searched for his own political identity. The Civil War student may not find this part of the story as fast paced as that of the war, but it is certainly important in understanding Duke the man. It is also important in understanding Duke's worldview, which he so candidly expressed in his editorials for the *Southern Magazine.* I believe that the reader will find these editorials to be the most revealing and interesting of Duke's writings.

What follows is more than just a Civil War history. It is an American history. It is the story of one man's long life, of the times he lived in and the impact that he had on the people and events of his day. Basil Wilson Duke deserves that.

Acknowledgments

In writing this book, I have been fortunate to have the assistance of people who were, not only knowledgeable, but also very interested in the subject matter of my endeavor. Foremost, I want to acknowledge the invaluable direction of Mike Courtney of Lexington, Kentucky, who foresaw a need for this book. His knowledge of Southern history, nineteenth-century manuscripts, and special collection repositories was shared with me enthusiastically, at all hours of the day. I also want to thank James A. Ramage and Nathaniel Cheairs Hughes Jr. for their review of the manuscript. Their comments were more valuable than they could possibly ever know. Dr. James Klotter of Georgetown College has my gratitude for his incisive direction as to Kentucky's nineteenth-century political history. Marshall Hier of St. Louis was very helpful on the topic of Missouri on the eve of the Civil War.

I owe a number of people at institutions across the country special thanks too. Jim Holmberg, curator of special collections at the Filson Historical Society, has always gone out of his way to help me on this project. Bill Marshall and Claire McCann of the Margaret I. King Library at the University of Kentucky were extremely helpful. Lynn Hollingsworth of the Kentucky Historical Society directed me to manuscript collections that were extremely helpful. Special thanks to Dennis Northcott of the Missouri Historical Society, James C. Morris of Duke University, Robert Glass of Centre College, Glen Edward Taul of Georgetown College, B. J. Gooch of Transylvania University, Nancy Baird of Western Kentucky University, and Wallace Dailey of the Houghton Library, Harvard University, as well as the staffs of the Indiana Historical Society, the Wilson Library, University of North Carolina, and the Tennessee Historical Society. Rebecca Rice of the Filson Historical Society, Charlene Smith of the Kentucky Historical Society, and Jason Flaharady of the University of Kentucky were all extremely helpful in assisting me in choosing the illustrations for this book. I especially want to thank Jeremy Music of Lexington, Kentucky, for his assistance in creating the maps that have enhanced the Civil War chapters of the book.

This book, as did I, needed some constructive oversight during the final stages of its preparation. I owe much thanks to the University Press of Kentucky and particularly to my editors, Joyce Harrison and David Cobb. I thank my copyeditor, Joseph Brown, whose comments and suggestions were very helpful.

There are two people to whom I owe a special thanks for their persistence in pushing me forward until this book was completed. My special friend Burl McCoy of Lexington, Kentucky, was ever enthusiastic and supportive of my writing this book. Of course, my wife, Dawn Kay Matthews, had to bear most of the unpleasant burdens associated with being married to a writer. Granted they were ameliorated somewhat by her living in Lafayette, Indiana. She has edited the manuscript and put together the bibliography and, in doing so, learned to appreciate Southern history. I thank her so much for her support during this process.

1

The Right Man in the Right Place

THE EARLY MORNING HOURS OF July 19, 1863, at Buffington, Ohio, were foggy and hot as twenty-six-year-old Colonel Basil Wilson Duke and hundreds of other young Kentucky and Tennessee cavalrymen were in the midst of fighting one of the most impressive rearguard actions of the Civil War. Under the command of Confederate General John Hunt Morgan, Duke and his men had been in the saddle for seventeen straight days, riding more than four hundred miles through three states, two of which were north of the Ohio River. Duke, along with Colonel Adam Johnson and fewer than a thousand exhausted Confederate soldiers, held in check a combined force of between six and eight thousand federal troops long enough to permit Morgan and most of his command to escape. When the Union pressure intensified, Duke tenaciously continued to hold his position, allowing Johnson and three hundred of his men to follow Morgan out of the trap. Finally, out of ammunition, Duke and his men begrudgingly surrendered. Morgan and those who escaped with him continued on, penetrating deeper into the Northern heartland than any other significant Confederate force before their capture near the Ohio-Pennsylvania line six days later.

It is hard to imagine a story more interesting than Duke's true-life career during the Civil War. Born into the landed aristocracy of the Bluegrass country of Kentucky, Duke was raised in the Southern tradition that bespoke of both honor and violence. Accepting slavery as a prerogative of the states, and fired by youth, he resented Northern intrusions into what he viewed as the Southern way of life. Nurtured on the rhetoric of Southern nationalism, by the time he moved to St. Louis in 1858, at the age of twenty-one, to begin a career in law, he had become a firebrand of secession. Despite his youth, people gravitated to his leadership, enabling him to assume a prominent role in Missouri's attempt to march into the Southern fold. Traveling south to acquire weapons for the fledgling Missouri secessionists, he met Jefferson Davis for the first time. Duke would cross paths with the Confederate president later in the war, during Davis's flight south from the Union army after the fall of Richmond.

It is, however, Duke's twenty-six-month tour of duty with his brother-in-law, John Hunt Morgan, that is most captivating to students of the war. Morgan became Duke's best friend, and Duke became Morgan's most trusted lieutenant, leading many to believe that Duke was the brains behind Morgan's success. There are many pieces of evidence that would lend truth to such a conclusion. Morgan's failures were certainly more abundant during Duke's absence and his successes more pronounced during his presence. Yet, as is the case with most military drama, things are not as simple as they seem. What is certain is that, largely because of Duke's own efforts, his military prowess has been overshadowed by Morgan's exploits.

Morgan and Duke initiated a partnership that was more deserving of success than either one of them could achieve alone. The charisma and leadership qualities exhibited by Morgan were balanced to perfection by Duke's tactical and organizational abilities. It must, however, never be forgotten that Morgan was the leader and that it was to his standard that the Kentucky and Tennessee boys flocked. But, once they had gathered around the standard, it was Duke who organized that band of haughty blue bloods into an effective fighting force. Duke understood his "boys" well and recognized the limits of their discipline. He, like they, learned on the job. He learned his trade well, and, after Morgan's death, he succeeded to the command, earning his brigadier star in the process.

Duke's appearance and demeanor were well suited to a popular young cavalry officer. The thick dark hair and beard often gave the handsome, sunburned cavalryman the appearance of what one Northern reporter termed a "Spanish bandit."[1] Although Duke was of slight build and medium height, his well-kept uniform and poise in the saddle enhanced his martial bearing. Although he was friendly and outgoing, his courage and sense of command demanded respect from his troops as well as from the enemy. His wit was as sharp as his sword, and, of course, like most Southerners, he was a proponent of the maxim that a good story is always better than the truth.

The Morgan-Duke adventures are well known and will be retold in depth from Duke's perspective in the chapters to follow. Duke's military feats in and around Sumner County, Tennessee, will be emphasized as evidence of his tactical soundness in battle—a soundness somewhat questioned by the action at Augusta, Kentucky. His rearguard performance at the crossing of the Rolling Fork River during the Christmas Raid of 1862 was certainly well handled and a forewarning of a repeat episode at Buffington the following summer. Wounded at Shiloh and the Rolling Fork River, Duke experienced two near-fatal events that professed his courage and endeared him to his men. Yet all these exploits pale in comparison to the Ohio Raid. Even today, on the secondary roads in southern Indiana and Ohio, dozens of historical markers bear witness to the impact of the raid on local history. The raid itself, as Duke admitted later, was of little military consequence. But raids seldom are. They are, instead, the mortar of lore and legend that makes something in all of us want to ride into history with Morgan and Duke.

The season of war did not hamper Duke's heart as he married Morgan's sister Henrietta in June of 1861. Tommie, as family and friends called Henrietta, was a fine match for Duke. Beautiful and intelligent, she endured and fought a war that is often lost in the military exploits of her husband. Giving birth to two children during the war, Tommie lived in Union-occupied Lexington, Kentucky, until she found that doing so was against her best interests. A refugee in her own country, she sought comfort and safety for herself and her children among friends and family in the Deep South. Weathering Duke's wounds and his imprisonment in Ohio, she endured most of the war with scant knowledge of his whereabouts or condition. Finally, in the late summer of 1864, she was able to live with Duke in his field headquarters at Abingdon, Virginia.

The Ohio Raid ended with the beginning of thirteen months of captivity for Duke. This was an experience that tested his mettle sure as any shot fired at him in the heat of battle. Confined and humiliated, he learned to cope with disappointment and defeat. Still, the Duke family, which had maintained strong ties with the North, made sure that he was not wanting to any great degree during his imprisonment.

Duke rejoined John Hunt Morgan in August 1864 only days before Morgan was killed by a Yankee cavalryman in Greeneville, Tennessee. By this time, Duke was resigned. Even the promotion to brigadier general and the assumption of what was left of Morgan's command did not dissuade him from recognizing the inevitable outcome of the war. Nonetheless, he took over Morgan's beleaguered command and tenaciously employed his organizational skills to instill an esprit de corps in the unit. Under the command of John C. Breckinridge, Duke performed well in the battles that occurred that fall in southwestern Virginia.

The end of winter in 1865 presaged the end of the Confederacy that spring. Marching with other units from southwestern Virginia, Duke's now-horseless troops headed east, hoping to unite with Lee's Army of Northern Virginia as it retreated west from Richmond. It was not long before Duke and his men heard of Lee's surrender. Undaunted, Duke refused surrender, believing that it was his duty to continue to fight as long as Joseph Johnston's army was still in the field. Duke's men, now mounted on mules, overwhelmingly supported his decision and followed him into North Carolina. It was here that Duke crossed paths with Jefferson Davis once again. Davis was intent on carrying on the war and had planned to reach the Army of the Trans-Mississippi for that purpose. Duke and his men, remounted on horses, joined several other cavalry units as an escort for Davis and members of his cabinet. It was not long before Duke saw the error in carrying the war on any further. He, along with the other field officers in the escort, tried to convince Davis of the futility of further resistance and the harm that it would cause. In the end, Davis acquiesced to his officers' advice and rode west, thinking of escape, as Duke assumed the responsibility of protecting the Confederate gold until its disbursement.

The Civil War was not all adventure and dashing cavalry engagements, as the histories of men like Morgan and Duke might make it appear. It was also the story of people, and Kentuckians in particular, who were torn apart by the violent nature and consequences of a war of brother against brother. These were terrible times, and, wherever soldiers went, the populace suffered. It was the story as well of military occupations, of disenfranchisement for some Kentuckians and freedom for others. These were times when raids took on a political as well as a military significance. All this would haunt veterans, such as Duke, in the life that followed the war.

The Civil War certainly was the apogee of Duke's life, and it was his intent that it not be forgotten. Written within two years of war's end, Duke's *A History of Morgan's Cavalry* was one of the first books to immortalize the "Lost Cause." Depicting a gallant band of Southerners, surviving on their wits and off the countryside, the story unfolds as a fight against impossible odds. Eulogies such as this would dominate Duke's postwar writing and speaking career. His own wit and charm would propel him to the status of one of Kentucky's most popular raconteurs, a feat, by Kentucky standards, of no small consequence.

Try as he might, Duke was not a great success as a lawyer in postwar Kentucky. He moved to Louisville in 1868 and worked hard at his profession, but he was always looking for more secure forms of employment. Duke seems to have been ill suited to the often dry and frustrating aspects of the practice of law. His life had been one great adventure, and, like many veterans, he found it difficult to thrive in an often mundane and sedentary profession. Finally, after nearly twenty years of struggling to build a law practice, Duke joined the legal staff of the Louisville and Nashville (L&N) Railroad.

Most notable about Duke's tenure with the L&N was the role he played as the railroad's chief lobbyist. His background as a Confederate general, in tandem with his rhetorical skills, made him very successful, albeit in some circles notorious, as a representative of the L&N in the political arena. This aspect of Duke's life is somewhat complicated. One wonders, with some justification, whether the character of his employment compromised his ethical standards. In order to belie the more unsavory aspects of his behind-the-scenes machinations, Duke positioned himself as an early proponent of sectional reconciliation and Henry Watterson's "New Departure" economic policies. Perhaps he, like many of that era, viewed his contributions as no more than business as usual. Whatever his motivations, Duke was a very effective lobbyist.

The years between the Civil War and World War I witnessed an era of political discontent unrivaled in Kentucky history. Although a holder of only minor government offices, Duke played a prominent role within the dominant Democratic Party.

Bourbon Democrats ruled Kentucky for over thirty years, setting a pattern of political dominance eagerly adopted by all Southern states after Reconstruction. Duke thrived in this environment and soon became a powerful member of the party's inner circle. In time, however, he grew disenchanted with the direction the party was taking and openly opposed several Democratic candidates for governor.

The combination of politics and the railroad proved to be highly combustible during William Goebel's bid for governor in 1900. Goebel was an antiestablishment candidate who for years had feuded with Duke and the L&N. In one notable instance, Goebel boldly stood in front of Duke and glared at him while he ate dinner at a Frankfort hotel. Undaunted by Goebel's attempt at intimidation, Duke finished dinner and the next day began to carry a revolver. The feud took on a very personal nature during the campaign as Goebel's polemics ignited Duke's ire more than once. The vote narrowly went against Goebel, but the Democratic-controlled legislature was intent on voiding the election and placing Goebel in the governor's mansion. What followed was perhaps one of the darkest episodes in Kentucky history. Goebel was assassinated just before the legislature was to meet to invalidate the election results. He did live long enough to be sworn in as governor, dying shortly thereafter. His cronies immediately identified the L&N and Duke as suspects in the murder. Although neither Duke nor anyone else associated with the L&N was ever indicted for the crime, for years many people considered them more than innocent bystanders.

It is not in the cigar-smoke-filled back room or at the state Democratic convention where Duke's legacy to posterity can be found. Rather, it is on the bookshelves and in the magazine archives of our nation's libraries. Although it was shortly after the war that Duke quickly authored *A History of Morgan's Cavalry,* it was another ten years before he picked up the pen to address other aspects of his wartime experiences. Most noteworthy of his attempts is the still widely cited *Southern Bivouac* article "After the Fall of Richmond," on the flight of the Confederate government. Several other important wartime articles, including "Bragg's Campaign in Kentucky" and "The Battle of Shiloh," were published in the *Southern Bivouac,* a historical journal, of which Duke later became the editor. As editor, Duke turned the *Southern Bivouac* into a literary magazine before its sale to the *Century Magazine* in 1886. The printer's ink was now in Duke's blood, and, several years later, he took over the *Southern Magazine,* crafting it into a superior literary journal. Of particular interest are the series of editorials he wrote for it. The fact that these editorials address so many different issues brings the reader to an understanding of Duke's worldview. Unfortunately for Duke, times were tough, and the magazine was eventually sold, only to meet its demise shortly thereafter.

One measure of a man's character and the esteem in which he is held is the number and quality of his friendships. There was no "exaggerated ego" to be found in Basil Duke's personality. Instead, a wonderful wit and pleasant charm, in combination with a gentle modesty, endeared Duke to many people. Yet he was a man of conviction and not one to be trifled with. These were qualities that earned him more than his share of respect from friend and foe alike.

Duke possessed an impressive catalog of close friends, but no friend quite so distinctive as Theodore Roosevelt. The friendship began in the 1880s when Roosevelt was in Louisville attending to research for a book he was writing on the West. Duke was a frequent visitor to the White House during Roosevelt's presidency, and the two maintained an avid interest in each other's historical works throughout their lives. There is a story that Duke visited Roosevelt to secure a federal judgeship for a fellow Kentuckian only to learn that the president intended to offer Duke himself the position. Duke graciously turned down the offer. There is another story that Roosevelt visited Duke in the hospital just hours before his death, sneaking up the back stairs to gain access.

A man who maintained a degree of modesty that even his friends found difficult to understand, Duke exemplified the characteristics of both the warrior and the gentleman. He was imbued with the dynamics of a culture that identified him with a code of honor that had become an essential part of his life. And, although hardened by the realities of postwar life, he never lost his love for all things Southern. He often wrote and nearly always spoke in hyperbolic terms about the Kentucky of his youth, drawing sustenance from memory. During the latter years of his life, he authored a series of articles for the regional agricultural journal *Home and Farm.* At the urging of his friends, he eventually assembled these articles and published them collectively as the *Reminiscences of General Basil W. Duke, C.S.A.* This book is an eclectic collection of stories and anecdotes about and reflections on Duke's life. Many of the stories in the book reveal Duke's love for Kentucky and its people, both of which were such an integral part of his complex and eventful life. In many ways, the story of Basil Duke is the story of nineteenth-century Kentucky.[2]

2

The Bluegrass

By LATE MAY, SUMMER HAS come to the Bluegrass, and it was hardly different in 1837. Gray limestone fences defined the boundaries of verdant pastures, while majestic pin oaks spread their limbs from one side of dusty country lanes to the other. Horses and cattle meandered across a landscape more akin to that of England or Ireland than the American South. The end of foaling season having arrived, farmowners eagerly examined each new foal for hints of racing greatness. The young thoroughbreds were still awkward, but, in the hands of the like of James K. Duke, these horses, with their impeccable bloodlines, would lend propriety and distinction to a sport that was to become synonymous with the Bluegrass.

Duke's farm, Richland, just eight miles north of Lexington, consisted of approximately one thousand acres of choice Bluegrass farmland. The original farm was part of a Virginia land grant awarded to Duke's father-in-law, Colonel Abram Buford, for his service in the Revolutionary War. Buford homesteaded the farm, building the beautiful main house in 1791, and, over the course of the next thirty years, developing his land into one of the premier farms in central Kentucky. Duke, having married Mary Buford in 1822, took over the farm after the death of his father-in-law and, by the 1830s, had developed a reputation for fine thoroughbred horses with excellent bloodlines. Duke was one of the most popular breeders and turf men of his day and was a charter member of the Kentucky Association, an organization of Kentucky's leading thoroughbred breeders.[1]

Richland, like most large farms and plantations in the South, dispensed hospitality as a matter of course and pride. James developed a reputation as one of the more exceptional hosts in the Bluegrass. The Dukes took part in the constant interchange of visits between families of the local farms. An early history of Fayette County, Kentucky, described James as "a man of great intelligence and well stored mind" who "was at all times entertaining; affable, polite, manly at all times, of winning presence with a suavity of manner that rather wooed than repelled approach."[2]

That May found Duke's younger brother Nathaniel and his wife, Mary, comfortably ensconced at Richland, having recently moved to Kentucky from Richmond, Virginia. Nathaniel, a career navy officer who was often away at sea for long periods of time, most likely wanted to establish a permanent home for his pregnant wife. It is also likely that he brought Mary to Richland so that she could enjoy the warmth and reassurance of his sister-in-law's presence during her confinement and childbirth. Mary Buford Duke was the mother of ten children and would have been a comforting influence during any woman's pregnancy.[3]

Nathaniel and Mary would have quickly discovered that the Bluegrass region and its people had evolved into a complex society. Lexington had become a cultural and educational center. The city supported a university and a well-read and educated population. The social scene for Lexington's elite was just as charming and demanding as that which existed in other Southern cities of the time. Parties, dancing, and barbecues were especially popular, with none of these social activities lacking at Richland. This male-dominated society also demanded conformity and certain faithfulness to traditional Southern values, including honor and bravery. It was into this atmosphere of wealth, society, and Southern tradition that Basil Wilson Duke was born at Richland on May 28, 1837. He was to be the only child of his parents. The lack of siblings was more than offset by the ten cousins with whom Duke shared his early life at Richland.[4]

Basil Duke's American ancestry was remarkable even by the standards of the Bluegrass gentry. Although he was only a second-generation Kentuckian, his American lineage could be traced to Maryland within a generation of the landing at Plymouth Rock. These early ancestors, like many colonists, tended to be sedentary, living in Maryland and Virginia, raising families, and prospering until the advent of the American Revolution. Kentucky at that time was merely a part of Virginia's distant and isolated western frontier.[5]

In an attempt to bring order to the confusion that existed on its western frontier, the commonwealth of Virginia enacted legislation in June 1781 that resulted in the appointment of a commission to review and settle warrants and land grant disputes. This commission was composed of William Fleming, Samuel McDowell, Caleb Wallace, and Colonel Thomas Marshall, Duke's maternal great-grandfather. The commission members arrived in Kentucky during the late fall of 1782 and immediately began to resolve some of the more complicated land issues. During his tenure with the land commission, Marshall became enamored with Kentucky and made plans to settle his family in the region.[6]

When Kentucky achieved statehood in 1792, the Bluegrass region was well on the way to becoming a thriving agricultural area, with Lexington serving as the hub for commerce and trade. The population of the state was growing rapidly, and Lexington developed quickly to become the state's first commercial capital. Although the traffic on the Ohio River ultimately diverted commerce to Louisville,

Lexington remained the heart of the Bluegrass and attracted its fair share of well-educated professionals and skilled artisans.[7]

The entire region quickly became agriculturally self-sufficient and economically strong, albeit with a dependence on Southern trade, particularly with New Orleans vis-à-vis the Ohio and Mississippi Rivers. A middle- and upper-class gentry composed of large landowners and successful merchants added stability to the economy of the region. This stability was one reason why professionals and artisans were attracted to Lexington very early in the city's development.[8]

The first Duke in America was Richard Duke of Devonshire, England, who made the voyage to Maryland aboard the *Ark* in 1634. Richard, who became a prominent man in the early affairs of the colony, eventually returned to England in 1652 with all but one of his children. His son James decided to remain in Maryland, and family tradition deems him as the father of the Duke family in America. Very little is known of James, who was most likely born soon after Richard's arrival in America. Before he died in 1672, James fathered four sons, including one named James. The second James Duke started Brooke Place Manor, a large plantation in Calvert County, Maryland. He lived a fairly eventful life, being arrested and jailed once for apparently supporting the wrong side in a political controversy. He prospered and, on his death in 1693, was survived by only one son, also named James. The third James Duke, who died in 1731, increased the size of Brooke Place Manor and fathered the fourth James Duke. To this point, the family had been Roman Catholic, but the latest James joined Christ Church Episcopal, becoming the first Protestant in the family. He had eight children through two marriages, with John, born in 1734, being his fourth child. John's third son, Basil, was Basil W. Duke's grandfather.[9]

Dr. Basil Duke arrived in Lexington sometime in 1790. Born in 1766, he had studied and practiced medicine in Baltimore for several years before deciding to move to Kentucky. On reaching Lexington, Dr. Duke enjoyed a successful medical practice, which permitted him to purchase property and become active in the city's development. He was an innovative physician who studied and believed in the advanced theories of his day. In particular, he was a strong advocate of vaccination and one of the first doctors in Kentucky to vaccinate against smallpox.[10]

Several years before Dr. Duke's arrival in Lexington, Colonel Thomas Marshall and his family made the move west from Virginia to Kentucky, settling at Buck Pond, in Woodford County, approximately twelve miles west of Lexington. Marshall, who, during the Revolution, had commanded the Third Virginia Infantry Regiment and, later, a Virginia artillery regiment, was named the surveyor general of the lands controlled by Virginia that had been apportioned for soldiers as a reward for service. John, one of Marshall's sons, opted to remain in Virginia, where he had a flourishing legal practice and a promising political career. In 1801, President John Adams would appoint him chief justice of the U.S. Supreme Court.[11]

Shortly after his arrival in Lexington, Dr. Duke was introduced to the colonel's youngest daughter, Charlotte. Eleven years younger than her suitor, Charlotte was a very attractive match for Duke, offering him youth, wealth, and a connection to one of Kentucky's most prestigious families. The couple fell in love and married in 1794.[12] Duke and his wife, like so many early American couples, raised a large family. The first of their seven children, John, was born in Lexington in 1795. Following his appointment in 1796 to a committee to build an academy in Washington, Kentucky, the doctor moved his family to the town, where daughter Mary was born in 1797. Washington was located about sixty miles northeast of Lexington in Mason County, only a few miles from the rapidly growing Ohio River port of Maysville. The Dukes' new hometown was also experiencing rapid growth and newfound prosperity, the result of the sense of security that had swept over the area following the westward movement of the frontier. Dr. Duke continued to practice medicine, but he also successfully expanded his financial interests by entering the thriving dry goods business. In 1801, he and John Coburn ventured across the Ohio River and laid out Decatur, the first town within the limits of the territory that was to become Brown County, Ohio. In the meantime, the Duke family added a third child, James, who later graduated with a law degree from Yale College. It was love, however, and not law that dictated his future when James married Mary Buford and quickly adapted to the life of a gentleman farmer.[13]

Within a few years of the Dukes' move to Washington, Colonel Marshall also moved to Mason County, leaving his son Louis in charge of the original homestead. Louis was rapidly becoming a noted scholar and educator. Ultimately, his reputation spread from his father's central Kentucky farm to Lexington, Virginia, where in 1838 he was appointed president of Washington College, the predecessor to Washington and Lee University. In the 1850s, Louis returned to Kentucky to become president of Transylvania University.[14]

Through Virginia warrants and land grants, Colonel Marshall acquired extensive property in Kentucky, including some in Mason County. All the Kentucky holdings, including eight thousand acres on the Ohio River, he bequeathed to his daughter Charlotte. The Marshall and Duke families continued to prosper and appeared to have adjusted well to their new homes. During their years in Mason County, Dr. Duke and his wife added four more children to their family: Nathaniel Nelson, Basil W. Duke's father, born in 1806; John Marshall, in 1811; Lucy Ann, in 1814; and Charlotte Jane, in 1817. Unfortunately, Charlotte Duke died in 1817 a few months after Charlotte Jane was born.[15]

Aside from his service record, there is not much written about Nathaniel Duke. He was raised in Washington, Kentucky, along with the future Confederate general Albert Sidney Johnston, his lifelong friend. At the age of sixteen, Nathaniel left home and enlisted as a midshipman in the navy. He was a career officer, achieving the rank of captain before he died in 1850. The lack of a naval war to inspire promotion, the size of the navy at the time, and the general reluctance of the military to be generous with peacetime promotions suggest that Nathaniel Duke's attainment of such high rank can be attributed to his qualities as an officer. Years later, a distant family member remembered Nathaniel and wrote of him as "an accomplished gentleman and gallant officer."[16]

On October 4, 1833, Nathaniel Duke married Mary Curric in Richmond, Virginia. Mary's father, James, was a native-born Scot who had served for some years as a British naval officer before emigrating to the United States, he and his sister having been invited by a childless uncle there to be his heirs. Unlike her new husband, Mary came from a very small family. She had only one other sibling, a sister.[17] By the spring of 1837, Nathaniel had, as we have seen, moved his wife to his brother James's farm, Richland, in Scott County, a move made even more agreeable to Mary by the presence of his sister eighty miles away in Cincinnati.[18]

Soon after moving to Kentucky, Nathaniel and Mary became friends with James F. Wood, a young man who lived in Cincinnati. Wood, who was born in Philadelphia, moved to Cincinnati with his parents in 1827. Over the years, he developed ties of friendship with several Kentucky families, including the Dukes. In 1838, he traveled to Rome to study at the Vatican for the priesthood. On his ordination in 1844, he returned to Cincinnati, where he remained until moving back to Philadelphia in 1857.[19]

Wood enjoyed an especially close relationship with Nathaniel and Mary and was responsible for their conversion to Catholicism sometime between 1844 and 1847. Young Basil remained a Protestant of no particular denomination until his marriage to Henrietta Morgan. At the time of his baptism, however, James Wood stood as his godfather. The relationship between Basil and his godfather became particularly significant during Basil's time as a prisoner of war many years later.[20]

Nathaniel Duke's navy career necessitated his absence from home for long periods, as we have seen. During these absences, Basil was raised by his mother and, like most children, influenced by his environment. Living at Richland with his ten cousins and a socially active uncle, he experienced exciting events and had many opportunities to meet interesting people. In particular, he always recalled the old-fashioned Kentucky barbecue fondly, even writing of such entertainments in his *Reminiscences.* They usually took place on Saturday, and many people were invited from other farms and nearby towns. Preparations generally took most of the morning and early afternoon, and, by mid-afternoon, guests who were not already staying at the main house began to arrive and partake in the festivities. In addition to large amounts of food, there would be appropriate entertainment, such as the customary afternoon shooting match. The barbecue was usually not served until later afternoon or early evening, after the entertainment, but sometimes barbecue and entertainment coincided. The evening usually ended with dancing.[21]

Depending on the time of year, a horse race or two usually took place on Saturdays at the larger thoroughbred farms. Kentuckians had developed an early appreciation and affection for horses, and the Bluegrass farms had been breeding the best horses in the country for years. It was generally recognized by 1840 that Kentucky bred the best horses in the United States. Basil, along with other boys of his age, began to acquire a thorough knowledge of Kentucky-bred horses and their attributes for riding and endurance that was to hold him in good stead in the years to come.[22]

Although Duke recalled Richland and the festive events of his youth vividly in his later years, he rarely wrote publicly about his father and mother, mentioning them only once in his *Reminiscences.* This may be because of their early deaths, his mother's when he was eight, his father's three years later. The Richland that he remembered best would have been the Richland of his young adult years, without his parents.[23]

The South of Duke's youth was adrift on a sea of contradictions. Violence and gentility coexisted "in the same cultural matrix without paradox." A complex set of social mores, latched to the terms *honor* and *tradition,* governed the ethics of the community. To gain acceptance and respect within the community, Duke had no choice but to accept these values and to learn the social skills that were required of a young man who wanted to be considered a well-bred Southern gentleman. Like the landed gentry of the British Isles, most Kentuckians spent a considerable amount of time riding horses. Duke—no exception—became an accomplished rider. He also became proficient with the rifle and, later, the handgun. And, of course, he acquired the customary social amenities. As a contemporary traveler described the type: "A Kentucky planter has the manners of a gentleman, he is more or less refined according to his education, but there is generally a grave, severe dignity of deportment in the men of middle age, which prepossesses and commands respect."[24]

A man's honor played a significant role in Southern society and was upheld at all costs. The uncompromising nature of honor was evidenced by the prevalence of the code duello. This nineteenth-century code prescribed the rules for duels, by means of which gentlemen could honorably resolve their differences. Richland, situated on the Scott-Fayette county line, was historically a favorite site for duels. Its popularity stemmed from the confusion its location caused county prosecutors. These officers of the court were forever having difficulty determining which county had jurisdiction over cases involving duels, which were illegal. Duke's older cousin William used the farm for such a purpose in 1847 when a controversy with the future Confederate general Roger Hanson occurred. The two young men had a disagreement over the hand of the young woman who was to become William's wife. The disagreement was resolved with a duel, during which both participants were wounded, although no one died.[25]

There are few surviving written records of Duke's childhood years. This is probably due to the early deaths of his parents. However, John Castleman, a lifelong friend, remembered meeting Duke for the first time around 1850 when they were both about thirteen years old. Castleman grew up on his family farm no more than two miles from Richland. The boys were introduced when John accompanied his mother on a visit to Richland. When the two boys were left to themselves, Duke took Castleman to a sloping hillside behind his uncle's house. Near the hillside was a springhouse where Duke had hidden a small toy cannon, which was capable of firing live shot. Duke loaded the cannon with powder and salt, and the boys then fired at some of "Uncle Jim's" prized shorthorn calves, grazing near the springhouse. Fortunately, none of the calves were injured. Thus began a friendship that lasted for the rest of Duke's life.[26]

Even a young gentleman must go to school, and there was no lack of educational opportunities for Duke in central Kentucky. The social and cultural development witnessed by the Bluegrass region could not have occurred without a foundation of formally educated people. Many fine universities and colleges—such as Transylvania University in Lexington, Centre College in Danville, and Georgetown College in Georgetown—had been founded in the decades surrounding the Revolution and had become highly respected by the time Duke was old enough to consider attending. Precollege education was another matter. Public education was in its infancy and very disorganized, and college preparatory instruction was for the most part available only at private institutions. Fortunately for young Basil, he had perhaps the most respected educator in Kentucky in his own family. His great-uncle Dr. Louis Marshall was providing precollege schooling for young men in Woodford County. Duke attended Dr. Marshall's school and received his initial experience in organized education. He also attended a private school in Georgetown where the Reverend Dr. Lyman Seeley was the headmaster.[27]

Like most young men, Duke had a restless nature, not caring enough to devote the time necessary to achieve the status of a scholar. This must have frustrated his great-uncle, who had spent a lifetime educating young men. Despite his lack of effort, Duke did, however, prove to be quick and a fast learner. Ultimately, he was not unlike many young men, intelligent but undisciplined. And, under Marshall, he obtained the fundamentals necessary to move on to college. Unfortunately for the researcher, penmanship was not a subject that Duke appears to have mastered.[28]

In the fall of 1853, Duke and his cousin James entered Georgetown College, which was located only a few miles from Richland. Most private schools in the antebellum South were church affiliated, and Georgetown was no exception, being a Baptist-sponsored institution. The year before the Dukes enrolled as students, Dr. Duncan R. Campbell was elected president of the college. This was fortunate both for the college and for its student body because Campbell was an energetic president who maintained and promoted Georgetown's status in the academic community during the rest of the decade and the turbulent years ahead.[29]

When Duke entered Georgetown, its curriculum had evolved in such a way that it offered three distinct areas of study. There was the regular collegiate four-year liberal arts course, which Duke chose, a three-year English language and literature course, and a science course. As at most colleges of that era, students were expected to attend chapel daily and church on Sunday. Religion was an integral part of daily life and the educational process. Dr. Campbell was a traditional disciplinarian, and those students who did not attend class or chapel had to explain their absences to the president personally. Discipline was a way of life at the college, and those students who did not adhere to the program were quickly sent home.[30]

The Georgetown College records reveal that Duke registered as a sixteen-year-old student in September 1853. He is listed in the grade book for the first and second semesters, but it is not until the second semester that there are records of the courses in which he was enrolled and corresponding marks of achievement. This would tend to indicate that the first semester may have served Duke's needs in some remedial or preparatory manner. School records for the 1853–54 school year show that Duke took geometry, chemistry, composition, and declaration, among other courses. They also indicate that his grades were lower than most other students'. His, as well as his cousin's, lackluster performance may have been what convinced his uncle to find another college for the two boys to attend in the fall of 1854.[31]

The years in which Duke attended college were tumultuous ones. With the Compromise of 1850, the era of the great triumvirate of Henry Clay, John C. Calhoun, and Daniel Webster had passed. The sectional issues dividing the nation were growing and becoming more problematic with the western migration into Kansas and Nebraska. As a result of the Kansas-Nebraska Act, free soil and proslavery factions were moving onto the prairie to test the nation's resolve over the issue of slavery. At the age of sixteen, and in an academic environment, Duke was certainly aware of these political developments. It is in this type of environment, among peers and friends, discussing heated issues and formulating opinions, that budding political philosophies are nurtured. Duke's political development was most likely influenced by the opinions and beliefs that were shared with him by his fellow classmates. The Georgetown College catalog for the year of Duke's enrollment provides an interesting insight into what type of sectional sentiment existed at the school. Almost all the non-Kentucky students enrolled in the freshman class came from the South, including several from Mississippi and Louisiana. And these students without a doubt expressed the hardening conviction behind Southern grievances with the antislavery North, most likely bolstering Duke's passionate Southern political identity.[32]

Duke and his fellow Georgetown students probably had many interesting hours of discussion concerning the issues of the day. Being a Kentuckian and the nephew of a lifelong Whig, Duke had a natural tendency to be tenacious about protecting state rights. He most likely was a defender of slavery, at least to the extent of each state's right to self-determination as to whether the institution would be permitted within its borders. Duke, like most Kentuckians, may have insisted on the preservation of the Union, a legacy that he could have inherited from his uncle or, perhaps, from the Kentucky icon Henry Clay. Although these positions seem inconsistent, they are easily reconciled when the mid-nineteenth-century Kentuckian's love for both his state and his country is taken into consideration.[33]

It is not difficult to understand why its historically strong Southern attachments influenced the state during the sectional arguments of the 1850s. Kentucky was a slave state, its population was primarily Southern in origin, and it had strong economic and cultural connections with the South. Furthermore, Kentucky's northern border, the Ohio River, had always been a natural boundary between North and South. Yet most Kentuckians realized that their state was different from the other Southern states in that, owing to its close proximity to the North, a growing number of Northerners were settling there, a trend dating back to the 1830s and tending to develop Northern attachments. Such conflicting attachments might suggest that, by 1860, Kentucky was neither wholly Northern nor wholly Southern. However, no matter what the official position taken, the state would always have strong ties with the South. This feeling, perhaps more than any other, created the indecision that plagued many Kentuckians in the following decade.[34]

Sectional tensions were exacerbated by the appearance in 1851–52 of Harriet Beecher Stowe's *Uncle Tom's Cabin.* Although the novel was highly successful as a political weapon in the North and in Europe, in the South it tended to temper the enthusiasm of even the most ardent Unionist. It particularly angered Kentuckians because Stowe based much of it on visits to Kentucky, and particularly Garrard County, from what was at the time her base in Cincinnati. Still, in 1854, the breaking point had not yet been reached: "Northern personal liberty laws were obnoxious but many Kentuckians, who lost most of their slaves because of them, were bitterly opposed to secession."[35]

Slavery and the violence of everyday life that existed in Kentucky 150 years ago are difficult for Americans living today to understand—and even more difficult to explain. Racial prejudice was not found solely south of the Mason-Dixon Line. Indeed, Alexis de Tocqueville wrote in the 1830s that it seemed the strongest in those states where slavery had never been known. Although repugnant to today's sensibilities, slavery is a fact of American history. And it must be examined in its historical context as a way of life if we are to assess objectively many of the choices that Duke made and the actions that he took.[36]

Duke witnessed slavery on a daily basis as he grew up on his uncle's farm. Slave labor was suited to neither thoroughbred breeding nor the production of such Kentucky staples as hemp, cereal, and tobacco. Yet Richland, with its more than fifty slaves, was located in a county that boasted one of the largest slave populations in the state. This curious situation was due to the rapid growth rate of the Kentucky slave population and the inability of owners to dispose of excess or unwanted slaves without incurring substantial financial loss. Some Scott County farmers purchased land in Mississippi or Louisiana, where they not only sent their surplus slaves but also lived themselves for part of the winter. Others became "slave poor" owing to the overhead cost of maintaining slaves with little or no work to perform and, whenever possible, sold their extra slaves to out-of-state purchasers. Unlike slavery in the Deep South, the institution was on the wane in Kentucky.[37]

Duke's attitude toward slavery in the 1850s can only be surmised from his actions and later writings, for example, the *Reminiscences* and the editorials for the *Southern Bivouac* and the *Southern Magazine.* He acknowledged in the *Reminiscences* that he had no firsthand experience with slavery in the Deep South but concluded that the institution must have been harsher there than it was in Kentucky. The noted Kentucky historian J. Winston Coleman Jr. wrote: "Slaves of Kentucky, especially those in the Bluegrass, where the yoke of bondage rested lightly, had an instinctive dread of being sold south." And even Stowe admitted in *Uncle Tom's Cabin* that perhaps the mildest form of slavery that existed in the South could be found in Kentucky. More modern thinkers have concluded that the institution was heinous regardless of the degree of degradation. Duke was not a modern thinker, and he, as did most Southerners of his generation, believed that the Northern antebellum writers exaggerated conditions in the Deep South. He made no excuse for the institution and never apologized for its existence. He did, however, admit that it was a good thing that slavery was eliminated. He insisted that the slaves in Kentucky, particularly those owned by his uncle, were well treated. Of course, such statements in and of themselves are a testimony to their own incongruity and cannot ameliorate the deprivations of a system doomed to condemnation.[38]

In the fall of 1854, Duke and his cousin James enrolled in Centre College, located in Danville, Kentucky, approximately forty miles south of Lexington. Centre College's 1890 general catalog is the best source of information on its nineteenth-century students. Duke is identified as a nongraduate who attended the college in 1854. The 1855 catalog also lists him as a member of the junior class, while his cousin James is considered an "irregular." Like the Georgetown College catalog, the Centre College catalog lists students by class and identifies their hometowns. Of thirty-five students enrolled as juniors, seventeen were from Kentucky. Most of the rest were from other Southern states, with just a few from Illinois. The Southern political influence that Duke was exposed to at Georgetown College obviously continued at Centre.[39]

Few of the surviving Centre College records provide any indication of how well Duke performed in the courses in which he was enrolled. There is, however, published in the 1854 catalog a list of courses required to be taken by the junior class. So we do know that Duke was taking at least rhetoric, calculus, political economy, natural philosophy, evidence of Christianity, and moral philosophy (the last two owing most likely to the college's Presbyterian background).[40]

Duke attended Centre College for only one year. During that year he met a young sophomore student from Louisville, Thomas W. Bullitt, who became a lifelong friend, the two bonding both politically and philosophically. Although this friendship did not fully develop until after the Civil War, Bullitt, in his unpublished memoirs, fondly remembered meeting Duke at Centre. In addition to Bullitt, Duke became acquainted with other students at the college, including James B. McCreary of Richmond, Kentucky, W. C. P. Breckinridge of Lexington, and John Y. Brown of Elizabethtown, Kentucky. All would in some sense integrate their lives with Duke's in the years to come.[41]

While Duke was away at Centre, his cousin Patti Duke married a young first lieutenant in the U.S. Army. His name was John Buford, a Woodford County native who moved to Illinois the year Basil was born. John Buford was a career officer and rose to the rank of major general just before his death in 1863. In 1856, Patti's sister Caroline married Green Clay Smith of Richmond, Kentucky, who would also become a major general in the Union army.[42]

As the old Kentucky maxim has it, when politicians are out of office and have nothing better to do, they practice law. There is no reason to believe that, in his youth, Duke wanted to be a politician, but he did have an interest in the law that may have been influenced by his older cousin Basil and his uncle James, who were both lawyers. The only reputable law school in central Kentucky in the 1850s was at Transylvania University. Duke may have decided on Transylvania because that's where his older cousin went—or simply because it was close to home.[43]

Reputable or not, the Transylvania law school, much like the medical school, was in decline at the time. The decline can be attributed to a number of factors, but most likely is that, for many years, a law degree was not a prerequisite for taking the bar exam in Kentucky. Many aspiring young lawyers simply apprenticed with active members of the bar, studying law in the process, and taking the exam when they felt ready. However, as of 1855, Transylvania's law school was still attracting students and conducting classes. The faculty consisted of three professors, including George Robertson, who had a national reputation as a jurisprudence instructor. Robertson was the only remaining professor when the law school finally closed its doors in 1858.[44]

No records exist from the years Duke was enrolled in the Transylvania law school. In fact, there is no written record that Duke actually attended the university, let alone that he received a law degree. However, the earliest biographical sketches published during his lifetime all indicate that he did attend, graduating in 1858. Most noteworthy, in a series of unpublished papers from the 1890s concerning his Civil War experiences, Leeland Hathaway, a Winchester, Kentucky, lawyer and one of Duke's wartime associates, noted more than once that Duke attended and graduated with him from Transylvania's law school.[45]

Morrison Hall, the primary building in which Transylvania held its classes in the 1850s, faced south on Third Street directly across from what is known today as Gratz Park. The area around the park was considered one of Lexington's most affluent neighborhoods. Approximately one block south of the university is a house on the northwest corner of Second and Mill Streets called Hopemont. John Wesley Hunt built the house in the early nineteenth century. When Hunt died, he bequeathed Hopemont to his daughter Henrietta. Henrietta was married at the time to Calvin Morgan, an Alabama businessman with strong commercial ties to Lexington. When Calvin died, his son John Hunt Morgan succeeded his father as head of the Morgan family and caretaker of its business interests. John Hunt Morgan resided with his wife in a house directly across the street from Hopemont. Morgan's mother and several of his siblings, including his younger sister Henrietta, still lived at Hopemont. Morgan, a Mexican War hero, was a well-respected businessman, not only in Lexington, but also across Kentucky and in the neighboring states.[46]

Henrietta, whom Duke would marry in 1861, was affectionately nicknamed Tommie by her family. Tommie was ten months younger than Duke. Contemporary accounts describe her as beautiful, vivacious, and intelligent. The Dukes and the Morgans were both socially active families, and it is probable that Basil had known Tommie for years. When their romance began is difficult to ascertain, but it is hard to imagine that, during his tenure at Transylvania, Duke was not aware of Tommie or that they did not travel within the same social circles.[47]

When Duke graduated from law school, he had to decide where he was going to start his practice. Although Lexington seemed to be the logical choice, there were many reasons militating against it. To begin with, Lexington was overrun by lawyers. There were other Southern cities where Transylvania law graduates were finding better opportunities for a legal career. Duke's older cousin Basil already had a thriving practice in St. Louis, Missouri. St. Louis was a much larger city than Lexington and held greater opportunities for Duke, particularly if he could join his

Henrietta "Tommie" Morgan, the beautiful younger sister of John Hunt Morgan, is shown here in a ca. 1860 portrait. (Courtesy the University of Kentucky.)

cousin's practice. Duke was also impressed by the fact that, with more than 100,000 Kentucky natives living in Missouri, the state's politics and culture mirrored those of Kentucky. The attraction of the big city and a job with his cousin convinced Duke to move to St. Louis, which he did during the summer of 1858.[48]

3

Missouri

IN 1858, FEW AMERICAN CITIES could claim to be as exciting and full of opportunity as St. Louis. Situated at the confluence of the Missouri and Mississippi Rivers, the city had become the purveyor of America's western movement, creating a period of unparalleled economic and commercial growth. When Duke arrived in St. Louis, the city had a rapidly growing population of more than 100,000 people, including many German immigrants who had fled the failed revolts that spread across Europe in 1848. The Germans, in tandem with the established ethnic communities of St. Louis, made for a cultural diversity unique in the Mississippi Valley.[1]

Part of the diversity that attracted Duke was the city's many Southern influences. A large portion of the population originated in Kentucky and other Southern states. Missouri, like Kentucky, was a slave state but, unlike Kentucky, found slavery to be much more suited to its economy, in particular, to the types of crops growing in the fertile lands along the Mississippi and Missouri Rivers. The institution was repugnant to many in the state's large immigrant population, especially the Germans, who had firsthand experience with oppression. The Germans enthusiastically gave their political support to the Union and some form of abolition. This combination of Southerners, Northerners, and European immigrants tended to polarize the political situation, which was already sensitive to the nuances that went along with Missouri's status as a border state.[2]

Duke's older cousin Basil had moved to St. Louis in 1848 after graduating from Yale and receiving a law degree from Transylvania University. He had joined Geyer and Dayton, one of the more prominent law firms in St. Louis. Almost immediately thereafter, waves of immigrants began to arrive and settle in St. Louis, increasing the city's legal business proportionately. After several years of association with Geyer and Dayton, Duke's cousin left to open his own office. He quickly developed a successful commercial practice and for several years was the land attorney for the St. Louis and Iron Mountain Railroad. Like his father, James, he was an old-line Whig with Southern sentiments, but, unlike his younger cousin, he never became politically active.[3]

The younger Duke quickly passed the local bar exam and began his career as a Missouri lawyer. Even though St. Louis was a bustling commercial center, there was stiff competition for a young lawyer trying to build a practice. There is no direct evidence that Duke and his older cousin formed any type of partnership, but most likely the older lawyer acted as a mentor, encouraging and helping his younger cousin on a case-by-case basis.[4]

From the very beginning of Duke's legal career, it was obvious that his attention was held, not by the practice of law, but by politics. The situation in St. Louis tugged at Duke, who found the sectional issues affecting the country and the political atmosphere more confrontational in Missouri than in Kentucky. The undeclared war and civil strife raging in Kansas were influencing the political environment in Missouri. The Northern and Southern factions in Kansas had formed various paramilitary groups, the most aggressive being the antislavery Jayhawkers. The Jayhawkers purposely raided and terrorized proslavery groups in Kansas and even made occasional border incursions into Missouri. Although the border was more than three hundred miles from St. Louis, the brazen attitude of the Jayhawkers infuriated the proslavery faction in the city, including the increasingly truculent Duke.[5]

During the decade preceding the Civil War, militia units were popular, and, as the decade marched toward its end, new units began to form on a regular basis throughout the South. In Lexington, Kentucky, sectional sentiments had become so divided that rival militia groups were formed purely on the basis of ideology. John Hunt Morgan had formed a pro-Southern unit aptly named the Lexington Rifles. This unit would eventually form the nucleus for the Second Kentucky Cavalry, a regiment to which Duke was to become inextricably connected during the Civil War. By 1860, several militia groups had formed and were training in the St. Louis area. Much like the Kentucky militia organizations, the St. Louis units were politically divided. Several units, including the City Guards, had been officially incorporated into the Missouri state militia. The St. Louis brigade of the state militia reflected its Southern sentiment by parading wearing states' rights badges, a fact that did not go unnoticed by the Union sympathizers among the city's population.[6]

In 1859, John Brown's failed attempt to seize the federal arsenal at Harper's Ferry, Virginia, intensified Missouri's concern about a potential slave revolt led or initiated by the Kansas abolitionists. The election of Abraham Lincoln in the following year provided further impetus for an expedition by the St. Louis militia to the Kansas border.[7]

The election of 1860 was a watershed in American political history. The Democratic Party significantly reduced its chance of success when it split on the issue of

State and local militia units grew in popularity during the years leading up to the Civil War. The Kentucky state militia, shown here at a prewar encampment, grew rapidly and was composed of sixty-one companies by the beginning of 1861. (Courtesy the Kentucky Historical Society.)

the treatment of slavery in the territories. Separate conventions resulted in the Northern Democrats nominating Stephen Douglas and the Southern Democrats John Breckinridge. Of course, the Republicans—primarily Northern voters who were adamantly opposed to any expansion of slavery into the territories—nominated Abraham Lincoln as their candidate. Finally, a fourth party, the Constitutional Union Party, hoped to continue to resolve sectional issues through compromise.[8]

The Douglas Democrats in Missouri nominated Claiborne Jackson as their candidate for governor. Jackson's political views were more in line with those of Breckinridge and the Southern Democrats. However, during the election, Jackson did not give the voters any indication of which national candidate he actually supported. On election day, Missouri voters cast their lot with Douglas and the Northern Democrats. Duke at this point was a conditional Unionist who supported states' rights and the South but did not actively support Breckinridge during the election. Douglas's younger brother-in-law, James Madison Cutts Jr., had joined Duke's law firm the previous spring and may have influenced Duke's rapidly evolving political philosophy. Even at this early point in his life, Duke was politically astute. Although he was a Breckinridge Democrat, he supported Douglas, but only for the purpose of blocking Lincoln's election.[9]

Missouri was the only state in the Union where Douglas received all the electoral votes. The Southern Democrats and Breckinridge failed to capture the imagination of the Missouri electorate, receiving even fewer votes than the Constitutional Union Party, which took the second-largest bloc of votes cast in the state. St. Louis County was one of only two counties in Missouri in which Abraham Lincoln received a plurality of the votes cast for president. The election results indicated that Missouri would be far more moderate on the secession issue than had originally been thought.[10]

Claiborne Jackson rode the coattails of the Douglas vote and was elected governor. In St. Louis, however, the large German and Northern vote helped elect a substantial number of pro-Union state legislators, ringing the alarm bell for the city's secessionists. The secessionists and other Southern sympathizers realized that, without a substantial number of proponents of their cause in the state assembly, they would be politically isolated. The significance of these events was not lost on Duke. By now, he was determined to fight, if necessary, to secure Missouri for the Southern camp. To further his commitment, on January 7, 1861, he and four other young men formed a secessionists' organization called the Minute Men. His involvement with an organization advocating secession placed Duke in a dangerous position, particularly if the city's large bloc of Unionists organized and aggressively challenged the Southerners. He needed to organize support for the Minute Men as quickly as possible.[11]

Duke was only twenty-three years old and the acknowledged leader of the Minute Men. For the youthful Duke to have ingratiated himself in such a short time with the Southern community in St. Louis was a compliment to his character. Not only was he a natural leader, but also his outgoing nature and self-confidence endeared him to aristocrat and yeoman alike. His friends were likewise young, ambitious, and ardent proponents of their cause. The intensity of the times was to galvanize Duke's belief in the Southern cause. He was becoming a Southern patriot, a defender of states' rights, and, more than anything else, the protector of a way of life. For a man strongly tied to traditional Southern values, Duke was near the pinnacle of honor. To reach the heights, he would eventually have to fight for those values. And that fight, when it came, would become the embodiment of the Southern cause for Duke.[12]

Once Lincoln was elected, the Southern states began to call for assemblies to determine where they stood on secession. Lincoln had publicly announced that he was not about to destroy slavery where it already existed. The Deep South, however, believed its own fiery rhetoric and was convinced that the new president would eventually outlaw slavery. South Carolina stepped to the fore and passed a resolu-

Although he was only in his early twenties, Basil Duke was a respected leader within the secessionist circles of prewar St. Louis. (Courtesy the Kentucky Historical Society.)

tion of secession on December 20, 1860. Eleven days later, on New Year's Eve, the Missouri General Assembly convened. With no political party having a clear majority, not much was achieved other than the passage of a bill requiring a state convention to determine what, if anything, Missouri should do regarding its status with Washington. Delegates to the state convention were to be elected on February 18, 1861.[13]

During the first month of 1861, the entire nation held its breath as other Southern states passed articles of secession. In St. Louis, it was evident to both sides that whoever controlled the city and the large federal arsenal there could dictate the state's position during the impending crisis. Each side began to train its men for a possible armed confrontation. As Frank Blair's largely German American Union organization, the Wide Awakes, trained vigorously, Duke was elected chairman of the Minute Men. He quickly put his budding organizational skills to work forming the group into five companies and, more important, procuring shotguns and revolvers for his men. Duke relished the challenge of his first command and was not found wanting.[14]

The immediate objective of both the Wide Awakes and the Minute Men was to seize and protect the federal arsenal. Within the walls of the largest arsenal located in the slave states were between fifty and sixty thousand stands of small arms as well as thirty-five to forty pieces of artillery. Although these weapons were of various qualities and vintages, neither side could afford to ignore their importance. It soon became apparent that whichever side controlled the arsenal controlled the city.[15]

The results of the February 18, 1861, election of delegates to the Missouri constitutional convention were dramatic. Not one ardent secessionist was elected to the special convention. It was obvious that, since the fall election, many Missouri voters had either changed their position or moderated their support for the Southern Democrats. Originally, the state convention was to be held in the state capital, Jefferson City. However, the moderates, who were concerned about undue influence from Governor Jackson, were able to change the site to St. Louis. Former Missouri governor Sterling Price was elected chairman of the convention. Price appointed a committee, which concluded in a written report that the state should remain loyal to the Union and hoped that any differences that existed between the two sections of the country would be solved by compromise. This position was very close to that of the Constitutional Union Party and to the policy of consultation, compromise, and peaceful adjustment that the states of Virginia and Kentucky had adopted. The committee also went on record in its opposition to the use of any form of military coercion against the Southern states.[16]

Duke and the secessionists were sorely disappointed with the results of the state convention. In line with his aggressive character, Duke astutely rationalized that the only way for the South to gain Missouri was for the secessionists to act quickly and decisively. On March 3, 1861, the eve of Lincoln's inauguration, Duke planned to stir up some trouble with the Unionists, hoping that it would escalate into a showdown over the arsenal. Duke chose to incite the Unionists by clandestinely hoisting secessionist flags over the courthouse and his headquarters. The flags were intended to defy "the submissionist state convention." Since most of the Minute Men had gathered at their headquarters, the secessionist flag that Duke had raised over the courthouse was immediately removed, without interference, by a custodian.[17]

The headquarters of the Minute Men was located in the Berthold Mansion on the northwest corner of Fifth and Pine Streets, directly behind the courthouse. Over the years, there has been some disagreement as to the design of the flag flying over the mansion that night. Duke remembered that it was a yellow crescent with stars on a green field. Of course more important than the design was what the flag represented. Like a magnet, it drew an angry crowd of Union men to face a determined group of Minute Men, led by Duke, gathered in front of their headquarters. The Union men began to demand that Duke have the flag taken down. Duke had no intentions of backing down. His plan of disruption was unfolding before his eyes. However, when he refused to pull down the flag, only a few fistfights broke out. Since neither group was armed, the fracas did not escalate into the type of disturbance that Duke needed to legitimize the takeover of the arsenal. The next day several of the more moderate Southern sympathizers in town chastised Duke for his flag display, arguing that his actions were impetuous and imprudent. Duke was utterly dismayed by this attitude and felt that, if Missouri's Southern leaders planned to address the crisis with moderation, they would be making a critical mistake. He firmly believed that events required the secessionists to react much more aggressively if their desire was to secure the state for the South. This type of hesitation, Duke later reasoned, ultimately lost Missouri for the Confederacy.[18]

The results of the state convention did not completely convince Governor Jackson that it was too late for him to direct Missouri's political loyalties south. In order to turn the tide, Jackson needed to neutralize the Union forces in St. Louis. Once again, the arsenal was the key to success. Working under the color of state law, Jackson ordered the pro-Southern state militia to encamp, drill, and train next to the St. Louis arsenal during the first week of May. The location of the encampment would permit the militia, should the opportunity arise, to seize the arsenal.[19]

Although Duke's actions on the night of March 3 may have been viewed as imprudent by some Southern sympathizers, others, including the governor, appreciated his audacity and courage. Duke immediately became an important man for the Southern cause in Missouri. On March 23, a bill was passed by the general assembly to create a board of police commissioners for St. Louis. This bill effectively took control of the police away from the mayor and put it into the hands of the commissioners. The bill further authorized the governor to appoint four members to the police commission. Jackson appointed the avowed secessionists Duke, James H. Carlisle, and Charles McLaren and the Southern sympathizer John A. Brownlee. Duke's appointment was obviously very controversial. The Union men in St. Louis strongly criticized it, claiming that Duke was too young and inexperienced to hold such a critical position. The real objection, of course, was that everyone knew that Duke was a secessionist and an instrument of Jackson's political intrigues.[20]

Jackson's next move was both his most clandestine and his most aggressive to date. In late March or early April, he met with Duke and his fellow Minute Man Colton Greene. The governor now realized that, if his plan was to succeed, the state militia had to be adequately armed. By this time, seven Southern states had formed a government, establishing its capital in Montgomery, Alabama. Jackson was aware that the Confederates had seized and taken control of all but a few of the federal installations, including several arsenals, within their respective state boundaries. He asked Duke and Greene to go to Montgomery and meet with Jefferson Davis to request arms for the secessionist cause in Missouri.[21]

Although he recognized the gravity of the assignment, Duke also sensed the adventure that was in store for him and his friend. With Greene, he started out for

Montgomery on April 17, 1861. The two were bolstered by the news that the federal garrison at Fort Sumter, South Carolina, had surrendered after a twenty-four-hour bombardment. President Lincoln had immediately called for seventy-five thousand volunteers from the various states to help suppress what was now termed *the rebellion.* Missouri was asked to furnish four regiments. Governor Jackson indignantly responded to Lincoln's request for troops from Missouri: "Your requisition in my judgment, is illegal, unconstitutional, and revolutionary in its objects, inhuman and diabolical, and cannot be complied with. Not a man will the state of Missouri furnish to carry out such an unholy crusade."[22]

During their journey south, Duke and Greene witnessed and relished the excitement that many Southerners were experiencing during those spring days. They also noted that each state was organizing troops and that no one imagined the war lasting longer than a few short months. The trip south was by railroad through Cairo, Illinois, to Memphis, Chattanooga, and, finally, Montgomery. After arriving in Montgomery, Duke and Greene presented their credentials and were warmly received by Jefferson Davis and his cabinet. Duke, however, recalled that only Judah Benjamin, a brilliant lawyer from New Orleans, appreciated their problems with Missouri's Union element and the difficulties that they faced in bringing the state into the Confederacy. Davis agreed to provide Jackson the weapons and wrote to inform him that several howitzers and siege guns were being shipped for his use against the arsenal.[23]

When Duke and Greene learned that the arms were in the arsenal at Baton Rouge, they immediately left for Louisiana. The commander of the arsenal supplied them with two twelve-pound howitzers, two thirty-two-pound siege guns, approximately five hundred muskets, and a large quantity of ammunition. The two then traveled sixty miles downriver to New Orleans, where they chartered the steamboat *Swan.* As the Baton Rouge dockworkers loaded the cargo onto the *Swan,* Duke and Greene made sure that the guns and ammunition were discreetly stored and covered. There was a tremendous amount of river traffic on the Mississippi, and, if the *Swan*'s cargo was not well hidden, their chances of reaching St. Louis undetected were minimal.[24]

According to his and Greene's plan, Duke would take the railroad north to scout for the location of federal troops and adverse river conditions. This suited his proactive sensibilities much better than sitting on the riverboat and waiting for something to happen. He and Greene agreed that, unless he discovered a problem prior to the rendezvous, they would meet south of St. Louis at New Madrid, Missouri. Duke's trip north was uneventful until he reached Cairo, Illinois, which had just been occupied by federal troops. The troops were new volunteers and possessed little or no concept of military procedures. Duke observed that the Union soldiers were very relaxed and less than vigilant and was convinced that the *Swan* would have no problems when it reached Cairo. However, in Cairo Duke ran into James Casey, the brother-in-law of Ulysses Grant. Casey, also a secessionist, warned him that the purpose of his trip to Montgomery had become common knowledge in St. Louis and that there were people in Cairo who might try to have him arrested as a secessionist. Armed with this information, Duke quickly left Cairo for New Madrid. Before he left, however, he was able to send a letter by a reliable riverboat pilot to the state militia commander, General Daniel M. Frost, alerting him of his pending arrival in St. Louis.[25]

Traveling on the railroad, Duke arrived in New Madrid several days ahead of Greene and the *Swan*. The closer he came to St. Louis, the more cautious and suspicious of strangers people became. He was questioned several times about his reasons for traveling, prompting him to move out of his hotel to a less conspicuous room on the wharf in a dismantled riverboat. The move to the wharf also allowed him to be immediately aware of the *Swan*'s arrival. When Duke checked into his new hotel, the clerk informed him that several people in the bar had asked that he join them for a drink. Duke, not sensing a trap, proceeded unarmed, only to be met in the hall by two men with drawn pistols. He was taken to the bar, where a group of men had gathered. Before anyone said anything, Duke, sensing trouble, bluntly asked the purpose of the meeting. One of the men irately told him that, since his arrival, they had heard more than one story of his reason for being in New Madrid, raising their suspicions of his intentions. He then accused Duke of being a Yankee spy. Realizing the seriousness of his predicament, Duke, never at a loss for words, told the ringleader his real reason for being in New Madrid. The self-styled prosecutor was not impressed, suggesting to the group that they do away with Duke. On hearing this, a young man stood up and vigorously argued the feasibility of Duke's story. The rest had no lust for blood and were looking for an excuse not to kill Duke. They accepted the young man's argument, and Duke was released.[26]

Having learned a valuable lesson, Duke stayed close to his room and boarded the *Swan* as soon as it docked. The rest of the journey was uneventful, and, on May 9, the *Swan* arrived in St. Louis. As soon as it docked at the wharf, Duke and Greene delivered the weapons to a representative from the state militia. Duke quickly learned that, during his absence, Captain Nathaniel Lyon, the federal officer in charge of the arsenal, had distributed weapons from it to Frank Blair's militia while removing most of the balance across the river to Illinois. Lyon and his troops had also occupied the hills surrounding the arsenal. In the meantime, Governor Jackson had ordered the state troops from southwest Missouri to join the militia encampment in St. Louis. The militia had selected a grove of trees on the western end of town for its camp, naming it Camp Jackson in honor of the governor.[27]

Lyon was very outspoken and did not hide his abolitionist sentiments. He viewed the state militia encampment, which he intended to disperse with Frank

Blair's support, as nothing more than a nest of traitors who had gathered solely to upset the political situation in St. Louis. Although the arsenal was now largely a moot issue, the encampment had become a powder keg of potential problems for Governor Jackson. To make matters even more dangerous, General Frost had underestimated the aggressive designs of both Blair and Lyon. Frost had selected a good site for the camp but failed to take the proper defensive precautions. The militia and particularly John Bowen's troops were convinced by their own bravado that each of them could "whip five to ten times their own number."[28]

Lyon attempted to incite a confrontation by sending Frost a written demand that the four cannons used during the militia's expedition to southwest Missouri be returned to the arsenal. Frost refused to comply. The same day, Lyon, disguised as a woman, was driven through the camp by one of his men so that he could personally determine Frost's strength. Lyon then raised the ante, adding to the four cannons the weapons that Duke had just delivered to the militia. Lyon was skillfully manipulating Frost into the proverbial corner, a move that would permit the Union officer to deploy his force of between seven and eight thousand troops against the much smaller militia detachment.[29]

Alarmed by the volatility of the situation, the police commission scheduled an emergency meeting for the night of May 9. Duke, acting in his capacity as a commissioner, attended the meeting. During the meeting, he learned that Blair and Lyon were planning to move on Camp Jackson, possibly as early as the following day. Immediately after the meeting, Duke went to Camp Jackson to warn Frost of a possible attack. Frost nonchalantly brushed off the warning. Duke quickly grasped the situation, concluding that, not just Frost, but also his troops were entirely unconcerned about the situation. Even though the militia had been encamped for several days, the most rudimentary defensive precautions had not been taken. The troops, instead of training, were drinking, romancing, and generally having a good time. Frustrated with the evident lack of concern, Duke decided that his best course of action was to proceed to Jefferson City with his friend Colton Greene and warn Governor Jackson of the situation.[30]

The next morning, Lyon and his troops moved west through the streets of St. Louis toward the militia encampment. When the news of Lyon's approach reached Frost, he suddenly appreciated the seriousness of his situation and the camp's predicament. In an act of desperation, Frost, who now sought to avoid a confrontation at all costs, wrote Blair and Lyon, asserting the legality of the militia encampment, and denying any plans to attack the arsenal. Lyon was amused by the protest—which he ignored. With deliberate confidence, bolstered by his overwhelming superiority in numbers, the federal officer moved toward the militia camp. When Lyon reached the militia bivouac, he quickly positioned his small army on the dominating heights that surrounded the grove. Complying with military decorum, he formally demanded Frost's unconditional surrender, giving him ten minutes to meet the terms of his ultimatum. After taking the entire ten minutes allotted to him, Frost prudently surrendered, stating that he was unprepared to defend himself.[31]

Though Frost and the militia were offered an immediate parole by Lyon, he and his officers refused to take the required oath and, instead, surrendered and were taken prisoner. The enlisted men followed suit and stacked their rifles. The Union troops, made up mostly of German immigrants, lined up their prisoners and positioned a single file of soldiers on each side. They then marched Frost and his men through the streets of St. Louis. In a matter of minutes, crowds gathered on both sides of the street, visibly angry at the sight of the militia being guarded by immigrants. The crowd began yelling insults at the German troops. The yelling escalated into rock throwing. The parade of troops and prisoners was on Olive Street when a scuffle broke out between a soldier and a drunken civilian who pulled out and fired a pistol when the soldier threw him in a ditch. The nervous troops then responded to a command to fire low into the crowd. When the smoke cleared, at least twenty-seven civilians, including a twelve-year-old boy, were dead. Six soldiers died as well that Sunday morning, while seven were listed as wounded, one, it turned out, fatally. It was later discovered that several of the Union soldiers had been shot by their own troops.[32]

When Duke reached Jefferson City, he and Greene made their report to Governor Jackson, informing him of Frost's precarious situation. Duke candidly advised Jackson that Frost needed to either take the initiative or remove his men to safety. During the interview, word of the debacle at Camp Jackson and the tragedy on Olive Street arrived from St. Louis. This electrifying news caused great consternation and generated an immediate response from the general assembly, which was in session. The legislators were not only angered by but also fearful of Lyon's aggressiveness. Laws were passed quickly in an effort to curtail the growing strength of private militia organizations and federal involvement in state affairs. In an effort to ease the governor's concern that federal troops might march on the capital, the state militia began to collect in Jefferson City, within days numbering more than a thousand. Duke was called on to assist Captain Kelly, an ex–British army officer, to train and discipline the militia. Kelly often had Duke accompany him on his nightly rounds or made him the officer of the day. This may have been Duke's first experience with a professional soldier. He was a receptive student and astutely learned the necessity of discipline and the rewards of commanding well-drilled troops.[33]

A rumor soon reached the governor's mansion that Blair and Lyon were marching in full force toward the capital. Duke, once more anxious for action, was ordered to guard the bridge over the Osage River and, if necessary, destroy the structure to prevent it from being captured. The governor then ordered Colonel N. C. Claiborne to take a locomotive as far down the rail line as possible to determine the accuracy of the rumor. Claiborne was further instructed that, if the Union forces were actually advancing, he was to destroy the bridges over the Gasconade and Osage Rivers. When Claiborne reached the Osage River bridge, he repeated his orders to Duke and then went farther on down the line. On reaching Franklin, he found no evidence of either Blair or Lyon approaching. He then returned to the Osage River bridge and instructed Duke once again to destroy it if Blair or Lyon attempted to cross, suggesting various possible methods. Duke himself reasoned that the easiest way to destroy the bridge would simply be to set it on fire. And, to be on the safe side, he did just that, setting alight the western span. As Duke had predicted, the fire quickly spread and destroyed the bridge.[34]

Returning to Jefferson City, Duke asked his commander for a leave of absence to return to Kentucky for his scheduled marriage to Henrietta Morgan. The request was granted, but, prior to his departure, some of Duke's friends, including Asa Jones, the U.S. attorney in St. Louis, learned that he intended to stop over in that city. All were astounded at his audacity and strongly advised him against such a course of action. Jones sent him a message warning that he had been indicted by a federal grand jury for taking the arms from the Baton Rouge arsenal and risked arrest and a trial for treason if he did, in fact, return to St. Louis. This information convinced Duke to change his plans. The next day he started for Kentucky.[35]

The political situation in Kentucky was far less tumultuous than that which Duke had just experienced in Missouri. Life seemed to be the same as always, but beneath this surface calm was a current of concern. The Bluegrass families were strongly attached to Southern values and believed that slavery was a protected state right. Yet most Kentuckians had no desire to leave the Union. Although Duke was perplexed and to some extent annoyed by the less-than-ardent support for the Southern cause in his native state, he should not have been. The previous fall, Kentucky, much like Missouri, had split its votes between the Constitutional Union Party and the Democrats. Although the bulk of the Kentucky Democrats supported Breckinridge, they were astute enough to realize that a split in the Democratic ranks meant a state victory for the Constitutional Union Party. Breckinridge ultimately lost the state to the Constitutional Union Party candidate, John Bell of Tennessee, primarily because the Southern Democrats were viewed as strong proponents of secession in Kentucky. The majority of the state was still faithful to the Union in the fall of 1860, as evidenced by John Hunt Morgan's writing his younger brother that he hoped Kentucky and the rest of the South would give Lincoln a chance as president. Morgan felt that there was no reason, at that time, for Kentucky to leave the Union.[36]

For months after the election of 1860, Kentucky attempted to take the moral high ground, arguing that, as a border state, it was in a better position to understand both sides of the sectional dispute. Conceptually, this attitude permitted the state to postpone the inevitable decision concerning secession. Torn by the divided feelings and loyalties of its members, the state legislature was unable to accomplish anything, causing the state to languish in a political no-man's-land for months.[37]

By the middle of April, the events in South Carolina and Lincoln's demand for troops, including four Kentucky regiments, created a crisis in the state. To Lincoln's demand Governor Magoffin defiantly replied: "Kentucky will furnish no troops for the wicked purpose of subduing her sister Southern states." The governor's action placed Kentucky in a difficult position. For Kentucky's border policy to succeed, war had to be averted. Making one last attempt to avoid armed conflict, the legislature declared that the state intended to remain neutral during the impending crisis. Neutrality was a natural response to the frustration the state felt over the failure of its border policy. This was the atmosphere that prevailed in Lexington when Duke arrived for his nuptials.[38]

On June 19, 1861, Basil Duke and Henrietta "Tommie" Morgan were married at Christ Church in Lexington, Kentucky. Duke married into a large and very close-knit family. His new wife had six brothers, the oldest being John Hunt, who was followed by Calvin, Richard, Charlton, Thomas, and Francis Key. She also had one sister, Kitty, who was soon to marry Ambrose P. Hill, a future lieutenant general and corps commander in the Army of Northern Virginia. Although Tommie's father had died some years previously, her mother, also named Henrietta, was in fine health and a true matriarch.[39]

The Morgans were a family with strong Southern ties, both through blood and through commerce. They never tried to hide their Southern sympathies, and their political inclinations were well known in Lexington. This notoriety was bolstered by the fact that John Hunt Morgan was the commander of the Lexington Rifles. Although Southern in its sympathies, the Morgan family, along with other Kentuckians, was content to stay at home and, if needed, protect Kentucky's neutrality—all, that is, except young Thomas Morgan, who in early July left Lexington to join the Confederate army at Camp Boone, Tennessee. Camp Boone was a recruiting post conveniently situated on the Tennessee-Kentucky border. From this location, it was easy to lure enthusiastic young men from Kentucky into the Confederate army without violating the state's neutrality.[40]

Some historians have speculated that John Hunt Morgan delayed going south to join the Southern army because of his wife, Becky. Becky was an invalid who had been sick for many years. By the time of Duke's marriage, she had only a little more than a month to live. If her illness was a factor motivating the timing of Morgan's decision, her death freed him from any restrictive marital obligations. He, however, like most Kentuckians, waited until September, when there was no longer any hope that Kentucky could maintain its neutrality.[41]

Duke was not so patient. He had made his decision months earlier in Missouri, and he intended to go where he felt he could do the most good. He remained with his young bride for about a month before returning to Missouri. During his sojourn in Kentucky, Captain Lyon had been promoted to brigadier general and was in command of all federal forces in Missouri. The secessionists' hopes of Missouri joining the Confederacy were dashed when Lyon occupied the state capital on June 15, 1861, forcing Governor Jackson and soon-to-be Confederate general Sterling Price to seek refuge in the state's Confederate strongholds. Price reached Lexington, Missouri, where a small army had gathered. After taking command of the army, he evacuated Lexington and proceeded to the southwestern part of the state. On July 5, at Carthage, another small Confederate force defeated a federal contingent commanded by General Franz Sigel. The fight at Carthage was short but decisive. The victory enabled the Confederate units to consolidate under Price, increasing his army to eight thousand men. On July 9, Lyon learned of the consolidation and planned to attack Price at the earliest opportunity. The active military situation in southern Missouri forced Duke to change his travel plans. No longer able to take the direct route to join Price and his army in southwestern Missouri, he was forced to take the longer but less hazardous way through Arkansas.[42]

Immediately across the Missouri border in Arkansas at Pittman's Ferry was a force of several thousand well-trained Confederate soldiers under the command of General William Hardee. Hardee and his troops were as close to Lyon and his army as were Price and his troops. Hardee's encampment thus became Duke's logical destination.[43]

Duke did not reach Pittman's Ferry until July 22, 1861. He still planned to join Price in southwestern Missouri, but a friend, John S. Marmaduke, was more familiar with the military situation in Missouri and strongly discouraged him from making such an attempt. Duke prudently accepted Marmaduke's advice. Marmaduke told Duke that, if he were so inclined, there were some opportunities for him to serve in a staff capacity with one of the many regiments at Pittman's Ferry and offered to introduce him to several of the commanders. Duke's first introduction was to Thomas Hindman, the commander of the Second Arkansas Infantry. Hindman, a Mexican War veteran, was a native of Knoxville, Tennessee. He had moved to Arkansas from Mississippi in 1856. Although elected to Congress in 1860, he refused to take his seat as the wave of Southern nationalism spread through Arkansas. Hindman organized the Second Arkansas and was elected its colonel. The regiment was an unusually large one, comprising as it did seventeen companies, and Hindman appreciated the need for assistance in managing such a large organization. Hindman took an instant liking to Duke and invited him to join his regiment as a volunteer aide. Duke accepted the offer with the understanding that he would be neither given a commission or rank nor officially mustered into the Confederate army.[44]

Shortly after Duke's arrival at Pittman's Ferry, Hardee ordered his army north in accordance with a coordinated plan to advance on St. Louis. Hardee crossed the Missouri state line, advancing as far north as the city of Greenville. In Greenville, Hindman's adjutant, Lieutenant Patterson, became ill, and, at Hindman's request, Duke took over the adjutant's position. Several days later, on August 10, 1861, Hardee's troops learned that General Lyon was killed during the Confederate victory at Wilson's Creek, Missouri. This victory enabled Price and his army to occupy Springfield, Missouri. The Confederates now controlled most of Missouri south and southwest of St. Louis.[45]

Just prior to the Confederate victory at Wilson's Creek, approximately twelve thousand Confederate troops in Tennessee under the command of General Gideon Pillow crossed the Mississippi River and occupied New Madrid, Missouri, and the surrounding area. The objective of this maneuver was to allow Pillow to reinforce Hardee. In theory, a coordinated attack by Pillow's and Hardee's consolidated forces and Price's army should have led to a Confederate victory in Missouri. But Hardee's advance on St. Louis never materialized. He was never able to agree with Pillow on a final plan, and neither general was able to meet up with Price. This was a significant failure for the Confederates in the war. The critical contributing factor was the lack of a supreme commander to control the movement of all three armies. Duke later wrote that the real issue involved Richmond's decision to concentrate forces in Kentucky rather than Missouri.[46]

When Hindman's adjutant returned to duty, Duke became a scout for General Hardee. This duty suited him far better than staff work. Hardee was still intent on capturing St. Louis and ordered Duke on several scouting missions in the vicinity of the city. Duke was now in his element and enjoying every minute he spent on horseback. After several forays, he reported to Hardee that, with two companies of cavalry, he could do a significant amount of damage to several bridges below St. Louis. Hardee concurred and authorized Duke to recruit the two companies from existing commands. Duke was elated at the opportunity and immediately asked permission from Jeff Thompson, the commander of the Third Missouri Infantry, to recruit from his regiment. Thompson, who was something of a character, told Duke that the day before someone else had tried to recruit his Missouri troops into Confederate service. The attempt ended, according to Thompson, when his troops, brandishing fully loaded weapons, chased the man out of camp. Thompson then suggested that he could call his troops for a meeting some distance from their guns to enable Duke to get a head start if they reacted as they had the day before. After listening to Thompson's story, Duke abandoned his recruiting efforts.[47]

Duke's scouting forays were generally carried out with only a handful of men. In particular, Duke discovered two young friends from St. Louis to be especially adept at such missions. These friends were White Kennett and Harry Churchill, both of whom were unattached members of the Missouri state guard. Duke, who had not yet been sobered by the reality of the carnage that war was capable of producing, found the scouting missions to be of interest as well as great fun. Not only were they exciting and relatively free of bloodshed, but they were valuable lessons in the effectiveness of the hit-and-run technique.[48]

Hardee and his army retreated from Greenville on August 28, 1861, and returned to Pittman's Ferry on September 2, the same day that Union forces, under the command of Colonel Gustav Waagner, occupied Belmont, Missouri, a small town directly across the Mississippi River from Columbus, Kentucky. General Leonidas Polk, the Confederate commander in western Tennessee, considered the occupation of Belmont, together with Ulysses S. Grant's demonstrations across the Ohio River from Paducah, Kentucky, to be Northern acts of aggression and, in order to protect his flank, directed a Confederate force to occupy Columbus. Polk's order and the subsequent movement of Confederate troops from Tennessee into Kentucky were viewed by most Kentuckians as a direct violation of their neutrality. The Confederate occupation of Columbus also opened the door for a federal countermove. The Union army quickly crossed the Ohio River and occupied Paducah, Kentucky, and most of the northern half of the state.[49]

The federal advance into Kentucky did not go unchallenged. Jefferson Davis lost no time in ordering additional Confederate troops into the state. General Albert Sidney Johnston, a boyhood friend of Duke's father and the commander of the Confederate Department of the West, his headquarters in Nashville, was in charge of the defense of Kentucky. Johnston attempted to fortify a line across the southern part of the state and ordered General Simon Buckner, another Kentuckian, to occupy Bowling Green, which the Confederates intended to use for their headquarters. Although Johnston had aggressively countered the federal move, he was never allocated a sufficient number of troops to maintain the defensive line that Richmond had ordered established.[50]

The simultaneous Union and Confederate occupation of Kentucky created more than a little confusion. It was at this time that many Kentuckians made their personal commitment by enlisting in one or the other of the respective armies. John Porter, a young man from Butler County, Kentucky, recalled: "Every neighborhood was in confusion. It was not infrequently the case that persons on their way to join the federal army were met by others on their way to enlist in the cause of the South."[51]

When the Confederates returned to Pittman's Ferry, Duke once again considered making an attempt to reach southwestern Missouri. He discussed the idea with General Hardee, who suggested that, rather than going back into Missouri, Duke should go to Kentucky and raise a cavalry regiment. Impressed with Duke, both as a man and as a soldier, Hardee wrote his young friend a letter of introduction to be given to General Buckner when Duke reached Bowling Green, Kentucky.[52]

4

On the Green River

WITH THE END OF KENTUCKY'S NEUTRALITY, Union troops quickly occupied the key cities of Louisville, Frankfort, and Lexington. Almost immediately, the official attitude hardened, and the state's Southern sympathizers found themselves risking arrest and detainment. Although the state's Unionists initially welcomed the federal occupation, it was not very long before many Kentuckians became disenchanted with the government's political policies. In a matter of months, the state became particularly indignant over the suppression of the press and summary arrests of suspected secessionists by Union troops.[1]

Camp Dick Robinson, a federal recruiting and training center, was located only thirty miles south of Lexington. John Hunt Morgan and other local Confederate protagonists were opposed to the camp's existence. The day that Duke arrived in Nashville, September 18, 1861, the Kentucky General Assembly declared for the Union, which legitimized the existence of the camp. The next day, a regiment of federal troops arrived from the camp to occupy Lexington. The regiment bivouacked on the fairgrounds, just south of the downtown district on land presently occupied by the University of Kentucky. Rumors spread through the streets of the town that many Southern leaders, including John C. Breckinridge, would be arrested. When this news reached Morgan, he began to make plans to leave Lexington.[2]

On Friday night, September 20, 1861, Morgan and those men from the Lexington Rifles whom he personally trusted met at the Lexington Rifles armory. Morgan decided, with the support of these men, to take the guns and other useful military gear stored in the armory and ride southwest to Bowling Green, where he intended to join the Confederate army. As several of the men diverted the attention of passersby, the guns and military stores were loaded onto two wagons. The loaded wagons left Lexington and headed west on the Versailles Road. Approximately fifteen men remained and continued to drill and parade for several more hours to give the impression that nothing unusual had occurred. Morgan and his band moved fast until they reached Bloomfield, near Bardstown, some sixty miles southwest of Lexington, where they remained for a week. They then marched for two days, continuing on a southwest course until September 30, when the detachment made contact with a Confederate encampment on the Green River.[3]

While Morgan was on his southbound odyssey, Duke had arrived in Nashville with Hardee's brigade. Tommie was now pregnant, and the anxious Duke wanted to travel to Lexington to see his wife. His friend White Kennett was also newly married and suffering the same pain of separation from his wife. However, Kennett's situation was somewhat more complicated than Duke's. His wife was in St. Louis, where it was deemed too dangerous for him to attempt to visit. Kennett, with Duke's convincing input, reasoned that, if he could reach Louisville, he could at least communicate with his wife by mail. It had already become difficult for mail to travel through the lines, but regular mail service was maintained between Louisville and St. Louis.[4]

With little apparent concern for the Union troops positioned across their planned route, the two left Nashville and headed north by rail for Bowling Green and Munfordville. When they reached Munfordville, Duke met an old acquaintance, Roger Hanson, who was now commanding the Second Kentucky Infantry Regiment. From Hanson, Duke learned that all railroad traffic heading north from Bowling Green terminated at Munfordville. Although the Louisville and Nashville (L&N) Railroad was not damaged past Munfordville, both armies had closed the line at their respective forward positions.[5]

Undeterred, Duke and Kennett were able to ride north on a wagon until they reached Elizabethtown on Sunday, September 22, 1861. They were now only ninety miles southwest of Lexington. From Elizabethtown, Duke expected to travel by railroad to Louisville and then on to Lexington. Elizabethtown was full of constant rumors, the most recent being that of the imminent arrival of federal troops from Louisville. Since Elizabethtown was heavily pro-Southern, such a rumor caused no small degree of anxiety among its citizens. Some of the more aggressive townsmen took matters into their own hands and damaged the rail line running north to Louisville. The net result of this foray was that neither Duke nor Kennett could proceed any farther by rail. Consequently, the two hired a liveryman to take them by wagon the next thirty miles to Bardstown. However, the "exceedingly pious man" would not take his team out on the Sabbath. Duke and Kennett would have to wait until the next day.[6]

The strong Southern sentiment in Elizabethtown convinced Duke, who now had some time on his hands, that it was an opportune time to recruit his cavalry regiment. He had no difficulty arousing the enthusiasm of the town's young men, who were eager to join him. His recruits, however, all had a high opinion of their individual military attributes, considering themselves nothing less than officer material. In fact, on enlisting, most of the recruits demanded to be made captains.

Much to Duke's relief, a local judge came to his rescue and convinced the recruits of the need for each of them to start out as a private. The judge argued convincingly that this would allow them time to adjust and learn the ways of the army so that they would become better captains. Duke's recruiting effort netted him enough men to fill two full companies. As he was preparing the muster roll for his new recruits, a man came running down the street shouting the news that federal troops were marching into the north side of town. The two companies of potential captains dispersed so quickly on hearing this news that Duke gave up hope of ever getting them back together.[7]

Realizing that it was not in their best interests to remain in Elizabethtown for long, Duke and Kennett "took to the woods," leaving on foot. They headed east on a small country road in the general direction of Bardstown. This form of travel was not very agreeable to the young cavalrymen, and the following morning, after spending the night with a local family known to Duke, they returned to Elizabethtown in search of better transportation. When they returned to town, the Union troops paid them little heed. Feeling less threatened, they located the liveryman who the day before had agreed to take them to Bardstown. However, the federal arrival had alarmed the liveryman, and he backed out of the prior day's bargain, claiming that Duke and Kennett could be "rebels in disguise." Attempting to find alternative transportation, the two soon discovered that the presence of the Union troops tempered anyone's interest in moving them north. Their only recourse, they decided, was to walk north, in the direction of Louisville, along the side of the railroad tracks, with the hope of flagging down a northbound train. But first they had to walk through the federal encampment to reach the railroad tracks. Duke was aware that there were several Kentucky regiments in the camp, including one that had volunteers from central Kentucky. He felt that, if he were recognized, it could cause him some trouble. But, having no other options, he and Kennett pressed on. As it turned out, the walk through the camp was uneventful, and the two reached the railroad tracks north of town without any further difficulties.[8]

After they had walked for several miles north along the tracks, they heard a handcar carrying several federal soldiers approaching from the direction of Elizabethtown. It was obvious that the soldiers had seen Duke and Kennett. As the two stepped to the side to let the handcar pass, Duke pulled his hat down over his eyes, hoping to appear nondescript. Kennett, on the other hand, incredulously yelled out at the Union soldiers, asking them for a ride. Stunned by Kennett's audacity, Duke forgot his caution, looked up at the riders, and found himself face-to-face with several Union soldiers who knew him. Two of those soldiers were George Jouett and John Harlan, a future U.S. Supreme Court justice. Much to Duke's amazement, nothing happened as the handcar passed and continued down the tracks. Astonished at their good fortune, Duke and Kennett ran into a nearby field and hid there until they thought it was safe to return to the tracks.

Years later, Harlan claimed that, while he recognized Duke, it occurred to him that Duke was attempting to reach Lexington to be with his new wife. Some of the other Union soldiers, however, wanted to arrest Duke, believing that he was on his way to join the rebel army, and insisted that Harlan stop the handcar and take him into custody. Harlan refused, believing that, once in custody, Duke would most likely be considered a spy and treated accordingly. This was such a close call for Duke and Kennett that they decided to abandon any further attempts to reach either Louisville or Lexington. They turned around and made it back safely to the Confederate lines on the Green River. Duke always remembered what Harlan had done as "an exceedingly generous and kindly act."[9]

When Duke returned from Elizabethtown, not only was Hanson's Second Kentucky Infantry located on the Green River, but so too were several other Kentucky units. Within a week, John Hunt Morgan and the Lexington Rifles arrived from Bardstown. Duke was thrilled to learn that his brother-in-law had come south in command of a cavalry detachment. He immediately joined the Lexington Rifles as a private, but, shortly afterward, the men elected him first lieutenant, second in command to Captain John Hunt Morgan.[10]

Duke was the only member of the squadron who had extensive experience as a scout and he and Morgan the only ones who had any familiarity with cavalry tactics. Duke's practical experience as an adjutant with Hindman was something that Morgan immediately recognized would be helpful as he began to organize his command into a viable fighting unit. Thus began a partnership between Morgan and Duke that lasted for almost two years. Morgan's skill as a cavalry commander, partisan, and guerrilla fighter was to become well known to both sides during the course of the Civil War. The successes that Morgan enjoyed were in large part due to Duke's contributions to the command. The hit-and-run tactics that Duke learned as a scout in Missouri were quickly adopted by Morgan's squadron during its patrols on the Green River. Morgan's type of warfare had not, at this stage of the war, been fully developed. Many of the tactics that he later employed can be traced to operations conducted during his first thirty days on the Green River. This was a dangerous time for Morgan, Duke, and the rest of the men in the command. The squadron consisted of approximately seventy-five men who were unattached irregulars, or, more accurately, guerrilla fighters. Since none had been mustered into the Confederate army, they had no official military status, and, if captured, the federal authorities could easily consider them as outlaws or common criminals and deal with them summarily.[11]

Not even two years after the end of the war, Duke wrote the definitive history of the unit, *A History of Morgan's Cavalry*. More than any other event during the early postwar period, the publication in 1867 of this book helped immortalize Morgan, securing his reputation and his position in history as the quintessential Southern partisan. In time, Duke himself came to be recognized as one of the early proponents of the Lost Cause, and none of his subsequent writings concerning Morgan ever deviated from his original historical analysis of his subject. *A History of Morgan's Cavalry* became the foundation for most subsequent biographies of Morgan. It has only been in the last twenty years that Morgan's most recent biographer, James Ramage, has skillfully articulated a different, less idealized and romantic picture of Morgan's military tactics—as those of a guerrilla fighter.[12]

Whether it was Duke who inspired Morgan to adopt guerrilla tactics is a matter of conjecture. The arguments that Duke used in attempting to convince General Hardee of the advantage of using cavalry to strike behind enemy lines were probably reiterated to Morgan. Morgan understood better than others the effectiveness of such tactics, and they adapted well to his personality. On the Green River, guerrilla warfare was the perfect type of action for a group of unattached cavalry such as Morgan's unit. Morgan's men were independent and aggressive by nature. William T. Sherman respected and feared the Confederate cavalry in the West, writing: "War suits them and the rascals are brave, fine riders, bold to rashness and dangerous subjects in every sense, the best cavalry in the world." Such characteristics made Morgan's men in particular ideally suited to this type of combat. Morgan, a charismatic and born leader of men, soon acquired a flair for this type of warfare.[13]

Morgan, never the disciplinarian, had no need to train his men in strict cavalry tactics since his forays usually involved fewer than twenty men. Instead, the dangerous and exciting hit-and-run tactics that he employed required personal courage and audacity. These were leadership characteristics, which impressed his young men more than his understanding of traditional military regulations. Morgan tended to delegate such less-glamorous aspects of military command, including discipline, to his second in command, First Lieutenant Basil W. Duke. This did not mean that Duke became a martinet in any sense. Morgan's military organization was not structured to permit this to happen. As later events were to prove, a strict military disciplinarian would be unacceptable to these men. Morgan, however, from his Mexican War experience, realized that any effective military machine required an administrative cog in its wheel, and, for the time being, Duke filled that position better than anyone else in the command. And Duke was effective only because the men respected his bravery and aggressiveness in battle.[14]

Duke took his duties as adjutant seriously and was not shy in dispensing penalties, when warranted. One of Morgan's volunteers later wrote that, while on the Green River, the men had strict orders from Morgan not to steal anything from the local residences. Not withstanding this order, some of the troops, who were in need of everything from blankets to cooking utensils, tended to sneak out of camp and engage in a bit of pilfering. One veteran, for example, remembered an instance when his mess sorely needed a coffeepot, Morgan's men still having access to coffee. Once the coffeepot was stolen, it was hidden for a week for fear that Duke would discover it and punish the offenders severely. When the soldiers finally took their coffeepot out of hiding, however, it was only to discover that the bottom was corroded and, thus, useless.[15]

Several weeks later, Duke had his first experience with bored soldiers and alcohol. Civil War field officers were always concerned about the disruptive results of their troops having access to liquor, and Duke was no exception. Morgan's squadron had been pulled back from the Green River and was encamped at Bowling Green, and, except for routine camp duties, the men had no active service responsibilities. The troops became easily bored and were searching for diversions. They quickly located a nearby store, which had a plentiful supply of liquor. After several days in camp, Duke noticed that the men were getting drunk on a daily basis. It did not take him long to discover the source of his problem. Attempting to resolve the matter amicably, Duke secured the proprietor's promise not to sell his men any more liquor. However, within a few days, the troops were once again drunk, forcing Duke to take more drastic measures. He ordered five of his nondrinking men to go to the store under the pretext of being provost marshals with orders to confiscate the liquor. The men loaded the liquor on a wagon and hauled it to a tent at the Confederate camp. The troops soon discovered the liquor's new location, forcing Duke to triple the guard. Within hours of the confiscation, Morgan's brother R. C. (Dick) Morgan, who was then attached to General Breckinridge's staff, came to the camp to warn Duke that the proprietor of the store had gone to see General Johnston to complain about troops stealing his liquor. Johnston apparently surmised that the troops involved were Kentuckians and ordered Breckinridge to take care of the problem. Breckinridge then ordered Captain Keene Richards to search Duke's camp and arrest the perpetrators. That night, Dick Morgan and Duke removed the liquor from camp and returned it to the store. In the morning, when Keene Richards arrived at the camp to arrest Duke, he could not locate the liquor, and, as a result of the lack of physical evidence, the matter was dropped.[16]

While encamped on the Green River, Morgan's men were not always involved in raids or operating behind the federal lines. Sometimes they performed rudimentary military duties, such as picket duty for Colonel Hanson and the Second Kentucky Infantry. During this period when Morgan worked closely with Hanson, he attempted to procure uniforms and arms for his men. Even at this early stage of the war, equipping volunteers for the Confederate army was not an easy proposition. Morgan did the best he could for his men, but, as was typical of most Confederate regiments, their clothing was never uniform. Later, Morgan's men individualized their dress to such an extent that, arguably, very few wore a standardized or regulation uniform. On October 11, 1861, Morgan was instructed to procure horses for his squadron through the Confederate quartermaster. Weapons were another matter. Morgan was asked to obtain his own shotguns, while Colonel Hanson was ordered to purchase rifles for his infantry company as well as for Morgan's cavalry. Sabers were to be furnished by the army when they were available. Finally, Morgan was notified that his squadron needed to be mustered into the Confederate army for perhaps as long as twelve months.[17]

On October 27, 1861, Duke, along with the rest of the squadron, was mustered into the Army of the Confederate States of America. The ceremony took place on the steps of the Woodsonville Church, which was serving as Morgan's headquarters. Major William Preston Johnston, the son of the commanding general, administered the oath. After the ceremony, the men once again elected their own officers, with Morgan and Duke retaining their previous ranks. The squadron was designated as Company A, Second Kentucky Cavalry, CSA. At this time, two more companies, commanded by Captains Thomas Allen of Shelbyville and James Bowles of Louisville, were attached to Morgan's squadron. Accompanying Bowles was Duke's Centre College classmate Second Lieutenant Thomas Bullitt. Bowles's company, composed mostly of men from the Glasgow, Kentucky, area, had been combined with a smaller group commanded by a Lieutenant Churchill. Allen and Bowles were given command of their companies, which were designated Company B and Company C, respectively. Several days later, Morgan and his newly formed squadron were withdrawn from the Green River line and ordered to report to Bowling Green, Kentucky.[18]

The Confederate defense of Kentucky was more theoretical than actual. General Johnston was given the almost impossible task of defending the state along a line extending for several hundred miles from the Virginia border in the east to the Mississippi River in the west. Of particular concern to Johnston was the vulnerability of several points on the Cumberland and Tennessee Rivers. Johnston's engineer had pointed out to him that the forts built in Tennessee to protect the northern approaches on the two rivers would be far more effective if they were moved upstream into Kentucky. There wasn't time to move them, however, and Johnston was forced to play the hand he was dealt.[19]

It was Johnston's intent for Bowling Green to function as a defensive outpost and represent the first line of defense for Nashville, which was located sixty miles farther south. After the Confederate army settled into position, significant military action was at a virtual standstill for the remainder of 1861. However, the Union army had no intention that the war remain static for long. Johnston realized that time was of the essence and that his army could not simply wait for the inevitable

Thomas W. Bullitt attended Centre College with Basil Duke and was a lifelong friend. Bullitt joined Morgan's squadron in the fall of 1861 and was mustered into Confederate service the same day as Duke. (Courtesy the Filson Historical Society, Louisville.)

Union offensive. Lacking the strength for a major blow, he attempted to intimidate the federal troops with raids and a series of aggressive attacks. He hoped that these continuous attacks might confuse the Union command and perhaps even lull them into believing that Johnston's small army was larger than it really was. Part of this ruse involved the use of Morgan's squadron, which made a series of hit-and-run raids behind the Union lines. For a time, it appeared that the plan was working. But Johnston knew that this tactic could not be successful for very long and realized that it was only a matter of time before the Union army started to probe and apply pressure somewhere along his line.[20]

When he reported to Bowling Green, Morgan learned that his squadron had been transferred to General Thomas C. Hindman's brigade, which was camped at Bills Creek, about twenty-five miles from Bowling Green. According to Duke, Hindman and Morgan worked very well together. Hindman, much like Morgan, possessed a very aggressive nature. The general soon appreciated Morgan's personality and military effectiveness, so much so that he encouraged him to raid behind enemy lines. During this time period, the squadron's principal activity was harrassing the Union troops, small detachments attacking the enemy's advance picket lines, a practice that at the time the federal army condemned. These actions rarely involved more than a few dozen troops on either side and were over in a very short time. Such tactics resulted in no major engagements, principally because the Union cavalry stayed on the defensive and seldom ventured out to fight. But, while these raids were largely inconsequential individually, collectively their frequency intimidated the Union troops, which began to report Morgan's squadron in several places at the same time.[21]

Typical of the duties performed by Morgan's squadron was that which he reported on February 2, 1862. On the afternoon of February 1, Duke and his detail discovered a small Union detachment picketed on the north side of the Green River. They immediately dismounted, and, after his men were in position, Duke ordered them to fire at the federal pickets, forcing them to retreat in some confusion. After falling back a short distance, the federal troops regrouped and began to return the Confederates' fire. This exchange continued for some time until Duke, on hearing the rattle of artillery approaching the Union position, prudently decided to withdraw. He and his detail ended by patrolling the vicinity around Woodsonville. These types of forays were an essential part of Johnston's plan to keep the Union army in check. Morgan's squadron was very effective at this game and contributed significantly to Johnston's effort by creating confusion within the Northern ranks.[22]

As Morgan's squadron continued to patrol the Green River, the strategic situation in Kentucky changed dramatically when, on January 19, 1862, a Confederate force was defeated at Mill Springs, Kentucky. Although the battle itself was not large and casualties were only a few hundred on each side, the Union victory forced the Confederates to abandon their front line of defense in eastern and east central Kentucky.[23]

The debacle at Mill Springs shifted the Union army's strategic offensive focus to the Tennessee River. Johnston understood the dynamics of this strategy and sagaciously anticipated an attack by the federal army at Forts Henry and Donelson. These forts were the gateway to Nashville and the lower extremities of the Tennessee River, as far south as Alabama. A federal success there would make Johnston's position at Bowling Green untenable. When the federal attack came on February 6, 1862, Fort Henry was unprepared and was easily captured. Most of the garrison, however, escaped and safely marched the twelve miles to Fort Donelson. On Friday evening, February 7, 1862, Johnston met with Generals Beauregard and Hardee at the Covington House in Bowling Green, and the three decided that Fort Donelson could not be held for more than a few days. They then concluded that the army had to evacuate Kentucky, fall back to a more defensible position, regroup, and fight the next major engagement on ground of their choosing. On February 14, while the Union army occupied the ground around the fort, the federal gunboats attacked the Confederate position but were decidedly repulsed. The next day, the Confederates struck a strategic point in the federal line, punching through and opening the road to Nashville, but withdrew back into the fort and decided that the only course of action was to surrender.[24]

The surrender of Fort Donelson was a complete surprise to many of its defenders, who believed that they had effectively defended the fort and had won a "glowing victory." Over ten thousand Confederates, including many Kentuckians, were captured when the fort surrendered. In anticipation of the abandonment of the fort, Johnston had begun the evacuation of Bowling Green three days earlier to avoid being cut off from the rest of the Confederate army. He realized that, not just Kentucky, but most of western Tennessee was going to be temporarily lost to the federal army until he had time to regroup somewhere south of Nashville and begin his counterattack.[25]

Communication between the Kentucky Confederate soldiers and their families and friends behind the federal lines was undependable at best, and the situation deteriorated as the Southern army withdrew farther south. The most reliable way to have a letter delivered was to arrange for its passage through the lines either covertly or by flag of truce. By early February, six months had passed since Duke had last seen Tommie, now pregnant with their first child. During the first week of February, Duke, under a flag of truce, entered the Union lines with a letter to Tommie that he requested be forwarded. A Union officer graciously took Duke's letter and told him that it would have to be reviewed by the censors. Unfortunately, it didn't pass muster and wasn't forwarded. However, the federal officer wrote a personal letter to Tommie, explaining what had occurred and that her husband was well and in good spirits. Tommie certainly appreciated the Union officer's personal attention to this matter, for his letter survives to this day.[26]

The evacuation of the Confederate troops from Bowling Green and the Green River line was not only demoralizing but also costly for the Confederates. Huge quantities of food stores that were soon to be sorely missed were put to the torch. The Confederates left a path of destruction behind them as they moved south. Their primary target was the L&N Railroad. Most of the rail line between the Green River and Nashville was rendered impassable, and nine depots, the machine shop, and the engine house at Bowling Green were destroyed.[27]

Morgan's squadron was actively involved in this process and doing anything it could to impede the progress of the Union army. During the evacuation, the weather was extremely cold, which seriously affected the troops' ability to perform their duties. For Duke the retreat was more stinging than the weather as it became apparent to him and the other Kentuckians that the Confederate army could be abandoning Kentucky for good.[28]

During the retreat, Morgan's squadron was detached from Hindman's brigade and used principally to assist the rear guard in protecting the retreating army. When Duke left Bowling Green, he was aware that fighting was still going on at Fort Donelson and did not learn of the surrender until he reached Nashville. Johnston, by that time, had decided not to defend the city but to retreat farther south and join other Confederate forces at Corinth in northern Mississippi. However, the people of Nashville assumed that the Confederate army was going to stop and protect their city from the advancing Union army. When they learned otherwise, chaos immediately ensued. Johnston was aware of his responsibility to maintain order in the city as long as possible and ordered the First Missouri Infantry and Morgan's squadron to police the streets until the army had been completely evacuated.[29]

The Confederates anticipated that, with virtually no organized resistance between it and Nashville, the federal army would quickly occupy the city. The Union army, commanded by General Don Carlos Buell, however, moved very slowly and did not push or harass Johnston's army during its retreat from Nashville. It was not until February 23, 1862, that Union troops reached the outskirts of the city. During this time, Morgan's squadron was ordered to remain in the extreme rear of Johnston's retreating army to pick up as many stragglers as possible.[30]

Johnston's army continued to retreat in a southeasterly direction until it reached Murfreesboro, where it stopped to rest and reorganize for the final leg of its march to Mississippi. Morgan's squadron remained in the Nashville area to monitor supply routes and to ensure that the needed supplies were actually getting through the lines. Morgan chose LaVergne, a railroad station midway between Nashville and Murfreesboro, to position his command. From this encampment, the squadron began to clash with elements of the Fourth Ohio Cavalry for the first of many times. The Fourth Ohio soon became a familiar and respected adversary for Morgan and Duke.[31]

On the night of March 7, 1862, Duke was ordered by Morgan to take a detail of approximately twenty men to reconnoiter the area around Nashville. He was to push as close to Nashville as practical and gather as much information as possible about the Union troops in that area. The city was guarded with pickets positioned to detect any Confederate probe into their lines. Duke had to find a way to slip past without being detected. Fortunately, having been active in the area for several days, he was aware of the location of the pickets near the road he intended to use for his approach to Nashville. After riding several miles in the direction of Nashville, he discovered that the pickets had moved. Although he now had to proceed with caution, he was not dissuaded from continuing the mission. He ordered his men to take another road leading into Nashville.

Experience had made Duke wary of withdrawn picket positions, something that usually presaged an ambush farther on down the road. Several times he stopped to question local civilians but gained little insight into recent Union troop movements. Finally, he approached a crossroads approximately four miles from Nashville called Flat Rock. Duke dismounted his men, and, with the help of a local guide, they proceeded on foot toward Flat Rock, leaving five troopers behind to hold the horses. Approximately two hundred yards from the crossroads, Duke's instincts convinced him that the Yankees had set a trap there. It was now getting late, and his options were limited. There was not enough time left that night to find another route to Nashville. Either he could withdraw his troops, or he could engage an unknown number of Union soldiers. Duke, always extremely confident in his abilities, seldom shied away from a potential engagement with the enemy. Thus, choosing the latter option, he quickly put together a plan that took advantage of the deployment of the federal troops.[32]

The detail was heavily armed. The standard weapons carried by the patrol were revolvers and shotguns. Duke ordered that the men were to follow him in single file and that, if challenged by the enemy, the entire detail was to fire its weapons and run back to the horses. He specifically ordered his men not to reload or to stand and fight it out with the Union soldiers. Duke understood the dynamics of the situation, realizing that the chances were going to be better than average that he was heavily outnumbered. If his calculations were accurate, his patrol would be at a great disadvantage in a prolonged fight. The closer Duke came to the crossroads, the more confident he was of his decision not to enter into a protracted engagement. The noises he heard coming from the other side of the crossroads indicated to him that there was a fairly good-sized group of Yankees waiting in ambush.[33]

As Duke's men neared the crossroads, a sentry discovered their presence and ordered them to halt. A shot rang out from Duke's detail, and the sentry fell to the ground dead. Immediately, the entire federal position opened fire in the direction of the shot. Duke and his men had just passed a fence from behind which a whole line of Union soldiers stood up to fire. He ordered his men to fall to their knees, thus avoiding any casualties, as the federal volley passed over their heads. The men kept to their knees and fired their shotguns. The simultaneous fire from fifteen shotguns was more than effective. Only the width of the road separated Duke and his troops from the Union soldiers. The Union line staggered when struck by the blast from the Confederate shotguns. Following their orders, Duke's men emptied their guns, then immediately ran for their horses. As they hastily withdrew, they could hear the moans and cries of pain from the wounded federal troops. Other Union soldiers quickly gave chase and were close on the heels of the Confederates and had nearly surrounded Duke when he and his men reached their horses. Quickly mounting, Duke led his small detail off the road and into the woods, where, in the dark, he lost the Union cavalry a few minutes later.[34]

On March 18, 1862, Johnston instructed Hardee to order Morgan's squadron to fall back from Murfreesboro to Huntsville, Alabama. Morgan received these orders the next day and, much to the displeasure of the local citizens, began to move his troops out of town due south through Shelbyville and Fayetteville, Tennessee. The squadron remained in Huntsville for ten days. The town was Morgan's birthplace, and both he and Duke had friends there, including the Fackler family, which Duke had visited on his journey to Montgomery the previous year. During their stay, Morgan and Duke were the guests of the Facklers, who hosted a party in their honor. The Facklers' young daughter Gypsy sang for the soldiers, and, in appreciation, Morgan appointed her an honorary adjutant of the squadron. In typical cavalier style, Duke drafted and read to Gypsy and the guests her commission:

Commanding them all to pay attention
To matters I herein mention—
I straightway perform the pleasant duty
Of adding rank to youth and beauty,
Therefore let this commission show
And give all men concerned to know
That in the camp, or yet without,
Upon the march or on the scout,
On drill, on guard, or in the battle,
When killing hogs or stealing cattle
Among the woods or on the road
On Miss Fackler is bestowed
Of Adjutant the style & rank
With pay galore & powers blank.
Henceforth let every cavalier . . .
If any dares presume to thwart her
He starves a month on bread and water.[35]

The Kentuckians, all of whom had been pampered by the town's hospitality, reluctantly resumed their march to join Johnston's army in Mississippi and return to the war. As the squadron was moving toward Mississippi, Tommie gave birth—on March 30, 1862—to her and Basil's first child at her family home in Lexington. The child was a son, whom Tommie named after the husband she missed so much. Tommie had not seen her husband for over eight months and had no feeling for when she might see him again, if ever. It would be weeks before Duke received news of his son's birth.

On April 3, 1862, the squadron joined John C. Breckinridge's division at Byrnesville, Mississippi. The Kentuckians were now camped only a few miles from Johnston's army at Corinth. In a matter of hours, Morgan and the rest of the Confederate army began moving north to engage the Union army in a battle that was to change America's concept of warfare forever.

5

Shiloh, the End of Innocence

GENERAL HENRY W. HALLECK and his generals were far from idle as the Southern army trudged south during the first weeks of March. On March 15, 1862, the heavyset Halleck received news that he had been appointed commander of the western armies. This appointment encouraged Halleck to implement his ambitious plans to invest the Southern heartland. Several days before Halleck's appointment, General Ulysses S. Grant ordered William T. Sherman south with an expeditionary force to occupy portions of Tennessee and Mississippi. Within a week, Grant had concentrated some fifty thousand troops in the vicinity of Pittsburg Landing. On March 15, General Don Carlos Buell, now under the command of Halleck, was ordered to abandon his Nashville base and join forces with Grant as soon as possible. The spring rains hampered Buell's progress near Columbia, Tennessee. On March 29, 1862, Buell's Army of the Ohio, approximately 37,500 strong, broke the Columbia camp and began to march southwest in the direction of Pittsburg Landing.[1]

Sometime in March 1862, Johnston decided to strike Grant and drive him from southern Tennessee before Buell's army became a factor. For this plan to succeed, it was essential that the maximum number of troops be assembled as quickly as possible. Within days of his arrival in Corinth on March 22, Johnston saw his available troop strength jump to approximately forty-five thousand, thanks to an influx of reinforcements. And he eagerly awaited the arrival of Earl Van Dorn's trans-Mississippi army, which would augment his forces by another twenty-six thousand. However, by the beginning of April, Van Dorn and his army were many marching days away, and time was of the essence. Johnston's preemptive strike would have to be accomplished without them.[2]

Despite the disadvantages of an untested command structure and inferior weapons, Johnston and his aggressive subordinate P. T. Beauregard were determined to attack Grant's army at Pittsburg Landing. Several elements were critical to the success of their plan, but that of surprise was, perhaps, the most critical. Johnston was convinced, however, that the Union troops were overconfident—that Grant did not anticipate a preemptive strike—and that surprise could, therefore, be achieved. When he received reports that Buell was approaching from the northeast, he scheduled the attack for dawn on April 4, 1862. The troops were ordered to break camp and head north on April 3.[3]

Morgan's squadron moved out on the narrow and muddy Mississippi roads on schedule as part of Breckinridge's reserve corps. Duke had loathed the long retreat, and the chance to redeem Southern honor put him in good spirits. There was no question that his morale, as well as that of the rest of the troops, was high. Duke remembered that the march was "slow and toilsome," with the infantry trudging through the mud and cursing the cavalry for splattering them with even more. During this march, a good-natured rivalry began between the infantry and the cavalry, a rivalry that lasted until the end of the war. The infantrymen, of course, chided the cavalry for conveniently being absent at the first sign of danger, declaring that they had never seen a dead body wearing spurs. Duke and his troops retorted that those who chose to ride were obviously far more intelligent than those who chose to walk.[4]

Heavy rains and more mud delayed the progress of the army, and it became apparent that the troops would not be in position to launch their attack as scheduled. Breckinridge's reserve became so mired that his column was stretched out for miles. At five o'clock in the afternoon of April 4, Johnston gave the order to postpone the attack until the next morning. It continued to rain very hard all that night and well into the next morning, resulting in even further delays. When on April 5 the army was finally in position, it was far too late to start the attack. That afternoon, Morgan's squadron reached the site designated as their bivouac along with several other Kentucky infantry units. Duke, hoping to catch a few hours of sleep before the battle, searched for any semblance of dry ground. The bivouac area was also the squadron's starting position for the attack the next morning.[5]

The Confederate attack began a few minutes after five o'clock in the morning on April 6, 1862. Prior to the attack, there was enough intermittent fire between the two armies to have alerted the Union command that the Confederates were before them in force. In fact, Sherman, the federal commander on the field, had been aware of some Confederate presence in the area for two days. Nonetheless, the federal army was surprised to some degree. However, despite this advantage, the Southerners' late start contributed significantly to their failure ultimately to win the day. This was not fully appreciated until that evening, when the lack of daylight prevented the Confederates from delivering a knockout punch to Grant's reeling army.[6]

The initial Confederate attack that morning had been very sluggish. The battle lines were not cohesive, and the units, many of which had never fought together, were not accustomed to extending themselves along a two-mile front. Hardee's corps led the attack simply because these were the most experienced and seasoned soldiers in the attacking force. Bragg's and Polk's corps followed, with Breckinridge's division close behind. Duke later wrote that Johnston's plan was "to execute a grand wheel to the left with his entire army, his right advancing, his left more deliberately, and his heaviest blows delivered upon the federal left and center." As the battle began to intensify, Morgan's squadron was still attached to Breckinridge's division and held fast for orders. Hardee's advance was steady, and, by eight o'clock in the morning, the Confederates were within half a mile of the main federal encampment.[7]

At nine o'clock, Hardee discovered that General Patrick Cleburne's brigade, on the extreme left of his corps, was in trouble. Cleburne's troops had run into a swampy thicket that destroyed the continuity of the brigade's line, forcing the troops to break rank as they tried to get around the obstruction. The Union line immediately in front of the brigade was positioned on higher ground, and, when the federal troops saw Cleburne's troops break rank, they took advantage of their superior numbers and enfilading fire to cut the brigade to pieces. Hardee regrouped Cleburne's brigade along with several fresh regiments in a ravine out of the line of fire of Sherman's men. With Cleburne checked, the Confederate advance on Hardee's left came to a standstill. In order to retake the initiative, between ten and eleven o'clock in the morning Breckinridge's reserve, along with Morgan's squadron, was ordered forward to support Hardee's line. The stiff federal resistance on Hardee's left thoroughly disrupted the wheeling movement, causing the attack to evolve into a frontal assault.[8]

Duke waited impatiently for five long hours, listening as the noise of battle roared loudly to his front. When the squadron finally received the order to move forward, the men, with Morgan and Duke in the lead, rode carefully around the infantry, doing their best to keep abreast of each other despite the trees. The closer Duke came to the front lines, the more evidence he saw of the destructive capabilities of both armies. Many years later he recalled:

> I remember the first sight I had of the killed and wounded that greeted my eyes, which made anything but a pleasant impression. I came across a pile of three dead bodies of federal soldiers, one of these men had been killed by a bayonet thrust through his body up to the cross, the other by a shot between the eyes, and the third had his entire face torn away evidently by the explosion of a shell. My patriotic ardour and anxiety to take part in the battle was considerably dampened when I saw this evidence of what extreme pains were taken to dispose of combatants.[9]

Hardee, who was about two hundred yards distant, did not recognize the squadron when it moved into position. He asked one of his staff, Lieutenant Kearney of St. Louis, who happened to know Duke very well, to ride over and learn the identity of the cavalry. Duke sat mounted at the head of the squadron when Kearney rode through the smoke shouting, "What cavalry is this?" Duke yelled back that it was Morgan's. When Kearney recognized Duke, he told him that Hardee wanted to see either him or Morgan. Since Morgan had left the squadron to get a better view of the federal artillery, Duke followed Kearney and reported to Hardee. The general was pleased both to see Duke and to learn that Morgan's squadron was on the field. Hardee had grown fond of Morgan and respected the combat effectiveness of his men. "Well Duke," he said, "you young Kentuckians have been anxious to see some war, and I'm going to give you an opportunity. Inform Colonel Morgan that he is to form his squadron and when I send the word, charge that battery on the hill to our right."[10]

Duke relayed Hardee's orders to Morgan and then joined the rest of the troops, who were nervously watching the action on the battlefield. From their vantage point, they could see the carnage, particularly the dead bodies of the soldiers from both armies that littered the ground over which they had just ridden. As they waited for the order to attack, to their front a Union battery began to pound and rip open the lines of a Confederate infantry unit advancing across the open field. Duke, as well as the rest of the Kentuckians, had never seen anything like this on the Green River or anywhere else. Duke admitted that this was a part of the war that the men, himself included, had never considered. Whatever the romantic notions of war he harbored as he rode into battle, they were soon destroyed that Sunday morning.[11]

Soon the word spread throughout the squadron that Hardee intended to order it to attack the battery that was wreaking such destruction on the Confederate infantry. Duke confirmed the rumor and "congratulated" his men "upon their opportunity of winning a great deal of glory." Hoping to give his men confidence, he added: "I am going to form you in such a way that just as few of you will be killed before reaching the battery as possible, and the others of course, must ride over the guns and take their chances with the infantry behind them." Duke later admitted that his poorly chosen words were not well received and that his men "looked very grave over the situation," but still they showed "no sign of fear or hesitation."[12]

As Duke and his company made ready for the attack, a Kentucky infantry regiment marched past. Friends in both units recognized each other. Once again, the foot soldiers teased their friends. But, since by this time they all knew the grim reality of what was occurring that day and what they were shortly to face, the teasing quickly turned to encouragement. The effect was electrifying for both units.[13]

Duke was still attempting to steel himself in the face of the carnage, which continually unfolded before his eyes. He had been involved in small unit actions in both Missouri and Kentucky where the enemy had employed a cannon, but he had never seen an entire battery in action. He now recognized the horrible, deadly effect that massed cannon could have on an attacking force. He compared the Union battery to the "output of a volcano in active operation."[14]

The order to attack still had not come, and Duke was continuing to muse about the battery, when he remembered a soldier, riding an artillery horse, who had attached himself to the squadron earlier that morning. That the man rode such a mount convinced a desperate Duke that he must have been with an artillery detachment and probably possessed more knowledge in that direction than anyone in the squadron. Trying to capitalize on the man's assumed experience, Duke told him of Hardee's pending order to attack the battery and asked how it should be done. "Why good Lord Lieutenant I wouldn't do it if I were you," replied the soldier. "Why your blamed little cavalry won't be deuce high agin them guns." This was not what Duke wanted to hear, so he pressed the soldier to tell him the best way for cavalry to charge a battery. The soldier thought a few moments and said: "Lieutenant to tell you the God's truth there ain't no good way to charge a battery."[15]

Sherman's troops began to give ground to the Confederate pressure, and Johnston's advance once again gathered momentum. Much to Duke's relief, the renewed Confederate initiative forced the troublesome Union battery to withdraw. The federal troops were now falling back all along Hardee's line. Wanting to press his advantage, Hardee ordered Morgan's and Wharton's cavalry units forward. As his squadron moved to the front, Morgan was ordered to head to the extreme left of the line and to "charge the first enemy he saw."[16]

The Confederate line was moving so fast that the squadron had to ride quite a distance before it reached the extreme left of Hardee's line. Morgan immediately saw in the distance soldiers dressed in blue. He ordered Duke to take Company A forward and identify the blue-clad troops. Even after a year of war, there were Southern units still wearing blue uniforms. After riding a short distance, Duke rode forward and in a short time was able to identify the "Creole Patois employed by the Adjutant of the regiment" and learned that the unit was the Eighteenth Louisiana Infantry. Morgan's caution was well-founded in this instance.[17]

Shortly after the encounter with the Louisiana regiment, the squadron reached the northwest corner of Jones Field. Here, they observed both the Louisiana regiment and a portion of a Kentucky brigade pressing their attack against a well-disciplined Union force that was in the process of falling back. Morgan's men and Wharton's Texas Rangers were behind the Confederate infantry, which, because of a ravine on their extreme left, they could not get around. It was now after two o'clock in the afternoon, and Morgan caught sight of more soldiers dressed in blue at the opposite end of the field. This time, the blue-clad troops were skirmishers from an Iowa regiment. Morgan and Wharton advanced their units in the direction of the skirmishers and drove them back to the main Union lines. A Union prisoner, from the Sixth Iowa Infantry, later remembered: "Some of the cavalrymen, including Duke, charged into the group of retreating Union soldiers to do some close work with saber and pistol."[18]

With the order to advance, Duke led his company forward at a gallop. They easily broke through the federal skirmish line only to come up suddenly on the entire Union regiment. Duke wrote later: "We got close to them before the federals fired; they delivered one volley, the blaze seemed to almost leap into our faces and the roar was like thunder." Under fire, Duke was, according to John Castleman, "extraordinary, with a cool and deliberate demeanor. The more desperate the action, the more danger involved, the more quiet and undisturbed was Duke." These were leadership qualities, qualities that his troops admired and to which they responded throughout the war.[19]

There was never a question about Duke's courage. During the attack, he rode a little ahead of his company with Lieutenant James L. West and Sam Buckner, both of whom were killed during the charge. Undeterred by the danger, Duke continued on and, while slashing away at the enemy, was shot in both shoulders, one bullet narrowly missing his spine. Sergeant Pat Garner, of Duke's company, immediately shot the soldier who had wounded Duke through the head with a "squirrel gun, which he habitually carried." Duke lay on the ground, dazed, and was able to recall only the riderless horses that ran around him and the other wounded and dead troops. The company quickly retired, having had four men killed and several more, including Duke, wounded. The Union regiment suffered casualties of a dozen killed and several captured.[20]

Wharton was not as fortunate as Morgan, his unit having suffered many more casualties in the attack. In the attempt to reach the rear of the federal line, the men in his command had been stretched out into a single file approximately five hundred yards long. With their flank exposed, the Rangers were too tempting of a target, and, predictably, a Union regiment prepared an ambush. When the column was at its most vulnerable point, it was struck from end to end with devastating fire from a federal infantry unit. Five of Wharton's men were killed and twenty-six wounded.[21]

After Morgan withdrew from the field, he learned the disturbing news that, at approximately 2:00 P.M., as he rallied troops in preparation for a Confederate push against the federal left, Johnston had been shot. Johnston believed that at times a commander had to lead from the front. Previously, his luck had always held. This time, however, he was struck in the right leg behind the knee by a minnie ball, which cut through an artery, and, in a matter of minutes, he had bled to death. With the loss of Johnston, there was a void in the command on the Confederate right, and momentum was soon lost.[22]

General B. M. Prentiss, who had rallied a large force from his routed Union Sixth Division, occupied a wooded knoll that commanded the field of fire over which the oncoming Confederates had to cross. For most of the afternoon, the Confederates were engaged with Prentiss at this hotly contested position, aptly named the Hornet's Nest. They attacked repeatedly, and, by late afternoon, his casualties heavy and his ammunition almost exhausted, Prentiss had no choice but to surrender. The Confederates began to re-form their lines to begin the final assault on Grant's army, which by this time had its back precariously pinned against the Tennessee River. It was at this moment that Beauregard, who was now in command, decided against any further action that day.[23]

Early the next morning, April 7, the Confederates awoke to learn that Buell's army was being ferried across the Tennessee River and unloading at Pittsburg Landing. Grant had received approximately thirty thousand reinforcements during the night and had immediately gone on the offensive in the morning. The Confederates fought very well that second day, but, by 1:00 P.M., the Union superiority in manpower had forced them off the battlefield. Beauregard felt that, in order to save the army, he had no choice but to retreat to Corinth. Morgan, along with Terry's Texas Rangers, was ordered to cover the retreat.[24]

The losses suffered by both armies were immense, and even the Europeans were horrified when they learned of the extent of the carnage. Union casualties totaled 13,000 out of the approximately 67,000 troops engaged over the two-day period. The Confederate losses of approximately 10,700, although not as high as those of the federal army, represented 25 percent of the army.[25]

The Confederate army's march back to Corinth lasted from April 7 to April 10. Duke, being seriously wounded, most likely was taken to the field hospital at the end of the first day of the battle. The physicians of neither side were prepared for the overwhelming number of casualties. Fortunately, Duke's wounds were of a nature that did not require amputation to increase his chances of survival, but it would take some time for him to recover. Like most of the wounded, Duke traveled to Corinth by ambulance. This must have been a painful retreat, physically and emotionally, particularly following a battle that many of the soldiers, including Duke, believed they should have won.[26]

The news of the battle reached Lexington in only a few days. Frances Peter, an ardent Unionist and neighbor of the Morgan family, wrote in her diary on April 10, 1862, that a terrible battle had been fought at Pittsburg Landing but that she was unaware of the human cost to either army. Tommie Duke certainly heard the same news and would have wondered whether her husband or brothers were in the fight. Over the next week, more news arrived, but it was generally about the Union participants from Lexington. Tommie did learn about Duke's wounds, but, apparently, the information that she received was sketchy at best. She was not even sure that her husband was aware of the birth of their son. Then, in mid-May, her mother received a letter from her younger brother Thomas informing her that he and their brother Charlton had been captured. Thomas was a prisoner at Camp Chase, Ohio, and Charlton was evidently being held in Tennessee. Thomas also wrote: "Basil

Duke is recovering and will be perfectly well in a few days." And he added a postscript to the letter: "Son to Sister Tommie I heard of her good luck, Basil has heard also."[27]

Mrs. Morgan left Lexington for Columbus, Ohio, as soon as she discovered Thomas was at Camp Chase. She was able to visit with him and learned the latest news about her other sons as well as her son-in-law. When she returned to Lexington, an anxious Tommie was unable to find out from her as much news as she would have liked to hear about her husband. So she took matters into her own hands and wrote her brother, demanding more news about Basil. Unfortunately her letter has not survived, but Thomas's May 24, 1862, response has. Thomas was noticeably defensive:

You attribute to indifference upon my part in the speaking to Ma about Basil. I told Ma everything I knew with regard to him, about his health and also where he was when I left Corinth. Ma had so much upon her mind while here that I suppose she has forgotten what I told her about him. Three weeks ago I left him in Central Alabama at a very nice gentleman's residence in the mountains, who has taken quite an interest in Basil. He was walking about and had almost entirely recovered from the effects of his wound. He heard of his good fortune from a doctor in the Confederate army who was taken at Mill Springs and who had just arrived from Lexington. Basil was very anxious that his boy should be named after Bro Johnny.

Basil is a first lieutenant and adjutant of our squadron, is very much beloved by his command and also by all the officers in the army.

He is a great favorite with General Hardee & Stirling Price who have often and again offered him appointments upon their staffs.

Basil is a great favorite with all. I must close as we are restricted to one sheet. I've already transgressed beyond the limits.[28]

The laudatory language concerning Duke may have been a younger brother's attempt to smooth his older sister's ruffled feathers. Tommie was fairly well known in Lexington as being a spirited young lady. Frances Peter had noted in a diary entry made earlier that year that Tommie had hissed continuously at federal soldiers who were ordered to accompany a funeral procession for a Confederate soldier in Lexington.[29]

While Duke convalesced in Alabama, the war continued, and Morgan was anxious to get back in the saddle. The battle of Shiloh was not the type of warfare that best suited his sensibilities. On the Green River, and during the retreat from Kentucky, he enjoyed the independence of command as he sharpened his skills as a guerrilla fighter. Morgan had learned the hard way that charging artillery or massed infantry was not a good tactic. And he had also recognized that the large Union armies that had penetrated into the Southern heartland were extended tenuously like paper kites at the ends of very long strings. The strings, of course, were the armies' supply lines, which were hundreds of miles long. In Kentucky and Tennessee, these supply lines and the Louisville and Nashville (L&N) Railroad were one and the same. Instinctively, cavalrymen such as Morgan and Nathan Bedford Forrest recognized the vulnerability of these hard-to-defend targets. Both Morgan and Forrest focused their raids on the destruction of bridges and other types of railroad infrastructure. In a short time, Morgan and Duke were to become the principal predators of the L&N.[30]

With the introduction of Duke's innovative ideas, the squadron was beginning to learn the tactics of mounted light infantry. It was being trained to ride to the scene of the battle, dismount, and fight on foot. The long rifle and the shotgun were, therefore, the weapons of choice. This was not a new concept of how to conduct a cavalry raid, but it was one that Morgan and Duke were in the process of perfecting. Morgan, most likely at Duke's urging, now began to forbid the use of both the saber and the carbine. This order was easy to give but difficult to enforce. Morgan's men generally captured an assortment of enemy weapons, including carbines, and a captured carbine was hardly ever thrown away.[31]

Although Morgan was to be without Duke's services for nearly two months, he was anxious to strike behind the Union lines, preferably in Kentucky. He began to plan a raid into Tennessee and Kentucky with the primary goal being the severance of the Union supply lines. He would attack the railroad and create as much turmoil for the Union army as possible. This plan was very ambitious and called for a raid as far north as Lexington.[32]

Morgan's exploits around Nashville in March 1862 had attracted the eye of the Southern press, which had been searching for a hero who personified the image of a chivalrous knight fighting for his hearth and home. The newspapers had so quickly endeared Morgan to Southerners that, by the spring of 1862, he was being compared to Francis Marion, the "Swamp Fox," a hero of the American Revolution. Such good press was undoubtedly responsible, at least in part, for Morgan's promotion to full colonel, effective April 4, 1862. It also made it easier for him to sell his commander on the need for an aggressive raid.[33]

Morgan's request to raid Tennessee and Kentucky was granted on April 23, 1862. In preparation for the raid, he appointed Lieutenant Sellers to command Duke's company during his absence. The squadron strength had been increased to 325 men with the addition of a fourth company and detachments from other units. Over the course of the next three days, the troops were reequipped and made ready for the raid. Whether the command had been properly disciplined and trained was a question soon to be answered. As it turned out, it had not. In fact, the raid fell far short of everyone's expectations. Arguably, it was Duke's absence that was the key to Union victory.[34]

On April 26, 1862, Morgan rode out of Mississippi in a northeasterly direc-

John Hunt Morgan was Basil Duke's best friend. The guerrilla leader quickly captured the imagination of Southerners as both a dashing and an audacious cavalryman. (Courtesy the University of Kentucky.)

tion toward the Tennessee River. Hampered by the spring rains and swollen rivers, he finally arrived near Pulaski, Tennessee, five days later. At Pulaski, the squadron engaged two different units of federal cavalry, capturing approximately 268 of the enemy, including the son of General Ormsby Mitchell. The general's son was quickly paroled so that he could be exchanged for Morgan's brother Charlton, who had been wounded and captured at Shiloh.[35]

Several days later, the command was fifteen miles from Shelbyville, in central Tennessee, an area heavily occupied by federal troops. On May 4, Morgan skirmished with the enemy, inflicting some minor damage, and then continued to

Kentucky Unionists, such as Colonel Frank Wolford, also made fine cavalrymen. Wolford and his First Kentucky Cavalry would be Morgan and Duke's nemeses throughout 1862 and 1863. (Courtesy the Kentucky Historical Society.)

move north. In Murfreesboro later that afternoon, Union general Ebenezer Dumont, with one battalion and two regiments of cavalry, including Frank Wolford's First and Fourth Kentucky (Union), learned from his scouts that Morgan was approaching from the direction of Shelbyville. Dumont immediately mounted his troops and, after a five-mile ride, discovered that Morgan had cut cross-country and was moving in the direction of Lebanon. Dumont's advance had caught up with Morgan's rear guard and began to skirmish with them. At approximately 7:00 P.M., Dumont called in his advance, giving the impression to Morgan that he was heading back toward Murfreesboro. The ruse was successful, and Morgan, believing his rear now safe, moved on to Lebanon.[36]

That night, Morgan separated himself from his command and slept at a hotel in the center of Lebanon. In the meantime, Dumont saddled his troops and rode to within five miles of Lebanon, where he halted and planned his attack. At 4:00 A.M., Dumont remounted his men and moved into Lebanon. Owing to a heavy rain, the night was very dark. Morgan's undisciplined pickets, tired of standing in the rain, had moved into the buildings to dry off. There they stayed and fell asleep. There had been a total breakdown in discipline within Morgan's command structure. At dawn, as Morgan and his men were mounting to leave Lebanon, Dumont with six hundred troopers rode into the town undetected by the sleeping pickets. Morgan was taken by complete surprise.[37]

Drawing their sabers, the Union cavalry struck and scattered the Confederates gathering in the streets. Morgan frantically tried to assemble his troops, but the companies became intermingled, all sense of command was lost, and confusion became the order of the day. Dumont's troops were tenacious and pressed the Confederates until they were surrounded and broke. It was every man for himself. Many of the Southerners fled in panic, without order or formation, as fast as their horses could carry them, casting aside their weapons along the way. Others abandoned their horses and ran into the woods to hide. A large portion of the squadron headed toward Carthage. The fight and flight became known as the "Lebanon Races." Morgan's command was decimated. Morgan himself escaped on a horse not even his own, accompanied by barely a handful of men.[38]

The casualties inflicted on Morgan's command are difficult to ascertain. The federal officers claimed over 100 Confederates killed and nearly 200 captured, which is certainly an exaggeration. According to Duke's *A History of Morgan's Cavalry*, few men were killed or wounded, but nearly 120 were captured. The exact figure probably falls somewhere between the two extremes. More important than precise figures was the fact that Morgan's embarrassed command was now scattered in small groups throughout the Tennessee countryside, putting an end to his plan for a large-scale raid. The victory was a significant one for the federal cavalry, which had a history of being manhandled by its Confederate counterparts.[39]

The next day, after riding nearly fifty miles to the east, Morgan, and what was left of his command, reached Sparta, Tennessee. Morgan remained there for three days, trying to collect his troops as they straggled into town. Sparta is located in east central Tennessee, and, because of its distance from Lebanon, it provided Morgan with a temporary sanctuary in which to reorganize his troops.[40]

The men's morale was shaken from the rough handling that they received, particularly from Wolford's Kentucky cavalry. Although the time at Sparta helped raise their spirits, the raid that Morgan had planned was now beyond his command's capabilities. He had only 150 men, most of whom had lost their weapons. Since he was determined to enter Kentucky regardless, the raid that he did mount would have to be significantly scaled back. To better his chances of success, Morgan employed a local partisan to guide him through the Tennessee-Kentucky borderland region. The man was Champ Ferguson, whose name was fast becoming synonymous with the cruel guerrilla war erupting in east Tennessee and Kentucky.[41]

Morgan broke camp on May 9, 1862, and, for two days, he and his troops rode hard until they reached the outskirts of Glasgow, Kentucky. Learning from one of his scouts that there were over five hundred federal troops in Bowling Green, Morgan prudently decided to avoid that town, opting, instead, to strike the L&N mainline at Cave City.[42]

Leaving Glasgow, the raiders rode all night to reach Cave City. On entering the town, Morgan immediately captured the railroad station. He learned from the station attendant that a southbound passenger train was due to arrive from Louisville at noon. The raiders captured the train after a minor exchange of shots with federal soldiers on board, including some from Wolford's regiment. When the fighting was over, Morgan and his troops sat down and ate dinner with the passengers. Before leaving Cave City, Morgan destroyed forty-five freight cars, five passenger cars, and one locomotive.[43]

When Morgan returned to Tennessee, he learned that he had been transferred to the command of General Edmund Kirby Smith, then in Knoxville. He was also given the authority to reorganize the Second Kentucky. Duke had now fully recovered from his wounds, but he was still in Corinth. He had gathered around him about thirty of Morgan's men who, for whatever reason, were unattached. While Duke waited for his orders, two companies of Texas cavalry commanded by native-born Kentuckians Richard M. Gano and John Hoffman arrived and were given permission to join Morgan's command. Toward the end of May, Duke, along with Gano's and Hoffman's companies, was ordered to Chattanooga, where Morgan's command was in the process of being refitted.[44]

Morgan and the troops enthusiastically greeted Duke when he arrived in Chattanooga. Recognizing his own organizational ineptitude, which had resulted in the fiasco at Lebanon, Morgan immediately put Duke to work reorganizing the command. He continued, however, to be a poor disciplinarian, making Duke's job that much more difficult. The army too appreciated Duke's attributes and promoted him to lieutenant colonel.[45]

The Second Kentucky was soon ordered to Knoxville. In the meantime, recruits began to arrive, among them over three hundred men from the First Kentucky Infantry Regiment. This regiment had been formed in the spring of 1861 and served under an enlistment term of twelve months in Virginia. When that term was over, most of the regiment's men decided to leave Virginia and join the Kentucky Confederate units in the west. These veterans were a welcome addition, not only because of their numbers, but also because of the discipline learned and the experience gained in their regular army service. In addition to these Virginia veterans, another fifty recruits arrived from Lexington under the command of Duke's friend John Castleman.[46]

The new additions to the regiment were armed with whatever weapons were at hand. (It would be months before all the men in the command could be armed in a uniform fashion.) The choice rifle was the medium Enfield because it was shorter and easier to carry on horseback than the regular Enfield rifle. However, much to Duke's dismay, there were not enough of the medium Enfields to equip the entire regiment. Each man was also provided with at least one pistol and two when possible, preferably the federal Colt revolver. The pistol was by far the preferred choice of weapon for close-in fighting on horseback. Finally, the War Department gave Morgan two small mountain howitzers. Duke felt that these guns, affectionately called the "bull pups," were ideal for the cavalry. Not only were they light and easy to handle, but they also had an effective range of three hundred yards. The bull pups could fire shot, grape, or canister and were perfectly suited to Duke's style of warfare.[47]

Champ Ferguson once again had attached himself to Morgan, who tended to ignore the scout's unsavory reputation. Ferguson was a tough character who thrived in a violent environment. His wanton killings, particularly of prisoners, offended Duke's sense of honor and justice. Duke was appalled that Morgan had taken Ferguson under his wing, and he tried—unsuccessfully—to convince his mentor to disassociate himself from the scout. Finally, Duke decided that his only recourse was to control the man's bloodletting himself. He confronted Ferguson straightaway, telling him that he could not "kill prisoners taken by us." "Why Colonel Duke," he answered, "I've got sense, I know it ain't looked on as right to treat regular soldiers tuk in battle that way . . . but when I catches any one of them hounds I've got good cause to kill, I'm goin' to kill 'em." Duke was not charmed by this reasoning and knew that, if Ferguson continued to act as he had, the troops would be adversely affected during and after battle. He would keep a wary eye on Mr. Ferguson.[48]

Morgan received approval to make a second raid into Kentucky. Just prior to the beginning of what was to be called the "First Kentucky Raid," the regiment was joined by the "gentleman from abroad." The "gentleman" was the infamous Lieutenant Colonel George St. Leger Grenfell. Grenfell, an English-born soldier of fortune, was almost sixty years of age and had lived and fought in Turkey and Tangier as well as other parts of the North African coast. His life read like a nineteenth-century adventure novel, causing Duke to compare him to the popular *Ivanhoe* character Brian de Bois-Guilbert. Morgan immediately took to the Englishman as Jeb Stuart had to Grenfell's German counterpart Heros von Borcke. Morgan and Grenfell met in Mobile at the end of May, the Englishman taking an instant liking to the Kentuckian and deciding to join his command. Not only was Grenfell an interesting individual, but his military experience was also an untapped resource.[49]

Grenfell's experience was immediately put to use and quickly appreciated by both Morgan and Duke. Morgan's evolving type of warfare was very similar to that employed by both the French and the Arabs in North Africa. Since Morgan often operated behind enemy lines, he relied heavily on locals for intelligence about Union troop movements. This intelligence was essential, and reliance on civilians was a chancy proposition, as Duke had discovered at Flat Rock. To avoid this problem in the future, Grenfell helped train a select group of sixty of Morgan's men as a scout detachment. The scouts' primary purpose was to obtain reliable information through firsthand reconnaissance. The detachment was to be commanded by Tom Quirk and thereafter would be known as Quirk's scouts.[50]

When Grenfell arrived in June, Duke was already in the process of training the

Second Kentucky in the tactics that were to make the regiment famous. Historically, Morgan has been given the credit for being the inspiration behind these tactical innovations. Perhaps Duke, more than anyone else, perpetuated this tradition in his postwar *A History of Morgan's Cavalry*. Duke, who readily admitted his admiration for his brother-in-law, was attracted to Morgan by his charismatic personality, which may help explain the tone of the book. Throughout Duke's life, his modesty prevented him from boasting of his own accomplishments, especially if doing so would diminish his brother-in-law's. To some extent, this is unfortunate because the facts, which are substantiated by numerous contemporary accounts, clearly indicate that it was Duke who seized on these tactics (which were not new to warfare) and intelligently tailored them to the American Civil War.

Many years later, in his biographical sketch of Duke for the *Memorial History of Louisville,* J. Stoddard Johnston wrote: "So vivid was the impression that his character was being produced upon the Southern army that it was frequently remarked he was the 'soul and brains' of Morgan's brigade but an expression like this coming to his ears brought from him a denial in the most unqualified terms." Stephen Z. Starr, Grenfell's biographer and the author of *The Union Cavalry in the Civil War,* wrote that Duke was the genesis of the cavalry tactics ascribed to Morgan. More important: "The general opinion of Union officers who had the honor of meeting Morgan's command in battle was that the Louisville journalist George D. Prentice told the truth when he said someone might hit Duke on the head and knock Morgan's brains out."[51]

Morgan's military experience both in the Mexican War and with the Lexington Rifles was traditional as far as the use and deployment of troops were concerned. Duke's experience as a scout for Hardee in Missouri was less so. And it was during that time with Hardee that Duke first encountered the type of cavalry tactics that he would later teach the Second Kentucky. Again, Duke's approach was not revolutionary, but he understood how Morgan wanted to fight and adapted existing techniques so as to exploit Morgan's talents fully. Even more important was Duke's hand in the metamorphosis of the command from cavalry to mounted infantry. The mobility of such a fighting force was essential to Morgan's style of guerrilla warfare. A further advantage was that it was also far less time-consuming to teach the Kentucky cavalry Duke's tactics than to teach them traditional European tactics.[52]

Duke, who had been promoted to lieutenant colonel and given the command of the Second Kentucky, had integrated most of the influx of recruits into his regiment. The Second Kentucky was now composed of six companies and the fragment of a seventh made up of a group of Alabama boys commanded by Captain McFarland. All the Texans were placed under Gano's command, and they labeled themselves Texas Rangers. Morgan's revitalized command was now made up of Duke's Second Kentucky, Gano's Texas Rangers, a regiment of Georgia Partisan

Rangers, and a company of Tennessee Partisans, in all about nine hundred men. It was not quite brigade strength, a benchmark that would have qualified Morgan for promotion to brigadier general. Nevertheless, Morgan referred to his command as a brigade, and it was three times as large as the squadron that he commanded when he left Corinth in April.[53]

When Duke rode out of Knoxville on July 4, 1862, his level of confidence must have been high. He was now in command of the Second Kentucky, the linchpin of Morgan's brigade. And any concerns that Morgan might have had about commanding such a large force or repeating the mistakes made at Lebanon must have been mitigated by the return of Duke and the presence of Grenfell. Refitted, reorganized, and far better trained, the brigade was an imposing sight. The presence of Morgan, charismatic and loved by his men, and Duke, tall, handsome, immaculately dressed, and at ease with command, together at the head of the column must have increased the confidence of the brigade. Grenfell, colorful and legendary, was a bonus. Led by such men, morale and expectations were exceedingly high as the brigade headed north to Kentucky and home.

6

Partners in Command

WHEN MORGAN'S BRIGADE rode north to Kentucky, the political situation in the state was far from stabilized. There was a growing segment of the population that was fast becoming discontented with the Lincoln administration. This was a direct result of the military's occupation policies, particularly, the indiscriminate arrests of Southern sympathizers. These arrests were made usually without a stated cause and always without warning. All Kentuckians, regardless of political inclination, began to demand that they come to an end.[1]

Duke was well aware of the political developments in the state. There were no definitive battle lines in Kentucky and Tennessee, and, although movement between the states could be risky, it was also fairly fluid. News traveled as easily as people, and the Confederates usually had access to Northern newspapers. John Castleman had come through the lines from Lexington in May with firsthand observations, albeit biased, of the federal occupation. Armed as Morgan's squadron was with news of oppressive actions taken against friends and family, the raid took on an added perspective. And, even beyond such political motivation, it was necessary for the procurement of weapons and horses. Over two hundred of Morgan's men were unarmed, and more than sixty had been left behind in Knoxville for lack of mounts.[2]

The brigade crossed the Cumberland River twenty miles south of Tompkinsville, where elements of the Ninth Pennsylvania were bivouacked. Quirk's scouts were ordered forward to reconnoiter the town and soon returned with news that there were approximately 350 Union troops there. A plan to invest the town was rapidly put together. Morgan placed Colonel Archibald Hunt and his Georgia Partisans on the left of his line of attack, with the bull pups in the center and Duke and the Second Kentucky on the right. In the meantime, Gano circled the town and positioned his troops on the Glasgow Road to seal off any potential retreat by the Union troops. Because of the brigade's overwhelming superiority in numbers, there was no need for Morgan to hold any of his troops in reserve. The Kentuckians were ordered to dismount and attack on foot. Duke and his men ran across an open field and then, at about sixty yards from their target, executed a frontal assault. After only one volley from Duke's unit, the Pennsylvanians broke and ran. The fight lasted less than ten minutes. The Pennsylvania regiment was completely overwhelmed, and those troops that did not surrender immediately were captured by Gano's men as they tried to escape through the other end of town. The brigade suffered no immediate fatalities. However, a minnie ball shattered Colonel Hunt's leg, and, unable to ride, he was left behind in Tompkinsville, where he died several days later.[3]

Attached to the brigade was a well-educated Canadian-born telegrapher named George Ellsworth. Before the war, Ellsworth had lived in Lexington, where he became acquainted with John Hunt Morgan. He had joined the brigade at Chattanooga, and Morgan soon learned that Ellsworth knew how to intercept telegraph transmissions without alerting anyone else on the line to his presence. Morgan made good use of Ellsworth's talents on this and other raids, and, eventually, Ellsworth's telegraph antics became legendary. In time, the brigade gave Ellsworth the name "Lightning" in appreciation of his ability to "milk the wires."[4]

From time to time, Ellsworth's work on the wires would raise the suspicions of another operator. On one occasion, Ellsworth was even challenged and, as Duke reported, dodged the cross-examination in the following manner:

> "You are Ellsworth," wired the operator, who also happened to be a Canadian "and you damned bloke you can't make a fool of me."
>
> "The Almighty has spared me the trouble," retorted Lightning. "But don't you know, you Canadian ass, that Ellsworth is sick at Knoxville?"
>
> Then ensued a long and angry colloquy, in the course of which, however, Ellsworth succeeded in imbuing his skeptical auditor with the very belief he had intended from the first to induce.[5]

That afternoon, when the brigade left Tompkinsville, it moved north in the direction of Horse Cave. Once again, Ellsworth was called on to perform his magic for Morgan, this time in the middle of a summer thunderstorm. As lightning bolts shot across the sky, Ellsworth made contact with an unwary operator in Louisville who freely disclosed Union troop locations. Once this information was elicited, Morgan ordered Ellsworth to respond with vague reports about Confederate troop movements.[6]

The brigade turned and began riding in a northeasterly direction, toward Lebanon, which it reached on the afternoon of July 11, 1862. A brief skirmish with the troops garrisoned in the town netted Morgan another two hundred prisoners. The raiders' movements were now being reported daily in the Kentucky newspapers. The news that Morgan and his hard-riding veterans were nearing the Bluegrass caused much consternation in Louisville, where the bankers moved their money to safety. The news reached Lincoln via Andrew Johnson, the Union governor of Ten-

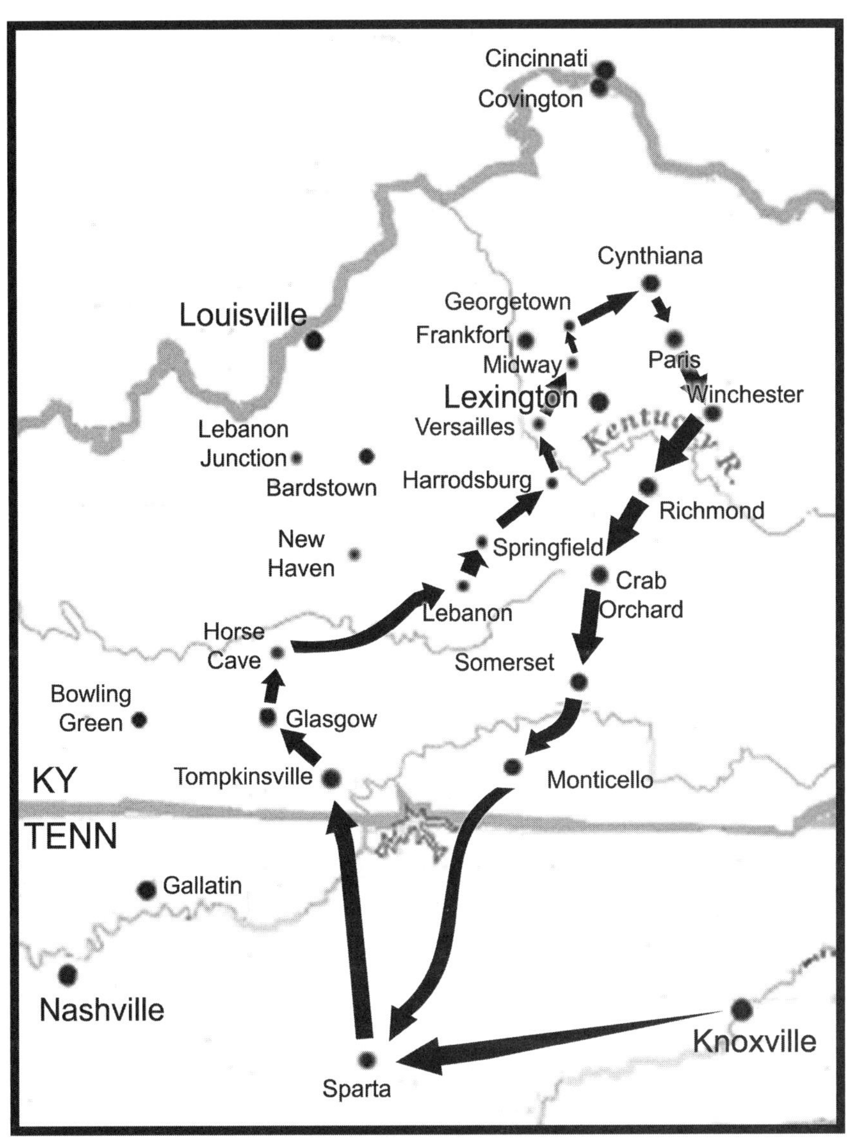

The First Kentucky Raid, July 1862.

Morgan's reputation varied depending on the newspaper. He is portrayed here, rather fancifully, as a bandit by the Northern press. (Courtesy the Filson Historical Society, Louisville.)

nessee, who was "in trouble and great anxiety about a raid into Kentucky." In Lexington, the Unionists were even more concerned for their own safety and requested additional troops for protection. Frances Peter's diary entry for July 12 noted: "Lexington is in a stir and . . . a dispatch [has] been sent to Cincinnati for more troops." She also wrote that Morgan had burned Lebanon. At the time Morgan captured Lebanon, he had also captured a large store of federal supplies, and that which was not plundered by his troops or the townspeople was burned. This fire is most likely the burning of Lebanon to which Peter refers in her diary.[7]

Morgan's men were reported seen almost everywhere, and the scouts, trained by Duke and Grenfell, were working to perfection as they scoured the countryside for information. When the brigade reached Harrodsburg, two companies were ordered to leave the town in different directions, a tactic that was often repeated to confuse the local populace of the raiders' true intentions.

Both Morgan and Duke were overly impressed, and perhaps more than a little willingly deceived, by the friendly and enthusiastic welcome that they received from the people of Kentucky. Each town seemed to go out of its way to share its hospitality and goodwill with the raiders. While in Harrodsburg, for example, the brigade was treated to an afternoon picnic by the ladies of the town. Duke easily misread this overabundance of Southern sympathy as validating his vision of himself as the liberator of his people. In a few short months, the reality of the situation would prove to be far different.[8]

When the column left Harrodsburg, it headed north toward Lawrenceburg, giving the impression that Frankfort was its intended target. Instead, several miles north of town, it suddenly veered east toward Versailles, a small town only twelve miles west of Lexington. Unknown to Duke, for several days Union sympathizers in Lexington had been venting their anxiety over the impending raid by threatening Tommie as well as other female members of the Morgan clan. That same day, the Union provost marshal in Lexington decided that he could not guarantee the safety of some of the older women, and ordered Mrs. Henrietta Morgan out of Lexington. In the meantime, brigade scouts were continuously being sent out in every direction to obtain the best information possible concerning the location of the federal troops. As the reports filtered back, it soon became apparent that the Lexington garrison comprised both cavalry and infantry and was numerically superior to Morgan's brigade. It would have been a tactical mistake for Morgan to fight a superior force in a strong defensive position, and, with Duke's input, he prudently decided against such a course of action. After spending the night in Versailles, the raiders moved on to Midway, eight miles farther north. Here, Ellsworth was once again given an opportunity to orchestrate confusion with his bogus telegraph messages. When Ellsworth was done, the column moved farther east in the direction of Georgetown, reaching it that night.[9]

Georgetown was protected by a small home guard unit that was in the process of preparing a defense when it learned that the raiders were at the edge of town. On hearing this startling news, it immediately abandoned its defensive efforts and began to withdraw toward Lexington. Duke, not one to miss the humor in any given situation, recalled that Will Webb, a Southern sympathizer who had been locked in the courthouse for several days, taunted the home guard in its precipitous retreat. Hanging halfway out of a second-story window, and pointing to the Stars and Stripes flying outside the courthouse, he yelled: "Are you going to desert your flag? Remain, and perform the pleasing duty of dying under its glorious folds, and afford us the agreeable spectacle that you will thus present." It is doubtful that Webb was quite as eloquent as Duke remembered, but it is noteworthy that his appeal had little effect on the the fleeing men, who kept on riding until they were safely out of town.[10]

Duke, along with the rest of his men, was exhausted after being in the saddle for twelve days and traveling approximately 350 miles. Georgetown was an ideal spot to rest. It was centrally located and heavily Southern in its sympathies. The raiders remained there for two days. During this layover, small companies of men were sent out to destroy railroad bridges and other viable military targets as well as reconnoiter the surrounding towns. Duke and his company commanders also took the opportunity to integrate the recruits that had been gathered—including John A. Lewis, who had just received a degree from Georgetown College, and Will Webb—into the Second Kentucky, where they formed an additional company. The lull in the raid also made it possible for some of the hometown troops to sneak into either Lexington or one of the other surrounding communities to visit friends or family. Such visits were always a dangerous proposition but well worth the risk to those who took the chance and succeeded. The risk of visiting Lexington would, however, have been too great for Duke, who could easily have visited Richland and learned as much about Tommie and the baby as was possible under the circumstances.[11]

Thomas Hines and John Porter may have precipitated the Lexington excursions. Prior to Morgan's arrival in the Bluegrass, these two scouts procured a buggy, dressed in civilian clothes, and ventured into Lexington to determine troop strength and what, if any, plans were being made to defend the city. After driving around the city for several hours, they boldly stopped at a local hotel to have lunch. Their daring was handsomely repaid as, while they dined, they overheard two federal officers speaking freely of defensive preparations. After lunch, the two once again audaciously rode around Lexington in their buggy to gather information, returning to the hotel only late in the afternoon. There, they discovered that units of the home guard from the surrounding communities were being assembled to guard the city. They also learned that "in a very few minutes or quite a short time all persons would be prevented from leaving the city, and perhaps would be forced to take up arms to defend the place from the anticipated attack." The two jumped into their buggy and left Lexington, heading east out the Winchester Road in the direction of Edgewood, only minutes before the pickets closed off the city. For the next several days, the two rode around the outlying Bluegrass communities enjoying various adventures until they were able to locate Morgan and the command in Georgetown.[12]

Even though he had earlier been dissuaded by Duke, Morgan was still very much interested in occupying Lexington and, consequently, ordered Gano to test the Union strength between Georgetown and Lexington. Gano worked his way toward Lexington, driving in all the Union pickets in his immediate path. The information gained in this exercise and Hines's report confirmed that Morgan and Duke had been right to avoid an attack on Lexington. In the meantime, Duke's cousin through marriage, Union General Green Clay Smith, arrived in Lexington with the balance of the Ninth Pennsylvania Cavalry and elements of other units to take command of the city and begin the pursuit of Morgan. With the arrival of Smith, the Confederates realized that it was time to leave the Bluegrass. However, to confuse Smith, the raiders first moved north toward Cynthiana. Cynthiana was between Lexington and Cincinnati, and it was hoped that this diversion would create the impression that the raiders' next target was Cincinnati. If the ruse worked, the federal pursuit would converge on northern Kentucky, gaining for the Confederates the necessary breathing space to turn east and then south to Tennessee.[13]

When the time came to leave Georgetown, a company under the command of

Captain John Castleman was a childhood playmate of Duke's. Shown here as a Confederate officer, thirty-five years later he would be a brigadier general in the U.S. Army during the Spanish-American War. (Courtesy the Filson Historical Society, Louisville.)

John Castleman was ordered to drive in all the pickets around Lexington and screen the movements of the column. Almost immediately, the young captain ran into a Union patrol, which he pursued and forced back to Lexington. Castleman, with the help of Hines, then set up an ambush at Mount Horeb Church, which is located near the present-day intersection of Iron Works Pike and Russell Cave Road approximately seven miles north of downtown Lexington. (The site of the ambush was only a few hundred yards from Castleman's home.) His target was a Union cavalry group sent from Lexington to determine the size and purpose of the force that had driven the pickets from their position. It fell into the trap and, after a short exchange of shots, headed back to Lexington, for the moment unaware of the threat to Cynthiana.[14]

Around noon, the commander of the Union garrison in Cynthiana, who had approximately 350 soldiers at his command, was alerted by telegram that the rebels were headed in his direction. A few miles west of Cynthiana, the Confederate column stopped and rested as Morgan and Duke planned their strategy. The Georgia Partisans were directed to attack the town from the north, Gano from the south. Morgan and Duke would take the Second Kentucky and attack from the west on the Georgetown Pike. In preparation, Duke deployed Companies A and B on the right and Companies E and F on the left of the road.[15]

At approximately 3:00 P.M., Duke began to drive in the Union pickets. As they fell back, Duke placed his artillery about three hundred yards west of the Licking River bridge and began to shell the town. During the cannonade, his troops dismounted and deployed for the main attack. The movement toward the bridge prompted some heavy and very accurate fire from the Union troops on the west side of the river. The deadly federal fire slowed Duke's advance, and his troops were repulsed several times before the Union troops withdrew across the bridge and back into the town, where they were able to find cover in the buildings and warehouses overlooking the river. Companies E and F of the Second Kentucky attempted to cross the river, but the water was too deep. Company A then crossed the river at a ford near the bridge and charged the federal troops defending the bridge, forcing them from their position and out into the street. At one point, when the outcome of the battle was still in doubt, Grenfell led several charges saber in hand, breaking up the resistance of a strong contingent of Union troops who had rallied at the railroad depot. Legend tells that Grenfell came out of the battle with a slight wound, but eleven bullets touched either him or his horse. New recruits, including John Lewis, were also thrown into the battle. Like most green troops, Lewis did not know what to expect, and his combat debut was a severe one. Still, he learned some valuable lessons that day, lessons that served him well for the remainder of the war.[16]

Almost at the same time as Duke's attack began, Gano had finished his flanking movement and attacked from the south, while the Georgia Partisans had placed themselves on the north end of town, completing the encirclement. The Union soldiers fought well but, once again, were overwhelmed by tactics and sheer numbers. Although some made good their escape, most were captured. The battle lasted not more than an hour, but the Confederate toll was eight men killed and twenty-nine wounded. The Union casualty list was seventeen killed, thirty-four wounded, and all but twenty-five captured. Early the next morning, the Union prisoners were marched six or seven miles north of town before they were released. They quickly reached Falmouth and boarded a train for Covington and Cincinnati, spreading the word of the Confederate victory at Cynthiana. This news created the necessary amount of consternation in the communities south of Cincinnati, diverting attention away from the brigade's intended retreat route.[17]

Once the prisoners were released, the column turned south toward Paris. Just outside Paris, a group of citizens waited anxiously to surrender the town to the Confederates. Word of the battle at Cynthiana had drifted back from Harrison County, and the good citizens of Paris wanted their town to avoid a similar fate. Meanwhile, General Green Clay Smith was finally venturing forth from Lexington to begin his pursuit of the raiders. He was moving north toward Paris with a force of approximately thirty-five hundred men. The Union commander seemed to act tentatively, moving cautiously, not taking advantage of his superior numbers, and never pursuing the raiders very aggressively. It was almost as if he knew that the Confederates were on their way back to Tennessee and, instead of initiating an engagement, was satisfied to follow them at a respectable distance and escort them out of the Bluegrass.[18]

Quite aware that Smith's force was three times as large as his brigade, Morgan was forced to ride east from Paris to the town of Winchester, which he reached around noon on July 19, 1862. Winchester was the home of Roger Hanson, the Confederate infantry commander with whom Duke and Morgan had worked on the Green River. Winchester, much like Georgetown and the other central Kentucky towns visited by the brigade during the raid, gave the Confederates a warm welcome. Mattie Wheeler, a teenage girl, noted the visit in her journal:

Col. John H. Morgan, with a great many of his men, variously estimated at 1500 to three thousand passed through Winchester. . . . We all went downtown and stood in Mrs. Turnbull's yard and talked to some of the soldiers. There was a good many of our acquaintances among them. . . . They got several recruits from this county, Jimmie Price, Marshall and Stone Street Van Meter and Joe Croxton. Two boys came in from Lexington. They stole off from there the night before. There were some of the nicest gentlemen among them that I ever saw. They did nothing wrong as far as I could see except swap horses.[19]

Concerned about the pursuit of Smith's cavalry, the brigade stayed only three or four hours in Winchester. The column now turned south in the direction of the Kentucky River and the ford located near the site of old Fort Boonesboro. The river was crossed just before dark, and the column rode all night in order to reach the city of Richmond. Once again, the Confederates perceived Richmond and the surrounding area to be almost entirely Southern in sentiment. Duke later wrote that it was Morgan's intention to make a stand at Richmond. From a tactical standpoint, this would have been a bad decision. The Union forces under Smith to the north and Wolford to the south were beginning to close in on the raiders. A stand at Richmond by the Confederate raiders could have been the final chapter in the history of Morgan's cavalry. After discussing the matter with Duke, Morgan changed his mind and, after incorporating into the command a company of recruits led by Captain William Jennings of Madison County, made the decision to veer to the southwest in the direction of Somerset. Prior to leaving Richmond, Morgan and Duke dined with Jennings and his wife, Lucy. Several weeks later, Mrs. Jennings wrote in a letter to Duke's wife, Tommie: "Oh! You can but poorly imagine what joy it was to see what my eyes had so long desired Morgan & his men. . . . After my breakfast was over Dr. Jennings came up from the hotel with Gen. Morgan Col. Duke. How I wished as your brother sat & talked & Col. Duke & Capt. Llewellyn all of them so little like heroes & so much like friends, you with your boy & your mother could have glided in my parlor & seen those who have yearned for one look, one word from those they so loved."[20]

For a few moments, Duke and Lucy Jennings were able to talk privately. She told him that, from time to time, she would receive a letter from a mutual friend mentioning Tommie and the baby. He asked Mrs. Jennings to write Tommie on his behalf. Then he admitted how much he missed his wife and how, although he had never seen his son, he often tried to picture what he looked like. He abruptly stopped and said that it "maddened" him and made him unfit for duty to think about his family but that he was confident that God would permit him to see them: "For we will come again so sure as the world stands." He then said good-bye to Lucy, reiterating his request that she write Tommie and "tell I am in perfect health and equal to any hardship to be borne." He then "parted with his large black eyes full of tears."[21]

The Madison County recruits added another 105 men to Morgan's ranks. The brigade left Richmond late in the afternoon, continuing south in the direction of Crab Orchard. It now entered an area of Kentucky that was not nearly as bountiful as the Bluegrass region. It was becoming difficult for the soldiers to obtain food, and, with hunger as an enemy and the federal cavalry within striking distance, this proved the most difficult part of the raid. The column was moving as fast as possible in order to elude a pursuit that was quite cognizant of Morgan's escape route. However, the federal forces failed effectively to coordinate their pursuit, and, by the time Morgan was south of Crab Orchard, they were too far behind to overtake the raiders. When the brigade reached Somerset, Kentucky, the telegraph office was immediately taken over by Ellsworth. Morgan once again put to very good use his telegrapher's skill, and false information concerning the brigade's whereabouts was soon flowing through the telegraph lines.[22]

On completion of his task, Ellsworth issued the following order, wiring it throughout the state of Kentucky:

Headquarters Telegraph Department of Kentucky, Confederate States of America—General Order No. 1.—When an operator is positively informed that the enemy is marching on his station he will immediately proceed to destroy the telegraphic instruments and all material in his charge. Such instances of carelessness as were exhibited on the part of the operators at Lebanon, Midway and Georgetown will be severely dealt with. By order of

G. A. ELLSWORTH,
Gen'l Military Supt. C.S. Telegraphic Dept[23]

The brigade arrived in Livingston, Tennessee, on July 28, 1862. At Livingston, the command was split into two forces, with Duke taking the Second Kentucky, along with Grenfell, to Sparta to rest, train, and be refitted. Morgan took the balance of the brigade to Knoxville, where he presented to General Kirby Smith his report on the results of the raid. Duke and the Second Kentucky remained in Livingston for another three days. While there, Duke's men suffered greatly from lack of food and other supplies. One of the troopers complained bitterly about the conditions and stated that he wanted to quit the regiment if he was going to be continually subjected to what he considered privations. Duke already recognized that the raid had revealed certain deficiencies in his regiment's discipline, and he had no intention of letting such a malcontent poison the morale of his men. He quickly stripped the trooper of his rank, removed him from the service, and then marched him out of camp in front of the entire regiment.[24]

Reflecting on the political importance of the raid, Duke disclosed that one of the primary objectives in going into Kentucky was to seek out and terrorize the principal Union man in each town the raiders visited. The unlucky soul was usually apprehended with the understanding that Morgan's purpose for entering the town was his specific arrest. Apparently, Morgan took some pleasure in frightening these men, who could easily imagine the outcome of their pending ordeal. They were always released with the knowledge that they had better curtail their actions against those of Southern sentiment because Morgan, like the proverbial bogeyman, could always return at a later date. This type of behavior, which was not customary for the regular Confederate army, illustrates, not only the independence of an unattached guerrilla commander such as Morgan, but also the personal nature of the war in Kentucky.[25]

Once in camp, and with Grenfell's competent assistance, Duke instituted a program of drill and discipline the intensity of which his troops had never experienced. During his tenure with Captain Kelly and the Missouri militia, Duke had learned the benefits of military discipline. He was far from satisfied with the regiment's performance during the raid and was convinced that, the more disciplined a combat unit became, the more efficient would be its performance in the field. To complicate matters for Duke, the regiment had grown to over seven hundred troops, many of whom were new recruits who had never experienced organizational, let alone military, discipline. Duke was determined that his regiment would not fail in combat for its lack of training and drill. As Stephen Starr puts it: "There would be no repeat of the Lebanon Races if Duke and Grenfell could prevent it." Extra guards were posted to keep the men from leisurely wandering away from camp in search of the nearest still. As we have seen, the young colonel had learned early in his military career on the Green River that bored soldiers and alcohol were a bad combination.[26]

The troops were drilled regularly and the manual of arms practiced daily. Other traditional military measures were tried on Duke's troops, generally under Grenfell's wary eye. However, despite Duke and Grenfell's best efforts, the Second Kentucky never attained the high level of military discipline to which Grenfell had become accustomed in his native Europe. The Southern soldier was very independent and not the type to readily accept discipline meted out with a heavy hand. Many of the Kentucky troops were well educated and considered themselves gentlemen and had no intention of submitting to the routine training method of humiliation. And Duke soon realized that the usual methods would be effective with few, if any, of the troops under his command. Nor did Morgan's personality and leadership style encourage discipline. Duke eventually achieved some degree of discipline among his troops, which were manageable under most combat circumstances. His Kentuckians fought, and they fought well, but they were never going to be the type of soldier that Grenfell envisioned. Duke was, nevertheless, satisfied with the results achieved during those few short weeks the regiment spent in camp at Sparta.[27]

In August 1862, two events occurred that illustrate Duke's distaste for what he considered to be the more repugnant aspects of military discipline. They also reveal that Duke's concept of discipline had some unique limitations. Two deserters had been captured. One had been fighting for a Union regiment; the other was on the run from charges involving a crime against a civilian.

Duke was ordered to execute the first man. Even though he clearly understood the purpose of such an order, Duke felt sympathy for the man himself and also knew that his men would have a very hard time acting in the cold-blooded manner that carrying out the death sentence required. When the man asked for a minister, Duke could not locate the regimental chaplain, who later admitted that he had purposely absented himself. (When Duke discovered what he considered to be the chaplain's inexcusable and dishonorable conduct, he became infuriated and summarily dismissed him from the regiment. This action later caused Duke some problems with his superiors, which he would have preferred to avoid.) He was, however, able to locate a minister in the ranks, and the execution went forward. Thomas W. Bullitt described the event: "The regiment was drawn up in dress parade; the deserter wasted to a post, facing the regiment; a detail of 10 or 12 men fired simultaneously he fell forward as the cords would permit—dead. It was the only execution that I witnessed; I believe the only one, which took place in the command. Desertions were very infrequent—though opportunities were constant."[28]

The sentence ordered for the second deserter was a flogging to be administered in front of the regiment. Although Duke never mentions the exact nature of the crime involved—there is some evidence that it may have been rape—it was evidently heinous enough that both Duke and his troops held the man in contempt. However, flogging was unpopular in the regiment, and selected enlisted men, representing each company, spoke with Duke about the punishment. The consensus was that the man should be hanged because no man in the Second Kentucky would degrade himself by volunteering to whip the deserter. Duke did not just agree with this logic; he was proud of his men for taking the initiative to come forward and voice their objections. Duke's acquiescence to their concerns was indicative both of the extent of his commitment to traditional discipline and of the mutuality of respect between him and his men.[29]

Duke was now in a quandary. How was he, as the commander of the regiment, to carry out the order if none of his men were willing to do the flogging? The quandary was resolved when a newly elected officer came forward of his own volition and volunteered for the job. Despite the fact that this solved his problem, Duke somewhat angrily tried to dissuade the man, asking him how, as an officer and a gentleman, he could step forward and assume the responsibility for an act that the enlisted men considered demeaning and dishonorable? Duke thereby revealed, not only that he was reluctant to enforce an order that in the regular army would have gone unquestioned, but also that far more important to him than military discipline was the maintenance of an officer's honor. Nonetheless, the officer persisted, and Duke finally acquiesced. The flogging took place the day after the execution, and once again the regiment was drawn up in dress parade. As Bullitt remembered: "The fellow was stripped to the waist; tied with his face to the post, his back to the regiment, and a strong man laid on the lashes, with a broad heavy leather, looking like a buggy trace. At every stroke a blue mark appeared across his back and the fellow withered in agony."[30]

This was, apparently, the only flogging that occurred in the command during the entire war. When it was over, Duke sent for the officer who had administered the punishment. The man reported as ordered, apparently expecting some form of commendation. Instead, Duke told him that he had forfeited his commission and asked him to leave the regiment. The man defended himself, arguing that Duke had no right to dismiss him. A point very well taken, Duke acknowledged, but, nevertheless, his actions were those unbecoming an officer, and Duke would not let his troops serve under such a man. The man eventually left, and Duke never saw him again.[31]

The federal cavalry was not unaware of Duke's presence in Sparta and, on occasion, advanced in his direction. In response to a report that elements of enemy cavalry were west of Sparta, Duke with fifteen men rode out to investigate. Approximately four miles west of Sparta was a covered bridge over a small stream. When Duke reached this spot, he instinctively felt that the enemy was hidden among the trees on the other side of the stream. As he approached the bridge, he decided to move forward for a closer look. He warned his troops to take care and be on the alert for any enemy troops that might be hiding inside the bridge. The road leading up to the bridge was not very straight, and, from his position, Duke could not see inside the structure. Then, as one of the Confederates recalled, the federal troops "dashed out . . . like an avalanche, in numbers about forty and those followed by 200 or 300 more on the far side that rapidly came charging over. Things were rather uncomfortable to say the least, and after firing a volley at them the Col. [Duke] ordered a retreat and then occurred one of those exciting and lively chases that a cavalryman is so accustomed to." The federal cavalry pursued Duke until he was met by reinforcements riding out from Sparta. The tide quickly turned, with the Confederates now in hot pursuit of the retreating bluecoats. The race ended when the federal cavalry reached McMinnville. Duke broke off the pursuit and returned to camp with no casualties—and with the knowledge that he had bested the enemy one more time.[32]

In July 1862, Braxton Bragg, whose army was separated from that of Kirby Smith's by Buell's Army of the Ohio, performed his most brilliant strategic maneuver of the war. He moved approximately thirty thousand troops on a 776-mile circuitous route by rail completely around Buell and his army to Chattanooga. Bragg had completely flanked Buell and now had a direct line of communication with Kirby Smith ninety miles to the northeast in Knoxville. At the end of July, Kirby Smith traveled to Chattanooga to confer with Bragg on a possible campaign against the federal army in Tennessee and Kentucky. In the meantime, Buell had separated his army from Grant's and was now moving across northern Alabama toward Chattanooga. When Bragg learned of this, he knew that he had been given an opportunity to regain the offensive but that he had to act quickly to take advantage of the situation. An advance by either or both Confederate armies into central Tennessee or even farther north into Kentucky could force both federal armies to move north to meet the threat, relieving the Southern heartland of the strains of occupation.[33]

Kirby Smith arrived in Chattanooga armed with a wealth of information provided to him by Morgan and Duke concerning federal troop concentrations in Kentucky. After the raid, both Duke and Morgan were extremely optimistic—perhaps a bit self-servingly so—about the chances of a major Confederate success in their state. They wrote glowing reports to Kirby Smith about the Kentucky political situation and concluded that the rise of discontent with the military occupation favored the Confederacy. Kentucky, it seemed, was a ripe plum that needed only the Confederate army to come north to pluck it from the orchard of federal tyranny. The two predicted that, on the arrival of the Confederate army, thousands of Kentuckians would rally to the Stars and Bars. Their enthusiasm was contagious, and Kirby Smith was certainly affected when, on August 11, 1862, he wrote Jefferson Davis that politically it was time to strike Kentucky: "Delay loses a golden opportunity and fall finds her people powerless and a large army between us and the waters of the Ohio." In his letter, he enclosed a letter from Duke that he described as "but one of many, representing the conditions of affairs in Kentucky and is interesting." Kirby Smith's letter introduced Duke to Davis "as the man of Morgan's regiment." This endorsement was a significant tribute from a soldier of Kirby Smith's rank. And it was not the first endorsement that Kirby Smith had given Duke. He had already written Bragg about his understanding that Duke was the man of the command: "He is said by all to do all the drilling, planning and fighting in which has gained his regiment such éclat, and as he is a modest man and intelligent gentleman I think his views are entitled to be well considered."[34]

Duke and Morgan both played significant roles in convincing the Confederate command of the high probability of military and political success of an immediate invasion of Kentucky. This optimism was based in large part on the enthusiastic reception that the raiders received from their fellow Kentuckians during the July 1862 raid. The people in the Bluegrass were genuine in their support of Morgan's men while they were in Kentucky. They were Kentuckians supporting Kentuckians—but not necessarily Kentuckians supporting the Confederacy. Duke and Morgan placed too much faith in their reception and, therefore, misinterpreted its meaning. What they did not fully understand was that family and friends back home were not necessarily as devoted to the cause as they were. The Confederacy had done little to convince the people of Kentucky that it was able to protect them. The Confederates' inability to occupy the key Kentucky population centers in 1861 and Johnston's swift retreat from the state in early 1862 had destroyed much of Richmond's credibility. It would take more than a cavalry raid to reestablish that credibility in Kentucky.[35]

When Kirby Smith and Bragg met in Chattanooga, they agreed on a simultaneous movement against the Union forces in Tennessee. Kirby Smith planned to move north and capture or neutralize the Union position at the Cumberland Gap. Once this objective was met, he would meet up with Bragg somewhere in middle Tennessee. If this scheme proved successful, the combined armies could then move on into Kentucky. However, before this plan could be implemented, there was another significant problem to be dealt with, one that was quickly identified by Kirby Smith but never adequately addressed by the Confederate government. In his August 11, 1862, letter to Davis, Kirby Smith astutely pointed out that it would be highly advantageous to have a high-ranking Kentuckian in command of the invasion. So convinced was he of the necessity of this that he even offered his command to Simon Buckner or G. W. Smith. It was evident to him that most Kentuckians would be more receptive to a native son commanding the invading army. Kirby Smith's advice went unheeded. In fact, Morgan's brigade was the only Kentucky unit involved in the invasion. John C. Breckinridge's division, which included the famous Kentucky Orphan Brigade, was in Baton Rouge.[36]

During the second week of August 1862, Morgan joined Duke at Sparta. Morgan had been ordered to move the brigade close to Hartsville and make ready for a raid on the Louisville and Nashville (L&N) main line twenty miles to the north at Gallatin. Seven miles north of Gallatin, at Big South Tunnel, the tracks went through an eight-hundred-foot-long tunnel. Obviously, if the tunnel could be destroyed or at least significantly damaged, then the flow of rail traffic between Louisville and Nashville—and Buell's supply line—would be interrupted indefinitely. Such an action would have the added benefit of assisting Bragg and Kirby Smith's plans to invest middle Tennessee.[37]

Morgan reached Gallatin on the morning of August 12, 1862. While en route from Sparta, the brigade was joined by a detachment of thirty men under the command of Captain Joseph Desha. Desha's men became Company L of the Second Kentucky. Captain Desha's abilities were immediately put to the test as he was ordered into Gallatin to capture the Union commander, who was staying in town with his wife, away from his troops. After Desha successfully accomplished his mission, Morgan convinced the captured federal commander to instruct the officer in charge of his troops to surrender. This ploy worked, and approximately two hundred men were captured without any bloodshed.[38]

The Confederates now turned their attention to the primary purpose of the raid, the railroad. Fortuitously, a southbound train with nineteen freight cars loaded with horse fodder and other provisions for the Union cavalry was captured as it tried to go through Gallatin. The train was quickly unloaded, and wooden ties were placed on the flat cars. The freight ties were set on fire, and the locomotive, on full throttle, was sent rolling down the tracks and crashing into a barrier erected inside Big South Tunnel. When the locomotive hit the barrier, it exploded, and the resulting damage was spectacular. It would take the L&N ninety-eight days to rebuild the tunnel. In the meantime, supplies would have to be carried by wagon from a newly opened railhead at Mitchellville over twenty-five miles of winding roads to the railhead at Goodlettsville, Tennessee.[39]

The brigade returned to Hartsville, where the men became involved in an activity that illustrates their unique mind-set. Several of the men found an abandoned printing press and a considerable amount of type. It so happened that Gordon Niles, Duke's acting adjutant, had been a capable printer prior to the war. In almost no time, Niles and several others began publishing a camp newspaper, called *The Vidette*. Of course, *The Vidette* was heavily inclined toward reporting news about the brigade, but it also contained political commentaries and sundry witty items written and contributed by officers and enlisted men alike. The newspaper was remarkably good for being printed in the field and, under the circumstances, should not be dismissed as an amateur publication. The life of *The Vidette* was relatively short, with issues appearing intermittently between August 1862 and early 1863.[40]

The first issue of *The Vidette* was published in Hartsville on August 16, 1862. Prominently displayed on the left-hand side of the front page was a column entitled "Morgan's War Song by B. W. D. one of Morgan's Brigade." This was a poem written by Duke, the lyrics of which were to be sung to the tune of "La Marseillaise."

The song was a hit with the men, who were soon singing it around campfires and on the march. Duke's poem was long remembered by the men of the command. The first stanza reads:

> Ye Sons of the South, take your weapons in hand,
> For the foot of the foe hath insulted your land!
> Sound, sound the loud alarm!
> Arise! Arise and arm!
> Let the hand of each freeman grasp the sword to maintain
> These rights, which, once lost, he can never regain
> Gather fast neath our flag, for 'tis God's own decree,
> That its folds shall still float o'er a land that is free![41]

On August 19, 1862, a twelve-year-old boy had been smuggled out of Gallatin, put on a horse, and told to find Morgan and "beg Him to come to the rescue" of the town. The boy was brought to Duke and excitedly told him that a federal cavalry detachment was in the process of rounding up all the male inhabitants of the town in "a most offensive manner." All the able-bodied men of Gallatin were in the Confederate army; only the old or the very young remained. Morgan decided that it was time to intervene and ordered his brigade north to Gallatin. While en route, Morgan heard various other rumors, for example, that the federal commander had ordered the execution of the townsmen if the "guerrilla Morgan" came to Gallatin and that the men were being taken to Nashville to be hanged as spies. Recollections of specific events that day vary depending on the source, but, in general, the situation can be reconstructed with some semblance of accuracy.

Duke wrote that the brigade caught up with the Union force and its prisoners on the road between Gallatin and Nashville that morning. The men in his command were angry because outside Gallatin they had found the dead body of one of their comrades, who had been shot by the federal soldiers. They became even angrier when the women in Gallatin told them that the dead soldier had been cuffed and kicked after he had been shot. Thomas W. Bullitt provides a somewhat different version of the events. According to him, when Morgan's command arrived in Gallatin, the women of the town reported that their men had been carried off by the federal troops and that they were afraid that they might have been killed. The women then pleaded for Morgan to kill the Yankees and take no prisoners. When the incensed Morgan caught sight of the federal detachment, he ordered an attack with the stipulation that no prisoners were to be taken; the fight was to be absolutely under the black flag. Both Bullitt and Duke confirm that the brigade inflicted heavy casualties on the Union force. However, when some of the federal troops began to lay down their arms, the Confederate subalterns refused to carry out Morgan's order. Bullitt further states: "I have it on undoubted authority (no less than general Duke himself) that Morgan coming up to Jake Cassell (of Company A) who had taken a number of prisoners, demanded angrily to know why his order had been disobeyed, Cassell quietly observed that if Colonel Morgan desired it he would execute this order at once. It called Colonel Morgan to his senses and Cassell's action was no doubt actually as well as formally approved."[42]

Morgan pursued the remainder of the federal detachment to the stockade at Edgefield Junction. Blind with rage, he ordered his men to make repeated frontal assaults against the structure even though it was well fortified and surrounded by a ditch. It was here that Captain Niles, the founder of *The Vidette,* senselessly lost his life. Shortly after Niles fell, Duke rode up and ordered the men to terminate the attack and fall back. Duke "saw no chance of reducing the work even with great loss." This incident aptly illustrates Duke's ability to act as a logical counterbalance to Morgan's less-disciplined nature.[43]

Interestingly, in his *A History of Morgan's Cavalry,* Duke addresses neither the black flag order nor Morgan's offensive behavior. The tone of the book, of course, prohibited such disclosures, which would have raised questions about Morgan's moral character. Some of Duke's contemporaries believed that he purposely omitted the incident from his book, "letting it die with the war," as Bullitt put it. This, of course, would be consistent with Duke's concept of honor and his intention to eulogize both Morgan and the unit as a whole.[44]

Following Morgan's raid at Big South Tunnel, Brigadier General Richard W. Johnson was ordered to gather a cavalry force of brigade strength and position himself to the west of Gallatin at Hartsville. This new brigade had as its principal objective the destruction of Morgan and his cavalry. Several days later, Johnson was given some vague orders to leave Hartsville and carry out his intended mission against Morgan. Johnson selected elements from the different regiments under his command and put together a force of 640 of his best-armed and -mounted men to search out and destroy Morgan.[45]

On the morning of August 21, 1862, Johnson rode out of Hartsville looking for Morgan. Morgan's men were also in the saddle early that morning and were preparing to accommodate Johnson or at least a federal force of cavalry, which they were aware was heading in their direction. Duke and the Second Kentucky were riding east on the Hartsville Road. He had ordered a strong force of pickets to move ahead of the regiment in Johnson's direction. Slightly east of Gallatin, the Hartsville Road reaches a junction with the Scottsville Road, which then branches off to the northeast. Morgan was riding with Duke that morning when, as they approached the junction, they heard shots fired. At the junction, the Second Kentucky had split off from the main force and was riding northeast down the Scottsville Road, while Companies D, I, and K proceeded down the Hartsville Road. The firing that Morgan and Duke heard was initiated by Duke's pickets coming in contact with elements of the Second Indiana Cavalry on the Hartsville Road. Apparently, when Duke's advance elements made contact with the enemy, there was some question in Morgan's mind as to whether the Confederates should escalate the engagement. Morgan had some reluctance to push the federal force because of an earlier report that infantry and artillery might be accompanying the Union cavalry and, therefore, ordered the main column down the Scottsville Road to avoid an engagement. Duke immediately became concerned that Morgan's maneuver might have exposed the column to a flank attack. After some discussion, Duke persuaded Morgan that he could "whip the enemy." Morgan, in full confidence of Duke's abilities, simply ordered his younger brother-in-law to "form his men and as soon as you check them, attack." Duke had grown fast in the art of command.[46]

In response to Morgan's order, Duke, along with three companies, galloped down the Hartsville Road in the direction of the firing. By this time, his pickets were being pushed back to the junction. To counter this pressure, Duke placed Company D in the woods north of the road and the other two companies in a cornfield south of the road.[47]

The commander of the Second Indiana, Lieutenant Colonel Robert Stewart, became alarmed when he saw Duke position his troops and immediately called for support. In response to his request, several more companies were brought forward to his aid. At this point, Stewart became aware of the Second Kentucky's main force on the Scottsville Road. As Duke had initially feared, Stewart with four companies wheeled to his right to strike the main force in the flank on the Scottsville Road. The two roads were very close together at this point, and the terrain was fairly level, so both Duke and Stewart could watch each other maneuver. As Stewart formed his troops for the attack, Duke ordered the main body of the Second Kentucky to dismount and take cover behind a rail fence. The strong defensive position that Duke had chosen for his men did not deter Stewart, whose men charged the Confederate position across an open meadow approximately three hundred yards wide, sabers drawn. Duke's troops had more than enough time to take careful aim. The first volley had a murderous effect on the charge and seemed to bring down two-thirds of the federal cavalry.[48]

Reeling from the Confederate fire, the Second Indiana fell back to re-form and charge a second time. As the Hoosiers began their second charge, Companies H and G of the Second Kentucky were coming up the Scottsville Road to support the companies bracing themselves for the new attack. These two companies were able to place themselves so that their fire enfiladed Stewart's line as it charged. The result was predictable. The Confederate fire was so intense and accurate that the Second Indiana broke and fled. In tandem with the action on the Scottsville Road, the three companies that Duke had placed in a defensive position on the Hartsville Road had also held off an attack by the Fifth Kentucky (federal) and were counter-attacking at the moment the Second Indiana broke. The impact of this counterattack, as candidly reported by Stewart, was "the Fifth Kentucky, panic stricken, fled the field in disorder."[49]

After witnessing the action, Johnson sent in reinforcements to support the crumbling federal lines. When the reinforcements failed to stop the Confederates, Johnson ordered a retreat down the Hartsville Road, intending to halt and re-form his command out of the line of fire. Several miles to the rear at the junction of Cross Lanes Road, Johnson tried to rally his men. Cross Lanes was perpendicular to the Hartsville Road and went in a southerly direction toward Cairo, Tennessee. While at the Cross Lanes junction, Johnson tried to buy some time by sending out a truce flag and requesting time to bury his dead. Morgan did not fall for this ploy and demanded that Johnson surrender. Johnson then ordered his men south down Cross Lanes toward Cairo.[50]

When the Confederate forces reached the junction at Cross Lanes, they were split into three columns, with five companies to the north of the Hartsville Road, four companies on the road, and three companies well south of but parallel to the road. These last three companies were in position to cut off any attempted federal retreat. After Johnson refused Morgan's demand to surrender, the Confederate forces positioned on the road and to the north moved on the junction. However, by the time they reached it, Johnson had extracted his force, which was now moving on the road south to Cairo. Duke, in the meantime, had caught up with his three southernmost companies, formed them into parallel columns of four, and picked up the pursuit. Lieutenant Colonel Stewart again candidly reported what happened next:

> We had gone about 1½ miles in the direction of the Cairo when the report came forward that the enemy was charging our rear. General Johnson here ordered me to force my men front to rear and resist the enemy's charge, which I expected, and had formed a line, when the Fifth Kentucky came dashing through in a style of confusion more complete than the flight of a drove of stampeded buffaloes, if possible disgracing their former inglorious conduct. There appeared to be a question of rivalry between officers and men for which should out vie in the disgrace of their cowardly scamper.

Stewart was, however, able to repulse Duke's attack, at least for the moment, and made an orderly withdrawal as Duke was re-forming his troops to resume the attack.[51]

Johnson's new defensive line was formed by the time Stewart caught up with the main body. The federal line was in the form of a V just below the top of a long hill. When Duke approached the rise, he immediately appreciated the significance of the form of the Union line below him, noting that the tip, or bottom, of the V was pointing up the hill directly toward him. If he directed the attack to proceed down from the top of the hill, his troops would have to go only about forty yards before they struck the federal line. Johnson realized that, as Duke's troops came over the hill on horseback, silhouetted against the sky, they would be easy targets. But Duke was by now too good a soldier to fall into this trap. He ordered his troops to dismount and advance on foot. When Duke's men charged, the peculiar shape of Johnson's line prohibited his troops from concentrating their fire while allowing the Confederates to fire on any part of the Union position. Johnson's men soon began to give way before the Confederate assault and fell back into a ravine. Duke ordered his troops to remount and sent part of his force to cut off any attempted retreat. In the meantime, Stewart realized that the game was up and safely withdrew his regiment from the engagement. Johnson, now left with only part of his command, decided to surrender.[52]

Morgan reported that the Second Kentucky had killed or wounded 180 of the enemy and captured 200 while suffering itself only 2 dead and 18 wounded. Several conclusions can be drawn from the battle. Was the Union cavalry in the west, as some military historians have suggested, truly no match for its Confederate counterparts, or was Johnson's hastily thrown together brigade unprepared to do battle with a competently led and cohesive unit such as the Second Kentucky cavalry? Most likely the latter. More evident in the battle than the Union unpreparedness was Duke's conduct. Morgan in his official report wrote: "Lieutenant-Colonel Duke led on his regiment, if possible, with more than his usual gallantry, and contributed, by the confidence with which he has inspired his men, to insure the success of the day." Although Morgan was present, it is apparent that Duke took Morgan's generic orders and, improvising, executed a battle plan while in the saddle. The battle also confirmed Duke's belief in the superiority of dismounted cavalry armed with infantry rifles over mounted cavalry armed with sabers and carbines.[53]

Johnson rode with Duke and Morgan at the head of the column back to Gallatin. As one story relates, a day or two before, Johnson had bragged to the people in Hartsville that he was going to capture Morgan and bring him back in a box. Johnson asked Duke that he not be taken to Gallatin, where he felt that he would be subjected to the taunting of the townspeople. Duke was empathetic and ordered the fences on the side of the road removed so that the column could cut through the fields and circle the town to get to camp.[54]

7

All the Kentuckians Wanted to Ride

THE LATE SUMMER AND EARLY FALL of 1862 was, perhaps, the only time that the Confederacy's sun shined bright over Kentucky. For six weeks, Edmund Kirby Smith and Braxton Bragg had the opportunity to solidify a strategy that could have resulted in serious consequences for the North. Bragg planned to unite with Kirby Smith and coordinate a joint invasion of middle Tennessee. The objective was to maneuver behind Buell's army and cut him off from his Nashville supply base, thus forcing him to retreat north to Kentucky. If, according to this plan, Buell either was defeated in battle or retreated north to Kentucky, the Confederates would then have the option to push on into Kentucky. After the Chattanooga meeting, Bragg felt that there was complete understanding between himself and Kirby Smith concerning the execution of this plan. Particularly encouraged by Morgan's and impressed by Duke's glowing reports on the conditions in Kentucky, Kirby Smith believed that he could march his army as far as Lexington without encountering any significant opposition. On August 9, 1862, he wrote Bragg, explaining that an attempt to take the Cumberland Gap would involve a siege that was likely to take more time than the two generals had budgeted at their meeting. Alternatively, he argued: "A move direct to Lexington, Kentucky would effectively invest [Union general George] Morgan, and would be attended with most brilliant results in my judgment, I suggest my being allowed to take that course." This decision, which was reluctantly agreed to by Bragg, effectively scotched the plan agreed on in Chattanooga. The question is why Bragg abandoned his original plan, which was militarily sound, without more resistance. The answer more likely than not lies in the Morgan and Duke dispatches.[1]

While Bragg and Kirby Smith prepared their plans, Morgan's brigade took a well-deserved rest at Hartsville. On August 24, 1862, Duke was ordered to turn over General Johnson and two other officers captured during the engagement on the Hartsville Road for transfer to Knoxville. This is the only significant military event, albeit administrative, that involved Duke during the last week of August.

Duke, like his soldiers, was eagerly anticipating a move north into Kentucky and home. He had still not seen his son and was obviously missing Tommie. On August 28, Morgan received orders to move north into the Bluegrass for a rendezvous with Kirby Smith and his army in Lexington on or about September 2, 1862. Kirby Smith had started his army north from Knoxville two weeks earlier. The general had not anticipated the bad roads that he encountered in eastern Kentucky, and his progress was significantly slowed. His army seemed to inch its way through the mountains and passes of that region. He wrote Bragg: "The country around here having been almost completely drained of all kinds of supplies, and the roads between here and east Tennessee being much worse than I had supposed, I find I have but two courses left to me." He could either return to Knoxville for supplies or continue on to Lexington. He advised Bragg that he had chosen the latter alternative. The invasion of Kentucky was now on in earnest.[2]

By August 26, 1862, Kirby Smith's army had gained momentum and was moving toward Richmond, Kentucky. Just as Morgan and Duke had predicted, except for the occasional bushwhacker, they had not met any serious resistance. This changed dramatically when the Confederate cavalry commanded by Colonel John Scott suddenly clashed with six hundred federal troops commanded by Colonel Leonidas Metcalfe approximately eighteen miles south of Richmond at Big Hill. Scott, who commanded a tough veteran force of approximately 650 cavalrymen, after a sharp fight that lasted about an hour and a half forced Metcalfe to retreat in disorder. Metcalf reported ten men killed and another ninety captured with no accounting for his wounded, Scott four men killed and twelve wounded. The engagement confirmed what many Unionists feared: that a major Confederate force was moving into Kentucky and that the federal presence was unprepared. With the news of the Confederate victory at Big Hill, frantic attempts were made by the home guard in Lexington to organize and prepare a credible defense. In a sense, this reaction was comic, considering the significance of the Confederate invasion, but, without considerable reinforcements, there was not much else that could be done.[3]

With Robert E. Lee threatening Washington, D.C., and Maryland, there was little chance that Lincoln had any intention of releasing eastern troops to defend Kentucky. The Union army closest to the Bluegrass was Buell's in Nashville. Although slow in reacting, Buell did recognize the significance of the Confederate advance into Kentucky and the vulnerability of Louisville and Lexington. Bragg had in the meantime left Chattanooga on August 27 and headed north into Kentucky, forcing Buell to enter into a foot race with the Confederates to the Ohio River. There is no evidence that Louisville was Bragg's intended target, but the city was in a near panic by early September.[4]

The rapidly approaching Confederate armies left the Union command no choice but to put together an army as fast as possible from the regiments scattered throughout the military district. Many of these regiments were either garrison troops or recently recruited units with no combat experience. General William Nelson was charged with the responsibility of organizing these troops and then putting them in the field against Kirby Smith's veteran army, a task that was well beyond his intellectual and material resources.[5]

Morgan broke camp at Hartsville on August 29, 1862, with approximately eleven hundred men, the majority of which were in Duke's Second Kentucky. This was the largest command that Morgan had taken north. The route chosen was through Glasgow and then northeast to Lexington. From the beginning, the men, perhaps Duke most of all, pushed their horses hard, all eager to reach Lexington as soon as possible.[6]

As Morgan and Duke rode the fifty miles from Hartsville to Glasgow, their passage was never challenged, nor did they see a single federal soldier. While they rode north, Kirby Smith's army was challenged on August 30 by Nelson's hastily organized force a few miles south of Richmond. General Horatio Wright, the commander of the Department of the Ohio, had instructed Nelson not to engage Kirby Smith south of the Kentucky River unless he was sure of success. The Kentucky River with its high, rocky palisades was a far more defensible position than the open farmland south of Richmond. Apparently, Nelson was not impressed with the defensive possibilities that the Kentucky River presented because he never conveyed Wright's instructions to General Mahlon Manson, his field commander at Richmond.[7]

Manson commanded approximately sixty-five hundred troops. After the federal cavalry had been repulsed at Big Hill, he was without adequate intelligence concerning the size and location of the Confederate units on his front—but nevertheless determined not to retreat. On the morning of August 30, the lead elements of Kirby Smith's army collided with Manson a few miles south of Richmond. In a very short time, the Confederates gained the upper hand and forced the Union troops off the field and back to Richmond, where they were trying to rally when Nelson arrived on the scene.[8]

As the battle raged, Scott's cavalry circled Richmond to the west and positioned itself to cut off any Union retreat in the direction of the Kentucky River and Lexington. Nelson, meanwhile, was able to rally and position a force of approximately twenty-five hundred soldiers along a ridge that ran through the Richmond Cemetery. However, after the Union line took only a few volleys, Nelson was struck by a bullet in the leg and fell to the ground, wounded. When they saw their commander go down, the green Union troops panicked, broke, and fled. The Union soldiers ran through Richmond searching for the road north to Lexington and safety; instead, they found waiting for them Scott and his gray-clad cavalrymen.[9]

Before the sun set, the Confederates had achieved a victory so complete that no other victory by either army in the entire war is quite comparable. Yet the battle wallows in relative obscurity. The Confederate army had 451 casualties, while the federal loss was 5,353, of which 4,303 were captured trying to escape. Some of the federal soldiers who did escape evaded Scott's cavalry by making their way north through Winchester, where Mattie Wheeler observed:

We heard the firing of cannon early Saturday morning and heard it till about ten o'clock. Ma called us all in to go to making bandages, though we knew nothing of the battle. Most persons thought it was Gen. Nelson practicing his artillery but we felt it was a battle. That night about 8 o'clock we heard some cavalry come dashing in the Richmond Pike & I never heard such swearing, just one oath after another, so we knew instantly what was a matter. It was the home guard of Winchester & part of Metcalf's men retreating to Winchester. The whole federal army was completely routed. I never heard of such a defeat, I believe.[10]

The gates were now open to Lexington and all central Kentucky for Kirby Smith and his army. Up to this point, everything that Morgan and Duke had told Kirby Smith and Bragg had been accurate. Duke and Morgan's advance into central Kentucky was not nearly as exciting as that of Kirby Smith and his army. On August 31, the brigade camped at Columbia, where it was joined by Duke's brother-in-law, Charlton, who brought with him the bull pups. The scouts also reported that no federal troops of any significance were between Columbia and Lexington, still several days' ride away.[11]

Kirby Smith did not stay in Richmond any longer than it took for him to bury his dead and care for his wounded. The lead elements of his army arrived in Lexington on September 2, 1862. The general, with the balance of the army, marched into the city later that day to a very enthusiastic welcome from its citizens, one that many of the gray-clad soldiers remembered for the rest of their lives. Women greeted the troops as liberators, hugging them as they marched through the streets. Some women even tossed flowers in front of Kirby Smith's horse as he rode at the head of the column. This friendly welcome seemed to add further credence to the accuracy of the Morgan-Duke reports. Several days later, Kirby Smith wrote his wife, emphasizing: "My entrance into the blue grass region of Kentucky has been a perfect ovation old and young have flocked to me with tears in their eyes have thanked God for their deliverance from persecution."[12]

The closer Morgan's brigade drew to Lexington, the more excited and anxious the native Kentuckians became. On September 2, just south of Danville, Duke, along with everyone else, heard the news of Kirby Smith's victory at Richmond. For Duke, this news confirmed his belief that the invasion would be successful and that, in a matter of days, he would be with his wife and child. Except for some persistent bushwhackers in Casey County, Morgan and his troops met no opposition throughout their entire ride. The brigade reached Nicholasville, a small town twelve miles south of Lexington, on the evening of September 3. The men wanted to continue on into Lexington that night, but Morgan had other ideas. It was his intention to make a grand entry into his hometown the next morning, and he insisted that his soldiers and their horses look their best for the ride down Main Street. So, instead of riding to Lexington, the men spent the evening cleaning equipment and uniforms and grooming horses.[13]

At ten o'clock the next morning, escorted by a local brass band, Morgan, Duke, and the rest of the brigade rode into Lexington. It has been written that they met with a welcome without parallel: that there were bands playing and Confederate flags waving and that "John Morgan could scarcely get to his home, the people almost carried him." Even an ardent Unionist like Frances Peter admitted that the church bells rang and that the "secesh [secessionist] ladies with the stars and bars in their hands & streamers of white & red in their dresses or bonnets" were in the streets cheering the Confederate cavalry. Miss Peter also provided a description of Morgan's troops that, although not flattering, is most likely fairly accurate: "A nasty, dirty looking set they were; wore no uniform but were dressed in gray & butternut jeans or anything else they could pick up, but were not quite so dirty as Kirby Smith's. . . . The officers were dressed in gray or black & wearing different kinds of flat hats & feathers with cockades or streamers."[14]

Almost immediately on the arrival of the Confederates in Lexington, the recruiting process began. Duke claimed that the men who came forward during those September days wanted to join the cavalry and Morgan's brigade in particular. These recruits claimed that they had been waiting for an opportunity to leave Lexington and make their way to Tennessee to enlist; however, Morgan's serendipitous arrival hastened their enlistment. Kirby Smith was having more difficulty than Morgan luring recruits. Barely enough to form one infantry company enlisted with his army. As Duke later emphasized in *A History of Morgan's Cavalry,* all the Kentuckians wanted to ride, and, "as a people, they are fond of horses, and if they went to war at all, they thought it a great tax upon them to make them walk." The cavalry recruits were so numerous that W. C. P. Breckinridge was authorized to form a battalion using his company from the Second Kentucky as a nucleus for the new unit. Gano was also authorized to raise a regiment, as were Leroy Cluke of Winchester and David Chenault of Richmond.[15]

The rally of recruits to Morgan's standard was an anomaly. The meager results of Kirby Smith's recruiting efforts were the first disappointment for the Confederates in the campaign and a forewarning of the attitude that actually prevailed in the Bluegrass. Contrary to what either Morgan or Duke wanted to believe, the friendly reception that the brigade received in many Kentucky towns during the July raid was generally from the women and, therefore, deceptive. Captain Paul F. Hammond,

Typical of the young men who rode with Morgan and Duke was sixteen-year-old J. Barlow. Brandishing three revolvers, the young Confederate appears to be ready for any action that might come his way.

of Kirby Smith's staff, noticed this fact when the army entered Lexington: "We could not fail to notice, even then that the crowds gathered to greet us were composed for the most part of women and children. The men, the bone and sinew of the land, the substantial property holders, even those who sincerely sympathized with the Confederate cause, with a few honorable exceptions, held cautiously aloof, while the Union men most violent of whom ran away at our approach kept closely in their houses." Bragg and his army would experience similarly disappointing results when they attempted to recruit in other parts of the state. The Confederates had brought twenty thousand extra rifles with them for the anticipated recruits promised by Morgan and Duke. The Kentuckians claimed only twenty-five hundred.[16]

During the brigade's encampment northwest of town on the Georgetown and Lexington Pike, the site later of the August Belmont horse farm, Morgan and his staff used the office of the *Lexington Observer and Reporter*, a local newspaper, as their headquarters. The *Observer and Reporter* had suspended publication prior to Morgan's arrival, but Lexington did not go without a newspaper. The *Kentucky Statesman*, whose publication had been suspended by the federal authorities in the fall of 1861, began to print again and was probably the only regularly published Confederate newspaper in the state during the war. The Confederates, particularly the publishers of *The Vidette*, had no intention of letting the *Observer*'s printing department sit idle while they were in Lexington. Morgan's printers published a large and varied assortment of military pamphlets, broadsides, and handbills during the occupation of Lexington. One of these documents bore the title *Tactics for Mounted Riflemen, by Colonel Basil W. Duke, Morgan's Power Press Print, John Hays Printer, Lexington, Kentucky.* The existence of this publication certainly lends credibility to the thesis that Duke was instrumental, if not key, in the development of the tactics used by Morgan and his men during the war.[17]

Unlike the previous September, when Duke's plan to reach Lexington and Tommie was foiled by the fast-unfolding military maneuvers of both armies, this time he was able to reach home and family as a conquering hero. Tommie did not care how her husband arrived; she was simply happy that they were together again. The strain of a year of occupation and general alienation was relieved the moment of her and Basil's reunion. For Duke, this heartfelt time proved that, as swiftly as his life in the saddle turned violent, just as swiftly it could revert to the serenity that he had prayed for that evening with Mrs. Jennings in Richmond in July 1862.

Once the initial euphoria of being in the Bluegrass wore off and the reality of the military situation became apparent, Kirby Smith grew increasingly concerned about the vulnerability of his northern flank. He realized that it was only a matter of time before the Union forces in the Cincinnati area began to probe south in his direction. Despite the large number of cavalry recruits, he was concerned that he did not have a sufficient number of veteran cavalry to screen his army adequately. To counterbalance the lack of veteran horsemen, Kirby Smith decided to rely on deception and ordered Duke and the Second Kentucky to northern Kentucky for the explicit purpose of annoying the enemy and giving the impression that the Confederates might threaten Cincinnati. Although he had a significant amount of combat experience, Duke had never before been given an independent assignment of this magnitude. Meanwhile, Morgan had received his own orders from Kirby Smith. He was to take the balance of the brigade to the southeast of Lexington and observe the movements of the Union troops under the command of George Morgan, who had evacuated his position in the Cumberland Gap and was advancing north through the hills of eastern Kentucky and seemingly posed a threat to Kirby Smith's eastern flank.[18]

To his Union counterparts, Duke appeared to be all over northern Kentucky and, by September 19, had destroyed three railroad bridges. His troops constantly fenced, sometimes on a daily basis, with larger federal patrols between Walton and Falmouth. This type of aggressive activity was exactly what Kirby Smith needed. It kept the federal forces off balance and continuously concerned about a possible major Confederate thrust toward Cincinnati. On September 27, General Horatio Wright, the commander of the Department of the Ohio, advised his superiors in Washington: "Against that great city [Cincinnati] the rebels may turn at any moment, and unless I can call upon the force here or obtain it in the mean time from Ohio I shall scarcely be in condition to offer a very successful resistance; of course I shall do the best I can."[19]

Wanting to exploit his opportunity to the fullest, Duke sent John Castleman north to check the fords on the Ohio River near Augusta, Kentucky. If it proved practical, Duke planned to cross into Ohio and make an aggressive feint toward Cincinnati. This tactic, if successful, had the potential to create pandemonium, not only in the Queen City, but also throughout the entire Ohio military district. If a rebel force crossed the Ohio, the federal troops near Walton would be ordered to withdraw to protect Cincinnati. Such a withdrawal would invariably relieve the pressure on Kirby Smith's northern flank. There was also another reason why Duke wanted to put in an appearance in Augusta. The home guard was using it as a staging area for patrols that were becoming increasingly aggressive on his front. Several had even come within a few miles of his position at Walton. Not only did Duke intend to cross the river into Ohio, but he also planned to disrupt or destroy the home guard's ability to continue its patrols in his sector.[20]

When Castleman returned from Augusta, he reported to Duke that there was an excellent ford over the Ohio River only a few miles below the town. This information was determinative, and Duke decided to take approximately six hundred of his troops and attempt to cross the river at the ford. Augusta is located on the Ohio River between Cincinnati and Maysville. It was typical of most small towns in that corner of Kentucky, loyalties being evenly divided. Regular troops were not garrisoned in the town. The only troops available for defense were the home guard in and around the town. However, Augusta did have a unique alternate defense force. Docked at the town's wharf were two small gunboats, one of which had a twelve-pound cannon mounted on its foredeck.[21]

The home guard was commanded by Majors Joshua T. Bradford and Joseph Harris and consisted of approximately one hundred men of varying quality and dedication. The town was under martial law and still a bit shocked by the news that Colonel Richard Gano had earlier that week ridden into and captured Maysville without firing a shot. Maysville was a far larger town than Augusta and was located only twenty miles farther up the Ohio River. Then, on September 24, about forty of Duke's men stopped at the home of Mrs. Mary Coburn two miles out of town demanding food for themselves and feed for their horses. These actions caused Bradford to position his pickets in a semicircle three miles from the center of town.[22]

When Duke and his troops rode through Brooksville, a small crossroads community less than ten miles to the south of Augusta, they captured some of Bradford's pickets and brought them along for the ride. At seven o'clock in the morning on September 27, 1862, Duke sat in his saddle on a two-hundred-foot rise overlooking Augusta, from which vantage point he was able to obtain a perfect picture of the tactical situation in the town. For example, he could see the two gunboats and elements of the home guard scurrying below in anticipation of his attack. What he could not see was that the majority of the home guard had already found defensive positions in houses and other buildings along the streets that his troops would use when they entered the town. In 1862, Augusta was a small, compact town nestled between the hills and the Ohio River and characterized by a tight network of streets. Street fighting was neither Duke's nor his men's forte. It also involved too many risks for those unfamiliar with the territory and without precise knowledge of the buildings occupied by the enemy. The effectiveness of the horse as a military weapon and the cohesiveness of a unit of cavalry are generally lost in such a combat environment.[23]

Duke ordered Company A to dismount and go to the eastern edge of town, next to the river. This position would permit it to harass the two gunboats as well as the enemy in town as Duke moved the remainder of his forces forward. Recognizing that horses would be useless in town, Duke dismounted the rest of his troops and ordered the bull pups unlimbered and placed on the rise overlooking the town. When Company A was in position, Duke ordered the bull pups to shell the gunboats. The gunboats immediately responded, one of their shells landing within thirty feet of one of the howitzers, forcing it to move to another position. The bull pups' fire was, however, more accurate, and, after a few more shells had been fired, one hit and damaged the deck of one of the gunboats. In tandem with the shelling from the howitzers, Company A concentrated its fire on the sailors who were manning the boat's cannon. This combination of fire was too hot for the gunboats and their captain, who, having lost the will to fight, ordered the boats to pull away from the wharf and steam downriver out of harm's way.[24]

After the gunboats departed, Duke anticipated the surrender of the home guard without much of a fight. Accordingly, he ordered two companies to enter the town. As Companies B and C rode down the hill into Augusta, they passed the edge of a vineyard the grapes of which had grown quite ripe. Duke's boys picked handfuls of grapes, eating them as they rode into town. The force divided when it reached the bottom of the hill, part riding down Main Street and then over to Front Street, meeting no opposition along the way. The only sign of life that this group saw was a white flag hanging out of a window. The other detachment was not so fortunate. Moving on to Upper Street, this group noticed that, as Thomas Bullitt recalled, "just opposite a church yard stood a double brick house, with five windows in the second story of the house fronting exactly on the sidewalk, with no yard in the front." When these men "marched past the house in a column, in the center of the street, a blaze of fire from all five windows was poured" in their direction. The troops instinctively sought cover in the churchyard across the street from the building. At the first sign of a fight, Duke ordered his troops to the right side of town to find cover, but there were so many of his men in the streets it was difficult for him to maneuver and coordinate his orders. The result was confusion and an increasing number of casualties.[25]

The bull pups began to lob shells into town, but their fire was not as accurate as it had been earlier, and several shells landed among Duke's troops, adding to the disorder. In spite of the confusion and chaos, it was only a matter of minutes before Duke restored order and brought the bull pups into town, where they were used effectively at point-blank range, firing grape and canister at the buildings believed to be harboring the Union resistance. Once again the white flag, this time in the form of sheets, was displayed in the windows, and the Confederates stopped firing. Believing that there was a general surrender, the Confederates stood up and began to walk toward the buildings to collect their prisoners and put out the fires started by the shelling. Whether some of the Union troops had not surrendered or the white flag had been a ruse to draw the Confederates out into the open is not clear. What is clear is that, as soon as Duke's men were exposed, the Union troops opened fire again, and several of Duke's men were killed. Duke wrote that only those who shook the white flag meant to give up and that the others continued to fight. However, a contemporary account found in a letter from Mary H. Coburn to her niece Mary E. Walton paints a different picture: "The women and children waived [*sic*] their white flags out of the windows and the men was behind them and done their shooting out of the windows they could not get them out of the houses and they [the Confederates] sit fire to the houses were [*sic*] the union men were firing out the windows."[26]

The Confederates naturally took this act to represent a blatant disregard of the rules of war. Duke himself was infuriated and ordered every house being used as a firing post by the Union soldiers to be set to the torch. Some of Duke's more vengeful troops entered the suspect houses with the express intent to kill anyone inside who wore a blue uniform. During the display of the white sheets, Captain Sam Morgan was shot and killed. His cousin Wash Morgan, Bullitt recalled, "became like a wild man; broke into the house and with his own hand shot every soldier he encountered, accepting no surrender, it was said that he shot one man hiding under a bed, all the time shouting and laughing at the distraction." This type of fighting could not go on for very long, and the Union commander surrendered. The toll on Duke's forces was twenty-one dead and eighteen wounded, while twelve Union soldiers were killed, three wounded, and approximately one hundred captured. Duke was obviously bothered by the circumstances surrounding the day's action. In *A History of Morgan's Cavalry,* he gives the names of and writes something personal about eight of the men who lost their lives during the fight.[27]

Although Duke had won the battle, the cost was disproportionate to the result. Duke had captured and neutralized the home guard, but the primary objective of the raid, the crossing of the Ohio River and the threatening of Cincinnati, had to be aborted. The command was emotionally drained and incapable of proceeding any farther. In many respects, Duke suffered a tactical defeat. His primary mistake was to commit his command to a street fight on the basis of an erroneous assumption: that the enemy would either surrender quickly or fight according to his rules. It was a costly mistake—and one that Duke never repeated.[28]

Duke stayed in Augusta for only two hours after the fight, which was more than enough time for him to form the impression that many of the townspeople were not enamored of the heavy hand of Washington. There was an underlying discontent that was growing throughout the state as a result of federal troops' impressing Southern men into the Union militia. Mary Coburn expressed this discontent by expressing no sympathy for the home guard. She felt that they "had been sporting for a fight" and got what they deserved, with no one to blame but themselves.[29]

The fight had lasted barely two hours, but the town of Augusta suffered significantly. The primary loss was caused by the fires, which destroyed several blocks containing some of the finer dwellings in the town. The total property damage was estimated at $100,000. Also, before Duke withdrew later that afternoon, in an exhibition of frustration and animosity toward the town several of his men did some uncustomary looting. Mary Coburn noted: "They broke open stores and took all they wanted and left town. . . . They took all the buggys and horses they could pick up. . . . They took the prisoners walking, they made them keep up with the horses, they left town." On leaving town, Duke headed first to Brooksville, where he paroled his prisoners, and then began his withdrawal toward Walton in full view of a pursuing Union force arriving from Maysville. As his column rode out of Brooksville, the Union troops unlimbered their cannon and fired a few parting shots at the retreating Confederates. Duke returned to Walton, from which position he continued to annoy the federal troops for the next week.[30]

On October 6, 1862, Duke and the Second Kentucky were ordered to return to Lexington. Buell had finally started to move his army out of Louisville and was heading in a general southeasterly direction searching for the Confederates. Meanwhile, the Confederate high command had come to the realization that the people of Kentucky were not going to rally to the flag in the vast numbers predicted by Morgan and Duke. Apparently, much more than the accomplishments of the Confederate army during the month of September was needed to motivate them. It seemed that it would take a significant military victory, the installation of a Confederate government, and the establishment of a permanent and substantial Confederate military presence in Kentucky to prove that the Bragg–Kirby Smith presence was something more than another transitory raid.[31]

During early October, there was very little optimism to be found in Kirby Smith's camp. All through September, Kirby Smith continued to court the civilian population. He had issued orders to all his commanders to make sure that their troops behaved in an orderly way "as otherwise the people cannot be favorably impressed." But, even as early as the middle of September, he was losing some enthusiasm and wrote to his wife of his disappointment in the number of recruits: "When I see their magnificent estates their fat cattle & fine stock I understand their fears & hesitancy they have much to lose." Two days later, he wrote a similar letter to Bragg, telling him that the people of Kentucky "are slow and backward in rallying to our standard. Their hearts are evidently with us, but their blue-grass and fat-grass are against us." After a year of federal occupation, most Kentuckians had accepted their lot, and, even though their sympathies "were altogether with the south," wrote Nathaniel Southgate Shaler, "reason kept them Unionist and they resisted the arguments of their secessionist comrades."[32]

By late September, many in Kirby Smith's army were asking what the situation was with Bragg. Several military historians, including Duke, believed that Bragg had squandered a favorable opportunity to confront Buell. Even during the first week of October, Bragg was still equivocating as to his next strategic move. It had taken him several weeks before he actually reached this point of indecision. When he had left Chattanooga, his army had advanced quickly into Kentucky and, on September 14, reached Glasgow in high spirits. At Glasgow, Bragg was positioned favorably between Buell to the west and Kirby Smith to the east, and the invasion plan seemed to be working like a finely tuned watch. Louisville was lightly defended and could be reached by Bragg, if he so desired, ahead of Buell. Alternatively, Bragg had the option of selecting a position of his choice and forcing Buell into a battle. The initiative certainly rested with Bragg, and, for the moment, Buell could only wait. Bragg, however, lost that initiative approximately twenty miles north of Glasgow.[33]

The Union army had constructed a strong defensive position on the southern bank of the Green River directly across from the small town of Munfordville. General James Chalmers, with the vanguard of Bragg's army, impetuously attacked the Munfordville garrison on September 14, 1862. The attack was not authorized by Bragg and was easily repulsed. Bragg was visibly upset when he learned of the debacle and concluded that he had no choice but to invest Munfordville. Munfordville, however, surrendered quietly to Bragg on September 17 after its commander conferred with several Confederate officers, who convinced him that any further resistance was futile. Some students of the campaign have argued, rather convincingly, that, after Munfordville, Bragg had time to position himself between Buell and Louisville or force Buell to attack his army at Munfordville. Politically and militarily, Buell could not let Bragg's army stay at Munfordville uncontested. Having seriously studied the campaign after the war, Duke concluded that Bragg's vacillations and timidity "unquestionably threw away his most favorable opportunity to strike a blow which would be decisive and sure to secure him permanent advantage, when he declined battle at Munfordville."[34]

At the time, Bragg viewed his situation quite differently. For several days after the capture of Munfordville, he was determined to fight but could not entice Buell into a battle. When Bragg realized that Buell was not going to attack him at Munfordville, he grew pessimistic about the campaign in general and decided that it was time to withdraw. In reaching this decision, Bragg may have concluded that he did not have sufficient manpower or supplies to make a protracted stand at Munfordville. He also had definitive orders from Jefferson Davis not to lose his army in Kentucky, orders that probably tempered his decisionmaking process. Bragg finally decided to withdraw, march to the northeast, and attempt to join up with Kirby Smith's army in central Kentucky.[35]

When Duke received Morgan's recall order, he immediately became concerned. He mounted his troops and rode all night so as to reach Lexington early in the morning. When he reported to Morgan at Hopemont, he was told that his regiment, along with the rest of Kirby Smith's army, had been ordered to evacuate Lexington and concentrate to the southwest near Harrodsburg. It was not difficult for Duke to detect the bitterness in Morgan's voice as he spoke of giving up the stakes without making any effort to win them. Duke's heart sank, and, for the first time, he began to lose faith in the cause. At that point, however, Bragg suddenly received intelligence that a heavy federal force was moving in the direction of Frankfort and, consequently, ordered Leonidas Polk to move from Bardstown and strike the enemy in his rear and flank while Kirby Smith advanced west from Lexington and attacked the federal force from the front. These orders were intended to supersede Polk's earlier instructions from Bragg issued on September 28 that, "if pressed by a force too large to justify his giving battle, [he was] to fall back in the direction of the new depot near Bryantsville." Unilaterally deciding to ignore Bragg's new order, Polk continued on to Bryantsville but advised his commander of this decision in time to prevent Kirby Smith's move west from being initiated, hence the move toward Harrodsburg. Bragg was now forced to abandon Lexington and Frankfort and establish a defensive line to protect his gains in central Kentucky. Duke, as well as the rest of his troops, was disappointed to leave Lexington, but he understood the order and hoped to soon return.[36]

Bragg's assumption that Buell was seeking a battle with Kirby Smith was incorrect. Only a portion of Buell's army, two divisions, was actually moving in the general direction of Frankfort. Buell's other three divisions had concentrated some fifty miles to the south of Frankfort, a few miles to the west of the small village of Perryville. There, near noon on October 8, 1862, a Confederate infantry division commanded by Benjamin Cheatham surprised lead elements of the federal army and attacked. The rebels initially rolled the Union troops back two miles until their attack stalled. Although the Confederates had gained a limited tactical success, the next morning Bragg withdrew from the battlefield to Harrodsburg. Over the next several days, Buell's army slowly started to deploy opposite the two Confederate armies. Numerically, a Bragg–Kirby Smith combination would have been somewhat larger than Buell's army. Duke believed that Bragg was attempting to form at Harrodsburg for the purpose of engaging the Union army and remembered conversations with some of Kirby Smith's staff on the night of October 11 indicating that "they were fully impressed with the belief that we would fight the next day and quite as strongly with the conviction that we would win a great victory." Stoddard Johnston, an aid to Bragg, had quite the opposite impression, believing that Bragg had decided to abandon Kentucky.[37]

That night, Duke and his regiment were in position with Morgan's brigade on the extreme left of the Confederate army. The night was cloudy and dark, and there was a steady drizzle, but Duke remembered seeing the long lines of campfires, each army having its own undivided character and each a "huge monster of wrath and ferocity." However, the next morning, the Confederates awakened, not to the anticipated battle, but to a quiet retreat toward Lancaster, where Bragg and Kirby Smith and their two armies went their separate ways. Morgan was ordered to cover the retreat and keep open the approaches to the Kentucky River at King's and Baker's Mills, where the Confederate infantry intended to cross. Duke and most of the Kentucky Confederates never really forgave Bragg for abandoning their state that autumn. Instances subsequent to the campaign between Bragg and John C. Breckinridge and other Kentucky commanders resulted in many Kentuckians harboring bitter feelings toward Bragg, feelings that lasted well beyond the war. Shortly after the war, Duke expressed his extreme wrath with Bragg in *A History of Morgan's Cavalry*: "The wrongs he did Kentucky and Kentuckians, the indignity which he bore down on the Kentucky troops, his hatred and bitter, active antagonism to all prominent Kentucky officers, had made an abhorrence of him part of the Kentucky creed. There is no reason why any expression of natural feeling toward him should now be suppressed—he is not dead, nor a prisoner, nor an exile." Duke eventually tempered his opinion, however, and, in 1885, when he wrote "Bragg's Campaign in Kentucky" for the *Southern Bivouac,* he simply concluded the article with the following statement: "With Bragg's retreat the pall fell on the fortunes of the Confederacy."[38]

After bivouacking for several days near Lancaster, Kirby Smith moved his army east to Richmond and then south to Knoxville. Morgan's brigade served as the extreme rear guard of Kirby Smith's army and did not leave Lancaster until October 14. Several days later, Morgan received permission to break off from the army, double back to Lexington, and then proceed to southwestern Kentucky to attack strategic points on the Louisville and Nashville Railroad.[39]

Tom Quirk and his scouts had reconnoitered Lexington and reported to Morgan that the brigade's old adversary the Fourth Ohio Cavalry was camped approximately a mile and a half from the center of town at Ashland, Henry Clay's estate. The federal troops in Lexington were aware that some Confederate cavalry had crossed back over the Kentucky River but did not know the identity of the units. In fact, Morgan and Duke's entire command had crossed the river and was heading into Lexington from two different directions, on both the Tates Creek Pike and the Richmond Road. After conferring with Duke, Gano, and Breckinridge, Morgan ordered Duke to enter Lexington from the south on the Tates Creek Pike and then send two of his companies into the center of town, capture what troops were there, and position the balance of the regiment north of Ashland. Gano and Breckinridge were expected to place their regiments to the south of Ashland, completing the encirclement of the Fourth Ohio.[40]

The Second Kentucky moved into position north of Ashland as planned but soon began to receive fire from Breckinridge's newly formed regiment. To avoid any further confusion, Duke pulled his regiment back, content with capturing any Union soldiers trying to evade the trap. Moments later, as Duke was collecting prisoners, Gano's men opened fire on his unit. After these two near-fatal mistakes, the result largely of confusion between Gano's and Breckinridge's newly formed regiments, the Fourth Ohio surrendered. Unfortunately, during the battle, Morgan's cousin Wash Morgan was mortally wounded. He was carried to Hopemont, where he was propped in a bed so that he could smoke a cigar before he died. Except for some light casualties suffered by the Confederates, doubling back on Lexington was a successful maneuver resulting in the capture of several hundred Union troops and mitigating, somewhat, the frustration of the retreat.[41]

Later that day, a courier delivered to Duke a message from Kirby Smith for Morgan. Bragg had countermanded permission for Morgan to return to Tennessee through western Kentucky and was now ordering him to proceed to southwestern Virginia to guard the salt and lead mines in that region. Morgan's biographer James Ramage points out that being assigned to southwestern Virginia was a "veritable graveyard for commanders" and that Bragg was attempting to bury Morgan in obscurity. Obviously, Bragg believed that he had been misled by Morgan's and Duke's preinvasion reports and held the two partly responsible for the failure of the Kentucky campaign. The message was never delivered to Morgan; instead, Duke put it in his pocket, to be forgotten until after the war. Duke was too good a soldier not to realize that his act was in violation of everything that he and Grenfell were trying to instill in his troops and could justify his decision only on the grounds that there was already a sufficient number of troops in southwestern Virginia.[42]

The Confederate return to Lexington had completely bewildered the Unionists in the city, many of whom had been in hiding during the Confederate occupation and had just returned to Lexington, believing that the Confederates had completely withdrawn. Now that Morgan had returned, the question on everyone's mind was for how long. The answer was not long in coming: bulging with new recruits, the brigade left Lexington the very next day. Riding in a westerly direction toward Versailles, by nightfall it had crossed the Kentucky River "somewhere in the vicinity of Lawrenceburg."[43]

As they moved west, the raiders returned to their old activities of skirmishing with sundry federal units and destroying enemy supplies. This continued for several days. Finally, on the night of October 21, 1862, the brigade camped just north of the Green River, which it crossed the next day. Three days later, the weather suddenly turned very cold. That night, as the temperature continued to drop, the troops bedded down, with three or four sleeping together to take advantage of each other's body heat. The men slept very soundly, only to awaken in the morning to find that they were covered with six inches of snow. In fact, when Duke rode into camp before the troops had risen, he might not have found them had it not been for the guards. With the change in the weather, Morgan decided that his men needed a rest. The command moved to Hopkinsville, where, to the delight of the townspeople, it stayed for three days.[44]

Since leaving Lexington, Duke and the other regimental commanders had been having some trouble with stragglers, most of whom were new recruits. Prior to arriving in Hopkinsville, John Porter had been ordered to take charge of the rear guard for the day. Porter also had the responsibility of collecting and arresting all the stragglers. According to Porter: "Many were drunk and fell out of ranks. All of whom it was my duty to arrest, which I did, and when I reached Hopkinsville, which was about midnight, I had about seventy-five men in arrest, whom I gave over to the charge of the Officer of the day. Some of them were boisterous and troublesome."[45]

As Bragg's and Kirby Smith's armies and Morgan's cavalry left Kentucky, the failure of the state's large population of Southern sympathizers to rise and rally behind the Confederates was a deep disappointment to and, to a certain degree, created bitterness in Bragg's army. Yet, when Bragg left Kentucky, it took two and a half days for his train of wagons, overloaded with provisions, and the trailing livestock to pass a given point. Bragg may not have raised a division of new recruits in Kentucky, as Morgan and Duke had promised, but he did leave the state well provided.[46]

Morgan and Duke arrived in Springfield, Tennessee, on November 1, 1862, moving on to Gallatin three days later. At Gallatin, Morgan was in perfect position to picket the right flank of Bragg's army. The brigade also welcomed the addition of a new regiment, the Ninth Tennessee. This regiment was still green, untested and in need of training before it could be integrated as an effective fighting unit within the brigade. The Ninth Tennessee was composed primarily of men from Sumner County and was commanded by Colonel James Bennett and Lieutenant Colonel W. W. Ward.[47]

The men felt that they were going to be given a well-deserved and much-needed rest after completing the retreat from Kentucky, but General Breckinridge had other ideas. Breckinridge was now at Murfreesboro and had learned that the Union army had collected about three hundred boxcars north of Nashville at a railroad junction near the town of Edgeville. General William S. Rosecrans, who had replaced Buell on October 30, 1862, had been collecting the boxcars in anticipation of the opening of Big South Tunnel. They were lined up on railroad tracks running along the river but close enough to the town to be protected by the Union garrison. Artillery had also been placed on a hill to cover the rail junction. In tandem with an assault on the rail junction, Breckinridge had planned a diversion using Nathan Bedford Forrest's cavalry and some Kentucky infantry units on the south side of the river.[48]

Duke and the Second Kentucky were ordered to lead the assault. However, at first light, when the attack was scheduled to start, alert federal pickets spotted the movements of the Second Kentucky and initiated an exchange of fire with the Confederates. Even though Duke was able to drive back the pickets, killing several in the process, the garrison was alerted. When Duke reached the rail yard, a strong force of Union infantry had already taken up position behind a railroad embankment. He immediately realized that concentrated fire from such a heavily fortified position was going to jeopardize the success of the attack. Meanwhile, on the other side of the river, Forrest created as much noise as possible, all to no avail. The Union troops in the rail yard realized that Forrest was a diversion and completely ignored his efforts. Tom Quirk was able to destroy about ten boxcars before Duke decided that the risk factor was too high and wisely pulled the Second Kentucky out of line and retreated. The Union cavalry pursued Duke for several miles. At one point they began to drive in Duke's pickets, causing some concern that his flank might be vulnerable to an attack. In order to ascertain the exact strength and position of the enemy, Duke along with Gano and several others fell in behind the rear guard. This was the only time Duke recalled seeing Gano frightened. Duke and Gano had stopped to observe the Union cavalry, and it was not long before their presence began to attract fire. Gano was wearing a Mexican blanket trimmed in deep red, and, as a bullet clipped the blanket, it sent the red material floating into the air between him and Duke. Initially, both men thought that Gano had been hit. All that a much-shaken Gano could manage to say was, "Why Duke they're shooting at us."[49]

Morgan moved his men and encamped for a well-deserved rest four miles from Lebanon. Duke later recalled Morgan receiving a visit from Nathan Bedford Forrest, and it may have been at this camp that that visit took place. Forrest was very interested in Morgan's Kentucky campaign, and Morgan in turn was interested in Forrest's capture of Murfreesboro the prior summer. It was during this meeting that Duke heard Forrest use an expression that he found at the time to be amusing and later often quoted in one variation or another. Morgan wanted to know how Forrest had been able to capture Murfreesboro when the entire countryside around the town was full of federal troops. Forrest—apparently recalling Beauregard's advice to Bragg, "Be careful always to move by interior lines and strike the fragments of your enemies' forces with the mass of your own"—reiterated this concept to Morgan in his own words: "I just took the shortcut and got there first with the most men."[50]

8

December Battles

On November 24, 1862, Duke and the Second Kentucky were ordered to Fayetteville, Tennessee, for a much-needed rest. Not only had Duke's regiment participated in a major Kentucky raid and the Bragg–Kirby Smith invasion, but it had also been very active on its return to Tennessee. The fluid nature of cavalry movements in Morgan's field of operations had involved Duke and his regiment in some sort of action on a daily basis. To further complicate matters, the new Union commander, General William S. Rosecrans, had reinforced the garrisons at Gallatin and Hartsville, thereby increasing the threat to the Confederate presence in that part of Tennessee.[1]

In early December, Duke, Tom Quirk, and Grenfell were ordered to Bragg's headquarters in Murfreesboro to meet with Morgan. Morgan had determined, correctly, that the garrison at Hartsville was isolated and had petitioned Bragg several times to permit him to return to Sumner County. Bragg finally acquiesced and organized the raid, authorizing Morgan to take a combined force of no more than eighteen hundred men, composed of cavalry, infantry, and artillery, and attack the garrison at Hartsville.[2]

Bragg had, apparently, tempered his displeasure over Morgan's and Duke's unfulfilled Kentucky prophecies and was now focused on their military utility. In early December, Bragg's faith in his cavalry was so strong that, according to Grady McWhiney, his biographer, he believed that the combined operations of Morgan, Wheeler, and Forrest could eventually force Rosecrans to withdraw from Nashville.[3]

Rosecrans had no intention of withdrawing from Nashville and was in the process of preparing for the inevitable clash with Bragg. The fighting spirit of his army was suspect, however, and his first task was to instill a sense of esprit de corps in his men. As Rosecrans worked to strengthen his army, he quickly realized the Confederate cavalry's superiority and its ability to interrupt his communication and supply lines. Pleading for an able cavalry commander, he petitioned General Halleck to give him Brigadier General David S. Stanley, claiming: "He can do more good service by commanding a cavalry than an infantry division. I beg you for

Basil Duke was described as the personification of the ideal cavalier. This photograph of Duke, possibly taken during his imprisonment at Fort Delaware in the spring of 1864, does not belie that description. (Courtesy the Filson Historical Society, Louisville.)

that reason to send him to me. You know the expense of cavalry, and what the rebel cavalry has done. Stanley will double our forces without expense." Stanley was given the job.[4]

The twenty-five-hundred-man garrison at Hartsville was designated as the Thirty-ninth Brigade, comprising the 104th Illinois Infantry, the Second Indiana Cavalry, the Thirteenth Indiana Battery, Company E of the Eleventh Kentucky Cavalry, and the 106th and 108th Ohio Infantry under Colonel Absalom B. Moore of the 104th Illinois. There was, however, at Castalian Springs, a scant six miles from Hartsville, a much larger force of six thousand men commanded by Duke's old friend General John Marshall Harlan. Morgan believed that he could capture Hartsville before reinforcements could arrive from Castalian Springs. Part of the motivation for Morgan's assuming this risky venture was the usual lure of badly needed arms. In particular, Morgan's men coveted the Colt revolvers issued to the Union cavalry.[5]

The engagement at Hartsville was to be a unique venture for Morgan and Duke. For the first and only time during the war, Morgan was to be the field commander of a force that included two infantry regiments and a battery of field artillery. For the first time, Duke was to command a brigade-strength cavalry unit. The cavalry would, however, be without the services of the Second Kentucky. The regiments assigned to Duke for the engagement were Gano's, Bennett's, Cluke's, and Chenault's as well as Stoner's battalion. The immediate command of the Second and Ninth Kentucky Infantry regiments was placed in the competent hands of Colonel Thomas H. Hunt. The total force numbered approximately fifteen hundred cavalry and seven hundred infantry plus Cobb's artillery battery.[6]

Morgan's small army broke camp and marched in the direction of Hartsville early on the morning of December 6, 1862. The weather had been cold, but that particular morning seemed to be the coldest of the season. Duke described the cold as intense. Adding to the infantrymen's problems was a layer of snow on the ground that, a few miles into the march, turned into mud. When the cavalry joined the infantry later that morning, Morgan ordered a "ride-and-tie" march. The cavalry and infantry started the march together with the cavalry in front. After the cavalry had ridden three or four miles, the men would dismount and tie their horses to trees or fence posts and march on ahead. When the infantry caught up to the horses, they would mount and ride until they were several miles ahead of the cavalry, at which point the process would be repeated. Neither the cavalry nor the foot soldiers cared for the ride and tie in cold weather. The feet of Hunt's men had become damp and even wet during the long march, and, when they mounted the horses, their wet socks and shoes were prone to freeze. This would have been less likely to happen if they had continued the march on foot. When their shoes and socks began to show signs of freezing, they became uncomfortable and wanted to dismount. After the troops changed for the second time, the shoes and socks of the cavalrymen began to freeze as well. Despite these problems the combined force of infantry and cavalry was able to cover thirty miles of muddy and icy roads and cross a river in twenty-four hours.[7]

The Cumberland River had become the dividing line between the Union and the Confederate armies in middle Tennessee. The plan that Morgan and Bragg conceived called for Morgan's force to ford the river at two different locations. With more than one ford in use, the small army theoretically could cross the river in one night and be in position to attack the enemy at dawn. The infantry regiments and the artillery battery arrived at their designated ford, a few miles above Puryear's Ferry, around ten that night. Although the river had risen since it had last been reconnoitered, making it impossible for the infantry to wade through, the scouts were able to locate two small boats at Puryear's Ferry several miles below Hartsville. The condition of these boats was questionable at best, but they turned out to be very useful and helped the infantry cross the river in a timely fashion. Concerned that the operation would take too long, Morgan personally urged the foot soldiers to move as quickly as possible. Although tired and wet, the infantry responded favorably to Morgan and crossed the river with time to spare.[8]

Duke with his cavalry was to cross the river at a ford located a few miles below Puryear's Ferry. But, when Duke reached the ford, he discovered that the rising water made it impossible for his men to cross there. With no boats in sight, he was forced to use valuable time searching for another place to cross. If one was not found quickly, the cavalry would not be in position in time to support the infantry. Morgan would then be forced to cancel the attack. The ford that Duke finally chose would be difficult but not impossible to use that night. The approach to it was along a bridle path that descended to the river. But the path was narrow, the men had to ride in single file and cross the river one at a time, and the process took longer than planned. Not only was the river continuing to rise, but it was flowing very fast as well. These conditions, when coupled with the dark night, compounded the difficulty of the crossing. Any one of these problems would have significantly slowed the crossing, but, together, they made for a long and difficult night for the cavalry.[9]

When Duke's troops finally reached the river, they discovered that the bank was a small bluff approximately four feet above the water. The height of the bluff was not an insurmountable obstacle, but each trooper would have to jump with his horse off the bank into the fast-flowing water. When man and horse splashed into the river, they were momentarily submerged, and, when they reached the opposite bank, they were thoroughly soaked. To be cold was bad enough, but to be wet and cold was unbearable. As time passed and more men crossed, both banks of the river became virtual mudslides.[10]

Many of the troops were literally freezing in their wet clothes when they reached the opposite bank, a condition that R. T. Bean, a trooper in the Eighth Kentucky, remembered as being "anything but pleasant." The men could not continue on like this, and Duke ordered them to build small fires to dry their clothes. Others, such as Leeland Hathaway, were ordered not to make fires and were forced to "get warm and dry by exercise." All this was taking far more time than Duke could afford and still be in position on schedule. A few hours before the dawn attack, Duke realized that it was impossible for all his cavalry to cross the river in time. Bowing to the inevitable, he ordered the troops who had not crossed to join him at Hartsville as soon as possible and then, cold and damp, rode the five miles to rendezvous with Morgan. When Duke arrived, it was nearly dawn. After a quick conference, Morgan ordered Duke to press ahead and not wait for the other regiments. As his men began to deploy, they immediately ran into a line of strong pickets within a half mile of the main Union line. The element of surprise that Morgan had hoped to achieve was now lost.[11]

As the sky began to lighten, Duke noticed a depression to his immediate front, followed by the crest of a low hill on which he could make out the figures of Union soldiers hurriedly forming an impressive defensive line. The federal line was composed of elements of the 104th Illinois positioned in the center and, to the immediate right, a battery from the Thirteenth Indiana. The 106th Ohio was on the left and the 108th Ohio on the extreme right of the line. The 108th Ohio formed itself in the trees overlooking the left flank of Morgan's line. The Union commander had his entire complement of troops in line and the Confederates perhaps half as many. As Duke watched the enemy deploy, he looked over at Morgan and said: "You have more work cut out for you here than you bargained for." "Yes," Morgan answered, "but you gentlemen will have to whip these fellows and get away from here in less than two hours, or you'll have 6000 more on your backs."[12]

The Ninth Tennessee, Bennett's relatively new regiment, was ordered to circumvent the Union line and enter Hartsville, capturing any enemy troops in the town. Morgan then ordered Duke to form Cluke's and Chenault's regiments facing the right flank of the federal line. Duke positioned these regiments opposite the 108th Ohio and then ordered his men to dismount and advance on foot. The cavalry wheeled to the right, counted off in groups of five, with every fifth man given the task of holding horses, and then dismounted. Men who were unarmed rushed along the line hunting for guns among the horse holders, who gladly gave up their weapons. Not counting the horse holders, Duke had approximately 450 men available for the attack. Cluke was opposite the Ohio regiment and Chenault to the left of Cluke but at an obtuse angle. This alignment gave Chenault the ability to stage a flank attack on the 108th Ohio. Hunt's infantry was opposite the federal center with Cobb's battery facing the Union left flank.[13]

In the meantime, Stoner's battalion and the bull pups had moved up and begun to unlimber across from the Union camp on the south bank of the Cumberland River. Knowing that the effective range of the bull pups was well short of the intended target, Morgan instructed Stoner to aim and fire anyway in order to give the impression that range was not a problem. Stoner and the bull pups were a diversion to distract the Union artillery long enough for the Confederates to form and start the attack.[14]

The Confederate troops had formed within five hundred yards of the federal line. This advanced position minimized the amount of time it would take to close with the enemy and bring weapons within effective firing range. Cobb's battery, which was supported by the Ninth Kentucky Infantry, opened the attack. The federal artillery battery did not return Cobb's fire until it realized the bull pups were nothing more than a ruse. Once the commander of the Thirteenth Indiana Battery realized his error, he began to respond to Cobb's battery, and the action became general all along the line.[15]

Cluke's and Chenault's regiments immediately advanced and pushed back the skirmishers in their front. As they started to move up the hill, the commander of the 108th Ohio formed his regiment into a classic defensive formation of two tight ranks, maximizing his firepower on any given point. Although the Ohio regiment outnumbered Duke's two regiments, Duke had deployed his men so that Chenault's regiment actually overlapped the federal line. Recognizing the tactical advantage of Chenault's position, Duke ordered the regiment to attack the Union flank and, if possible, move to its rear. He still felt some anxiety about how either or both of his regiments might react under fire, but their performance during this stage of the attack quickly dispelled his concerns.[16]

Just as Duke's men reached the ravine in front of the federal position, the Ohio regiment began to fire volleys by rank. Normally, such fire would have been very effective. However, the depression not only provided cover but also caused the Union fire to sail high over the heads of the Confederate cavalrymen. Duke moved his men forward and, when they were within sixty yards of the federal line, ordered them to commence firing. Their fire was so rapid that it stunned the federal troops. Chenault completed his flanking maneuver at this time and began to fire on the Ohio regiment from their rear. The Buckeyes tried to turn and meet Chenault's threat, but the casualties resulting from the simultaneous fire from two directions created large gaps in their line. With scores of their comrades on the ground and no slack in the intense fire from the Kentuckians, the 108th Ohio broke and ran. Unrelenting, Duke continued to press, forcing the federal right flank back on its center, making their line resemble the letter V. At this point, the Kentucky infantry attacked. The Second Kentucky led the attack, followed by the Ninth Kentucky, both units smashing into the center of the federal line, causing it to stagger. When the Union center tried to turn to re-form its right flank, it collapsed on itself. At this moment, Duke's men came crashing into the once-cohesive line. When the federal center and right flank merged, all order was lost. To add to the problems already facing the Union commander, Gano with another hundred men arrived and was quickly thrown into battle. Pressed by the Confederate infantry, the 104th Illinois re-formed behind two of the Thirteenth Indiana's cannons below the brow of a hill. It continued to fight but was soon overwhelmed and forced to surrender.[17]

Captain John Wadleigh of the 104th Illinois Infantry later complained that, after the surrender, the Confederates abused the prisoners by not feeding them and taking their winter coats. The rebels, on the other hand, were exercising the time-honored rule that the spoils go to the victor. Richard Bean recalled this postbattle activity with relish, remembering the comfort of the added clothing along with sampling federal rations over a warm breakfast fire. Leeland Hathaway also found the Union camp a cornucopia of everything "a soldier covets, flour, meat, sugar, coffee, blankets, etc."[18]

The entire plan had been based on surprise and speed. Time was of the essence, and, in order to avoid any further complications, the Confederates needed to withdraw from Hartsville as soon as possible. Morgan's pickets on the Castalian Springs Road reported the advance of a large federal detachment estimated at five thousand men. Cluke's regiment was sent to delay their advance and act as a rear guard to gain enough time for all the captured wagons to be loaded with arms, ammunition, and supplies. Harlan's troops aggressively pressed Morgan's rear guard, but Cluke was able to keep them at a safe distance during the withdrawal.[19]

Morgan was extremely pleased with the capture of the Hartsville garrison. He received accolades from the military, the government, and the press, and his picture appeared on the cover of the *Southern Illustrated News,* the only illustrated newspaper published in the South during the Civil War. Although the Battle of Hartville was celebrated in the South, its significance has been variously interpreted. Morgan's modern biographer concedes that, with the opening of Big South Tunnel the previous month, the raid had no serious impact on the federal supply lines. In Nashville, Rosecrans attributed the loss to his lack of cavalry, an argument that was brushed aside in Washington, putting the blame instead on Moore and the 104th Illinois. Nevertheless, the raid was a well-executed attack using a combination of cavalry, infantry, and artillery units that had never fought together before. In his official report, Morgan gave credit where it was due. In particular, he wrote of Duke's actions: "Colonel Duke, commanding his cavalry was as he has always been the right man in the right place. Wise in counsel, gallant in the field, his services have ever been invaluable to me."[20]

On December 14, 1862, Morgan married Mattie Ready at Murfreesboro. General Leonidas Polk, an Episcopal bishop, performed the service as Bragg, Hardee, Cheatham, and Duke stood by Morgan as his best men. The guests later chided Morgan that the Union garrison at Hartsville was his wedding present to his new bride. Some historians have pointed to Morgan's wedding as the turning point in his military fortunes. They have argued, with some merit, that his aggressive nature and audacity were tempered by his love affair with his new wife. This argument is subject to debate and beyond the scope of this book, but, if Morgan had, in fact, lost his audacity, the Ohio Raid might never have occurred. More likely, his postmarital military reversals can be traced to more concrete factors. For example, by 1863, the Union cavalry had finally become an effective fighting force, a fact first evinced in Virginia at the Battle of Kelly's Ford in March of that year. Also, the winter of 1862–63 was a harsh one for the Confederate cavalry in Tennessee. Food and other supplies often ran low, both man and horse suffered, and neither was in any condition to carry on an aggressive campaign until late spring. More fundamental, perhaps, were Morgan's limitations as a commander, limitations that became more apparent as the number of men that he commanded increased. What made Morgan such a successful guerrilla fighter did not prepare him for the multifaceted demands of a division command. Finally, and most significantly, Morgan's setbacks nearly always occurred while Duke was absent from the command.[21]

The Hartsville raid did gain Morgan his brigadier's star, which he received personally from Jefferson Davis. At the same time, Duke was promoted to full colonel. The brigade strength at that point stood at four thousand men dispersed among seven regiments of cavalry. Such a large force would be difficult for one man to manage in the field, so it became necessary to form the regiments into two brigades. The command of a brigade is generally given to the most senior colonel, and Adam Johnson, of the newly arrived Tenth Kentucky, was senior to all the regimental colonels, but he declined to accept command of either brigade. Duke—who had, in fact, been acting as a regimental commander for quite some time even before his promotion—and Breckinridge were then chosen as the brigade commanders. Duke's First Brigade comprised the Second, Third, and Eighth Kentucky Cavalry regiments plus Palmer's battery of four guns. Breckinridge's Second Brigade comprised the Tenth, Eleventh, and Fourteenth Kentucky Cavalry regiments plus the Ninth Tennessee.[22]

The division bivouacked in the vicinity of Alexandria, Tennessee, during the third week of December. Each brigade numbered about two thousand men—with perhaps as many as two hundred without arms. As Morgan began to implement the new command structure, Grenfell, who had been acting as Morgan's adjutant general, resigned from the command. (Bragg subsequently appointed him inspector of all the cavalry, a post that he held for only three months before moving on to greener military pastures.) It turned out that Grenfell greatly disliked Breckinridge and had expected that he himself would be promoted to brigade commander over Breckinridge. At the same time, Grenfell's overbearing attitude was wearing thin with his fellow officers, who considered his interference with the affairs of the command unwarranted. Nevertheless, Duke liked Grenfell, had learned a great deal from him, and maintained a friendship with him that survived the war.[23]

Three days before Christmas 1862, the division broke camp to head north once again to Kentucky. Morgan as well as Forrest had received permission from Bragg to conduct a raid before the end of the year. With the reopening of Big South Tunnel and the construction of a series of new stockades along the Louisville and Nashville (L&N) main line, Bragg's staff and Morgan decided that the "most sensitive" targets on the railroad were the two five-hundred-foot-long trestles at Muldraugh's Hill. The trestles were only eighteen miles south of Louisville and just north of Elizabethtown. Morgan's objective, besides taking out the trestles, was to attack and break the Union communications and supply lines between Nashville and Louisville. Additionally, Morgan was authorized to create the kind of havoc that his raids usually engendered. The seasonal timing of this foray has caused it to be referred to as the "Christmas Raid."[24]

The L&N Railroad during the Civil War epitomized a corporate culture that could be fully appreciated by today's international corporations. It was an economic and not a political creature. It had made significant profits transporting Northern goods to the South prior to the federal occupation of Kentucky and now was making even greater profits delivering war materials and supplies to the Union army in

Tennessee. It also benefited from the assistance of the Union army, which, in order to keep its supply lines open, diverted as much manpower as necessary to damage repair and infrastructure maintenance.[25]

On December 22, 1862, in the early dawn light, Morgan's men were, as Duke reported, "in high spirit's, well armed, well mounted, in good discipline and in perfect confidence with their commander, and with hearts longing for the hills and valleys, the bluegrass and woods of dear old Kentucky." It was a magnificent body of troops, the pick of the youth of Kentucky. Duke's brigade, and the Second Kentucky in particular, took the lead as the column began its ride north. The morning was warm and almost springlike, with little or no evidence of clouds in the sky. With artillery in tow and the shortness of the winter day, the division could move only about thirty miles a day. At the end of the first day, it camped on the north side of the Cumberland River, but it was not until the next evening that it crossed into Kentucky. For the third time since May, Duke was returning to his home state. This time, however, a visit to central Kentucky was not on the agenda. Still, the troops were happy, and James McCreary, a future governor of Kentucky, wrote in his journal on December 23: "Tonight we are camped in the sacred soil of old Kentucky and it fills my heart with joy and pride to know that I am once more on my native heather."[26]

As early as December 16, 1862, the Union army had been warned that Morgan was planning to raid Kentucky. Rosecrans almost immediately advised General Horatio Wright, General Jeremiah Boyle, the Union commander in Louisville, and General Robert S. Granger, the officer responsible for guarding the L&N, of the possibility of a raid. Despite being forewarned, however, Rosecrans was having a difficult time ascertaining Morgan's whereabouts. Then, on December 21, Charles Mersham, a deserter from Morgan's division, told the Union officers to whom he surrendered that Morgan was about to "raid the L&N railroad" and that the camp bakers had prepared enough bread for eight days. This information convinced Rosecrans that Morgan intended to strike the railroad somewhere in Kentucky.[27]

The day before Christmas, the raiders were on the road between Tompkinsville and Glasgow, the same route they had taken in August, and, just as in August, not a federal soldier was to be seen. Traveling through Union-occupied territory did not affect the convivial mood within the ranks as several of the men made homemade brandy to celebrate the season and to help themselves adjust to the cold weather. Morgan was not one to deprive his men of their Christmas cheer or to pass up a good time himself, but he also realized that it was only a matter of time before the Union cavalry was on his trail. He was right. On December 23, Union headquarters in Nashville alerted Frank Wolford that the Confederate cavalry was on the move. Even though Gallatin was identified as the intended target, Wolford soon realized the error in this intelligence and turned his column to the northeast

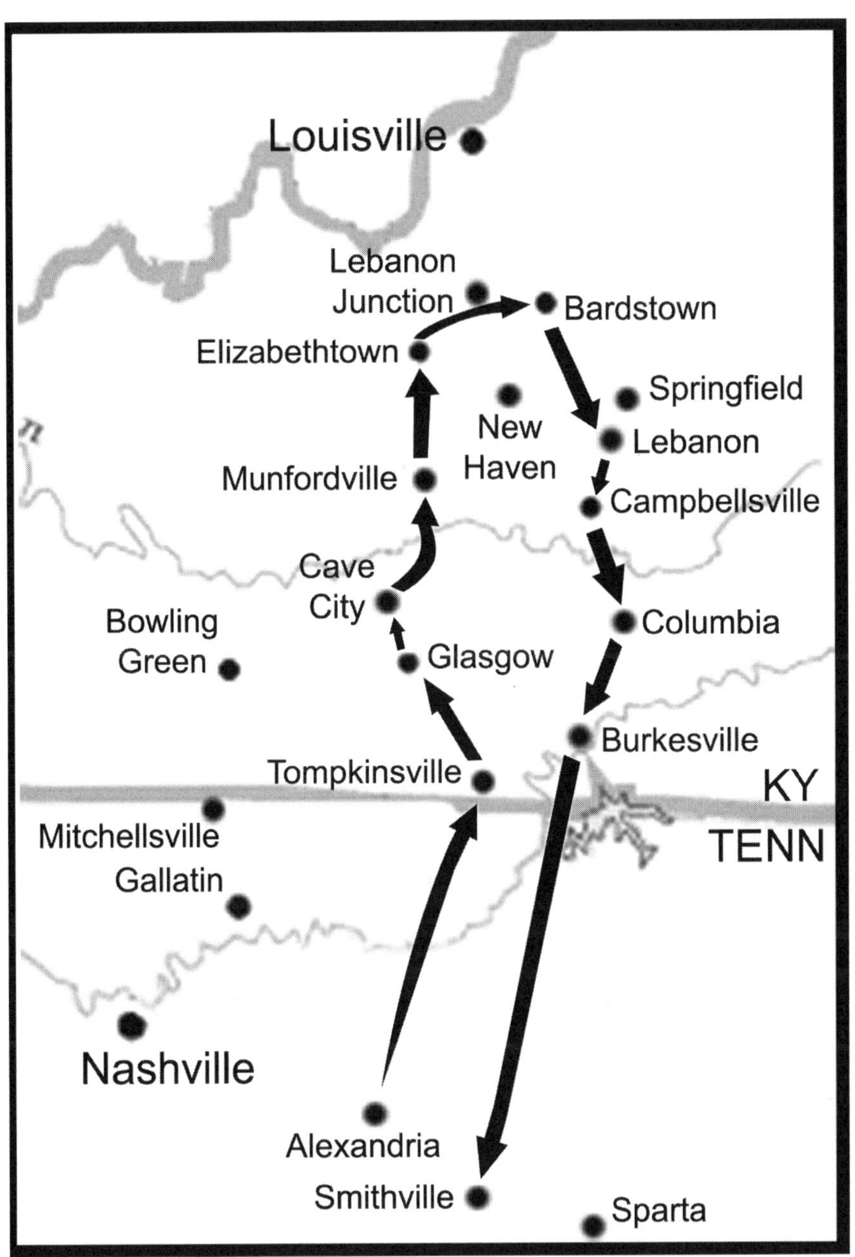

The Christmas Raid, December 1862–January 1863.

in an attempt to intercept Morgan at the Cumberland River. Arriving too late, Wolford's only recourse was to give chase to the fast-moving and elusive raider.[28]

As the raiders approached Glasgow, Breckinridge ordered Captain William Jones from his brigade to determine whether there were any federal troops in the town. The raiders then camped for the night a few miles south of Glasgow. Since it was Christmas Eve, some of the men could not resist drinking and singing to celebrate the holiday. McCreary noted in his journal that there was a superabundance of whiskey and that the men celebrated merrily. In the meantime, Jones's detachment had entered Glasgow at the same time as a battalion of the Second Michigan Cavalry entered the opposite side of town. The two patrols collided near the center of town, and a skirmish began immediately. It was dark, and the troops from each patrol became confused and had difficulty identifying their enemy. When Jones was shot, his patrol retreated, leaving behind seven of their fellows, six wounded and one, Will Webb of Georgetown, dead. The wounded men were captured. The Second Michigan beat a hasty retreat and rode to Cave City, where their commander telegraphed Nashville, announcing the Confederates' presence in Glasgow.[29]

On Christmas Day, the raiders resumed their march north. Quirk and a detachment of fifty scouts rode in the direction of Munfordville, hoping to induce the Union command into believing that that was the intended target and at the same time screen the division's movements. Quirk encountered several small cavalry patrols, none of which were of any consequence. However, later in the day, he ran into a battalion of dismounted cavalry—two companies of the Fourth and Fifth Indiana—who were ready to stand and fight. When Morgan learned of their presence, he ordered Duke forward with two companies in support of Quirk. As Duke moved forward, Quirk was advancing on the Union cavalry, unaware that another company of the Fifth Indiana was hidden from view. The cavalry in his immediate front withdrew after firing several volleys. Quirk moved up to give chase but was struck by a blast of carbine fire from the undetected company of Hoosiers. The unexpected fire caused some momentary confusion in Quirk's ranks; however, by this time, Duke was moving up, and the Indiana cavalry withdrew at the sight of the reinforcements. The Confederates then crossed the Green River and continued in the direction of Elizabethtown, camping at Hammondsville that evening. Although the coveted trestles were still some distance away, the L&N main line was running parallel to the raiders' route, always providing an alternate target in the event the attack on the trestles had to be aborted.[30]

The next morning, the troops woke up to deteriorating weather conditions. The temperature had dropped significantly, and the men were pelted by ice and rain as they saddled their horses. Prior to leaving camp, it was decided to burn two nearby bridges at Nolin and Bacon Creek. Earlier in the war, the Second Kentucky had destroyed the bridge at Bacon Creek, and there were many men in the regiment who were familiar with the structure. This experience gained the regiment the task at hand. Since Duke's promotion to brigade commander, the Second Kentucky was under the command of Lieutenant Colonel John Hutchinson. Duke accompanied Hutchinson and the Second Kentucky to the bridges but astutely did not interfere with Hutchinson's role as regimental commander. The Bacon Creek bridge was protected by a well-defended stockade, as was the nearby bridge at Nolin. Although neither stockade was completely finished, both were still formidable defensive positions. On reaching the bridge at Bacon Creek, Duke broke off from Hutchinson and, along with the bull pups, headed toward the bridge at Nolin. There, he unlimbered the bull pups in view of the garrison, attempting to intimidate the stockade commander. One of the Union officers tried to convince his commander that the bull pups were not powerful enough to destroy the stockade. This effort was to no avail because, after a conference with Duke, the stockade was surrendered without a fight. The garrison at the Bacon Creek stockade put up a strong fight, however, and surrendered only when Morgan rode up and personally convinced the Union commander that it was in his best interest to terminate his resistance. The end result was the destruction of both bridges.[31]

The next day, the raiders stopped short of Elizabethtown while Morgan, Duke, and Breckinridge determined how best to capture the town without a costly engagement with its six-hundred-man garrison. Lieutenant Colonel Harry S. Smith, the commander of the Ninety-first Illinois, was not in the least intimidated when he learned that Morgan was about to attack his position. He matched Morgan's audacity by sending a messenger under a flag of truce to inform Morgan that the Confederates were surrounded and that he intended to compel Morgan to surrender. Duke later referred to Smith's act as "the most sublimely audacious I ever knew to emanate from a federal officer." Smith's bluff was quickly called and, during the time that he and Morgan exchanged messages calling for each other's surrender, the Confederate artillery began to unlimber on the Nolin Pike. Duke and Breckinridge had already positioned their brigades to attack on the right and left of the town, respectively.[32]

Time was running out for Smith as he continued to haggle with Morgan over surrender terms. Finally, when Smith declined his latest offer, Morgan ran out of patience and ordered the attack to start. The bull pups opened fire, and Cluke's and Stoner's men advanced on foot toward the town. Stoner's men quickly overran the outlying buildings, where some of the Union sharpshooters had been positioned. Many of the Union troops withdrew to the center of town and took cover in a large brick building that Smith was using as his headquarters. Duke ordered Palmer's battery brought forward, and the shelling of the brick building began. Smith's men continued, nevertheless, to pour a hot fire into the streets, forcing Duke to bring one of the guns in for closer work. He positioned the gun along with a company from the Ninth Kentucky on a railroad embankment opposite the building. Duke positioned the gun away from the building's windows so that, each time the gun fired, Union troops had no recourse but to rush out of the building and fire at Duke's men as they tried to reload. The troops from the Ninth Kentucky would then return the federal fire, forcing Smith's troops back into the building. This exchange went on for several minutes until one of Morgan's staff ordered the support company to charge the building. The company charged as ordered and was immediately exposed to a withering fire from Smith's troops. Almost at once an officer from the Ninth Kentucky countermanded the staff officer's order and instructed his men to fall back. Sensing an opportunity, the Union troops charged out of the building and advanced up the street, shooting several of the gunners manning the cannon. The artillery officer in command of the gun held his ground and, once again, forced the federal troops back into the building. Several minutes later, Smith raised the white flag, and his entire garrison, along with all of their weapons, was captured.[33]

After the Union garrison surrendered, several young Kentuckians, including James McCreary, were riding past a house when three ladies invited them in for refreshments. McCreary and his friends accepted the invitation. As they entered the house, they noticed three dead Union soldiers on the floor, apparently having met their demise from an artillery shell that had sailed through the window and exploded as they were taking cover. The three ladies walked contemptuously past the three dead soldiers as they lead McCreary and his friends through the room. That night, a barrel of whiskey was brought out to the Confederate camp from town as a gift from a local merchant. The merchant obviously considered this a cheap price to pay to keep the troops in camp and out of town that night. The ransom may have been for naught, for a Louisville paper reported that many of the Union shopkeepers were "liberated" of their goods that night.[34]

The weather improved during the night, and it was unseasonably mild the next day, December 28, when the raiders left Elizabethtown. They continued north along the same path that Duke and White Kennett had followed the previous year in their unsuccessful attempt to visit their wives. After a few miles, the two large trestles at Muldraugh's Hill could be seen in the distance. It had become standard practice for the Union army to build and garrison a blockhouse at each important bridge and trestle on the railroad between Louisville and Nashville. Troops of the Seventy-first Indiana garrisoned each of these two trestles and their respective blockhouses. Duke was assigned the task of reducing the blockhouse and destroying the upper, or northern, trestle, Breckinridge its southern counterpart. The two brigades attacked their targets simultaneously. The resistance was determined, but, after several hours of shelling, the defenders surrendered, and the trestles were set on fire and destroyed. Scouting detachments also destroyed three smaller bridges.

That night, the raiders camped a few miles east of the burnt trestles near the Rolling Fork River.[35]

With the primary objective of the raid successfully completed, it was time for the raiders to head back to Tennessee. But the return trip was going to be difficult. Rosecrans was intent on capturing or at least significantly mauling the Confederate cavalry in battle. To accomplish this end, he had dispatched three separate infantry commands, each with a small contingent of cavalry, from different directions to intercept Morgan. However, matters soon became complicated for Rosecrans when he learned that Forrest had also been turned loose to raid in west Tennessee. With significant elements of cavalry separated from the main Confederate army, Rosecrans recognized that an opportunity was at hand to strike Bragg and wrote Halleck: "The detachment of Forrest to West Tennessee, and of Morgan will materially aid us in our movement."[36]

John Harlan commanded one of the three infantry detachments ordered by Nashville to pursue Morgan. He had begun his pursuit at Gallatin on December 25, and, after a forty-hour trip on the railroad, he and his troops finally reached Munfordville. The trip had exhausted the men and was very hard on the horses, which were neither fed nor watered the entire time on the train. Still, Harlan felt compelled to move on as soon as possible. After resting for two hours, and reinforced with two regiments of cavalry, he resumed the chase at three in the morning on December 28, pushing his badly worn out troops into Elizabethtown twenty-four hours later.[37]

On December 29, 1862, Morgan's division reached the Rolling Fork River. Prior to the crossing, Morgan ordered the destruction of the railroad bridge over the river, five miles below the point of crossing. Major Robert S. Bullock and the Eighth Kentucky were assigned this task. An additional detachment of approximately three hundred men was assigned that of serving as rear guard. Because of the recent rain, which had swelled the river, more time was needed to complete the crossing. Unknown to the raiders, Harlan had sent his cavalry units ahead of his main force, and they were rapidly closing in on the Confederate rear guard. When he reached the crossing, Harlan could not believe his good luck. He had caught a portion of Morgan's command in the middle of a river crossing. Recognizing his opportunity, Harlan ordered his pickets to advance, unlimbered his artillery, and immediately began to shell the last of Morgan's regiments as they tried to cross the fast-moving river.[38]

The exact moment that Harlan's shells began to fall on the retreating Confederates, Duke, along with Breckinridge, Cluke, Hutchinson, and Stoner, was seated in a brick house on the south bank of the river. He and his fellow officers were in the process of conducting a field court-martial of Colonel John Huffman for his alleged mistreatment of prisoners captured at the Bacon Creek blockhouse. The court-martial ended with Huffman's acquittal, and, when the officers filed out of the house, each heard Harlan's artillery fire in the distance and grasped its significance. Rushing to the ford, Duke immediately assumed command and directed the formation of a defensive line and reserve with the troops who had not yet crossed the river. He would have to hold the ford until Bullock and the Eighth Kentucky returned from burning the railroad bridge. If he could not, Bullock would be isolated and, most likely, captured. As Duke dug in on the riverbank, Morgan rejoined the rest of the division and rode toward Bardstown.[39]

Using approximately three hundred men, Duke formed his defensive line and sent a dispatch to Bullock, advising him of the situation, and urging him to bring his regiment to the ford as soon as possible. Duke had placed his men in a depression about eight hundred yards long with the bank of the river to his right and a thick wooded area to his left. This position provided an optimum amount of cover and field of fire for the troops but very little protection for the horses. Still, Duke felt prepared "for the game he was about to play" and confident that he could defend the crossing until Bullock arrived. Harlan, however, had approximately three thousand men at his disposal. Whether Duke was cognizant of the size of the federal force at the time of the battle is not known, but, given his choice of action at Buffington Island, it seems likely that he would have taken the same action here whether facing an enemy large or small. What mattered to him was the need to hold the line, regardless of the odds, until he could extract as many of his men as possible.[40]

The Union artillery kept up a fairly steady barrage as Harlan slowly and somewhat indecisively positioned his men for the attack. As the shells began to land among Duke's men and their mounts, Bullock and the Eighth Kentucky finally returned. Palmer too had returned with Bullock, bringing with him several small six-pound cannons from his battery. Not wanting to escalate the battle or throw the six pounders into an unequal brawl with Harlan's larger-rifled parrot guns, Duke stuck to his plan and simply tried to get as many of his men as he could to the other side of the river with as little loss as possible. Harlan's first attack was so easily repulsed that Duke's audacious nature sensed that a counterattack was the last thing the indecisive Harlan expected and could buy him the additional time he needed to pull his men across the river. He then received a dispatch from Morgan ordering him to withdraw. Duke decided that the withdrawal could succeed only in conjunction with the counterattack. As he moved among his men on horseback, shouting the order to counterattack, he was struck in the head by a fragment from an exploding artillery shell. He fell unconscious into the water at the river's edge. Seeing Duke fall and then lie motionless in the water, his men concluded that he was dead and began to shout the news to the troops further down the line. Breckinridge was so upset by this turn of events that, as one man remembered, "tears streamed down his manly cheeks" as he urged the rear guard "to hold their

Tom Quirk was the captain in charge of Morgan's scouts. The feisty Irish immigrant pulled a wounded Colonel Duke from the waters of the Rolling Fork River during the Christmas Raid of 1862. (Courtesy the University of Kentucky.)

ground till Duke could be safely carried over the river." The Union soldiers also heard Duke's men shout and reached the same conclusion. Harlan wrote in his official report that Duke had certainly been wounded during the engagement and "is believed to be the life and soul of all the movements" of Morgan's command.[41]

When Duke fell wounded, Breckinridge assumed command of the rear guard and carried out the final phases of the withdrawal. Captain Virgil Pendelton was carrying out Duke's counterattack, with three companies of the Eighth Kentucky. His abrupt charge carried him over the hill, forcing part of the Union battery to retreat, and effectively silencing the Union barrage for fifteen minutes. During Pendelton's attack, Breckinridge ordered the men to mount and cross the river as quickly as possible. As the main body of troops began to cross the river, Tom Quirk rushed to Duke's side, lifted his limp body out of the water and placed it across his saddle, and then urged his steed into the swollen river. Dr. John Wyeth, a future biographer of Nathan Bedford Forrest, witnessed Duke's rescue and concluded that he would have drowned had it not been for Quirk. Once across the river, Quirk found a wagon at a nearby farm and placed the still-unconscious Duke in it.[42]

The Confederate line pulled back and broke off the engagement, but not before Bullock and the Eighth Kentucky as well as the rear guard successfully crossed the river. When the Confederate rear guard reached the horses, many were found to have been killed or scattered by the shelling. Fortunately for the Confederates,

Harlan decided not to press his advantage, and the rear guard was able to gather up the wounded and cross the river safely. Harlan did not cross over to the north bank until December 31, claiming that his force was exhausted from the forced march and the engagement.[43]

The division camped at Bardstown that night. Several soldiers carried Duke up the stairs to a second-story doctor's office. One observer looked at Duke's wound and noted a "piece of skin and bone behind the ear was gone." Duke allegedly opened his eyes during the examination and said: "That was a pretty close call." Much to everyone's relief, the surgeons determined that the wound was not fatal. For the remainder of the raid, Duke would ride in Quirk's wagon or a buggy.[44]

That night, at Bardstown, some of Morgan's troops engaged in looting and generally harassing the local Union merchants. Morgan's biographer James Ramage noted: "Duke was considered by many to be the conscience of Morgan's command and it may have been more than coincidence that discipline broke down that night . . . as he lay wounded in bed." As was generally the case, Morgan did nothing to the perpetrators, believing that the Union shopowners deserved such treatment.[45]

Riding southeast from Bardstown, the division reached Springfield on the afternoon of December 30, only to learn that a large federal force was in Lebanon, just a few miles farther down the road. It was obvious to Morgan that, if Harlan was closing in on his rear, he could easily be surrounded by the federal cavalry. To avoid such a trap, it was imperative that he evade the federal force at Lebanon. In order to do so, Morgan ordered an all-night ride around Lebanon. Not only were the men fatigued from being in the saddle for days, but the weather had once again turned cold, with sleet falling for most of the night. The night was, in fact, so dark that some of the regiments became disoriented and the command inadvertently split. It took some time to reunite it, but this was accomplished before morning.[46]

It was the first day of the new year, and, like a bad dream, Champ Ferguson's wanton bloodletting once again crossed Duke's path. Ferguson's wartime forte was killing Union bushwhackers. On this particular night, he was looking for Elam Huddlestone, who had on more than one occasion advertised that he wanted to kill Ferguson. During the raid, Ferguson had discovered where Huddlestone was living and decided to put an end to the feud once and for all. Having accomplished his mission, Ferguson returned to the column and told Duke what had happened. Evidently, one of Huddlestone's men fired his pistol at Ferguson and his men when he heard them approach the hideout. Ferguson simply ignored the guard, burst through the front door, and killed Huddlestone and another man with his knife. Duke, being wounded, was a captive audience, forced to listen to Ferguson as he told his loathsome tale. At one point, Ferguson showed Duke his knife and explained how he used it on his victims. Duke later recalled: "The sight of that knife still covered with red blood thoroughly nauseated me."[47]

The night march had gained the raiders twenty miles, or twelve hours' riding time, on the pursuing federal cavalry. This did not satisfy Morgan, who was obsessed with the need to farther outdistance his adversaries. Instead of halting at Columbia, the raiders camped for a few short hours south of the town and then, after riding again all night and reaching Burkesville, crossed the Cumberland River on January 2, 1863. Morgan paused long enough at Burkesville to write a letter to his wife describing the success of the raid as well as Duke's wound. Three days later, the division rode into Smithville, Tennessee, ending the raid.[48]

The destruction of the trestles at Muldraugh's Hill did not have quite the impact on Union supply lines the Confederates anticipated. Prior to the raid, Rosecrans had turned Nashville into a supply depot and stored enough supplies to withstand a minor siege. Still, the Christmas Raid was a success, resulting in over eighteen hundred federal soldiers captured and over $2 million worth of property, including the two trestles, destroyed. In Logan County, Kentucky, a minister-farmer noted in his diary: "Since the railroad had been torn up Union soldiers were scouring the countryside for provisions principally if not exclusively from Southern Rights men, giving receipts for quantity but not price." The loss to the command was slight—only twenty-six men during the entire ten-day, five-hundred-mile-long raid.[49]

Although Bragg had authorized the raid, he had had a change of heart shortly after Morgan left Alexandria and had sent messengers to recall the raiders. However, the messengers never were able to catch the fast-moving column. In the meantime, Rosecrans was, as we have seen, delighted that both Morgan and Forrest had gone raiding. Their absence made his task of contending with Bragg's army, and particularly the Confederate cavalry, less difficult. On December 26, he gave his army its marching orders.[50]

The two armies clashed outside Murfreesboro between December 31, 1862, and January 2, 1863. On the first day of battle, Bragg initiated the offensive and significantly battered the Union army. He was unable to follow up on his success the next day, however, both armies lying dormant owing to the inclement weather. On January 2, however, he ordered Breckinridge's division to make a frontal attack against the strongly entrenched Union right flank. Roger Hanson was killed almost immediately, and, not long after, the attack was repulsed. After sustaining another tactical defeat, Bragg and his generals became estranged, pointing the finger of blame at one another for the failure at Murfreesboro.[51]

9

We Found Pies Hot from the Oven

THE WOUND THAT DUKE RECEIVED in the fight at the Rolling Fork River crossing was fairly serious, and it was not until January 8, 1863, that he was able to write Tommie about the recent campaign. To diffuse her concerns, he attempted to minimize the seriousness of his injury. Fortunately, she missed hearing the premature reports of his death circulating in Lexington at this time because she had already packed up and headed south. Morgan apparently had sent a messenger to inform his mother that Duke was only slightly wounded, but the courier evidently told others in Lexington that he would not survive. Aware that Tommie had left Lexington, uncertain of her exact whereabouts, and concerned that her safety could be threatened by troop movements, Duke advised her to stay away from Huntsville and consider taking up residence in east Tennessee or even Georgia. Later in the war, Tommie made every attempt to be with her husband, but, in 1863, the division's movements were too fluid to permit such a luxury. Several days later, Duke's wife joined him in Tennessee, where she spent the next two months as he recovered from his wound and regained his strength.[1]

With Tommie's attention and comfort, Duke's rehabilitation progressed rapidly during the winter months, and, by March 1863, he was able to rejoin his brigade. During Duke's convalescence, Bragg had entrenched the Army of the Tennessee along the Duck River just above Tullahoma. Duke's brigade, with the rest of the division, had been positioned along Bragg's right flank. The brigade was under the temporary command of Colonel Gano and was stretched out along a twenty-mile picket line with camps in several different locations. Camp size varied, depending on the assignment, and could range from several companies to regimental strength. The scattering of Duke's troops enabled the brigade to patrol the area between McMinnville and Woodbury effectively. The brigade's position was almost at a right angle to the Union army, with Woodbury being the extreme northern edge of the Confederate presence.[2]

The winter of 1862–63 was extremely cold and bitter and, according to Leeland

Hathaway, "a very hard one for soldiering." Hathaway, a young officer in Breckinridge's Fourteenth Kentucky, elaborated: "There was scarcely a day which was not made miserable by the rain, snow and sleet. Often raining far into the night, then snowing, sleeting and freezing for the next several hours. The camps were only open rail pens when we had any shelter and from those we were called almost every night. There was no 24 hours without the report of the enemy advancing on the pike or the dirt road." The severity of the winter and Richmond's general inability to supply its troops in the field created severe shortages of clothing, ammunition, and basic food items. By the middle of the winter, the lack of sufficient fodder and oats for the horses became so acute that many of the animals deteriorated physically and were unable to be used even for routine picket duty. The lack of adequate provisions had a corresponding detrimental effect on the men's morale and general combat effectiveness. From time to time, the division quartermaster was able to work minor miracles and procure the much-needed supplies, but it was never enough. Nonetheless, Duke was enraged by the supply system employed by the Confederate army and considered the root of the problem to be "incompetence and malfeasance." Adding to the problems of the men in the ranks, pay was irregular, when it appeared at all. One soldier in Morgan's command was pragmatic about the whole concept of pay, conceding that, while it was essential for the infantryman, who was restricted to camp and forced to rely on his pay to acquire his necessities from the local sutler, it was less so for the more mobile cavalryman, who was able to scour the countryside for his "square meal" and other needs.[3]

As the winter dragged on, supplies became even more of a problem, particularly in February, when two new regiments, the Fifth Kentucky, commanded by D. H. Smith, and the Sixth Kentucky, commanded by Warren Grigsby, joined the division. If supplies were scarce, military bureaucracy was abundant. Orders were soon issued to Morgan requiring him to regularly brigade the division. This resulted in Duke's brigade being reorganized. The brigade now consisted of the Second, Fifth, Sixth, and Ninth Kentucky as well as the Ninth Tennessee. Since both Smith and Grigsby were senior to all the other regimental colonels, either could legitimately have been appointed its commander. According to Duke, both refused to take command, citing as their rationale their newness to the division, thus permitting him to retain his position. In truth, they were aware of Duke's reputation and popularity with the men and "would not have presumed to oppose his appointment as their commanding officer." Adam Johnson, the commander of the Tenth Kentucky, summed up Duke's appointment to the command of the First Brigade as Morgan's effort to guarantee continuity of leadership: "Morgan . . . fixed the succession absolutely on him in the event of the disability or death of the famous cavalryman. Nor could Morgan's mantle have fallen on a more worthier successor;

an accomplished gentleman, ever successful in fight, I hold him to have been the ablest officer of his age in the Confederate army." At the same time, Breckinridge replaced Gano as temporary commander of Duke's brigade, while the Second Brigade was assigned to the more-than-competent Adam Johnson.[4]

During the winter of 1863, Morgan's cavalry had little success and several reversals in the field against its Union counterparts. Except for a small Kentucky raid in February by Cluke's regiment, the federal cavalry generally bested Morgan during these months. This was a new experience for Morgan's men, who, except for the Lebanon Races, had always enjoyed the upper hand against their Union foes. Perhaps the single worst episode during this period of time occurred on March 20, 1863, at Milton, Tennessee. Morgan was in hot pursuit of a retreating Union infantry column and, despite being warned by Quirk that he would be facing odds of three or four to one, was determined to attack. When he made contact with the federal rear guard, the bluecoats halted and, taking advantage of a small hill with large rocks, began to form an almost impregnable line. He challenged the position by ordering a frontal attack that resulted in a predictable disaster. The Confederates suffered significant casualties and were forced to withdraw. One wonders what might have happened had Duke been present during the battle. Most likely, he would have sensed that the attack had little chance of success and would have tactfully restrained Morgan's impulsive behavior, as he had done at Edgeville.[5]

In early April, Morgan suffered another reversal at Snow's Hill near Liberty, Tennessee. Federal troops had moved into Liberty, and Colonel Gano had taken up a defensive position along the ridge of a string of low hills just east of town, hoping to prevent any further Union advance in that direction. Early the morning of April 3, a Union cavalry force composed of elements of the Third and Fourth Ohio commanded by Colonel James W. Paramore advanced toward Gano's line. Colonel Paramore skillfully turned Gano's left flank, forcing him to withdraw to form a secondary defensive line. Observing the withdrawal, the Union commander ordered his troops to press the attack. The Union troops responded, hitting Gano's troops in the middle of their withdrawal. Paramore's pressure had the desired effect of turning what had been a strategic withdrawal into a rout. It was at this point that Duke, who had just returned to active duty, met up with some of Gano's sullen troops as he was riding in the direction of the gunfire. He attempted to rally the men, but they were in no mood to continue the fight that day, and his efforts largely failed. Such indifference was a new and troubling experience for the duty-minded Duke, who soon became disgusted and rode forward to where some troops had rallied to the colors. It was there, Kelion Peddicord, one of Quirk's scouts, recalled, that Duke was able to stabilize a portion of the line: "Retreating over a mile, we met Colonel Duke, who took command, to the entire satisfaction of all, and formed his line of battle. This was done to no purpose; however, for when the Yankees struck the main road they took the Liberty end, expecting to capture at least a portion of the command. In this they were mistaken, for we had withdrawn in time. They went back to Liberty and encamped, while Duke kept the hill."[6]

While Snow's Hill was the first active duty that Duke had seen since December, he had in early March returned to his administrative responsibilities, immediately setting about a reorganization and upgrading aimed at improving the combat readiness of his men. By April 1863, he had regained his full strength and assumed all the duties expected of a brigade commander, including, when time permitted, using his talents to benefit the entire division. For example, the success attributable to Quirk and his scouts gave him the idea, which he proposed to Morgan, that a squadron of scouts could be a very effective weapon. He also turned his attention to the supply problem, which was less pressing now that spring had arrived but nevertheless an issue. "There is still," he wrote Morgan, "abundance of forage about the camps to judge from the quantities I saw hauled in & we are getting plenty of wheat & bacon. Van has just hauled about 6,000 pds. of meat from Lebanon and is still getting more. I have just heard of a widow lady living at Trousdale who has 700 lbs. of corn, 100 bus. of wheat & 1,000 pds. of meat which she wishes to sell us." The abundance of supplies that Duke described was highly unusual. The cavalry was generally supplied with "great difficulty and great oppression of the citizens," forced as it was to live off the land, which resulted in large areas being "literally stripped of meat, grain and everything edible."[7]

With the advent of warmer weather, a federal raid in Mississippi may have motivated Morgan to propose to Bragg a raid across the Ohio River. To convince Bragg that the risky venture was militarily sound, Morgan argued that it could divert enough federal troops to impair Rosecrans's expected summer offensive. Benjamin H. Grierson's successful cavalry raid from La Grange, Tennessee, due south 450 miles through the entire state of Mississippi to Baton Rouge, Louisiana, was, indeed, impressive. And Morgan, who had been searching for some way to raise the morale of his cavalry, found such an action appealing. A similarly successful raid into the Northern heartland would convince his troops that their lackluster performance against the federal cavalry the previous winter was an anomaly. Bragg found himself in a bad tactical position. He knew that Rosecrans was under pressure from Washington to mount a summer offensive, and he was not prepared to meet such a thrust. A properly planned and executed diversion could possibly, as Morgan argued, provide Bragg the time he needed. Morgan had an additional incentive; much like Stuart after Brandy Station, he needed to reclaim his status as one of the South's preeminent cavalry commanders in the eyes both of the Union army and of his superiors in Richmond. A stunning raid across the Ohio River might achieve both Morgan's and Bragg's objectives.[8]

If Rosecrans's garrison and reserve forces are excluded from the computations, the relative strengths of his and Bragg's armies were fairly equal at this time. Bragg had, however, not only a qualitative advantage, but also a numerical superiority of six thousand men in his cavalry divisions. This disparity had always concerned Rosecrans, who realized that the Confederate superiority in cavalry made it extremely difficult for him to maneuver his army without being detected. Rosecrans also surmised that his surest avenue to victory was to maneuver Bragg into the open and then force him to give battle. Quarrels and dissension continued to play a prominent role in Bragg's headquarters, and, although Bragg had been at Tullahoma for months, William Preston Johnston, aide-de-camp to President Davis, reported that he "did not learn from any general of any projected movement."[9]

In *A History of Morgan's Cavalry,* Duke maintained that Morgan met with Bragg and proposed another Kentucky raid, mainly targeting the Louisville and Nashville Railroad, but also creating general havoc among the federal troops in Kentucky. According to Duke, Morgan suggested that he also be permitted to cross the Ohio River and carry the raid into Indiana and Ohio, crossing back into Kentucky or Virginia somewhere east of Cincinnati. To prove the feasibility of his plan, Morgan had some weeks earlier ordered Duke to send scouts to reconnoiter the fords on the upper Ohio River. The mission was assigned to Captain Sam Taylor, who, after scouting all the fords, including the one at Buffington, Ohio, reported that there were several that were shallow enough to afford Morgan safe passage to Southern soil. Morgan's argument and fieldwork were impressive. Bragg approved the raid into Kentucky—but strictly forbade Morgan to cross the Ohio and take his troops north of Kentucky.[10]

Official records, however, tell a different story. In his official report of November 7, 1863, General Joseph Wheeler indicated that, on June 13, 1863, he received a dispatch from Morgan "stating that the enemy at Louisville, Kentucky, was but 300 strong" and asking for permission to raid the city. Wheeler sent Morgan's request to Bragg, who authorized the raid the next day. Wheeler then communicated Bragg's decision to Morgan with the stipulation that Morgan could take only fifteen hundred of his men on the raid. Morgan was also ordered to return to Tennessee and fall on Bragg's rear if he heard that Rosecrans was "advancing for a general engagement." When Morgan received this order, he petitioned Wheeler to allow him to increase his force for the raid to two thousand men, arguing: "To make the attempt with less, might prove disastrous, as large details will be required at Louisville to destroy the transportation, shipping, and Government property." Wheeler relayed Morgan's request to Bragg, who authorized the increase. Bragg intended to use the balance of Morgan's division as a screen for his army during the anticipated summer campaign. Wheeler emphasized in his November report that "not one word was said about his crossing the Ohio River; but, on the contrary, he was urged by me to observe the importance of his returning to our army as rapidly as possible."[11]

There is no direct evidence to substantiate Duke's claim that a meeting took place between Bragg and Morgan. In fact, in January 1891, almost twenty-five years after authoring *A History of Morgan's Cavalry,* Duke wrote an article for the *Century Magazine* in which he admitted receiving the information of the alleged meeting secondhand, from Morgan. In the same article, Duke emphasized that Bragg had issued orders that Morgan was not to cross the Ohio, but he also revealed that Morgan intended all along to "disobey them," that "the emergency, he believed, justified disobedience." Morgan was, according to Duke, "resolved to cross the Ohio River and invade Indiana and Ohio. His command would probably be captured, he said; but in no other way could he give substantial aid to the army." Of course, what is important here is, not whether a meeting between Bragg and Morgan actually took place, but that Duke obviously had full knowledge both of Bragg's orders restricting the scope of the raid and of Morgan's decision to ignore those orders. The prior year, at Augusta, Duke had planned his own, ultimately frustrated crossing of the Ohio. Can that earlier failure account at least partly for the fact that Duke quickly succumbed to Morgan's enthusiasm and confidence despite being apprehensive about the plan? Or was it simply that Duke's uncompromising devotion to his brother-in-law clouded his reasoning concerning the proposed raid as well as his estimation of "General Morgan's remarkable genius"? Whatever the reason, Duke acquiesced remarkably readily to his commander's decision to ignore Bragg's orders.[12]

In early June, Morgan had ordered Captain Tom Hines on a special mission. With approximately eighty men, Hines was to cross the Ohio and enter Indiana. Since neither Hines nor Morgan filed a report, the exact nature of Hines's mission is not certain, but subsequent events make it fairly obvious that the scouting trip to Indiana was meant, first, and most important, to gather intelligence regarding the river crossing at Brandenburg, Kentucky, and, second, to determine the strength of the federal presence in southern Indiana.[13]

Hines left Tennessee with his handpicked contingent and, after a costly misadventure northeast of Elizabethtown, crossed the Ohio River with a much smaller force. Hines operated in southern Indiana for almost a week before he lost all but twelve of his men attempting to cross the Ohio back into Kentucky, where his alleged antics included the destruction of a train near Frankfort. After this latter incident, Hines prudently kept a low profile in and around Brandenburg as he waited for Morgan to arrive.[14]

When time permitted, Duke put aside his commission and addressed family matters. Tommie was both pregnant and a refugee behind Southern lines. A concerned Duke wrote his mother-in-law to advise her that he had found a place—La Grange, Georgia—that would serve as a safe refuge for Tommie and their young child. Apprehensive, however, that Tommie would find La Grange boring, he also suggested the alternative plan of finding someone to take her to Knoxville, where she could stay with friends. Unknown to Duke, the Union army was planning to advance into east Tennessee, thus presenting a threat that Tommie could not ignore. After careful consideration, she would go to La Grange.[15]

Toward the end of May 1863, Morgan ordered his troops to concentrate at Liberty and Alexandria, Tennessee. Duke noted that, at Alexandria, "the horses were in better condition and the men better provided for in every respect than at any period since the December raid. New and excellent clothing had been issued them while on the Cumberland—a thing unprecedented in the history of the command—and their general equipment was much superior to what it had been at the close of the winter. All were well armed and with the kind of guns which were always preferred in Morgan's cavalry." Duke began to drill and train his troops in anticipation of the upcoming raid and posted guards to ensure that the brigade was not infiltrated by spies or debauched by the local moonshine. The veterans correctly surmised that such activity indicated that a major raid was about to start.[16]

Morgan arrived at Alexandria on June 10, 1863, attired in a splendid new uniform, much to the delight of his men. That afternoon, he ordered the division to be prepared to march the next day. On June 11, Morgan received an ominous letter from his uncle, S. D. Morgan, posted from Talladega, Alabama: "You say you want to go into Ohio and can stay in Illinois & Pennsylvania for 2 months. This plan of raiding is a favorite one of mine. Still as things now stand in the North West, I have doubts as to the expediency of such a movement. It might at this particular time do harm & hinder, situated as our army in Tennessee is, I don't want you away. If you and Forrest had been with Bragg at Murfreesboro, I have not a doubt that Rosecrans would have been badly whipped." These comments were more prophetic than S. D. Morgan could ever have realized. However, it was not until the end of summer, after Bragg had been skillfully maneuvered into the hills of northern Georgia, that Morgan's presence was sorely missed.[17]

On the evening of June 11, Morgan received orders to intercept a federal raiding party, reportedly near Monticello, Kentucky. If the report was accurate, the Union cavalry was in a position to threaten Knoxville. The weather suddenly turned bad, raining constantly for several days, making the roads impassable at times. When the Confederates reached Albany, the threat of the federal raid had passed. The division then turned west and rode toward the Cumberland River, where it camped on its south bank until July 2, 1863, poised to launch a raid into Kentucky and points farther north.[18]

The rains had abated by early July, and Morgan was anxious to cross the Cumberland River and begin his raid. Although Bragg's orders limited his force to two thousand men, Morgan was taking twenty-five hundred and leaving only the Ninth Kentucky in Tennessee to assist Bragg. Even at that, several companies of the Ninth Kentucky detached themselves from the regiment to go on the raid. Morgan and Duke now met with the regimental commanders and outlined the plan to cross the Ohio River. Duke was aware that Lee had invaded Pennsylvania and that, if the opportunity arose, Morgan intended to attempt to link up with him somewhere north of the Mason-Dixon Line. Morgan had confided to Duke that he was quite aware of the possibility that, if he crossed the Ohio, he might lose his entire command, but he had so much confidence in the ability of his men to outride any pursuit that it appeared to Duke to be only a fleeting concern.[19]

The Cumberland had risen considerably as a result of the June rains and was going to be difficult to cross. On July 2, 1863, Duke crossed at Burkesville and Scott's Ferry, two miles farther up the river, while Adam Johnson and his brigade crossed at Turkey Neck Bend. The men were in good spirits and sang to the health of both Morgan and Duke as they prepared to cross the river. Morgan was splendid in his new uniform, and Duke, as always immaculate in dress and martial in bearing, had added a plume to his hat. The men sang "My Old Kentucky Home" as they entered the river. Several canoes were lashed together and used, along with two small flatboats, to ferry the men and the artillery across the river while the horses swam. Duke was quite surprised by and critical of the Union command's failure to post pickets on the opposite shore. For weeks, Union cavalry had been in the vicinity of Burkesville, but, apparently, they assumed that the river was too high to cross. At least, Duke's brigade met no initial resistance. In time, however, Frank Wolford showed up with almost three hundred men, and a short but brisk engagement ensued, resulting in only one man seriously wounded, but that man was Tom Quirk. Thus, at the very beginning of the raid, Morgan lost his best scout. By nightfall, the raiders were seven miles beyond Columbia.[20]

The forward elements of Morgan's command reached the banks of the Green River on the night of July 3. During the night, they heard the sound of ringing axes on the other side of the river at a point called Tebbs Bend. The noise was being generated by elements of the Twenty-fifth Michigan Infantry, which garrisoned the stockade at Tebbs Bend. That night, they were working outside their stockade, building a defensive perimeter out of sharpened tree limbs hammered into the ground at an angle. Duke and the First Brigade were positioned behind Johnson's Second Brigade and did not "come up" until after the action the next morning. When Duke arrived, he was duly impressed with the site chosen for the stockade, it being one of the strongest natural positions he had yet seen. Not surprisingly, Morgan, once again, did not share Duke's appreciation for a strong static defensive position.[21]

The next morning, when Morgan demanded that the garrison surrender, the patriotic federal commander appropriately responded that it "was a damn bad day to surrender." It was, after all, the Fourth of July. Having been rebuffed in a manner

The Indiana-Ohio Raid, July 1863.

reminiscent of the response he received the previous December in Elizabethtown, Morgan ordered his troops to charge the position. Adam Johnson, like Duke, immediately recognized the strength of the federal position and pleaded with Morgan to flank the position and get on with the raid—but to no avail. Morgan reiterated his order to charge. The attack was carried out tenaciously, but it ended in disaster, with thirty-six men killed, including Colonel Chenault, Major Thomas Brent, and Captain Alexander Tribble. Finally, recognizing his error in judgment, Morgan called off the attack and moved on. Tactically, the attack had been senseless, and, even if it had been successful, the stockade, but for its weapons, was of little value to the raiders. Duke and Johnson had realized that all such an attack could do would be to slow down the raiders while giving the federal cavalry time to intercept them before they reached the Ohio River.[22]

Leaving Tebbs Bend, the raiders continued north through Campbellsville and on toward Lebanon, Kentucky. Garrisoning Lebanon was the Twentieth Kentucky Infantry (federal) under the command of Lieutenant Colonel Charles S. Hanson. Charles Hanson was the brother of Confederate General Roger Hanson, who had been killed at Murfreesboro while leading the Orphan Brigade. The Hanson family, much like the Dukes, embodied the division that the war had caused in many Kentucky families. It was truly a war of brother against brother, more often than not pitting lifelong friends against one another.[23]

When the Confederate column approached Lebanon on the morning of July 5, Morgan demanded that Hanson surrender his command. Hanson had 350 veteran troops with orders to hold Lebanon. He had also been promised reinforcements: two regiments of Michigan cavalry and an artillery battery from Stanford, forty-two miles to the east. Hanson was a fighter and had no intention of surrendering before he and his troops had done their duty that day.[24]

Hanson's obstinate refusal to surrender was an invitation for the Confederates to attack. Duke was in position on the right of the road leading into town, the artillery was in the center to the left of Duke, and Adam Johnson and his brigade were farther to the left. Simultaneously, both brigades advanced and quickly cleared the houses on the edge of town of any Union soldiers. Hanson with the majority of his troops withdrew in an orderly fashion and concentrated in a large brick railroad depot. The depot was a strong defensive position. The building had numerous windows from which its defenders had an excellent view and field of fire. Grigsby's and Ward's regiments had occupied several buildings to the right of the depot from which they directed a steady fire at the Union troops. Cluke's and Chenault's regiments were in a similar position to the left of the depot.[25]

The Confederates were finding the railroad depot a hard nut to crack. Hanson's men were fighting well, their accurate marksmanship well documented by the mounting Confederate casualties. It was a typically hot Kentucky midsummer day, and the Confederates were beginning to suffer both from thirst and from the heat. The attack continued for several hours without any success when word arrived that the promised reinforcements were approaching from Danville, which was to the east. If this report was true, then the depot had to be taken soon, or else the engagement could escalate, with unforeseen results. Duke's immediate tactical problem was that Cluke's regiment had been pinned down by fire from the depot for some time. To relieve Cluke, he ordered the veteran Second Kentucky, which had learned some tough lessons in the streets of Augusta, to take the depot. Major Thomas Webber moved the regiment forward, and his men were able to pour an effective and heavy volley of fire through the depot windows. This concentrated small-arms

Young Thomas Morgan was a favorite of the command. He was killed at Lebanon, Kentucky, in July 1863 during the early stages of the Ohio-Indiana Raid. (Courtesy the University of Kentucky.)

fire from the Kentuckians forced the Union defenders away from the windows and back into the building. Realizing that the windows were momentarily clear of defenders, Duke ordered the Confederates to close on the depot. Accepting the hopelessness of his situation, Hanson finally surrendered after resisting for seven hours. Sadly, just before the surrender, Duke's young brother-in-law Thomas Morgan, a favorite of the men, was killed. The nineteen-year-old was in the lead during the final charge on the depot when he received his mortal wound. His brother Calvin caught him in his arms as he fell, where he died a few minutes later.[26]

The seven-hour engagement cost the Confederates nine killed and twenty-one wounded. Soon after Hanson surrendered, he exchanged pleasantries with many of Morgan's men, including J. L. Wheeler, his brother-in-law. Hanson was immediately paroled in Lebanon, but the rest of his command was marched nine miles in the July heat to Springfield. In addition to the Union troops, the raiders captured the garrison's medical supplies. This was an addition welcomed by the regimental surgeons, who, like most Confederate army doctors, were always in need of supplies. As an added bonus, unarmed Confederates were given one or more of the captured weapons.[27]

The raiders were within twenty miles of Bardstown. Morgan planned to get as close to Louisville as possible before he crossed the Ohio River. If, as Morgan hoped, Louisville appeared to be the raiders' primary target, then the Union commander should logically concentrate the majority of his troops in and around the city. Such a concentration, Morgan concluded, should leave the Ohio River crossings either to the east or to the west of the city unguarded. It was also improbable that the Union command considered the crossing of the Ohio River as an objective of the Confederates. Consequently, the column rode in the direction of Bardstown, which was only thirty-seven miles south of Louisville. The raiders paused briefly in Bardstown after the advance units had skirmished with and then captured a small Union detachment. At Bardstown Junction, a few miles west of Bardstown, George Ellsworth went to the telegraph office and began to intercept any pertinent information concerning troop movements and any speculation concerning the Confederates and their whereabouts. Ellsworth soon learned that the Union command was massing significant forces to the south and expected the Confederates to head for Louisville. It was also discovered that the Union command had swallowed the bait and was concentrating in Louisville. This news convinced Morgan that he needed to move quickly before the Union command realized its mistake. From this point forward, time and mileage were to be critical to the success of the raid. The raiders' new destination was Brandenburg, a small Ohio River town, to the west of Louisville.[28]

Since there was no ford at Brandenburg, it was unlikely that the Union authorities would anticipate a Confederate attempt to cross the Ohio River at this point. Thomas Hines had thoroughly scouted Brandenburg for several days and was about to provide Morgan with some valuable information concerning, not only Brandenburg, but also the results of his visit to Indiana. The young scout had discovered that riverboats, large enough to ferry the raiders to the Indiana shore, routinely docked at the Brandenburg wharf. Therefore, it was absolutely essential for such a boat to be captured before anyone in the town was aware that the raiders were in the immediate vicinity. In order to accomplish this task, Captains Sam Taylor and Clay Merriwether with elements of the Tenth Kentucky rode ahead to Brandenburg to locate and assist Hines. To confuse the Union army further, Captain William Davis with two companies was ordered to cross the Ohio River east of Louisville at Twelve Mile Island. Once across into Indiana, Davis was to create confusion among the local population and divert as much of the Indiana militia as possible to the east of Louisville and miles away from the actual crossing at Brandenburg.[29]

On the evening of July 4, 1863, Frank Wolford and his cavalry brigade had received their marching orders. Early the next morning, Wolford started from Jamestown, Kentucky, near the Tennessee border, and, by the afternoon of the next day, was at Lebanon. He was twenty-four hours behind Morgan and Duke. At Lebanon, he combined his forces with those of Generals Edward Hobson and James Shackelford. These were the federal forces massing behind Morgan that Ellsworth learned about at Bardstown Junction.[30]

The main body of Morgan's cavalry reached Brandenburg midmorning of July 8, 1863, after an all-night ride from Bardstown. The previous day, Captain Sam Taylor and his men had concealed themselves in a wharf boat and captured the steamboat *John T. McCombs* when it docked. Taylor immediately ordered the captain of the *John T. McCombs* back out onto the river to intercept another steamboat, the *Alice Dean,* that was paddling downriver toward Brandenburg. With the use of distress signals, the budding pirates were able to lure the *Alice Dean* alongside the *John T. McCombs,* enabling them to board and capture it without a fight.[31]

From midmorning until midnight, the two steamboats ferried the raiders and their horses across the Ohio River. Just before the first boatload of Confederates left Brandenburg, a group of militia with cannon on the Indiana side of the river attempted to contest the crossing. The Confederates immediately reacted by unlimbering several parrot guns and, with deadly accuracy, firing at the Hoosier militia. The third round from the parrot guns made a direct hit on a piece of artillery, causing the militia to disperse.[32]

Prudently, the Confederates posted a guard in the steamboat pilothouse to make sure the pilot did not try to sabotage the ferry operation. Years later, Duke recalled the story of one particularly tough-looking rebel who was assigned this task. As each crossing took time and the day dragged on, the pilot of the boat tried to initiate a friendly conversation with his guard by telling him his name was Smith and asking the guard his name so "he might remember the person to whom he owed the pleasure of this visit." The guard informed the pilot that he was not particular about whom he met and that his name was Tom Boss. During their conversation, the pilot learned that Boss was on duty for four hours. When the boat was unloading on the Indiana shore, Boss asked Smith if he had anything stronger than water to drink on the boat. "Why certainly," said Smith, who then ran down to the barroom and asked the bartender to make him two "real stiff toddies as quick as you can." When the pilot, who was looking forward to having a drink with his newly discovered rebel friend, returned: "Out shot both of Mr. Boss's long arms, a glass was grasped in each hand and drained." Then Tom told the pilot: "You needn't fetch any more until jest before I'm relieved, I don't like to drink too much while I'm on duty."[33]

The first troops ferried across the river were from the Second Kentucky and the Ninth Tennessee. These troops arrived on the Indiana shore without their horses. Once ashore, they quickly secured the landing area and sent out skirmishers to challenge any remaining militia. At noon, a small Union gunboat, the *Springfield,* arrived on the scene and, for several hours, threatened the crossing, until the Confederate artillery forced it to retreat. For the rest of the day, the crossing continued without incident. Toward midnight, the advance elements of Hobson's cavalry made contact with McCreary's Eleventh Kentucky, which was acting as the Confederate rear guard. McCreary kept the Union cavalry at bay for several hours until all the troops had crossed into Indiana. Then, under the cover of a dense fog, he withdrew with his men and crossed into Indiana.[34]

When McCreary and his men were safely ashore, Morgan ordered both riverboats put to the torch. The *Alice Dean* was immediately burned, but Duke, knowing Captain Ballard of the *John T. McCombs,* countermanded Morgan's order. Duke's family had used the *John T. McCombs* for commercial purposes for many years. In consideration of Duke's generosity, Ballard took the boat to Louisville, depriving Hobson and his men of its immediate use.[35]

As Duke rode into Indiana, leaving the Ohio River and the Kentucky shoreline behind him, it was not possible for him to know that it would be almost two years before he set foot again on his native soil. That night, Duke and his brigade camped approximately six miles north of the river crossing. Duke recalled that, when they camped that night, the civilians in the neighborhood had fled and left their homes wide open, sometimes with their half-eaten suppers still on the table. In the meantime, Hobson and his full brigade arrived in Brandenburg. With the *John T. McCombs* on its way to Louisville and no other riverboats available, Hobson had to wait for one to arrive before he could start ferrying his troops across the river.[36]

On July 9, 1863, the raiders, with Johnson's brigade in the lead, advanced on Corydon, Indiana, where the local militia had gathered approximately 450 men, most of whom were farmers with no military experience but determined nevertheless to make a stand. Not overly concerned that the militia could sustain a fight against his veterans, Morgan ordered Johnson's brigade to attack. After a frontal assault was repulsed, Johnson regrouped his troops and attacked from several different directions simultaneously. The militia had held its line for approximately twenty-five minutes, but a multidirectional attack was more than it bargained for that afternoon. Completely confused, the men broke and ran. The raiders suffered at least ten killed and thirty to forty wounded.[37]

After dispatching the militia at Corydon, the raiders rode north on the Salem Road for approximately eighteen miles. News of the Confederate invasion stunned Union officials. There was an immediate concern in General Ambrose Burnside's headquarters that Indianapolis was the target of the raid, and efforts were made to gather troops to protect that city. However, the vast majority of well-trained and veteran Union troops were in the South, and, to Morgan's credit, this was one factor that he had considered and depended on while planning his raid. Realizing the improbable situation the raid had forced on the local militia, the commander of the military district quickly ordered that some form of resistance—preferably a pursuit—be organized. In Indianapolis, General Lew Wallace was ordered to organize a force of "minutemen" and proceed by rail to southern Indiana with hopes of capturing the Confederates at either Madison or Lawrenceburg.[38]

All through southern Indiana, local militias tried to organize and prepare credible defenses. Such was the case at Salem. The Indiana militias generally were not very aggressive, however, and that at Salem was easily dispersed by the Second

Kentucky. The Confederates stopped at Salem for a short time to feed and water their horses. During this interlude, small detachments were sent out to locate and burn any local bridges. Duke noted that, while at Salem, the troops began a practice of wholesale plunder that neither he nor any of the other officers had witnessed before. For Duke, there was a simple explanation for this behavior. This was the first time his troops had been on Northern soil, and they realized that they might never have another opportunity to replicate, albeit to only a minor degree, the destruction of property maliciously visited by Union troops on Southerners. As the looting continued, Duke noticed the popularity of calico cloth, many of his men leaving Salem with bolts of it draped over their saddles. One enterprising soldier even carried a birdcage with three live canaries in it for two days, while another left town with seven pairs of ice skates dangling around his neck. Some of the troops were a bit more practical in their selection of goods. Curtis Burke wrote in his diary: "Tap Carpenter got two pair of new boots and gave me one pair of no. sixes." It did not really matter what a young Confederate took as long as it was Yankee property. Usually, the items were discarded after several days or after an individual need for retribution had been fulfilled. But for an order from Morgan instructing the troops not to destroy a certain factory, Duke did not try to interfere with the looting, actually condoning it somewhat by his acquiescence.[39]

The column now turned east toward Vienna, unaware that Hobson had crossed the Ohio and was a mere twenty-five miles behind. Shortly thereafter, however, the Confederates captured the telegraph office at Vienna before the operator was able to signal the alarm, and Ellsworth was able to learn of the disposition and location of most of the federal troops, including Hobson's, in southern Indiana. Armed with this knowledge, the command began to zigzag through the countryside, giving the impression that it was heading in more than one direction at any given time. This thoroughly confused the already anxious Union high command, which could not determine whether the reports it was receiving were accurate or exaggerated claims from worried civilians. To further complicate matters, several units, such as D. H. Smith's, were dispatched to feint in a direction different from that being taken by the main column. According to Union General Orlando Willcox, all "this was a nice piece of work. Morgan baffled the federal calculations while doing damage to various railroads." At least for the time being, no federal commander was able to pinpoint the raiders' location.[40]

All through Indiana and Ohio, Duke was impressed with each state's large population and evident abundance of material wealth. He was well aware that this abundance was indicative of a strong and vibrant nation, conditions diametrically opposed to those in the South. This epiphany enabled Duke, unlike other Southerners, to comprehend the dichotomy that existed between North and South. What Duke witnessed was evidence of the great economic boom in the North, which

Safety Guard

The Woolen Factory at Salem Ind. the property of Messrs Allen Manley & Co. is hereby protected from violence by the Confederate troops. Any Command passing through here will obey and respect this

By Order of
Jno H Morgan
Brig Genl
C. S. A.

July 10/1863

Not all Northern factories were at risk of being destroyed during the Ohio-Indiana Raid of 1863. This order from Morgan prohibited the Confederate raiders from destroying a factory in Salem, Indiana. (Courtesy the Kentucky Historical Society.)

began in 1863 and lasted through 1865. For a multitude of reasons, including the federal naval blockade and the absence of the adult-white-male population, beginning in 1863 conditions in the South worsened significantly. Even in Kentucky, the realities of war had a far greater impact on society and overall living conditions than what Duke discovered in Indiana and Ohio. The standard of living of Southern sympathizers, particularly those living in rural Kentucky, was similar to that of their brethren farther south and grew worse each year the war continued. William Lafferty, the son of a Confederate soldier, remembered growing up in Kentucky: "During that year [1863] they [the home guard] took away all of the meat hogs and our chickens, milked our cows when they chose and took all the horses we had. . . . As winter [that of 1864–65] came on we had little food to subsist on. Our meals until late in the spring of 1865 consisted of corn meal, bacon and occasionally potatoes. Instead of coffee we used parched rye and sweetened it with a cheap coarse brown sugar. Enough wheat had been saved to provide biscuits once a week."[41]

Smith and his regiment rejoined the column at Vernon, where a relatively large federal force of two thousand volunteers was waiting for the raiders. Brigadier General John Love, who was intent on making a stand, commanded the Union force. When intimidation failed to convince Love to surrender, Morgan's first impulse was to attack, but Duke and Johnson demurred, so, instead, he turned east and rode toward Dupont. The raiders now rode all night and were in the saddle as much as twenty-one hours a day. During these long days, the Confederates would begrudgingly abandon their broken-down mounts even though they were prized by the pursuing federal cavalry, which often pressed them into further service. Morgan's tired band reached Dupont on a Sunday morning, and, as they rode through town, some of the men became rejuvenated and plundered a nearby meatpacking plant. Hams and other meats literally dangled from the men's saddles as they left town.[42]

The next day, July 13, 1863, the raiders crossed into Ohio to the northwest of Cincinnati. Once again, detachments were sent in several different directions to confuse the Union army as the main column rode in the direction of the city. Several hundred men of the local militia, with cannon, had built a strong defensive position on a hill overlooking the main road, and, when the Confederates approached, they began to shell the road. The advance guard, which included Leeland Hathaway, attacked the hill and dispersed the militia. Duke and Morgan rode up and watched as their troops, screaming the rebel yell, took the position. Both Morgan and Duke wanted to know who led the charge. When Duke found out it was his old law school classmate Leeland Hathaway who was the first one over the breastworks, he took Hathaway "by the hand and swinging his hat shouted hurrah for old Transylvania." Morgan then immediately promoted Hathaway, an event that thrilled Hathaway for the rest of his life.[43]

In Ohio, Duke noted "that on more than one occasion in deserted houses we found pies, hot from the oven, displayed upon tables conveniently spread." The first time this phenomenon occurred, Duke noticed that his men stood around the table staring at but making no effort to eat the pies. Baffled, Duke asked what was stopping them. One of the soldiers responded that the men were afraid the pies were poisoned. Hearing this, Duke laughed and assured them that the pies had been set out for their benefit, and, to prove his point, he began to eat one. These particular pies were filled with apples, and, after two or three minutes watching Duke enjoy himself, the men took hold of the balance of the pies and ate them "ravenously." A veteran riding with Hobson's pursuing cavalry noted that the women of Ohio and Indiana were, of course, even more open and notorious in their efforts to see that no man "of General Hobson's force went hungry longer than 60 seconds."[44]

After eleven days in the saddle, Morgan and his troops were near the point of exhaustion. Just north of Cincinnati, Captain Sam Taylor met up with the command. Taylor had been inside Cincinnati for several hours that day and reported to Morgan that the city was in near panic, under martial law, and convinced that the Confederates were going to attack at any minute. Morgan never seriously considered attacking Cincinnati, but he did order diversionary feints toward it. He believed that, once he was past Cincinnati, the greatest threat to his men would be over and that, to reach safety, he simply had to outrun the Union cavalry. That evening, Morgan ordered a night ride around the city. The men were naturally worried about the horses and their ability to continue for any extended period of time. The horses that they had captured in Indiana and Ohio did not have the stamina of their Kentucky- and Tennessee-bred mounts. Typically, the Confederates would ride the Northern-bred horses and not abandon their Kentucky-bred mounts unless they were totally broken down; instead, they "allowed them to travel light and only used them in great emergencies." The men themselves began to wonder how much longer they or the raid could continue under these circumstances. All knew they were fairly close to the Ohio River, and they speculated as to where and when they might try to cross back into Kentucky.[45]

Hour after hour the men rode. Never had they been so tired, and never had so much been expected of them. Unable to fight off the exhaustion, many slept while riding, spurred on by the knowledge that Hobson was not far behind. All realized that they were now riding for each other and that, to survive, they might have to die for each other. Every bridge they crossed was burned. Every attempt was made to slow down their pursuers. Duke believed the most difficult aspect of that night ride to be keeping the column together: "It was a terrible, trying march. Strong men fell out of their saddles, and at every halt the officers were compelled to move continually about in their respective companies and pull and haul the men who would drop asleep in the road—it was the only way to keep them awake." Some of the raiders were not so lucky and were later found by the pursuing Union cavalry so worn out and exhausted that, in the military sense, they could hardly be called stragglers. Finally, at 4:00 P.M. on the afternoon of July 14, too exhausted to go any farther, the raiders camped twenty-eight miles east of Cincinnati in the small town of Williamsburg. They had ridden ninety miles in thirty-five hours.[46]

After they ate and fed their horses, most of the men fell into a deep sleep. When they awoke, many began to look for fresh horses to replace their worn-out mounts. By and large, the people of Williamsburg and the surrounding area remembered the Confederate visit with some affection. Ulysses Grant, a native of the area, wrote in his memoirs that the county did not care much for Lincoln and that many of the women prepared meals for the rebels, the task "no doubt a far pleasanter duty for some families than it would have been to render a like service for Union soldiers." The men were well behaved and troubled the locals only during one of their infamous horse swaps. One farmer by the name of Solomon Mershon was victimized by several horse swaps. Intent on recovering his horses, Mershon boldly marched into the rebel camp and almost immediately spotted one of his animals. Mershon and the horse's new owner were soon embroiled in an argument, which they decided they could settle, to the delight of the soldiers, with a fair fight. A space was cleared, and hundreds of rebel cavalrymen circled the two men to watch them fight. The farmer and the soldier pounded each other until Mershon forced the gray-clad warrior to quit. Mershon then mounted his horse, and, as he rode out of the camp, he received "round after round of rebel yells." His horse was never swapped again.[47]

Early the next morning, the raiders were in their saddles riding farther east. Curtis Burke was becoming anxious, as were many others, to cross the Ohio River. The men were reading the local newspapers and knew that a large force of Union cavalry was chasing them. Anticipating crossing east of Cincinnati, Morgan ordered Hines to lead a detachment of scouts to Ripley, Ohio, a small town across the river from Maysville, Kentucky, and determine whether it was feasible to cross there. Hines found the river too high to ford and the crossing itself too well guarded. The only alternative left for Morgan was to ride east another hundred miles to the next ford at Buffington. Two days later, a Cincinnati newspaper reported that the Ohio River was only thirty inches deep at Buffington.[48]

Duke noted that the Ohio militia was much more aggressive than its counterparts in Indiana. The Buckeyes did whatever they could to impede or slow Morgan's advance. Although they never seriously contested or confronted the Southerners, their acts of harassment were constant. They repeatedly blocked the roads or fired at the column. Of all the actions, no single one was significant, but, in the aggregate, they had the desired effect. James McCreary wrote in his journal that the Confederates captured hundreds of prisoners, "but, a parole being null, we can only sweep them as chaff out of our way."[49]

10

The Boys Were Sorry That Duke Was Captured

ON THE AFTERNOON OF JULY 16, the raiders crossed the Scioto River and burned the bridge before they entered the small town of Piketon. It was at Piketon, Duke wrote in 1891, that he received the news of the surrender of Vicksburg and Lee's retreat from Gettysburg. It seems that Duke should have learned of this news many days before he reached Piketon. He had been north of the Ohio River since July 9, and the men had been reading the local newspapers at almost every opportunity. The Northern newspapers were reporting news of Vicksburg and Gettysburg when the rebels had crossed the Ohio River. It is not hard to imagine the impact that the news of these two major military reversals, whenever it was discovered, had on Duke and the rest of the men. The significance of these events must have discouraged almost everyone. In the meantime, the raid was also getting its fair share of publicity. One federal soldier was convinced that the raiders would be caught, but, as the days passed, he started to believe that "none would be caught" and that after a "masterly raid through the states they would escape to Virginia."[1]

By July 15, 1863, the Union commander of the Ohio military district, General Ambrose Burnside, realized that Buffington was the only logical place left where the raiders could ford the Ohio River. While Hobson and the others were pursuing the Confederates from the west, Burnside had ordered General Henry Moses Judah to Portsmouth and the gunboats commanded by Lieutenant Commander Fitch "to check the enemy at Pomeroy and Buffington until our men get up." Portsmouth was midway between Cincinnati and Buffington, placing Judah to the south of the raiders and on their right flank. After his troops disembarked, Judah began to ride up the old Pomeroy Road in a northeasterly direction, planning to intercept Morgan somewhere between Piketon and Buffington.[2]

The weather on July 17 was pleasant enough. Early that morning, Curtis Burke had been sent out to forage for the rest of the men in his company. It was Friday morning, and Burke and his detail were riding through the countryside a few miles to the west of Jackson when they reported:

A couple of us went to a house and found no person at home but a couple of little children. We looked into the cupboard and found some milk and little bread and then we get into a large jar of honey and eat as much as we wanted. We saw the lady of the house coming and covered up the honey again. When she came in view we asked her to cook some bread for us. She willingly went to work at it saying she was a butternut or a copperhead as the abolitionists called them.

Later that day, Burke and a few others, while still scrounging for food, earned Duke's ire for getting ahead of the column and stirring up quite a bit of dust. A distant cloud of dust where Duke did not expect his men to be could have easily been taken as a sign that the federal cavalry was approaching. That night, as Burke bedded down, he intuitively felt that the raiders should have kept on riding all night until they reached the Ohio River and safety. Burke wrote in his diary: "Several of the boys remarked that we ought to keep moving although they were in need of rest. Nothing disturbed us during the night, and I slept fine."[3]

All that day, the Ohio militia had harassed the Confederates, blocking roads, and doing anything else it could to slow the raiders' progress. This highly successful tactic was the direct result of an order issued several days earlier. The harassment was so effective that Duke referred to the militia as "embarrassing their [the raiders'] march."[4]

Early on the morning of July 18, 1863, near Pomeroy, Johnson's brigade skirmished with and then swept past part of Judah's advance elements. Although Judah had pushed his men hard, it had not been hard enough, and he was too late to intercept the Confederates before they reached the Ohio River. He immediately sent a dispatch to Burnside, notifying him that he was only three hours behind Morgan's main column and was trying to reach Buffington before the Confederates. A Union soldier, paroled by Morgan, told Judah that the rebels thought Hobson had given up the pursuit and that they had no knowledge of his whereabouts. Sensing that he might be able to trap the Confederates at Buffington, Judah sent a message to Hobson to press hard.[5]

To Duke, it seemed as if the raiders were constantly skirmishing, almost as if they were running a gauntlet. Nonetheless, they were now only twenty-five miles from the Ohio River, and everyone's confidence was growing as the distance shortened. Perhaps because he was overconfident, Morgan halted for nearly two hours at Chester. It was this time spent at Chester that many, including Duke, have argued prohibited the raiders from crossing the river that night. The river is only eighteen miles from Chester, but, because of the stop, they did not reach it until after nightfall. Adam Johnson shared Duke's opinion and recalled receiving orders from Morgan to arrest anyone on the road to Buffington. Johnson's advance guard almost immediately picked up an old man riding toward them. Morgan began to question the man, who told him about an alternate crossing "that was about twenty miles down river but the ford was much deeper." Based on this information, Morgan decided to continue on to Buffington. In spite "of all this," Johnson believed that they could have crossed the river had they arrived there before nightfall. When they did reach Buffington, the Confederates discovered that Union infantry, with artillery, were entrenched near the ford. Duke felt that it was far too risky to launch a night attack based on pure guesswork. The Confederates were also "ignorant of the ford and without guides." Taking all these factors into consideration, Morgan decided to wait until morning to assault the entrenchments and cross the river.[6]

When Morgan camped that night, he was still unaware of the presence of the gunboats and their proximity to the ford. He was confident that all his troubles would be resolved in the morning. He did not even send out scouts that night to locate the pursuing federal cavalry, nor had he organized an effective rear guard to protect the crossing in the morning. There may be a practical reason for these failures. Morgan and his subordinates, including Duke, were, quite simply, exhausted. The responsibility for this lapse in vigilance must be shared by Duke, who, by this time, was something more than a competent brigade commander. Morgan did, however, order Lieutenant Peddicord, one of Tom Quirk's veteran scouts, to take ten men and cross the river into Virginia to determine whether there were any usable boats on the other shore. When Peddicord and his patrol reached the riverbank, the fog had become so dense that they could not even determine the width of the river. Peddicord unilaterally decided to wait until morning when the fog had cleared to patrol the opposite shore.[7]

The ford at Buffington was, as late as July 17, not "boot deep in places and very narrow," according to Leeland Hathaway. By the next day, the river had risen so fast that, as Hathaway learned from an old woman who lived near the ford, only twice before in the last sixty years had it been witnessed rising so fast. The rise of the river permitted the Union gunboats to maneuver on the water and, on the night of July 18, place themselves close to Buffington. The following morning, at least one of these boats would be close enough to bring Morgan and his troops well within range of its guns.[8]

A thick layer of fog hanging over the river greeted the first hints of dawn, completely covering the Union gunboats and the Virginia shore. Earlier, Morgan had ordered Duke to use two of his regiments to capture the earthworks blocking the ford. At first light, Duke met with D. Howard Smith and instructed him to use his Fifth Kentucky and Grigsby's Sixth to carry out Morgan's order. When Duke and Smith formed to attack, they learned that the earthworks had been abandoned and the cannons spiked. Duke then ordered his two subordinates to take their regiments approximately five hundred yards to the south down the Pomeroy Road, where he supposed the Union troops had retreated. As the two regiments began to advance down the road on foot, the fog began to lift, revealing the unexpected presence of Judah's lead regiment. The Confederates could not believe that the Union cavalry was on their immediate line, in force. The raiders grasped the initiative, fired, and charged, all of which, coming as a complete surprise, caused the enemy to withdraw in confusion. The Confederates captured about fifty men, including Judah's adjutant, and wounded perhaps a half dozen others in the process. Duke reformed the two regiments near the abandoned earthworks and, being satisfied with their position, rode to Morgan to brief him as to what had just happened. With the arrival of Judah's cavalry, both Morgan and Duke realized that the river crossing was going to be contested. Morgan told Duke to hold the enemy in check until he and the rest of the men crossed the river and to call for reinforcements if necessary.[9]

Pursuant to Duke's orders, Smith posted the two regiments at the southern end of a valley with a ridge running on his right flank and the river to his left. Morgan started to gather his force to begin crossing the river near seven o'clock that morning. Then, as the fog began to dissipate, a Union gunboat, the *Moose,* commanded by Lieutenant Commander Fitch, made its appearance and began to shell the congested group of Confederates on the shore. Within half an hour of the gunboat's arrival, Judah's entire force had taken position and begun to advance on foot down the Pomeroy Road. This time, the Union troops were far more aggressive and quickly captured two of the Confederates' parrot guns, turning them on the raiders as they tried to withdraw. Grigsby led an unsuccessful counterattack, trying to recapture the guns, and was forced to fall back. As the Confederates fell farther back, part of the Fifth Kentucky was flanked and cut off. The Union troops, experiencing this sudden success, began to press harder. Sensing that his line might break, Duke sent several couriers to Morgan asking for the Second Kentucky to be posted on his right to help reinforce his hard-pressed line. Duke was unaware of the mass confusion and pandemonium that the shelling from the Union gunboat had caused to his rear. Horses, men, and wagons were all thrown together, and it was a miracle that the Union shells did so little physical damage. The Second Kentucky had become commingled with the other regiments and never responded to Duke's request for reinforcements.[10]

At approximately eight o'clock that morning, Hobson's cavalry finally started to make an appearance from the west on the Chester Road. Johnson immediately formed his command to block Hobson's advance. At this point of the battle, neither Hobson nor Judah was aware of the other's presence. Fortunately for the Union cavalry, Hobson's advance coincided with that of Judah's and gave Duke the impression that the federal troops were mounting a coordinated attack all along their lines. Johnson's troops on the Chester Road immediately opened fire when contact was made with Hobson's troops, but they were eventually driven back by the pressure of the numerically superior Union cavalry.[11]

The Confederates were now receiving fire from three directions—Hobson to the west, Judah to the south, and the gunboats on the river. As Johnson fell back, his line began to form at a right angle to Duke's. Johnson momentarily stabilized his line, and, with Duke continuing to hold, Morgan saw his opportunity and headed north out of the river valley with as many men as he could extricate from the scene. While Morgan was forming for his withdrawal, a regiment of dismounted Michigan cavalry occupied the ridge to Duke's right and began to add a steady fire on the already hard-pressed Confederates. It was now only a matter of time before Duke's heavily outnumbered troops would be overwhelmed. Even with the Union cavalry closing in hard, Duke was able to hold out long enough for Johnson and Morgan to disengage and lead their men out of the valley. Johnson and Morgan rode to another ford fourteen miles upstream. Forming his troops in columns of four, Johnson began to lead the Confederates across the river into Virginia. The water was deep, and the men had to swim their horses across the river. Johnson was able to extricate 360 men before the gunboats showed up to shell the troops as they tried to cross. Morgan was almost across the river when the shelling started. It was very effective, and several of the Confederates were killed or wounded. Morgan saw that approximately seven hundred of his troops were stranded on the Ohio shore. Without any hesitation, he turned his horse around to rejoin his men.[12]

Duke had been fighting a losing battle for quite some time, and his fatigued troops either were completely out of ammunition or had at the most two or three cartridges left. Finally, with the pressure being applied by both Judah's and Hobson's troops, the Confederate line broke. Most of the men took off on foot and headed for the woods on the hills along the river. Duke and about forty men withdrew into a deep ravine surrounded by dense foliage. It was Duke's plan to hide in the ravine until dark and then try to escape. However, there were just too many Union soldiers in the area, and it was not long before he and his men were discovered. Duke realized that his only option was to fight his way out. When he climbed to the top of the ravine, however, he immediately saw that he was significantly outnumbered, and, since his men had almost no ammunition, he prudently surrendered.[13]

The fog had completely dissipated by the time Duke surrendered, and the July sun beat down mercilessly as the Confederates were collected in a nearby wheat field. Over seven hundred of them had been captured, but, because of Duke's holding action, Morgan, Johnson, and almost two-thirds of the raiders had escaped. The Union soldiers were, at first, unaware that they had captured Duke until one of his men inadvertently disclosed his identity. The Union officers immediately separated Duke, who "bore himself with dignity" as he was taken to General Judah. The two officers discussed the day's battle, with Duke admitting that "he could not have been more surprised at the presence of Judah's fire had it dropped from the clouds" on the Pomeroy Road that morning.[14]

Many years later, Duke wrote that the raid did have the immediate benefit of distracting at least some Union forces so that they could not participate in the Battle of Chickamauga. It is more likely that, as one historian has concluded, the benefits of the raid were minor, perhaps delaying Burnside's move into east Tennessee a month. In exchange for this minor advantage, Morgan's cavalry was almost completely destroyed, and, as Duke wrote, "much the larger number of men captured lingered in the northern prisons until the close of the war." More important, Duke recognized that the raid impaired, not only Morgan's prestige with his superiors, but also his ability to obtain a new command. Others speculated about the political consequences of the raid. As the historian Allan Nevins has pointed out, Senator Lyman Trumbull of Illinois wrote that Morgan had settled all doubts concerning Ohio's tenacity in prosecuting the war, as evidenced by the victory of the radical Republicans in the fall election. Trumbull concluded that "no campaign before ever damaged a political friend so much as Morgan's damaged Vallandigham," the Democratic "peace at any cost" candidate.[15]

Judah immediately sent Burnside confirmation of the victory at Buffington. Burnside reported Duke's capture to Halleck the next day. Then, on July 22, 1863, Burnside reiterated the importance of Duke's capture, emphasizing to Halleck that his prisoner "has been the managing man of all Morgan's raids." The capture of Duke and the Battle of Buffington were rapidly reported in both the Northern and the Southern press. If there was excitement over the capture of the Confederate raiders, it was tempered with the realization that Duke had given the Union army only a partial victory. Morgan and Johnson had escaped, and it was to take all Burnside's resources and another week of pursuit before he was able to capture the raiders—a mere twenty miles from the Pennsylvania line. Duke was now recognized by the Northern press as being something more than one of Morgan's brigade commanders. Shortly after the war, John S. C. Abbott wrote of the Morgan-Duke combination during the raid: "The cool, wary, crafty rebel chieftain, Basil Duke, aided the impetuous Morgan in the reckless enterprise. It was said that Duke furnished the thinking brain, and Morgan the impetuous hand which guided and nerved the lawless band, as it swept a tornado path of destruction through three states."[16]

One staunch Kentucky Unionist, who had a very disagreeable impression of Morgan, wrote in a letter to his cousin his own opinion of the raid and Duke's capture:

> I know you are all grateful at the capture of so many of Morgan's men and the possibility of capturing him with the remainder. My own opinion is that Morgan has about a half-million in greenbacks and is striking for Canada with the intention of converting these to gold and going to Europe. And he wants his men captured is the idea. That the fewer he has with him the smaller will be his divide. I do hope they will catch the scoundrel and hang him. Any other death is too honorable for him; I have some sympathy for Basil Duke but none for Morgan.[17]

Curtis Burke was also captured and, while surrounded by guards in the middle of the wheat field, noted: "Col.'s Duke and D. Howard Smith with about 100 more of our command was brought in. The boys were sorry that Duke was captured, but they cheered him when they found he was unharmed." Leeland Hathaway recalled the afternoon with mixed emotions. Surrendering his horse was a traumatic event, eased somewhat by a chance encounter with a Union officer who had some distant connections with the Hathaway family. Once the connections were established, the Union officer procured for Hathaway a bottle of Kentucky whiskey that he gratefully shared with those around him.[18]

The Union troops issued bacon and "army crackers" to their prisoners that evening. The exhausted Southerners opened up bundles of wheat, which were stacked in the field, to use for bedding that night. Hathaway and many of the other Confederates were so tired and slept so soundly that, when they awoke the next morning, they were surprised to discover that they had slept through a heavy rain.[19]

The next day, the Confederates were marched under the hot July sun for ten miles and then loaded on riverboats destined for Cincinnati. During the march, Duke's leg became lame, causing him much difficulty toward the end of the day. Although the river below Buffington was navigable, it was still low, and the riverboats made slow progress. During the passage to Cincinnati, one enterprising Confederate cut his hair, shaved off his beard, changed into some civilian clothes he had stolen during the raid, and leisurely walked over to the deck reserved for civilian passengers. When the boat docked, he casually walked off with some of the civilian passengers and, subsequently, rejoined the Confederate army. Other Confederates who were sleeping on the hurricane deck jumped overboard that night and swam to shore and eventual freedom.[20]

It took three days for the steamboats to reach Cincinnati. Duke felt that the guards treated him and the rest of the officers with courtesy, and, although the enlisted men were crowded together on the hurricane deck, the guards did their best to make them as comfortable as possible. Finally, on the morning of July 23, 1863, across from Covington, Kentucky, the boats began to make arrangements to unload the prisoners at the downtown Cincinnati wharf. The news spread on both sides of the river that Duke and Morgan's captured raiders were on the boats. Crowds gathered on both sides of the river, and, when it was learned that the Confederates were going to disembark in Cincinnati, hundreds began to gather at the Broadway Street wharf hoping to get a glimpse of the men who had created so much excitement during the past two weeks.[21]

As the prisoners disembarked, Duke, who was still suffering from his lame leg, and Dick Morgan, who was wounded, were placed in a carriage at the head of the column and paraded through the streets of Cincinnati. The prisoners looked more like brigands than an elite Confederate cavalry unit as they made their way to the city jail. They wore a variety of types of dress, including parts of captured Union uniforms. The soldiers sarcastically explained to the crowd that, because they had outrun their own quartermaster, they were forced to rely on the Union army for their clothes. Duke, himself, was dressed in blue jeans with a plain white linen shirt and a dusty broad-rimmed hat. He was described by a New York reporter as being a man of small stature, well built, with dark hair brushed carelessly aside, penetrating eyes, and a mustache and goatee. The same reporter wrote of Duke as having a pleasant smile and being cordial in his manner, emphasizing that he had been termed by some the "brains" of the raid. Another newspaper reporter described Duke as looking like a Spanish bandit on a small scale.[22]

The officers were separated from the enlisted men at the wharf and marched to the city prison on Ninth Street. The enlisted men remained on board the riverboats until the next day, when they were taken to the railroad depot and transferred either to Camp Douglas in Chicago or to Camp Morton in Indianapolis. The officers' march through the Cincinnati streets brought out huge crowds. The soldiers remembered a mixed reception as friends and family who had crossed the river from Kentucky earlier that day cheered their men while others pelted the Southerners with curses and things other than words. The Cincinnati newspapers reported that Duke seemed to have many acquaintances in the city, for, as he rode through the streets, he lifted his hat to many different people.[23]

A correspondent for the *New York Evening Post* interviewed Duke and several other of the captured officers during their stay in Cincinnati. Duke's "pleasant smile" and cordial demeanor apparently charmed the reporter, who did not expect a prisoner of war to be in good spirits and such a willing conversationalist. Although Duke freely admitted that he and the men were fatigued, he was confident that Morgan would escape. After interviewing several other officers, the reporter left with the distinct impression that Duke was a gentleman and quite the favorite of those imprisoned with him.[24]

Duke and his officers spent three days in the Cincinnati jail before they were once again marched through the streets. Large crowds again appeared, but this time they were more curious than anything else, and many climbed buildings to get a better vantage point to view Duke and the other officers. Finally, the Confederates reached the Hamilton and Dayton Railroad station on Central Avenue, where they boarded a train scheduled to take them north to the prisoner-of-war camp on Johnson's Island near Sandusky, Ohio. Just prior to leaving Cincinnati, Duke learned of Morgan's capture. He and the rest of the officers "hoped and almost felt confident that Morgan would escape." Morgan was to follow Duke to Cincinnati several days later.[25]

While Duke was in the Cincinnati jail, his old St. Louis law partner James Madison Cutts Jr., now a Union captain and the judge advocate of the Ohio military district, sent a letter to Burnside denouncing him for incarcerating Duke and his men in a civilian facility. Cutts argued, as had the Southern newspapers, that Duke and his men were prisoners of war and should be treated as such. Unknown to Cutts, Burnside had used the Cincinnati jail only as a temporary solution until he was able to find a more permanent residence for the prisoners. Prior to sending his letter to Burnside, Cutts had written a letter to Lincoln, advising the president that it would be in the Union's best interests to remove Burnside and replace him with General Hooker. Such ill-advised meddling only exacerbated Cutts's existing problems, problems that stemmed from his having been caught in an act of voyeurism at a Columbus hotel. Burnside soon after fired Cutts.[26]

General in Chief of the Union army Henry Halleck had for more than a year been embarrassed and frustrated too many times by their raids to be anything but relieved when Morgan and Duke were captured. Halleck was now determined that the elusive Morgan and his key officers were to be put safely away, with little or no chance of exchange. Within twenty-four hours of Morgan's capture, Halleck was in contact with Governor Tod of Ohio to determine whether there was room in the Ohio State Penitentiary for Morgan and his officers. Tod, also having an axe to grind owing to the Confederates' recent ramble through his state, was initially more than willing to accommodate Halleck and consented to the use of the state prison for the raiders. On July 30, 1863, S. A. Meredith, commissioner for exchange, notified his Confederate counterpart: "Morgan and his officers will be placed in close confinement and held as hostages for the members of Colonel Streight's command."[27]

Halleck's use of the Ohio State Penitentiary for Confederate prisoners of war was unprecedented. The Northern press attempted to give it the color of legality by arguing that the Confederacy had set the precedent by holding Colonel Abel D. Streight and his men, captured on a raid in northern Georgia, in a Richmond, Virginia, jail, treating them not as prisoners of war but as common criminals. It was irrelevant that this story was untrue because neither Halleck, nor Burnside, nor Tod felt it necessary to explain their actions to the Confederate government. Morgan had become a larger-than-life threat in the minds of many Northerners, and the penitentiary minimized the prospects of his returning as a raider. Southern newspapers, on the other hand, predictably complained, and even some European publications, such as *Blackwell's Edinburgh Magazine,* censured Halleck's action: "That the Yankees when they captured Morgan and a large part of his command last summer, should have confined them in a penitentiary, and subjected them to all manner of indignities, is a disgrace to them and not to Morgan and his brave followers. If they had been accused of anything contrary to the rules of war, they ought to have been tried by court-martial, but such a pretense was never set up."[28]

During Duke's trip from Cincinnati to Johnson's Island, large crowds gathered at every railroad station where the train stopped. It seemed to Duke that the people's opinion of the raiders had changed dramatically over a two-week period, from indifference to the rebels during the raid to outright hostility after their capture. When Duke reached Sandusky, he and the others were put on a ferry for the twenty-minute ride to the prison island. On the island, they were taken to the adjutant's office, where they were told to turn over any money or weapons in their possession. They were not searched, and the adjutant accepted their word as to money and even as to weapons. The new arrivals were then admitted to the prison compound, where they quickly mingled with the other prisoners and began to search for friends and acquaintances. After only four days on the island, Duke received news that he and the other officers from Morgan's command were being transferred to another facility.[29]

Neither Duke nor any of the other officers had any idea where they were going until they reached Columbus on August 1 and were marched to the Ohio State Penitentiary. The penitentiary was a massive stone structure that Duke described as a "gloomy mansion of crime and woe." The "gloomy mansion" would test the young man's resolve. Duke, like many of his comrades, would soon discover that imprisonment could wilt the flower of Southern manhood to the point of depression. While standing in the cell-block alley awaiting his assignment, a prisoner called to Duke from behind a grated cell door. Duke looked at the man and, initially, did not recognize him. Then, as he listened to the man's voice, he was stunned to realize that it was Morgan. Morgan's hair and beard had been so neatly cropped that, with his "forlorn look," his appearance was far from that of the man Duke had last seen at Buffington.[30]

The next day, Duke and the Johnson's Island contingent were marched from their cells out into the prison yard, where they were stripped of their clothes and personal items. Duke watched as two African American convicts washed down the naked men as they stood in large wooded casks. He felt that this was an obvious attempt to humiliate the Southerners, and, when it was his turn, he argued in vain that he had just recently given himself a bath. Duke was then taken to the prison barbershop, where his hair and carefully cultivated beard were cropped like Morgan's. Two days later, Burnside wrote General Mason, commander of the federal prisoner-of-war camp in Columbus, who was at Camp Chase, that he did not think it advisable, "against their own will, to trim the hair or shave the beards of the officers who arrived from Johnson's Island." The prisoners were then assembled, and Warden Merion informed his new wards of the prison regulations, including the prohibition against visitors.[31]

Each prisoner was assigned an individual cell. The cells were on three levels, or *ranges,* as they were termed by the prison. Duke was assigned to cell 27 on range 2, the second floor. The dimly lit cells were small, measuring seven feet deep by three and a half feet wide, with ceilings only as high as the cells were long. Although

Charlton Morgan wrote that the Confederates were "subjected to the same regulations which govern the criminals," this statement was not entirely accurate. The soldiers were separated from the convicts and were not required to wear the classic striped prison uniform, nor were they required to do convict labor. Each day, for two hours in the morning and two in the afternoon, they were permitted to walk outside their cells into the corridor and mingle with each other. Nevertheless, they were required to conform to some rules applied to the general prison population. For example, twice each day they were marched from their cells to a large dining hall, where they were seated across from each other and forced to eat in silence.[32]

After several days of adhering to the prison regulations, Morgan complained to Governor Tod of the unusual treatment to which his men were being subjected. Tod arranged to meet with Morgan and personally visit the prison. When the governor did visit several days later, he was astonished that the Confederates had had their hair and beards cropped and realized that such treatment was contrary to military law. After Tod's departure, conditions at the penitentiary started to improve for the Confederates. They were granted more time out of their cells, permitted to talk during meals, and, on August 10, were permitted to purchase goods from outside the prison. The use of tobacco was reinstated, and, most important, the prisoners were permitted to receive packages from friends and family. The prisoners were now given military rations and permitted to visit the prison library. There is no question that, as a result of Tod's visit, the general conditions were far more agreeable and, to some extent, far better than those found in many Northern prisoner-of-war camps. Yet, even so, Duke mournfully found the most onerous aspect of prison life in Columbus to be the reality of confinement, evidenced by the stone walls surrounding the prison, which were over fourteen feet high.[33]

As early as July 29, 1863, Morgan learned that he and his officers were hostages of a sort. Each time he petitioned Washington that his officers be treated as prisoners of war or complained about the indignities to which his men were subjected, the Union army always responded with the same answer—that the treatment of his officers was not to be altered until Colonel Streight and his men were released. At one point, General Mason advised Morgan: "It is not a part of my military duty to require more than your safe confinement in the Ohio penitentiary, giving you as far as possible all of the privileges of prisoners of war."[34]

To date, no evidence has surfaced of a journal or diary kept by Duke either in prison or at any other time. This seems a little unusual since Duke was such a prolific writer after the war. Then again, the confinement and the generally depressive nature of his situation may have contributed to a reluctance to write. Duke was aware of his reticence and was constantly apologizing in his letters for being dilatory in his correspondence. A fellow prisoner even commented that Duke hated to pick up the pen.[35]

For the first four months of their imprisonment, the Confederates received mail and even packages of food from home. At night, they were permitted candles in their cells and could remain awake an hour beyond the normal prison curfew. Most of the men used this time either to read or to write their allowance of three letters per week. Although newspapers were not permitted, at least once or twice a week the prisoners, through the benevolence of the guards, obtained an edition. The smuggled-in newspapers were generally circulated from cell to cell until the news was too old for even the most ardent reader. When the news of the Confederate victory at Chickamauga reached the newspapers, the articles were read to the men in detachments, each one more anxious than the other to hear of the Confederate victory.[36]

There were times when one or more of the Confederates breached the prison regulations and was punished accordingly. Typically, the offender was taken from his cell and placed in solitary confinement. The cells used for these purposes were underground, with no windows and no other light source. They were ominously referred to as the *hole* or the *dungeon.* The dungeon was smaller than a normal cell, and the prisoners were usually required to remain standing in it for twenty-four hours. They were fed only the proverbial bread and water, and their solitary companion was the night bucket. Duke, who went through this ordeal, recalled that the stench from the night bucket could be a worse punishment than the dungeon itself, as it was never cleaned on a daily basis.[37]

Duke wrote that Captain Foster Cheatem was the first Confederate officer to experience the dungeon. Cheatem's alleged transgression was an attempt on his part to purchase alcohol from one of the prison guards. Cheatem was placed in the dungeon for the obligatory twenty-four hours and, according to Duke, learned a lesson he never forgot. Cheatem was soon followed by Major Higley. Although Higley was visibly shaken by his ordeal, he did not lose his sense of humor and gave Duke and the other prisoners a spirited account of his experiences in the dungeon. Duke's opportunity to visit the dungeon occurred in December. His crime was talking to a fellow inmate after curfew. He spent a day and a half in solitary confinement, including a very cold night. He had only the clothes on his back to keep him warm.[38]

In September, Colonel Cluke and another officer were removed from the penitentiary to be tried for violating an oath taken prior to entering the Confederate army. Cluke was found not guilty and sent to Johnson's Island, where he died in 1864. After Cluke left, three prisoners were brought to the Ohio penitentiary from Camp Chase. Two of the men were being punished for trying to escape and the third, Major Thomas Webber, for writing a letter. Webber and the other two officers, in accordance with Burnside's August 3 order, refused to have their hair or beards cropped. Separated from and not permitted to speak with the rest of the Confederates, Webber had plenty of time to muse about his situation. The problematic letter had been written to a friend in Kentucky and contained the following language, which both the censors and the War Department found objectionable: "I cannot tell how long we will be prisoners. Until the end of time, yes, until eternity has run its last round, rather than our Government shall acknowledge the doctrine of Negro equality by an exchange of Negro soldiers. I hope all Negroes captured in arms and their officers be hung. I am willing to risk the consequences." Duke endorsed a subsequent letter that Webber sent to the War Department complaining about the retaliatory nature of his punishment. Webber felt that the very fact that a prisoner's letters were censored gave him the right to use the language of his choice. Duke thoroughly agreed with Webber and felt that an officer should not be punished merely "for expressing sentiments hostile to the policy of the United States Government." Webber was ultimately released in 1864 and spent the remainder of the war serving under Duke.[39]

Most of the men who shared these trying days with Duke became his friends for the rest of his life. Like Duke, they were well educated and came from the best of Kentucky families. They were an extraordinary group of individuals. Hart Gibson, for example, who had been raised in Lexington, received one of the finest classical educations in the world for that time. A graduate of a highly respected European university, Gibson was fluent in French and, as part of his daily routine, conducted French classes for prisoners interested in learning the language. Thomas Hines, a prewar professor and postwar judge, was a self-styled cloak-and-dagger expert who masterminded his and Morgan's escape from the penitentiary that November. Hines was also instrumental in engaging midwestern Copperheads to assist him in a daring attempt to free the Confederate prisoners at Camp Douglas, Illinois, in late 1864. James McCreary, who spent five days in the dungeon, was twice elected governor and once U.S. senator from Kentucky. Thomas W. Bullitt, Duke's classmate at Centre College, also a lawyer, who practiced in Philadelphia prior to the war, perhaps adapted better to his surroundings than any of the men. Much like a content monk, he enjoyed the intellectualism permitted to him by time alone in his cell. Bullitt religiously wrote in his prison journal, but, unlike others who wrote about their experiences, he reflected on the philosophical aspects of his life and life in general. His journal is almost entirely devoted to self-examination, with very few comments regarding the day-to-day events of prison life.[40]

In early September 1863, Duke's mother-in-law, along with Hart Gibson's mother, traveled from Lexington to Columbus hoping to see their sons and other relatives. Several weeks earlier, Duke had written and advised her not to come to Columbus unless she had specific permission to visit the prisoners. Hard as she might try, Mrs. Morgan could not convince Warden Merion to let her visit with her sons and Duke. Mrs. Gibson was also unable to obtain the permission to visit with her son. The warden, according to Charlton Morgan, made one small concession. The mothers were permitted, as a special privilege, to peer through the iron grating at their loved ones.[41]

However, it was only several weeks later that Duke's aunt Mary and his cousin Abe Duke were permitted to visit with him for two hours. Unlike Mrs. Morgan and Mrs. Gibson, Duke's aunt had significant federal connections. Mary and her husband, James K. Duke, had remained loyal to the Union, and, through the intercession of her son-in-law General John Buford, of recent Gettysburg fame, she was able to obtain the necessary permission for the visit. Duke's spirits were obviously lifted by the visit, which helped him through the difficult days ahead. Because he was ill, Uncle James was unable to make the trip to Columbus. He died several weeks later.[42]

On August 18, 1863, Tommie gave birth to her and Basil's second child, a daughter. The baby was named Thomas Morgan Duke in memory of Tommie's younger brother, who had been killed that July in Lebanon, Kentucky. This must have been another painful experience for Duke, not to have been present at his daughter's birth. Duke's situation was further exacerbated by the difficulty that Confederate prisoners encountered in maintaining a reliable correspondence with anyone behind the shifting battle lines. Mail from the South was so erratic that, more often than not, letters sent north either never reached their destination or, when they did, arrived in bunches or out of sequence. Willis Jones, a major from Woodford County who was assigned to the Bureau of Conscription in Richmond, was married to Duke's cousin Mary Buford. Mary had remained in Kentucky to run the family farm. Since the farm was now within the federal lines, it was easy for her to send and receive letters from Duke. She would then relay to Willis what her cousin had written, and he, in turn, would send this information on to Tommie. In an effort to circumvent this tedious process, Willis wrote Tommie and offered to improve her ability to communicate with Basil:

> Write if you wish to write to Bas or to your mother I will give you the directions and I will most cheerfully attend to the sending there for you—write one page of the letter on—cap paper, put in an envelope leave it opened, enclose in another seal it, and direct to Major Willis L. Jones Bureau of Conscription, Richmond Va, and I will send them for you every week, write nothing about the army, but you can mention anything you please about yourself, where you are, and what your plans are, in fact anything save about the army, this letter or letters I will send by flag of truce, or if you wish to write a strictly private letter, seal it and send it to me, and I can send them every few days by underground.

Duke's imprisonment was a trying time for Tommie. Correspondence was erratic at best, and often she had to learn news of her husband from secondhand sources. (Courtesy the University of Kentucky.)

Tommie's brother Dick wrote her on September 16, informing her that Basil and brother Charlton were writing to her on a regular basis but had no idea whether she was receiving the letters. Apparently, Duke's initial depression was quite noticeable as Dick noted to Tommie that her husband was doing much better than at first, "when he was morose and unspirited," but now "he is as gay and lively as the balance." Duke would, as would many of the other prisoners, continue to struggle emotionally with the long days of confinement.[43]

As the days passed, each merged into an endless stream of monotony for Duke, with no apparent relief in sight. He was well aware that the exchange cartel had been suspended the previous May, but he also knew that, through negotiations, some exchanges were taking place. What he hoped for was an extraordinary event, such as a Confederate victory resulting in the capture of a significant number of high-ranking federal officers. The Confederate success at Chickamauga appeared to be such a victory. As Duke and the others assessed the totality of the Confederate victory, they began to assume that, with the large number of federal officers captured, their chances of being exchanged increased dramatically. Their hopes were misplaced, however, and, by October 24, 1863, Charlton Morgan noted: "There seems to be no immediate hope of our release or exchange." As the chances of exchange seemed to diminish, Duke wrote a lengthy poem entitled "The Captive's Dream." The first stanza reads:

At midnight, in his grated cell,
Bright visions to the captive came,
And o'er his spirits sank a spell,
As potent as the magic flame
In which the wrapt disciple reads
The future's unaccomplished deeds.
He dreams his turn of stay is done,
His dungeon's door is open thrown,
And the stern warder bids him go
Forth from these walls of crime and woe:
He dreams that Jeff at last relents—
To slacken up, and straight consents;
And by some apt negotiation
Redeems him from the Yankee Nation.[44]

Any chance of an exchange for Duke or any officer was subject to Halleck's approval, and Halleck certainly had no desire to go in that direction. Even the whims of war, as evidenced by Chickamauga, seemed not to deter his resiliency. Morgan and his officers began to realize that their only other option was escape.[45]

Several of the Confederates had attempted to escape almost immediately after their arrival in prison. Captains Jacob Bennett and Merriwether of Johnson's old Tenth Kentucky regiment were sent to Camp Chase for making just such an attempt. Captain Ralph Sheldon soon joined Bennett and Merriwether. Then, when it seemed that the prisoners' frustration had reached its height, Thomas Hines devised an ingenious escape plan. Hines was in the process of reading Victor Hugo's *Les misérables,* and it was Hugo's main character, Jean Valjean, who impressed him with his improbable escapes through the subterranean tunnels of Paris. One quiet day in late October, while musing in his cell, Hines noticed that his floor was dry and free from any mold. The cell was on the first range and close to ground level. After further examination, Hines discovered that the floor was dry even at the rear of the cell, which never received any sunlight. He reasoned that the only logical explanation for the floor's dryness was that, because the cell was on the bottom floor, it must rest on an air chamber. If this assumption was correct, he surmised, then the air chamber could be used as a tunnel to reach the prison yard.[46]

All through the night, Hines formulated his escape plan and, in the morning, presented it to Morgan. Morgan did not hesitate; he immediately approved the plan with only one change. The number of prisoners attempting to escape had to be limited to Morgan plus six others, including Hines, whose cells were the closest to the air chamber. Since Morgan's cell was on the second range, it would be necessary for him to be moved on the night of the escape to the first range. For two of the prisoners, Captains Bennett and Sheldon, it would be their second attempt to escape.[47]

Thomas H. Hines planned and executed his and John Hunt Morgan's escape from the Ohio State Penitentiary. (Courtesy the Filson Historical Society, Louisville.)

On November 4, 1863, the civilian prison authorities transferred the responsibility for the day-to-day management of the Confederates to the Union army. The civilian prison guards continued to watch them each night; however, during the day, they were within the exclusive control of the military. The most conspicuous changes resulting from this new arrangement were that the civilian convicts no longer cleaned the cells and that the military eased the rigorous cell inspections. Both these changes significantly assisted the Confederates' escape.[48]

The next day, Hines began to dig through the floor at the back of his cell. While he worked on the tunnel, Tom Bullitt sat at the front of his cell, reading Gibbon's *History of the Decline and Fall of the Roman Empire,* or trying to master one of Hart Gibson's French lessons. Bullitt was in perfect position, not only to act as a decoy for Hines's tunnel work, but also to give immediate warning if a guard approached. The air chamber turned out to be six feet wide by four feet high and to run the length of the range of cells. Its location allowed a prisoner to knock out a hole in his floor, drop down into the chamber, and crawl to the tunnel under Hines's cell. As the tunnel work advanced, Dick Morgan made a rope approximately thirty-five feet long out of bed ticking. The prisoners also pirated the iron poke from the hall stove and fashioned it into a hook in the nature of a grappling iron to be attached to the end of the rope.[49]

The prisoners who were to take part in the escape began to sleep at night with blankets covering their heads. After several days, the guards became accustomed to this practice and soon took it for granted that the men were in their cells. Duke wrote that, on November 26, Morgan learned that a new military commander had been appointed for Columbus and logically concluded that he eventually would want to inspect the prisoners and their cells. Morgan, of course, wanted to avoid this risk and, therefore, decided that, just after midnight, the escape was to take place. The escape plan worked perfectly, and all seven made it over the wall, with Morgan eventually reaching Richmond, Virginia, to a hero's welcome.[50]

Duke and the remaining prisoners did not receive a warm welcome from Warden Merion the following morning when the guards discovered the escape. The prisoners on the first range were immediately taken to the third tier, where each one was stripped and thoroughly searched. Then, for the next fifteen days, the men were confined to their cells and forbidden to talk to each other. Duke's trip to the dungeon was due to his violation of this gag order. During the days following the escape, the responsibility of guarding the Confederates reverted to the civilian authorities. Finally, on December 8, 1863, Governor Tod permitted the prisoners to leave their cells for two hours of exercise. As James McCreary described it, all the officers looked "ghostlike and ghastly" when they emerged. The men were given a new set of printed prison regulations, tailored to make any future escape attempt impossible. The new regulations provided, in pertinent part, that there was to be no talking or noise after the convicts were locked up and that no prisoner was allowed to sleep with his face covered. Correspondence was now limited to two one-page letters of a strictly personal nature per week. The prisoners were no longer allowed to purchase supplies or receive them as gifts. In addition, a list of eleven conduct restrictions was made part of the new rules. Among the conduct restrictions were prohibitions against visiting another cell and, once again, talking while in the dining room.[51]

Extremely upset by the new round of "harsh and rigorous treatment," the officers chose Hart Gibson to petition Governor Tod for their removal to a military prison. Gibson's letter, dated December 10, 1863, referenced Burnside's July 30, 1863, commitment to Morgan that they were to be "restored to the ordinary footing of prisoners of war upon the release of Colonel Streight and his officers." Logically, Gibson argued, because of Burnside's statement and Streight's release earlier that fall, they were "entitled to be moved to a military prison prior to Morgan's escape." Governor Tod forwarded Gibson's letter to W. Hoffman, commissary general of prisoners, with the urgent request that he give the matter his immediate attention. Hoffman forwarded the letter to the secretary of war with the statement: "It is thought advisable to remove these officers from the penitentiary." The letter finally reached the desk of Major General Hitchcock, commissioner for exchange, who, on December 22, did not "recommend any change of locality for these prisoners."[52]

Duke learned to work within the new system of regulations and began to avoid situations that could send him to the dungeon. He was not a defeated man, only more careful. For most, the new restrictions were just another hurdle to overcome as they planned more escapes. It was soon Christmas, a particularly difficult time for the prisoners. There was a general sense of depression among the men, being away from home and family with no light at the end of the tunnel. On Christmas Day, the prisoners were served a special meal, which James McCreary referred to as a "ridiculous burlesque." McCreary took particular umbrage at the molasses cake, describing it "hard enough to have been fired with considerable effect from a mortar gun."[53]

11

A Convivial Evening in Philadelphia

Except for two companies, Breckinridge's Ninth Kentucky did not participate in the Ohio-Indiana raid. The regiment was attached to Wheeler's cavalry corps and, at the end of December 1863, was with General Joseph Johnston's army in northern Georgia. The Ninth Kentucky had not forgotten Duke and the rest of the men in Columbus, and, when Morgan escaped, they were eager to be placed once again under his command. D. H. Llewellyn, Breckinridge's adjutant, wrote Morgan from Augusta, Georgia, and told him: "The cavalry all look to you as our leader. . . . [Y]our escape has been to the expedition which Cave City was to Lebanon." Little did Llewellyn realize that, although Morgan was a hero to some, his superiors were outraged that he had knowingly misled Bragg and Wheeler on the purpose as well as the scope of the raid. Although Morgan was the delight of the Richmond social circles for the time being, he was persona non grata with his superiors.[1]

Llewellyn's letter also disclosed that he had visited with Tommie in La Grange and, possibly at her prompting, went on to question Morgan about the likelihood of the prisoners in Ohio being exchanged. Willis Jones continued to be helpful and was also eager to obtain news about Duke's exchange. Jones was, however, a bit too optimistic when he wrote Tommie on December 28, 1863, that he was sorry Basil had not received her letter, but that it was his understanding an exchange was about to take place, and that, if her husband were lucky enough to be chosen, he would be with her in La Grange within ten days. Duke was not one of the lucky ones, and Tommie's hopes must have been crushed. Forced to care for two small children on her own, Tommie found life trying at best, as would any woman, Northern or Southern, in similar circumstances. Her moral fortitude and character during this difficult time rivaled her husband's and should never be discounted. Certainly disappointed, Tommie might have felt a bit better had she known that, two days after Jones wrote her, Basil finally received one of her letters.[2]

The long, cold Ohio winter dragged on into late January. Then, at the instance of some of his Union friends, Duke was transferred on February 1, 1864, from the penitentiary to Camp Chase, a military prisoner-of-war facility also located in Columbus, Ohio. When Duke arrived at the camp, he was given an immediate parole "not to pass the limits of the camp with out the authority from the war Department, nor to have any communication with any person by word or in writing except with the permission of the camp commander."[3]

Duke's parole permitted him to go anywhere in the camp and even to visit other prisoners and talk with the guards. He readily admitted that his situation was no worse than that of the federal officers stationed there. The day after Duke arrived at the camp, he received a cordial invitation from one such officer for dinner and conversation. That night he dined with Colonel Porter and Absalom Y. Johnson. Johnson kept a meticulous diary, and his entry for February 4, 1864, described the evening with Duke. Naturally, the major topic of interest was the war, of which Duke spoke freely. The Northerners were interested in Duke's personal assessment of the condition of affairs in the South. They were not disappointed as Duke spoke both candidly and pragmatically, believing that the South's prospects were "gloomy."[4]

A series of letters between Duke and Mrs. Henrietta Morgan from February through May 1864 has survived. Although they contain few specific details about day-to-day life at the camp, the letters do give a good sense of Duke's state of mind during this period. Several dating from a two-week period shortly after his transfer to Camp Chase indicate that the sudden advent of freedom of sorts had lifted his spirits and loosened his tight writing hand. The first, dated February 18, 1864, in which was included a photograph of Duke taken at the camp, advises his mother-in-law that Bishop Purcell had visited and brought him favorable news concerning Charlton's probable exchange. It ends, almost impassively, with: "I no longer wonder that I had to serve a time in the penitentiary." What Duke did not say was that, three days earlier, he had sent a note to Colonel Richardson, the camp commander, asking for his parole to be revoked and to be returned to the Ohio State Penitentiary. Apparently, his conscience could not feel "satisfied as long as he was a prisoner and the recipient of privileges and comforts from which his friends were debarred." He regretted not being able to write his friends at the penitentiary and wished that someone else had been transferred to Camp Chase.[5]

Toward the end of February, Duke finally advised his mother-in-law of his decision to return to the penitentiary. He had also written John Hunt Morgan to investigate his chances of being exchanged. Morgan forwarded Duke's letter to E. M. Bruce, a Confederate representative from Kentucky, who had been working on Duke's exchange. Bruce wrote Duke: "If the federal authorities will send you to City Point an officer of equal rank will be returned unless there are special reasons against such exchange." This was the first positive news Duke had received concerning his exchange.[6]

In compliance with Duke's request, the Union commander revoked his parole and returned him to the Ohio State Penitentiary on February 28, 1864. On his return, Duke encountered an even more dismal environment than that prevailing before he left. During his monthlong absence, the prisoners had devised a plan to obtain knives to use in an attempt to capture Warden Merion and force their way out of the prison, but they had been moved to another part of the prison before it could be put into effect. Unfamiliar with the floor plan of this new area, they were forced to reevaluate their plan. Neither Duke nor any of the other prisoners were given an opportunity to formulate a new plan. The day after his return, Duke was transferred to Fort Delaware, to be followed in several weeks by the remaining prisoners.[7]

Absalom Johnson's final diary entry mentioning Duke was that for March 1, 1864, and it said simply: "Colonel Duke was taken to the Ohio State Penitentiary this evening to be sent to Fort Delaware." Within twenty-four hours of his return to the penitentiary, Duke was taken to a Columbus railroad station to be put on a train bound for Philadelphia. At the station, standing attired in a full Confederate uniform and a large floppy hat trimmed with gold braid, Duke was introduced to Major Johnson of General Heintzelman's staff. The major informed Duke that he, along with an escort of six enlisted men, had been ordered to take Duke to Fort Delaware. It was a very cold night, and Duke, who had no overcoat, was happy to board the train quickly. Johnson's behavior had been very professional and cordial, but still Duke found his demeanor to be quite cool.[8]

Johnson seated himself and Duke in a coach occupied by several ministers who had just attended a religious convention in Columbus and a group of soldiers returning to the Army of the Potomac. Once the train was on its way, Johnson began to warm and soon produced some brandy, sandwiches, and cigars, which he offered to share with Duke, saying that it was going to be difficult to sleep on the train so they might as well enjoy themselves. Duke did not hesitate to exploit Johnson's hospitality, and, for the next several hours, he and the major enjoyed themselves as they ate, drank, smoked, and entered into a lively conversation on many different topics.[9]

Major Johnson remained somewhat reserved with Duke until the two were interrupted by the soldiers, who were by that time drunk. The soldiers were harassing the ministers and behaving quite rudely to the rest of the passengers. Finally, one of the ministers asked Johnson to intervene on their behalf. Johnson spoke to the soldiers, who quickly settled down. On returning to his seat, he and Duke had a good laugh about the soldiers' behavior. This episode apparently broke the ice, and Johnson began to open up, telling Duke that the Columbus authorities had warned him that Duke was extremely dangerous and, if given the chance, likely to slit his throat and escape, hence the six-man guard. Johnson, a much larger man than Duke, took pride in his athletic abilities and was embarrassed that his superiors believed that he could not manage Duke. Realizing that Duke was not a physical threat, Johnson apologized for not having the authority to grant him a parole while on the train. Duke found the situation humorous, particularly since there was little likelihood that he would attempt to escape, dressed as he was, without a winter coat, and deep behind Union lines.[10]

A few minutes later, a young man entered the coach who recognized Duke from his days in St. Louis. Duke rose from his seat to greet and talk with his friend. During their conversation, the young man slipped a roll of bills into Duke's pocket. Duke immediately pulled the bankroll out and gave it back, saying that, although he appreciated the gesture, it was not necessary. All this transpired in front of Johnson. The young man looked over at Johnson, the bills prominently displayed in his hand. He was obviously frightened that his effort to help Duke would subject him to arrest by Johnson. When he realized that Johnson was not going to take any action, he quickly returned to his coach, leaving the two officers to another good laugh.[11]

Johnson, like most people, found it very easy to like Duke. The next day, the major was much more congenial, and, when the train arrived in Philadelphia, he discharged the escort and took Duke with him to the Continental Hotel. Duke, still dressed in his Confederate uniform, was an instant celebrity when he walked into the crowded hotel lobby. Several people introduced themselves and began to ask Duke questions about his military and prison exploits. Neither Duke nor Johnson was aware that some of these people were newspaper reporters. The newsworthy Duke gave several impromptu interviews, which turned out to be excellent material for the local newspapers.[12]

To Duke's utter amazement, after he and the major checked into the hotel, Johnson decided that he wanted to take Duke to the theater. Even Duke realized that it might not be prudent for a Confederate prisoner of war to attend the theater with a Union officer in Philadelphia and cautioned Johnson that they might want to do something that would attract less attention. Still not resigned to spending the night in the hotel room, Johnson convinced Duke to have dinner with Clement Barclay and several other Union officers. Duke acquiesced and had a very good time that evening. Barclay, a wealthy civilian, was a benevolent individual who had developed a habit of arriving on the Virginia battlefields immediately after a major engagement to set up a private field hospital for the wounded of both sides. The dinner party was very friendly, and conversation lasted late into the night. The next day, Johnson turned Duke over to the authorities at Fort Delaware.[13]

It was several weeks before Duke saw Johnson again. This time, Johnson was very agitated when the two met. The Philadelphia escapade had been reported in all the major newspapers in the city, making Johnson and Duke instant celebrities.

One of the articles had speculated that the purpose of the dinner meeting with Barclay was to plot some sort of rebellion in the city. Although this story was nonsense, the publicity and Johnson's instant notoriety had put him in some very deep and hot water with his superiors. In time, however, Johnson "got through it all right," and Duke was always grateful for his courtesy.[14]

By mid-1864, Fort Delaware could easily be identified as one of the Union's proverbial prison hellholes. Such conditions—which prevailed to some degree in all prisoner-of-war camps, Northern and Southern—were, of course, not intentional, but the result of neither side having the foresight to prepare to manage the vast number of prisoners that ultimately would be taken. The commander of Fort Delaware was Polish-born Albin Francisco Schoeph, a veteran of several Kentucky battles, including Perryville. Schoeph's eyesight had deteriorated to such a degree that he had been removed from field command and relegated to being the jailer of Fort Delaware.[15]

After the Battle of Gettysburg, Fort Delaware's Confederate officers were transferred to Johnson's Island. When Duke arrived at Fort Delaware, there were eight thousand enlisted men and only one other Confederate officer housed at the prison. The officer was Jeff Thompson, Duke's old acquaintance from Missouri. Duke was quartered with Thompson, and both were segregated from the general prison population. The two officers obtained the services of a young enlisted man as their orderly, and Duke felt that he was "pleasantly situated," with his condition being similar to what it had been at Camp Chase. In both *Reminiscences* and *A History of Morgan's Cavalry,* Duke never mentions any instances of the Confederate prisoners being tortured or treated inhumanely while he was at Fort Delaware. It is, however, hard to imagine that he was totally oblivious to conditions among the general population. More likely, he was embarrassed, as he had been at Camp Chase, by his special treatment and opted to remain silent about the enlisted man's lot.[16]

It was not very long after his arrival at Fort Delaware that Duke concluded that Schoeph was kind, courteous, and generous and that he did everything he could to "ameliorate" conditions for the prisoners in his charge. Rarely did captors fraternize with their prisoners, and most prisoners regarded guards as their enemies. Yet there was a concentrated effort on Schoeph's part to ensure that Duke and the other officers received a different standard of treatment than that experienced by the enlisted men. Duke, for example, received an immediate parole for the confines of the island on his arrival. According to Leeland Hathaway, prior to the war Schoeph had taught school in Lexington and was "well acquainted" with Duke and Dick Morgan. Hathaway was not so well acquainted and was placed in a pen "apart from the building" and, thus, saw little of Duke.[17]

The day Duke arrived at Fort Delaware, he was introduced to Dr. Isaac Handy, a Presbyterian minister and political internee from Portsmouth, Virginia. During his interment, Dr. Handy faithfully kept a journal, which was published in book form after the war. This journal provides an insightful description of the personalities and demeanor of the Confederate prisoners, including Duke, and their interactions both with each other and with the prison authorities. There is evidence in the journal that Handy too was not totally aware of the severity of the conditions experience by the enlisted men and agreed with Duke's assessment of Schoeph. Handy was certainly angry with the federal government over his detainment and, given the opportunity, would surely have exposed any infractions on the part of the Fort Delaware officials of which he was aware.[18]

Jeff Thompson was, at the time of his capture, a lieutenant colonel with the Third Missouri Infantry; however, by 1864, he was styling himself as, and had evidently convinced the Union authorities that he was, a brigadier general. A flamboyant individual, Thompson loved to sit for the camera dressed as a general. The two roommates became close friends and, in time, thoroughly entertained the other prisoners with their wit and humor.[19]

On March 11, 1864, Duke forwarded to Schoeph a copy of E. M. Bruce's February 26 letter setting the conditions arranged for his exchange. Duke wrote Schoeph: "I will be greatly obliged, general, if you will call the attention of the proper officer of your Government to this proposition." Two weeks later, Schoeph delivered to Duke a letter from W. Hoffman, commissary general of prisons, stating that Duke's "request could not be entertained while others had precedence over his claim." The denial was just the latest in a long series of frustrations that forced Duke to become resigned to the fact that his exchange might still be months in the future, if it was to take place at all. By this time, confinement had seasoned Duke's resiliency, and he did not let his personal disappointment interfere with his relations with the other prisoners, continuing to cultivate his friendships with Jeff Thompson and Isaac Handy.[20]

Dr. Handy continued to spend a considerable amount of time with both Duke and Thompson. He described Duke as being of "light frame, about five feet ten inches in height, of dark complexion, and wears a brown goatee and light mustache. He has a small, keen, chestnut eye, pleasing face, and good teeth. His forehead, which is low, is overhung with heavy eye-brows." Handy wrote that Duke and Thompson talked freely about many different subjects. According to Handy, the two had their own accustomed style of entertaining the other prisoners. Both were great raconteurs and were constantly weaving anecdotal tales of their "battles and hair breadth escapes." Duke was considered by Handy to be a person who improved and cultivated his mind through experience. He also noted that Duke read more than Thompson and exhibited a considerable knowledge of the classics. A more noticeable distinction between the two men was Duke's modesty, a trait that others recognized in him throughout his life.[21]

Religion was a topic that Dr. Handy never grew tired of discussing with anyone. Inevitably, Handy's intellectualism tested his two young friends' philosophical and religious beliefs. He concluded that Duke and Thompson were freethinkers, both having a "warm side for the Roman Catholic Church." He also wrote that both repudiated the general teachings of the Bible. Thompson apparently was fairly radical, with less substance in his arguments than Duke, who based his arguments on reason and what he had read. Handy also complimented Duke on his ability to appreciate the opinions and arguments of those who did not agree with him.[22]

It was not long after his arrival at Fort Delaware that Duke received a visit from an old friend of his parents, James F. Wood, now a bishop in Philadelphia. Wood became aware of Duke's arrival at Fort Delaware when he read of his memorable night out on the town in the Philadelphia newspapers. The bishop was allowed to visit Duke on March 18, 1864. Duke was thrilled to see Wood and wrote the same day to his mother-in-law: "I shall always remember his agreeable visit with pleasure and his kindness with gratitude." Several days later, on March 21, being concerned about Duke's religious and physical well-being, the bishop had a book on Catholic missions and an overcoat delivered to his young friend. In the letter that accompanied the gifts, Wood made it clear that, in order for him to be helpful, Duke needed to reciprocate by being "open and frank about his needs." The gift of the book may have been the good bishop's gentle attempt to persuade Duke to consider following his parents' path to Catholicism. Although the bishop was unsuccessful in this regard, Duke did find the book thought provoking, and it helped occupy his mind during the long and depressing days of imprisonment.[23]

Armed with Wood's book, Duke proceeded to enter into a discourse with Dr. Handy about the comparative successes of the Catholic and Protestant missions. Not surprisingly, Duke took the position that the Catholics were far better evangelists than the Protestants. Handy of course took exception and noted that Duke was thoroughly prepared during the several "arguments elicited by the debate." He also noted that the colonel had been reading an elaborate work on the subject of missions sent to him by the bishop and that, if he was only part "Romanist before, he seems now to be thoroughly indoctrinated with the teachings of Mother Church."[24]

On March 18, 1864, the commissary general of prisoners ordered the Confederate prisoners at the Ohio State Penitentiary and the "rebel officers" at Camp Chase to Fort Delaware. With the arrival of the new officers, Duke and Thompson were placed in a large room with W. W. Ward of the Ninth Tennessee, Hart Gibson, Dick Morgan, Charlton Morgan, Cicero Coleman, and Colonel Tucker. The men immediately formed a mess and were living "very well," so well, in fact, that, according to Ward, on March 31 they decided to "give a Negro woman $7.00 per week for cooking, $10.00 for washing." The next day, they purchased furniture for their room at the cost of $5.95 per man. The increase in the number of officers, however, caused the camp officials to be more concerned about escape attempts. Several days after the new officers arrived, the number of camp guards was increased, and, for a time, fraternization with political prisoners was forbidden.[25]

With the arrival of the contingent of prisoners from Columbus, Duke learned that four of their number had taken the oath of allegiance while in Ohio. Duke reasoned sympathetically that, under certain circumstances, it was understandable that men would choose such a course of action, but only if they "would have done nothing else prejudicial to the cause which they abandoned, or that would have compromised their former comrades." Duke had no sympathy, however, for the man who had also informed the prison officials of the plans for the attempted breakout in February, an action so dishonorable that, as Duke wrote, "his name must not be given so that those of his family and relatives who served under the Confederate banner were not associated with his shame."[26]

In early April, there was still no word that an exchange was pending for Duke—or anyone else. In fact, the correspondence between Secretary of War Stanton and Major General Butler indicated that the Union army's only concern was that the Confederates had not released a sufficient number of federal officers to "equalize the whole number between us" and that the exchange business needed to be cleared up in a few weeks "so as to be out of the way by the spring campaign." Schoeph continued his cordial relationship with the Confederates, meeting with the paroled officers, including Duke, on April 6, 1864, for over an hour in the sutler's private room. The conversation was friendly as Schoeph continued to assure the officers that it was his intention to continue to treat each of them with kindness and consideration. Jokingly, Schoeph told them that, if he was ever unfortunate enough to be captured, he wanted to fall into the hands of Morgan's men, from whom he would expect the best treatment. He half jokingly told Duke that General Morgan "was not worth much without him; and he intended to keep him [a prisoner] as long as possible."[27]

Duke had been a prisoner of war for over eight months, and the days of captivity were long and depressing. Duke was well aware that the military situation in the South had reached a critical stage and that the campaign of 1864 could be decisive. With the coming of spring, he expected the North to begin its offensive at any time. The ranks of the South's frontline officers had been so depleted by the battles of 1863 that field officers with both combat experience and leadership qualities were desperately needed. With the Union unwilling to commit to any large-scale exchange agreement with the Confederacy, the absence of Duke and other competent Confederate officers from the battlefield that spring would not go unnoticed. This realization was certainly disheartening to a man with Duke's patriotic zeal and aggressiveness. Yet Duke did not convey any form of outward depression to his fellow officers or to his correspondents. He did, however, constantly complain to his mother-in-law about the lack of letters from his wife but finally qualified his annoyance and acquiesced to the fact that letters from the Deep South rarely reached a destination north of the Mason-Dixon Line.[28]

Of all the officers in Duke's mess, perhaps Hart Gibson was the most fortunate during his stay at Fort Delaware. Gibson's wife, Mary, was a very tenacious lady. When she learned that her husband was at Fort Delaware, she made every attempt possible to visit him at the camp. Not only was she successful in her efforts, but, during an April 1864 visit, she stayed at General Schoeph's quarters with him and his wife. She then returned on May 9 and, apparently, stayed with Hart at a tavern on the island until May 28, when, as Ward noted in his diary: "Capt. Gibson's wife left for home & he came up to his room again." This remarkable incident would be all but unbelievable had it not also been noted in Handy's journals as well as Colonel W. W. Ward's diary.[29]

In the meantime, Morgan was having a very difficult time putting together a command. His superiors in Richmond were reluctant to trust him with another command, particularly one that would grant him the same independence that he so flagrantly abused during his last raid. Morgan proved unable even to have "Willie" Breckinridge's Ninth Kentucky Cavalry reassigned to him. A frustrated Breckinridge wrote Morgan from Tunnel Hill, Georgia, on April 26, 1864: "Officers and men are very eager to be with you, but their hope is fast dying away. I have done everything in my power to keep them cheered up by the hope of finally being ordered back; but this late order rather makes my faith in ever returning to your command, so long as General Bragg supreme control. When Duke is exchanged the desire of the regiment to return will if possible be increased." Hart Gibson was also frustrated and wrote Morgan about the exchange situation, expressing his belief that he and the other prisoners would most likely be held at Fort Delaware for the duration.[30]

Finally, Morgan was given a command in southwestern Virginia. The troops assigned to this command were vastly inferior to those assigned to his old division. Without the assistance of Duke or someone with similar abilities in organizing and disciplining his new command, Morgan found himself in an alarming situation. Nevertheless, he assumed command with confidence and a strong desire to raid Kentucky one more time. With his headquarters situated in Abingdon, Virginia, Morgan learned that this military district was strategically important because of the lead mines located in Wytheville and the saltworks at Saltville. His primary responsibility was to ensure that the federal cavalry did not successfully raid these two targets. For the impetuous Morgan, there was no satisfaction to be found in routine cavalry duties. Morgan the guerrilla was more interested in planning his next raid.[31]

Duke's mess at Fort Delaware. Duke is shown standing second from the right. (Courtesy the University of Kentucky.)

The prevailing topic of discussion among the prisoners at Fort Delaware—albeit one without resolution—was the same as it had been in Columbus: When were they to be exchanged? At least the month of May brought pleasant weather, alleviating somewhat their emotionally dreary confinement. Helpful too were opportunities to be photographed by a commercial photographer who visited the camp from time to time, opportunities of which the men took ample advantage, both individually and collectively. The surviving individual portrait photographs show that, even in prison, Duke was immaculately dressed and perfectly groomed, as does the collective photograph of Duke with his mess. The prisoners, including Duke, traded their photographs with one another, an event that was apparently a high point for at least one prisoner as it was noted several times in W. W. Ward's Civil War diary.[32]

Events taking place in Charleston, South Carolina, however, were to have a dramatic impact on Duke as well as forty-nine other Confederate officers. Charleston had been the subject of a determined federal blockade and siege for most of the war. The federal fleet and army siege guns on nearby islands were bombarding Charleston almost around the clock. On June 1, 1864, General Bragg received a letter from Major General Samuel Jones stating that "the enemy continues to bombard the city with increased vigor," "endangering the lives of women and children." In order to dissuade the Union bombardment, Jones suggested that Bragg take fifty Yankee prisoners and confine them "in parts of the city still occupied by citizens, but under the enemy's fire." Nine days later, under a cover letter from Confederate Adjutant and Inspector General Samuel Cooper, General Howell Cobb in Macon, Georgia, was instructed that President Davis had approved Jones's application and that Cobb was to pick the fifty Yankee prisoners to be sent to Charleston. When the Union commander at Hilton Head, South Carolina, learned of the Confederates' plan, he immediately wrote General Halleck, complaining about the situation, and proposing that President Lincoln authorize a like reprisal. Halleck ordered the commissioner of prisoners to turn over five general and forty-five field grade officers to the appropriate officer to be transported to the Department of the South. Duke, Jeff Thompson, and many other officers at Fort Delaware were chosen.[33]

Duke and the other officers learned that the Union army intended to take them south to Morris Island, South Carolina. There they were to be placed in selected locations, in the line of the return fire of the Confederate batteries in and around Charleston. Fully aware of why they were being relocated, Duke and the others were elated to have been chosen. Duke knew that the accuracy of the large Confederate guns in Charleston was suspect and concluded that the chance of being injured was remote. Jeff Thompson characteristically speculated that there was a better chance of being struck by lightning than of being hit by a shell from one of the big guns.[34]

Two days before the Confederate contingent was to disembark, Major General Sam Jones wrote General Cooper in Richmond, advising him: "The right and expediency of confining prisoners of war in this city [Charleston] is eliciting some discussion in and out of the public print, and the actual facts of the matter do not seem to be correctly understood by the public." Jones had been in correspondence with Union General John G. Foster concerning the retaliatory measures being taken by both armies and requested permission from Cooper to publish this correspondence. More important, however, Jones asked for permission to enter into negotiations with Foster for an exchange of the officers. By the first week of July, Jones had opened a written dialogue with Foster at precisely the time that Duke and the other Confederate officers began their stay in the floating Union prison off Hilton Head Island.[35]

On June 26, 1864, Duke and his fellow prisoners boarded the steamship *Mary A. Boardman* in the Delaware River. The Confederates were still under the impression that they were to be taken to Morris Island, South Carolina. Duke was confident that the standoff between the two governments would, ultimately, end in the long-hoped-for exchange. The next day, the *Mary A. Boardman* began the long journey down the Delaware River, out into the Atlantic Ocean, and then south toward South Carolina.[36]

The voyage to South Carolina was the first time that Duke and many of the other officers had ever been on the open ocean. Most of the Confederates were from either Kentucky or Tennessee and, unlike Duke, had never even seen the ocean. The ride was relatively smooth as the small boat made its way down the Delaware River; however, when the boat reached the open ocean, it began to bob like a "green rider on a trotting horse." Duke was jammed into a small cabin on the upper deck with nine other men. Most of the other prisoners were below Duke, confined in a poorly ventilated area of the boat. Their plight was compounded by the fact that the ports and air holes were closed. It was only a matter of time before many of the prisoners, including Duke, became seasick. Duke recalled that, even though the Confederates quartered below him suffered much more from nausea than he did, the guards prohibited them from coming on deck until the boat arrived off Hilton Head, South Carolina.[37]

The voyage took three days, but it must have felt like an eternity to the seasick Duke. The Confederates remained on the *Mary A. Boardman* another two days until, on July 1, 1864, they were transferred to the USS *Dragoon,* a sailing ship. Little did the prisoners realize, however, that they were to remain on the *Dragoon* for four long, hot weeks. Within days of the Confederates' arrival at Hilton Head, the federal authorities had discovered that the report concerning the use of Union officers as targets for the federal siege guns was false. The plan to retaliate by positioning the Confederates on Morris Island was now moot. Still unaware of his ultimate disposition, Duke wrote Tommie on July 7: "We received as yet no indication as to what will be done with us. As long as our stay at this place be not long I earnestly hope as it is by no means an agreeable location."[38]

The weather in Hilton Head was extremely hot and humid, with daytime temperatures in the high nineties and little relief at night. Initially, when Duke was transferred to the *Dragoon,* he was placed below deck, where the temperatures were almost unbearable. In the beginning, the *Dragoon*'s captain permitted only two prisoners on the deck at a time. However, after having suffered through the first week, the Confederates were allowed on deck for an hour in two alternating groups of twenty-five during the daylight hours. While on deck, they tried to amuse themselves by fishing for one of the many small sharks that swam around the *Dragoon.* One day, the men caught a rather large shark, which was extremely difficult to kill once it was brought on board. Witnessing the shark's tenacious will to live—and, more important, to fight—convinced the prisoners that an escape attempt through the water was not in their best interests.[39]

Tommie and the children were staying in Madison, Georgia, when she learned that Duke was on the *Dragoon.* She had not seen her husband for over a year and was anxious for any news concerning him or his possible exchange. She constantly made inquiries with the Confederate authorities concerning these matters, and, when she learned that he was at Hilton Head, she immediately tried to secure permission to visit him. Although sympathetic, General Jones advised Tommie that her request was not likely to be approved by the Yankees but that her letters could be delivered by flag of truce. Tommie wrote Duke on July 25, 1864, telling him that she knew he was at Hilton Head and that their baby girl had been sick, forcing her to remain in Madison even though most of the town had been evacuated, fearing a raid by Sherman's cavalry. On a lighter note, she wrote that a family acquaintance had seen their daughter and remarked that the baby looked remarkably like his, Basil's, mother.[40]

Toward the end of July 1864, negotiations for the prisoner exchange were no longer at an impasse, and, on August 1, it was announced that an agreement had been reached. The next day, Duke and his fellow prisoners were transferred from the *Dragoon* to the *Cosmopolitan.* The *Cosmopolitan* left Hilton Head around ten o'clock in the evening with orders to rendezvous the next morning with the Confederate vessel *Chesterfield* in Charleston harbor. In the early morning hours, the fifty Union officers to be exchanged for Duke and the other Confederate prisoners were brought from Charleston aboard the *Chesterfield.* Standing on the deck of the *Cosmopolitan* as it maneuvered through the Union blockade, Duke was intrigued by his first sight of the monitor-class ironclad patrolling the harbor entrance.[41]

When the *Cosmopolitan* rendezvoused with the *Chesterfield,* the Union officers came on board the ship. After the formalities of the exchange were completed, a banquet was given for all the officers. The officers, whether Union or Confederate, found it difficult to believe the spread of food on the tables. Everyone enjoyed and appreciated the feast. When the meal was completed, the Confederates boarded the *Chesterfield,* leaving the *Cosmopolitan* on a positive note. Although there was an agreement to suspend shelling that day, both Union and Confederate batteries saluted the Confederates as the *Chesterfield* steamed into Charleston harbor under a cloudless blue sky.[42]

A cheering crowd gathered at the Charleston wharf and welcomed the returning Confederates warmly. Each officer was graciously taken to a private residence to spend the night. It had been one year and two weeks since Duke's capture at Buffington. The initial sense of relief was rapidly being replaced by a desire to see his family. However, Duke spent his first night of freedom with several other released prisoners at the residence of Major Huger. After supper, the men retired to Huger's veranda for what Duke anticipated would be a pleasant evening of conversation. Around 8 P.M., the suspension of the artillery barrage ended abruptly with simultaneous cannonades from each side. Caught off guard, Duke started fearfully to his feet, much to the amusement of his host. Huger laughingly assured Duke that there was no reason to worry because the shells never came within half a mile of his house. A short time later, a louder explosion produced the same reaction, and, after another great laugh, Duke's friends identified the noise as coming from the famous Confederate battery known as the "Swamp Angel."[43]

The next day, Duke was finally reunited with his wife and children. Several days later, he and his family traveled to Richmond, Virginia, but it was not until late August that he was able to join Morgan at Abingdon. Morgan was at the time the target of severe criticism as a result of yet another disastrous Kentucky raid that he had led that summer. Although his troops had managed to pull off three bank robberies, the overconfident Morgan had been soundly defeated by a superior Union force at Cynthiana, Kentucky. Reeling from the defeat, the command limped back to southwestern Virginia, many of the men deserting and remaining in Kentucky to join outlaw bands. Richmond was not at all happy about the bank robberies and certain other untoward incidents that occurred during the raid. Morgan's primary responsibility was to defend southwestern Virginia, a responsibility that he had ignored at a critical time.[44]

Morgan's command had deteriorated to such an extent that its ability to function as a combat unit was highly suspect. Further disrupting matters, several of Morgan's officers had filed their own reports about the bank robberies and requested an investigation of the raid. Morgan effectively thwarted the investigation by granting his inspector general thirty days' leave, infuriating his brigade commanders, who wrote Richmond and demanded a formal inquiry. As the controversy heated up, Secretary of War Seddon relieved Morgan of his command and scheduled an inquiry to be held in Abingdon on September 10, 1864.[45]

When Duke arrived in Abingdon, he was very surprised at Morgan's physical and emotional condition. He wrote that Morgan was "greatly changed" and seemed bitter, with none of his former enthusiasm. Then, within days of Duke's arrival, Morgan left Abingdon with approximately fifteen hundred men for Jonesboro, Tennessee, ignoring Seddon's orders. Duke prudently did not accompany him. Morgan reached Jonesboro on September 2, the same date Major Webber arrived in Abingdon from Richmond. Webber told Duke and W. W. Ward that he was very troubled with the condition of the command. Later that day, Duke and Ward talked privately about the problem and how the situation might be turned around.[46]

Morgan moved on to Greeneville, Tennessee, where he camped the night of September 3. As during his 1862 stay in Lebanon, Morgan stayed in town with his staff that night, convinced that the closest Union troops were no nearer than Knoxville. His troops, on the other hand, bivouacked approximately one and a half miles out of town in the direction of Bulls Gap. During the night, a local twelve-year-old boy whom Union soldiers had befriended when they were in Greeneville rode the eighteen miles to Bulls Gap and alerted the federal cavalry to Morgan's presence in the town. The rain that had fallen most of the night began to ease at daylight as the federal cavalry dashed into town undetected. During the melee that followed, Morgan was killed attempting to escape. There has been a considerable amount of controversy surrounding the circumstances of his death, in particular whether he had been betrayed. Years later, Duke admitted that, despite having visited Greeneville shortly after Morgan's death, he was still not certain exactly what had happened. To this day a consensus has not been reached.[47]

The Union commander ordered Morgan's remains delivered to the Confederates under flag of truce. Duke arrived at Carter's Station on September 5, 1864, to take possession of the body. When the coffin arrived, it was opened so that he could view Morgan's remains. Duke became very emotional and broke into tears when he saw his brother-in-law's body. This was certainly a traumatic moment for Duke, who had admired Morgan and considered him his best friend. After viewing the body, he sent a telegram to Major Llewellyn in Abingdon confirming Morgan's death and instructing him "to break the news to Morgan's wife." Morgan was quickly buried the next day, September 6, 1864, in an above-ground vault in Abingdon Cemetery. The Confederate government later gave Morgan a formal military funeral in Richmond. The general's body was finally returned to Lexington, Kentucky, in April 1868, where it was interred at Lexington Cemetery in the Morgan family plot.[48]

12

The Glory and Chivalry Seemed Gone

THE MILITARY AND POLITICAL SITUATION had changed dramatically since Duke's capture at Buffington. Militarily, the South was hanging on by a shoestring, and even its strongest advocates realized that victory was not likely to be obtained on the battlefield. Astute Southerners and their sympathizers in the North began to search for a political solution. It was a presidential election year, and the war-weary Democrats nominated the popular George McClellan to run against Abraham Lincoln. Many Southerners naively believed that a McClellan victory could result in a negotiated peace settlement. Even if such an optimistic assessment of McClellan was correct, Sherman's capture of Atlanta at the beginning of September 1864 proved to most of the Northern skeptics that the war could be won.[1]

By the summer of 1864, Governor Thomas E. Bramlette of Kentucky had become part of a strong opposition core that formed the nucleus of the state's Union Democracy Party. The Union Democrats strongly condemned the government's plan of reconstruction and its policy of enlisting African Americans into the Union army. They also supported McClellan's bid for the presidency. This infuriated General Stephen Burbridge and other Republicans in Kentucky, who threatened to use force to ensure a Lincoln victory in November. In an open letter to the people of Kentucky, Bramlette advised treating any interference with the election by the military with "indignant contempt" and "scorn[ing] obedience which implies perjury and cowardice to you," further increasing tensions. Although the nation elected Lincoln, McClellan won the state by thirty-six thousand votes. The results of the 1864 presidential election were to have a profound impact on Kentucky and on Duke's postwar politics and career.[2]

In Virginia, Morgan's death had a decided influence on Duke's attitude toward the prosecution of the war. He wrote: "When [Morgan] died, the glory and chivalry seemed gone from the struggle, and it became a tedious routine, enjoined by duty, and sustained only by sentiments of pride and hatred." What Duke seems not to have realized was that, during his thirteen-month absence from active duty, the dynamics of the war had changed dramatically. Having achieved an overwhelming superiority in men and material over the South, the North shifted its focus to the prosecution of total war, the destruction of the South's very ability to wage war. Glory and chivalry did not die with Morgan; they died with Grant and Sherman at Atlanta and, perhaps more significantly for Duke, at Buffington.[3]

The war in Appalachia may have appeared to be little more than a military sideshow and has certainly attracted less attention than the war in Virginia and Georgia, but the combat there was just as ferocious—and perhaps even more so. The Union armies under General Gillem in east Tennessee and General Burbridge in Kentucky were becoming more aggressive and, by September 1864, were pressing the Confederates on two fronts. Because of his treatment of civilians in Kentucky, Burbridge was already hated both within and without the state. His activities and those of his subordinates in eastern Kentucky in the fall of 1864 had caused many Kentuckians to desert the Confederate army and wage their own independent warfare "in their native mountains."[4]

The same day that Duke took possession of Morgan's body at Carter's Station, he received orders from General Echols to take command of Morgan's men. Echols's order was somewhat irregular because D. H. Smith was still senior in rank to Duke and first in line for the command of the brigade. Smith had, however, declined the command in deference to Duke—although Echols believed Smith's real reason to be that the command had deteriorated beyond repair. Notifying General Cooper of Smith's decision, Echols spoke favorably of Duke: "I am sure that he will improve the condition, as he is a most intelligent and efficient officer."[5]

With his orders in hand, Duke took command of the brigade, "comprised of Cassell's and Cantrill's Battalions," to find that there were only 273 effective troops and 50 serviceable weapons. It was a brigade in name only. The men were armed so poorly that Duke wondered "how they could fight at all." It was going to take a significant effort on Duke's part to raise the brigade to the level of combat effectiveness that he had always demanded of his troops. This would be a challenge since the majority of the enlisted men were not of the quality that Duke had commanded prior to his capture. Fortunately, competent officers such as Colonels Ward, Morgan, and Tucker, along with Majors Webber and Steele, were with Duke and ready to go to work. There were also representative elements of all the old regiments within the brigade, thus providing Duke a viable core with which to work as he began an intensive two-week reorganization and discipline program.[6]

Duke's brigade remained in and around Jonesboro for nearly two weeks following Morgan's death as the drills and inspections under the capable supervision of its veteran officers slowly but surely sharpened the troops' combat edge. W. W. Ward and Joseph Tucker took command of the two battalions and proceeded with the reorganization under Duke's watchful eye. On September 15, 1864, in the middle of this intensive training, Duke was promoted to brigadier general. The *Richmond*

(Va.) *Dispatch* reported his promotion the previous day, commenting: "Colonel Basil W. Duke known throughout the Confederacy as an officer of rare merit and gallantry has been placed in command of the late General Morgan's cavalry."[7]

After Duke was promoted to brigadier general, the brigade was officially known as Duke's cavalry. Visibly strengthened by Duke's discipline, the brigade had grown from 273 effective personnel at the time of Morgan's death to 578 officers and men by the end of September. Recapturing some of its old élan, Duke's cavalry was now prepared to take the field.[8]

In late September 1864, Duke left Jonesboro and, along with Vaughn's brigade, skirmished for several days with the Union cavalry in and around Greeneville. Then, when a small army commanded by General Burbridge began advancing from southeastern Kentucky with the obvious intention of raiding either Saltville or Wytheville, Echols ordered Duke to bring his brigade to Saltville. As the Confederates feared, on October 2, Burbridge struck Saltville. The day before, Duke, knowing that John C. Breckinridge had been appointed the new commander of the Department of Southwestern Virginia, sent him the following dispatch: "General: I received with my commission of brigadier orders to report to you for assignment to the command of this brigade. I am very desirous of reporting to you with the brigade at once and beg that you will order me to do so immediately. I wish to take part in the expedition against Burbridge, and at any rate to join you while my command is yet in a condition to do service."[9]

Duke admired and respected Breckinridge very much and probably personally hand delivered the dispatch to his new commander when he arrived in Abingdon. Abingdon was only twenty miles southwest of Saltville, and, when Duke arrived, he joined both General Echols and General Breckinridge and rode on to Saltville the next day. It was late in the afternoon when they reached Saltville. Burbridge had attacked that morning, and, except for the exchange of some intermittent fire, it appeared that most of the battle was over. Fortunately for the Confederates, Burbridge had not attacked when he arrived the prior evening. The overnight delay gave the Confederates the time they needed to assemble enough troops to score a hard-fought, last-minute victory.[10]

The usual early-morning fog covered the valley and the surrounding mountains when Duke awoke the next morning. Shortly after sunrise, many of the Confederates, including Generals Breckinridge and Duke, began to hear sporadic gunfire coming from the battlefield. Duke's first reaction was to assume that Burbridge had returned and initiated a new attack. The Union army was not, however, the source of the gunfire. Confederate soldiers from General John S. Williams's command as well as the notorious Champ Ferguson were roaming the battlefield murdering African American soldiers who had had the bad luck to have been left behind when Burbridge withdrew. George Dallas Mosgrove, a soldier with the Fourth

John C. Breckinridge had been a vice president of the United States, a major general in the Confederate army, and the last secretary of war of the Confederate States of America. He proved himself to be an able commander during the war in southwestern Virginia during the fall of 1864. (Courtesy the Filson Historical Society, Louisville.)

Kentucky Cavalry who had slept that night on the battlefield, also awoke that morning to the gunfire. Mosgrove was in front of Robertson's and Dibrell's brigades and immediately realized that "the Tennesseans were killing Negroes." As Mosgrove wandered over the battlefield, he came to a small cabin where half a dozen or more African American soldiers were inside huddled against a wall. Suddenly: "A pistol shot from the door caused me to turn and observe a boy, not more than 16 years old with a pistol in each hand. I stepped back telling him to hold on until I could get out of the way. In less time than I can write it, the boy had shot everyone in the room. Every time he pulled a trigger a Negro fell dead. Generally the Negroes met their fate sullenly. It was bang, bang, bang all over the field—Negroes dropping everywhere."[11]

The firing continued until Breckinridge and Duke rode up to the scene. Breckinridge was visibly angered by what he discovered and ordered the firing to stop immediately. The men promptly obeyed, but, as soon as Breckinridge and Duke were out of eyesight, they resumed their killing spree. It was at this time that Mosgrove saw what he described as "a bright looking mulatto boy" who did not seem to feel endangered until a young Confederate pointed a gun at him. The mulatto ran for cover screaming that General Duke had ordered him to remain there until he returned. Not impressed by what he heard, the Confederate shot the mulatto. Mosgrove wrote later that he heard that Duke had recognized the young African American as someone who had at one time belonged to either the Morgan or the Duke family.[12]

Later, Breckinridge wired General Lee with his "own condemnation of the atrocity." Felix Robertson, a brigadier general on loan from the Army of the Tennessee, was implicated as being instrumental in instigating the murders. Although his arrest was ordered, Robertson avoided a court-martial by returning to the Army of the Tennessee, where he served out the war in Wheeler's cavalry. His actions at Saltville, however, prevented the Confederate Senate from confirming any promotions that he had received above the rank of captain. Champ Ferguson was not so fortunate. Although never indicted for his role in the Saltville murders, Ferguson was arrested and tried after the war for other murders in which he was involved and, ultimately, met his death on the gallows during the summer of 1865.[13]

For several months following the Saltville murders, a rumor circulated in the Department of Southwestern Virginia that Burbridge intended to hold Duke's brigade responsible for the deaths of the African American soldiers. Mosgrove claimed that no Kentuckians took part in the atrocity, but B. F. Day of the Tenth Kentucky later recalled: "We did not let up while we could see a Negro." Duke was convinced, and there is no evidence to the contrary, that no one from his command took part in the October 3, 1864, murders. Concerned about his troops' as well as his own reputation, Duke wrote Burbridge, taking exception to any claim to the contrary. Finally, in February 1865, Burbridge responded in a perfunctory but satisfactory manner, writing Duke: "Your information that I propose to hold your command responsible for the murder of the Negro soldiers under my command at Saltville in October 1864, is incorrect." Burbridge's response apparently satisfied Duke, and there were no more innuendos concerning Duke's troops' involvement in the Saltville murders.[14]

The day after the battle, Breckinridge's scouts reported that Burbridge was retreating but was still within striking distance. The scouts accurately described Burbridge's escape route and pointed out to Breckinridge that there was an oppor-

Area of operations for Duke's cavalry, 1864–65.

tunity to intercept him before he left Virginia. Breckinridge ordered Duke, General Williams, and four other brigades of cavalry to pursue Burbridge. Duke was promptly in the saddle, and his brigade was ready to ride. For some reason, there was a delay, and Duke impatiently waited for either Breckinridge or Williams to join him and begin the pursuit. Mosgrove remembered the moment: "I have often thought of the brilliant young general's appearance on that morning. He was the personification of the ideal cavalier, a veritable Prince Rupert or Henry of Navarre. His agile, symmetrical form was in constant, nervous motion. Restlessly turning in the saddle, his dark eyes flashing, he impatiently awaited the ordered to advance. He was an attractive, martial figure."[15]

The Confederates finally started their pursuit and, with Duke in the lead, sighted the rear of Burbridge's retreating column late in the afternoon. The plan was for Williams to cut off Burbridge at Richlands while Giltner struck the Union detachment from behind, completing the trap. Owing to the terrain and the length of Burbridge's head start, Williams was unable to cut in front of him, and, although the Tenth Kentucky Cavalry skirmished briskly with his rear guard, the main body withdrew safely back to Kentucky.[16]

When he took over the command of the Department of Southwestern Virginia, John C. Breckinridge inherited a number of significant problems. With the war going badly for the South, desertions from the Confederate army increased daily. In retrospect, some of these desertions were, in a sense, justified, as many men returned home to protect their families and help them survive the desperate times. There were some deserters, however, who had little or no concern for their families, the cause, or their honor. These men were on the lookout only for themselves and, when they deserted, often joined outlaw bands preying on the weak, both Union and Confederate. One of these outlaw bands, called the Heroes of the New State, was operating in Floyd and Franklin Counties. On October 15, 1864, Breckinridge ordered Duke to take two hundred of his troops and report to General Echols for further instructions. Breckinridge qualified his orders by emphasizing Duke's "high character as an officer," which would characterize "the conduct of his command, in the delicate duties to be performed."[17]

Duke, with Major Webber and Dick Morgan, pursued the outlaws and captured the "lieutenant governor" of the "New State" and approximately two hundred of his men with little or no bloodshed. In concert with this action, Duke had sent Captain Cantrill with forty men to Grayson County to rid the area of outlaws. Attempting to evade Cantrill, the Grayson County outlaws headed for North Carolina. Cantrill in hot pursuit caught up with the deserters, and a short but bloody fight ensued. Cantrill's detachment killed twenty to twenty-five of the renegades before the remainder escaped and hid in the hills of western North Carolina. For the remainder of the war, the band posed no significant threat to the civilian population. "Duke has done most effective service," reported General Echols, "having arrested a large number [of] deserters and disloyal men, shot some, and driven them so effectually that many are coming in."[18]

For the next week to ten days, the brigade performed routine patrols, often skirmishing with local federal units. Finally, at the beginning of November 1864, Duke received orders from Breckinridge to report to Carter's Station. The Confederate line in east Tennessee was being probed by federal troops led by General Gillem out of Knoxville. Breckinridge decided that the best way to solidify and defend his position was to take the initiative away from Gillem. On November 10, Breckinridge moved his small army to the vicinity of Greeneville, approximately eighteen miles southeast of Gillem's force at Bulls Gap. The next day, Duke engaged the federal rear guard of approximately twelve hundred men at Lick Creek, driving it back to Bulls Gap.[19]

Twice later that afternoon and evening, the Union troops came out of Bulls Gap and attacked Duke's troops, only to be repulsed as the Kentuckian stood fast at his position. After dark, Duke finally requested permission to fall back and build some fires so that his men could keep themselves warm that night. In the morning,

Breckinridge arrived and spent most of the day assessing Gillem's position. That evening, he advised his brigade commanders of his decision to attack. Duke thought the plan that Breckinridge proposed "audacious almost to rashness." Gillem was well entrenched and outnumbered Breckinridge, whose small army lacked sufficient infantry to storm the federal position. These obstacles did not deter Breckinridge, who had planned a multidirectional attack. A demonstration, or diversion, of three hundred Confederates was to take place in front of the federal position, while Vaughn with about one thousand cavalry would flank the Union force and strike from the rear. At the same time as the diversion in the center, another was to take place on Gillem's left, while Breckinridge led Duke's and Cosby's brigades in what he hoped would be a surprise attack on the right. The attack was scheduled to begin early the next morning.[20]

For his troops to be in position in time for the early morning attack, Breckinridge was forced to send Duke's and Cosby's brigades out several hours before dawn on the morning of November 12, 1864. It was a difficult march in the dark as it involved traversing a steep ridge and riding over rocky terrain. Breckinridge had placed his troops so that his battle line was perpendicular to that of the Union entrenchment. He also discovered that the Union troops had constructed an earth fort in support of their line. Not deterred by the strength of the Union position, Breckinridge personally led the attack, assigning to Duke the assault on the left of the Confederate line. Duke advanced rapidly but ran into a sheet of fire when he was within thirty yards of the earthworks and could advance no farther. On the right, Colonel Ward initially "succeeded in carrying a line of earthworks" but could not hold his gain. After suffering significant casualties, Breckinridge ordered a retreat. Most of the Confederate troops involved in the attack were cavalry, but Breckinridge employed them as if they were infantry, with predictable results.[21]

The next day, the infantry troops that Breckinridge so badly needed to press his attack arrived from North Carolina. That afternoon, scouts reported to Breckinridge that Gillem had left Taylor's Gap, two miles below Bulls Gap, unguarded. This discovery altered Breckinridge's plans. He now decided to lead Duke's and Vaughn's brigades through Taylor's Gap and attack the rear of the Union position. In the meantime, provisions and, more important, ammunition were running dangerously low for the Bulls Gap defenders, forcing Gillem to send a dispatch for the needed supplies. Then, in the late afternoon hours, after learning of the arrival of the Confederate infantry, Gillem decided that it was in his best interests to evacuate Bulls Gap that night.[22]

That night, the moon was bright and the sky clear, providing Gillem with the optimum conditions for his withdrawal. Still hoping to receive his needed supplies that evening, Gillem delayed his evacuation for several hours. Finally, an hour after receiving a dispatch that the supply train was not coming, his troops began their withdrawal. Two companies of the Ninth Tennessee (federal) were in the lead, followed by a train of wagons, the balance of the Ninth Tennessee, the artillery, and two battalions of the Eighth Tennessee Cavalry. Gillem ordered the Thirteenth Tennessee Cavalry and the remaining battalion of the Eighth Tennessee to remain in their positions to give the impression that Taylor's Gap was still defended and operate as a rear guard. The withdrawal began at eight that evening.[23]

Breckinridge and Duke passed undetected through Taylor's Gap. The scouts discovered that Gillem was in the process of withdrawing and that his column was stretched out on the road, its flank completely exposed and inviting attack. When Breckinridge received this report, he recognized his advantage and ordered the rest of his troops, including the infantry and artillery, to come up through Taylor's Gap. The Union scouts, by this time, had discovered that the Confederates were in force on the Arnett Road, an artery that ran parallel to the road Gillem was using for his withdrawal. Gillem was confident that the Confederates were unaware that his troops were in the process of withdrawing and ordered his wagons and artillery to leave the road and to travel four miles farther west to cross the Holston River at Cobbs Ford. He also sent back orders to the rear guard at Bulls Gap to withdraw and follow the road taken by the wagons and artillery. This disposition of troops would place Gillem and his cavalry between the wagon train and the Confederates. Thus, no longer encumbered with the wagons and the artillery, he proceeded with the rest of his force to Russellville, where he planned to engage the Confederates.[24]

Just as Gillem was completing the disposition of his troops, he received a dispatch that the supply wagons along with six hundred men were approaching. With these reinforcements, Gillem concluded, he could now make a successful stand against the Confederates. He ordered the reinforcements to Russellville, where they were to form their battle line at the intersection of the Knoxville-Greeneville roads and, if attacked, defend the position until he arrived. Gillem then ordered the Ninth and Eighth Tennessee to the front of the wagons and then on to Russellville. Duke had received orders to move ahead to the other side of Russellville and cut off Gillem's retreat, while Vaughn was to strike the strung-out Union column on the road. In the event Duke could not get around Russellville in time, he was to "take the enemy in the flank." The Confederate cavalry attacked Gillem's column shortly after midnight on November 14, just before it reached Russellville. The Union troops initially responded well to the attack, but, as more Confederate units arrived, they began to fall back in some disorder, causing the predictable confusion within their lines. Most of Gillem's column retreated so rapidly that they were on the other side of Russellville before Duke arrived, leaving him no choice but to attack the rear guard.[25]

Gillem and his staff tried to rally the disorganized troops, but they were able to get only "a fraction" of the men in line. The Ninth Tennessee (federal) fought well in the hotly contested action, holding Duke and Vaughn in check for nearly an hour. The reinforcements that Gillem expected turned out to be only 302 men, all either infantry or dismounted cavalry. The commander of these troops argued with Gillem concerning their disposition but eventually relented and formed his men on the crest of a hill on the Knoxville Road. A few minutes later, the rear guard withdrew and, with an assortment of other troops, joined this makeshift line. At that moment, the Confederates came into view and formed into two lines as they prepared to attack. The federal troops fired one volley when the Confederates attacked and then broke and ran. Gillem's last line of defense was completely overrun, and his troops fell back "panic stricken." The Confederates, sensing victory, pursued hot on their heels. What ensued was a running battle that lasted for twenty-five miles and ended only when Gillem crossed the Holston River and re-formed at Strawberry Plains just east of Knoxville. In his postbattle report, he admitted losing six pieces of artillery, 61 wagons, 71 ambulances, 300 horses, and about 150 men.[26]

When Breckinridge reached the east bank of the Holston River, his scouts reported that Gillem was well entrenched at Strawberry Plains, with artillery and infantry reinforcements arriving from nearby Knoxville. The flanks of the Union position were well protected, and a frontal assault was out of the question. Breckinridge remained opposite Gillem for several days, exchanging artillery fire, skirmishing, and even crossing the Holston River, at one point, to make a strong demonstration toward the federal rear. However, with his primary objective accomplished, Breckinridge decided to withdraw, leaving Vaughn's brigade to monitor the situation.[27]

While Duke was at the Holston River, a woman brought her wounded young daughter, who was probably not more than three years old, to Breckinridge's headquarters for medical attention. The little girl had received a gunshot wound from a Spencer rifle, a weapon issued to some Union cavalry regiments. She and her mother were immediately taken to Breckinridge's medical officer for attention. Duke, who was with Breckinridge when the woman arrived at headquarters, offered his services to the doctor. The doctor most likely asked both Duke and Breckinridge to help hold the girl still on a table while he operated. During the operation, Duke became unnerved at the sight of a little girl struggling with her pain. He became noticeably ill and sick to his stomach. His only recourse was to get some fresh air. He ran out of the house before he embarrassed himself any further. In a few moments, a nauseated Breckinridge followed Duke outside. The two men, who had seen and taken part in so much mayhem, looked at each other and laughed at their own sensitivities. Unfortunately, the outcome of the child's operation is lost to history.[28]

Vaughn was ordered to remain in position on the Holston, while Duke and his brigade, along with the rest of the army, withdrew to Russellville. In Knoxville in the meantime, General George Stoneman, intent on regaining the initiative from

The capture of Colonel Dick Morgan and eighty-five other men of Duke's command on the Clinch River in December 1864 initiated a winter campaign in southwestern Virginia, which culminated in the Union raid on Saltville. (Courtesy the University of Kentucky.)

Breckinridge, planned and ordered a two-pronged attack consisting of approximately four thousand troops under Burbridge striking from the north through southeastern Kentucky and another two thousand troops, which he would personally command, advancing from Knoxville. It was not until December 1, 1864, when Burbridge began advancing south from Kentucky, that Breckinridge became aware of the new offensive. After the reports of Burbridge's advance were confirmed, Duke was ordered to Rogersville, while Vaughn withdrew from the Holston and fell back to Greeneville. The two brigades were within twenty miles of each other and, prudently, established a line of couriers enabling them to react and support each other on a timely basis if attacked. Feeling satisfied with the position of his brigade, Duke placed his brother-in-law Dick Morgan in command and then went on to Abingdon.[29]

On December 12, 1864, Breckinridge learned that Gillem was advancing from Knoxville toward Kingsport, Tennessee, with fifteen hundred men. The next day, Gillem bumped into Duke's brigade, still under the command of Dick Morgan, at Rogersville. Morgan withdrew, skirmishing with Gillem for twenty-five miles until he reached Kingsport. He then crossed the Clinch River and tried to position the brigade to contest Gillem's crossing of the river. He was overextended, however, and could not guard all the fords. Gillem easily slipped across the river and engaged Morgan, whom he soundly defeated. Morgan along with eighty others was captured, as were all the brigade's wagons. The following day, Stoneman filed an exaggerated report claiming that he had killed or captured "most of the brigade" and that "all consider the command completely destroyed." Such claims were a bit premature, for Colonel Napier had extracted "most of the brigade" and met Duke in Bristol. With Stoneman in hot pursuit, Duke continuously skirmished with the Union cavalry as he withdrew farther east to Abingdon, Virginia. Being greatly outnumbered, he declined to make a stand at Abingdon and abandoned his position, leaving only a small picket force that Stoneman easily brushed aside. Duke then joined Breckinridge at Saltville on December 15, 1864, with what was left of his brigade. The addition of Duke's men increased Breckinridge's effective strength to only fifteen hundred men. Outnumbered four to one by the combined armies of Stoneman and Burbridge, Breckinridge was hard-pressed to formulate a viable defensive plan.[30]

Vaughn, in the meantime, had withdrawn from Greeneville and, with Gillem in close attendance, entered the town of Wytheville on December 16. Fewer than twenty men, commanded by J. Stoddard Johnston, were available for Wytheville's defense. When Vaughn evacuated the town, Johnston did his best to delay Gillem by negotiating for over an hour for the surrender of the town. During the negotiations, Johnston was able to remove a large quantity of supplies. Gillem eventually tired of Johnston's polemics and entered the town, destroying anything of value to the Confederates.[31]

Stoneman was momentarily content to leave Breckinridge behind his defenses in Saltville while his own troops wreaked havoc on the railroad around Marion. Breckinridge, however, was not satisfied to sit on his hands in Saltville while the Union troops had their way. When he received assurances from local authorities that the enemy could not shut down the works for an extended period of time, he took to the field against Stoneman's rear. Duke left Saltville with a 150-man scouting force to determine whether the information that Breckinridge was receiving concerning federal troop movements was accurate. Riding toward Wytheville, he discovered a large federal force much closer to Saltville than anyone anticipated. After he drove in its pickets and ascertained that this was the main body of federal troops, he fell back a mile and settled in for the night to observe its movements.[32]

A stroll during the night almost earned Duke another stay in a federal prisoner-of-war camp. Walking alone to the rear of his position, Duke came on a large group of soldiers who he thought were Giltner's men. Almost immediately, he discovered that they were Union cavalry armed with Spencer rifles, all of which were pointed in his direction. Challenged to surrender, Duke, clothed in Bishop Wood's dark blue overcoat, cleverly excused himself from their presence by claiming to be from a federal Kentucky unit. Daylight revealed to Duke that a detachment of Union cavalry, perhaps as many as twelve hundred men, had placed itself between him and Saltville. He was now sandwiched in between two significant federal forces, either of which could have easily destroyed his command. His only choice was to withdraw as quietly as possible. However, when he called in his pickets, the Yankees misinterpreted this movement as the arrival of reinforcements and withdrew. Duke returned to Saltville and briefed Breckinridge on what he had learned on his patrol. After listening to Duke's report, Breckinridge decided to move on Marion that night.[33]

On December 17, 1864, taking with him no more than one thousand men, having left four hundred to defend Saltville, Breckinridge advanced on Marion, where he collided with two of Burbridge's brigades at a covered bridge on the Holston River. The Holston at this location was little more than a large stream. Quickly taking the offensive, Duke easily crossed the river and pressed the Union left until just before dark, when the Union troops in his front disengaged. Securing a position approximately half a mile in length along a ridge that stretched in a southeasterly direction from the creek and at an obtuse angle with the balance of Breckinridge's forces, Duke settled in for the night. At the end of the day, Duke and his troops were the only Confederates positioned on the other side of the Holston. The river was shallow enough, however, so as not to break the continuity of Breckinridge's line. Although the Yankees probed, they did not push hard against Duke's position that night. This was probably a reconnaissance ordered by Stoneman, who had arrived and was trying to sort out Burbridge's mess before he made any plans to attack. Anticipating a concentrated attack on his position the next day, Duke ordered his men to prepare breastworks during the night.[34]

With the coming of dawn, and aided by the height of his position, Duke was able to ascertain that Stoneman's entire force had arrived during the night. William J. Davis, a member of Duke's staff, estimated that 220 men held Duke's half-mile-long line, with 12 men below the ridge holding the horses. These men were deployed roughly six to ten feet apart in a line "thinner than a shoestring." Potentially, Duke faced an attacking force of some 5,500 federal troops. Fortunately for him, it took Stoneman some time to prepare before he attacked. When he did attack, he struck Breckinridge's center and was easily repulsed. For the next several hours, he probed the Confederate line until he finally decided to concentrate on Duke's position. By that time, Duke had received reinforcements of approximately 60 men. The additional men permitted him to close the gaps in his line slightly and repulse several attacks. The continued pressure from the Union attacks nearly exhausted his ammunition. Duke ordered Sam Murrell, a member of his staff, to work his way to the rear where the ammunition train was posted and bring back as many rounds as possible. Murrell was eventually able to distribute ten rounds of rifle and fifteen rounds of pistol cartridges to each man in a timely fashion.[35]

That afternoon, Stoneman concentrated his attack against Duke's position. Two lines of federal infantry, each twelve to fifteen hundred men strong, formed in front of Duke and his men. This attack was far more sustained, and a brigade of African American soldiers led the first line and drove Duke's line out of its breastworks and turned his right flank. The Confederates fell back approximately one hundred yards before the Union troops were repulsed. The second attack was very similar to the first, with Duke's command suffering few casualties primarily because the Union volleys, although heavy, were too high. Duke's men, fighting tenaciously, finally repulsed the attack and, led by Colonel Napier, charged downhill after the retreating Union soldiers and pushed them into another line forming to attack. The counterattack by Duke's men stunned the federal soldiers, and many broke and ran. On returning to their position, Duke's men were greeted by yells from Giltner's men, who witnessed the attack and counterattack. They called Duke's troops the "Bulldogs," a nickname that stayed with the brigade for the rest of the war. Later that day, when Duke finally abandoned his position, there were 187 dead Union soldiers in his immediate front.[36]

Late in the afternoon, Duke decided to follow up on the momentum generated by his counterattack and made a tactical move around Stoneman's left flank. This move was moderately successful and caused Stoneman to go on the defensive for the remainder of the day. By nightfall, Duke's men, along with the rest of the Confederates, were almost out of ammunition and completely exhausted. Breckinridge had also received reports that a large federal force had passed around his right and camped to his rear. Knowing that, for the last two days, his men had fought and bested a significantly larger force, Breckinridge was forced to leave the field to Stoneman. Although Breckinridge withdrew from the field of battle, he adroitly maneuvered his force to Stoneman's rear and was once again prepared to pounce on his enemy. Stoneman, however, was so completely fooled by the maneuver that he was convinced that the Confederates had retreated into North Carolina, thus freeing him to attack Saltville, and inadvertently checking Breckinridge's skillful maneuver.[37]

When Breckinridge discovered that Stoneman had moved and was now deploying his force in the direction of Saltville, he ordered Duke to gather from among all the brigades a contingent of the least-exhausted men he could find to reinforce the town's garrison. Duke was able to gather a force of three hundred and pressed hard toward Saltville, stopping only for a few hours of rest. It was a bitterly cold day as Duke sent a detail forward to confirm what everybody believed, that Saltville had fallen to the Yankees. William Davis was so cold that, when the detail halted before Saltville, he was unable to dismount. Fortunately, Colonel Diamond of the

Tenth Kentucky held to Davis's "willing lips a canteen of pine top hot from the still of a moonshiner, he urged as a recommendation." Davis remembered that the stuff was so ineffably vile that "the very recollection of its flavor nauseates me, but the draught thawed my half frozen limbs and as Diamond would always have it, saved my life from being shot." Duke confirmed that Saltville had fallen and waited patiently for the Union force to leave.[38]

The cold intensified as Duke closely followed Stoneman north from Saltville. At Hayter's Gap, the federal force split, with Stoneman returning to Knoxville and Burbridge and his men continuing north through the mountains. Duke followed Burbridge and his troops toward Kentucky. If possible, the weather seemed to get colder, and both man and horse suffered. Soon, however, the Confederates began to see evidence that the weather was having a greater and more severe impact on the retreating federal army. Dead horses frozen in every imaginable position littered the road ahead of Duke and his men. There were so many dead horses that William Davis remembered they actually impeded the pursuit. At one particular point, Davis counted two hundred dead horses in a one-mile stretch of the road. The road was verily littered with cartridge boxes, saddles, broken wagons, and even artillery pieces, all indicating the pathos of a retreating army.[39]

What might have been considered, under normal circumstances, as skirmishing with Burbridge's rear guard Davis more accurately described as nothing more than running into groups of Union stragglers unable to keep up with the main army. These troops surrendered without any resistance. It was impossible for Duke to take these men with him as he pursued Burbridge. Those of his own men who were too exhausted to continue were ordered to find shelter in local houses with their Union prisoners. In some of these houses or along the roadside, the Confederates discovered half-frozen Union soldiers who were suffering the final moments of a horrible death.[40]

Approximately fifty-two miles from Saltville, at Wheeler's Ford, Duke halted. He counted only fifty of his original three hundred men fit to go any farther. Reluctantly, he gave up the pursuit and returned to Saltville. He had, however, been able to capture more than one hundred Union troops, the majority of which were stragglers. Stoneman's raid had caused significant damage at both Wytheville and Saltville. The lead mines at Wytheville were inoperable for three months, and, although the saltworks at Saltville did not take nearly as long to return to operation, a significant amount of mined salt and equipment was destroyed. Burbridge had also taken the African American slaves who had worked the mines with him when he retreated.[41]

For three months, Duke had been engaged in primarily defensive actions against an aggressive and numerically superior foe. This type of warfare was far different from the freewheeling raids of 1862–63 and demanded a determination and fervor that evaded many Southern soldiers. Duke was both committed and tenacious, and, although he knew the game was about up, he delivered more than a creditable performance that fall. With his troops and horses nearly exhausted and winter having set in, he wrote Breckinridge on the last day of the year that his "men want to be paid, guns, saddles, cartridge boxes" were all needed. However, he was also pragmatic and, understanding the constraints under which Breckinridge was working, told his commander that he "was prepared to wait with patience until your quartermaster and ordinance officer can furnish the articles requested." He also asked Breckinridge to move his brigade from Wytheville to Abingdon for the winter. Duke spent the next three months with his wife and children at Abingdon, a pleasant novelty for all concerned.[42]

The fall fighting in southwestern Virginia had stripped the land clean of grain and fodder. The rail system had been disrupted throughout the South and in some locations had been completely destroyed, making it nearly impossible for Duke and his troops to rely on receiving supplies from other parts of the Confederacy. Unable to feed his horses in Virginia, Duke reluctantly ordered his brigade dismounted and sent the horses with Colonel L. Napier to North Carolina to be fed and given a chance to recuperate during the winter months. Duke's troops were upset when they learned that they were to be separated from their horses. The men were concerned that they might never see their "best friends" again, thus becoming an infantry unit by necessity. It took some skillful arguing on Duke's part before his men acquiesced.[43]

During those long winter months, Duke's inactive troops, although subjected to the predictable winter-camp problems, maintained a higher level of morale than most soldiers. However, Duke did have problems, including some desertions, which were attributable to the brigade's close proximity to Kentucky. Recognizing this problem, on February 20, 1865, Duke told an army inspector: "The interests of the service would be enhanced by removing these troops from this department." The inspector concurred with Duke's opinion and advised Richmond: "Their propinquity to their homes, the nature of the country in which they operate, together with the loose and irregular manner in which they have, until recently, been managed, renders it exceedingly difficult if not impossible, to keep them together in camp, recruiting their ranks in Kentucky being usually the pretext for wandering over into that state." It was too late in the war for Richmond to resolve such issues.[44]

William Davis wrote his girlfriend on February 22, 1865: "We have been comparatively quiet since Stoneman's last raid in the department and are quite comfortable in our winter quarters." W. W. Ward confided to his diary that his quarters were also comfortable since he remained indoors throughout most of the very cold winter with "little to do and doing little." A report filed by the army medical inspector two weeks later stated that, except for a few cases of diarrhea, the health of the command was very good. What the medical report and Davis's letter failed to say was that, although the troops were warm and healthy, they were half starved for lack of provisions.[45]

Giltner's brigade, in winter camp to the west of Duke, had less of a problem as far as securing forage for his horses. Giltner wrote Duke on January 31, 1865, that he had split his brigade into smaller components and posted them at different locations, each of which had an abundance of forage, enough, in fact, to last until the first of March or later. He also reported that he had had little contact with the enemy and was more concerned about the large number of deserters in his area who had taken the oath and were operating as bushwhackers.[46]

Interestingly, the winter hiatus and Duke's horseless cavalry did not dissuade the Union command in Kentucky from being intimidated by the Abingdon Confederates. Duke's reputation as a raider had followed him, and, as late as February 2, 1865, E. H. Hobson in Lexington was writing his superiors that he was convinced that Duke was concentrating with considerable force at Abingdon for the sole purpose of invading "Kentucky at an early period."[47]

Hobson failed to realize that, unlike Morgan, Duke operated in conjunction with, and not independent of, his department commander. Even with healthy horses, it is highly unlikely that Duke would have given serious consideration to an independent raid. He was more concerned with maintaining control of his troops, a concern that had always been his trademark, and the winter months of 1865 were no exception. But not all Duke's problems were caused by Yankee cavalry. For example, without his knowledge, several of his men had received furloughs through the headquarters of the Department of Southwestern Virginia. Obviously, his primary objective was keeping his command together, and having accurate knowledge as to his men's whereabouts was absolutely essential. Duke reacted to the departmental furloughs with a sharp letter to Stoddard Johnston: "When you will after this time furlough men of this Brigade—as you frequently do without my knowledge and consent, please send me copies of such furloughs and orders, so that I may know what has become of men [for] whom I am responsible and will be able to give a satisfactory explanation of the disorganized and demoralized state into which such practice throws my command."[48]

The lull in activity also permitted Duke time to focus on an exchange for Dick Morgan, who had been captured at Kingsport, and Charlton Morgan, who was still a prisoner from the Ohio Raid. On January 8, 1865, Duke wrote his mother-in-law discussing Dick's recent capture and his efforts to arrange a special exchange, which he felt confident he could accomplish. He also touched on Charlton's situation, advising Mrs. Morgan that General Vaughn was arranging an exchange for Charlton but that he, Duke, had not received a recent update on the matter. Several weeks later, Duke wrote a censorious letter to Charlton, chastising him for complaining about the lack of letters from his friends, and reminding him of the efforts of the many people working to effect his exchange.[49]

The last official inspection report filed on Duke's brigade, dated February 28, 1865, shows that the command consisted of four battalions of cavalry. Then, in March, after moving to Lynchburg, Duke received reinforcements consisting of three hundred released prisoners from the Ohio Raid. This brought his effective strength to just over six hundred men. His troops were, however, still dismounted and, therefore, began to do duty as infantry, which not only disgusted the cavalrymen but also severely challenged their tempers.[50]

13

We Looked at Each Other in Amazement

The beginning of April 1865 found Duke and his troops once again under the command of General John Echols, who, on March 30, 1865, had replaced Jubal Early as the commander of the Department of Southwestern Virginia, Early having replaced Breckinridge, who in January had been summoned to Richmond to be offered the office of secretary of war. With the rapidly deteriorating military situation, Echols found himself in an unenviable position. Sherman had been pushing north from South Carolina, intending to destroy Joseph Johnston's army and the railroads that the Confederates could use during their retreat. Consequently, he ordered Stoneman's cavalry to set out from Knoxville and destroy the railroad between Charlotte and Columbia. By the time Stoneman's cavalry entered North Carolina, Sherman's troops had moved east of Charlotte, making the cavalryman's orders moot. Grant then ordered Stoneman to destroy the Virginia and Tennessee Railroad in southwestern Virginia. With the majority of Echols's army marching toward Lynchburg, the only resistance the Confederates could offer Stoneman was Giltner's brigade, which enjoyed a minor success against elements of Stoneman's cavalry near Wytheville.[1]

The small army that Echols commanded consisted of Duke's, Vaughn's, Cosby's, and Giltner's cavalry brigades and some five thousand infantry. As Giltner withdrew from Wytheville, Lee and what was left of the Army of Northern Virginia were retreating west from Richmond. On April 2, 1865, Echols issued orders for his army to evacuate southwestern Virginia. His plan was to march toward Lynchburg and try to join up with Lee. By April 10, Echols had concentrated near Christianburg, where he decided to wait until he received news of Lee's movements. He was still confident that he could unite with Lee, perhaps somewhere near Danville, and that the two armies could then turn south and merge with Joe Johnston's army in North Carolina. That evening, while Echols, Duke, and several other officers discussed these plans, a rider approached with a dispatch from General Lomax. Echols's face turned pale when he read the dispatch, and Duke realized that it contained bad news. Folding the dispatch in his hands, Echols asked

Duke to step aside with him for a moment. Leaving the other officers behind, Duke walked with Echols. When they were alone, Echols read the dispatch to him, revealing the news that Lee and his Army of Northern Virginia had surrendered the day before. Lomax, along with remnants of Fitzhugh Lee's and Rosser's cavalry divisions, was trying to make a juncture with Echols. Echols and Duke were both stunned by this news and agreed that only the brigade commanders should be told about the disaster. They felt that it was in the army's best interest to keep this news from the troops until they had formulated a viable plan or at least were aware of the policy that Jefferson Davis intended to pursue. However, no sooner had Duke and Echols ended their conversation than they both noticed that the camp was buzzing with excitement. The news was already spreading throughout the camp. The men's reaction was predictable. There could not have been greater surprise and consternation had the sun fallen out of the sky.[2]

That night, rumors ran rampant as both officers and enlisted men sat around and discussed their options. Duke remembered that each group built a great fire and every man had an opportunity to present his opinion. The suggestions ranged from fighting a guerrilla war to going to the Trans-Mississippi and on to Mexico. Most of the men, however, realized that there were only two real options: surrender or march toward Johnston's army in North Carolina. Echols knew that he had to talk to his troops and give them some direction. The next morning, he called a meeting of his brigade commanders. By this time, many of the men had slowly and reluctantly acquiesced to the inevitable conclusion that the war was lost. Duke, however, still refused to entertain the possibility of surrender and felt that it was his duty to continue to fight as long as Johnston's army was still in the field.[3]

After learning from their officers that the infantry troops had decided against marching to join Johnston's army, Echols recommended that they be furloughed for sixty days with the understanding that, if the Confederate government was still in existence at the end of their furlough, they would rejoin the ranks of the Confederate army. The artillery was to be disbanded, and each artilleryman was to be given the option of joining the infantry or the cavalry. That left only the four brigades of cavalry to attempt the juncture with Johnston's army. Cosby and Giltner felt that to continue to fight was a mistake and not in the best interests of their men. They intended to take their brigades back to Kentucky and surrender as soon as was practical. Vaughn and Duke were adamantly opposed to the idea of surrendering. Duke reiterated his feeling that they had a duty as officers to continue to fight as long as the Confederate government had a viable army in the field. After listening to both arguments, Echols told the brigade commanders that he planned to issue a written order instructing them to be mounted at four o'clock that afternoon and ride with him to join General Johnston in North Carolina.[4]

When the meeting was concluded, Duke met with his brigade to inform them of General Echols's proposed order. Duke had always been popular with his men, and they respected not only his military prowess but also his judgment. Their response was as he anticipated, with no more than ten men declining to follow him to North Carolina. There being no apparent issue with morale, Duke's major concern was how to solve the more practical problem of mounting his troops. To help resolve this problem and reward the resolute Kentuckians who were soon to distance themselves even farther from home, Echols ordered the artillery horses and wagon mules released to Duke. This enabled Duke to mount all his Abingdon veterans as well as some of the recently paroled men from the old command. The latter he was able to arm with the rifles from the furloughed infantry. Unfortunately, he was unable to mount all Morgan's old men, most of whom he reluctantly left behind. Some of these men tried to follow on foot later that afternoon.[5]

Giltner and Cosby had also talked to their troops, but their assessment of the situation was a more pragmatic one. With tears in his eyes, Giltner told his Fourth Kentucky Cavalry that, with Lee and his army no longer in the field, to continue the fight was only to delay the inevitable, that the best they could do for themselves was to ride to Kentucky and surrender, that he himself was going to Kentucky, and that it was up to each of them to decide for themselves whether to follow him or to fight. There was no coercion on Giltner's part, and his men respected and appreciated his candor. Most decided to follow him to Kentucky. There were, however, some who did not want to surrender the next day, and they decided to join Duke's brigade.[6]

At four o'clock that afternoon in a driving rain, Duke's and Vaughn's brigades reported to General Echols. Vaughn's men cheered Duke and his brigade as they rode past and formed in ranks for the march south. With the rain still pouring down, Echols rode to the head of the column and began the march to North Carolina. Duke's men must have made quite a spectacle. Freshly mounted, with no saddles and few bridals, they struggled with the newly acquired and very obstinate distant cousins of their usual mounts. The next day, approximately ninety men from Giltner's brigade caught up with the column and joined Duke. Although Duke was, apparently, angered that Giltner and Cosby had decided to surrender, his only published comment concerning the situation was that the men who had refused to go back to Kentucky and had joined his brigade believed as he did that no soldiers "had the right to quit the service in which they had enlisted, and so long as the Confederate government survived it had a claim upon them that they could not refuse."[7]

To the east of Echols were Jefferson Davis and his cabinet. They had evacuated Richmond at the beginning of April to reestablish the government in Danville, Virginia, a small town on the North Carolina border. The Confederate government remained in Danville until April 10, 1865, when it received the news of Lee's surrender. This prompted Davis to move farther south to Greensboro, North Carolina, to be nearer Johnston and his army. Davis and his cabinet arrived in Greensboro on the afternoon of April 11 to the "cold unconcern" of the city. Just two days later, his staff and cabinet recommended that Davis move the government to Charlotte, North Carolina.[8]

Shortly after starting south, Echols began to receive reports that federal cavalry could be patrolling the passes and gaps leading through the mountains into North Carolina. Although unsubstantiated, these reports worried Echols, who knew that it would be easy for even a relatively small force to effectively block any of the passes. The most obvious pass for the enemy to contest was "Fancy Gap" on the Virginia–North Carolina border, approximately fifty miles northwest of Greensboro. Fancy Gap was a natural passage through the mountains ending in a steep descent onto the North Carolina Piedmont. A very narrow wagon road ran through it, making it very easy to defend. Just before entering the gap, Stoddard Johnston, Echols's chief of staff, gave Duke and Vaughn instructions on how to proceed. Abounding with an imaginative sense of humor, Johnston concluded his instructions with the following verse:

Now, if the Yankees, d——n their eyes
Shall seek to take us by surprise,
And hope to catch us in a nap
As we file through this Fancy Gap;
Wycher will skirmish to the front,
While Duke and Vaughn abide the brunt,
Meanwhile, the old Tycoon and staff
Will mount a hill apart and laugh.[9]

Much to everyone's relief, the column passed into North Carolina without incident. Two more days brought Echols to Statesville in central North Carolina, where he left Duke and Vaughn, hoping to reach Johnston sooner without the burden of the two brigades. Duke and Vaughn also split up, with Vaughn going in the direction of Morgantown and Duke toward Lincolnton, where he expected to find Colonel Napier and the brigade's horses. This was the last official contact that Duke had with Echols during the war. Echols, however, filed a post-Appomattox report with General Lee that mentioned Duke: "The bearing of General Duke's command which with unbroken ranks faced the hardships of a march which was leading them at every step further from home and to a destination full of danger and uncertainty was beyond praise. Even had they been fully equipped their bearing would have been worthy of praise, but when it is remembered that they were mounted on barebacked horses and mules with blind bridles, and nevertheless preserved the same discipline and order as upon a regular march, their conduct reflects great honor upon them."[10]

A report alerted Duke that Stoneman's cavalry was also moving in the direction of Lincolnton. This development complicated Duke's plans, particularly if Stoneman reached Lincolnton before the Confederates and captured Napier and the horses. In a matter of hours, Duke's scouts made contact with elements of Colonel William J. Palmer's first brigade on a road less than three miles distant, running parallel to the one being used by the Confederates. When the troops began to skirmish, it was evident that Stoneman's horsemen were going to maintain the upper hand over Duke's men, whose mobility was hampered by their mules.[11]

When Duke was within three miles of Lincolnton, his skirmishers reported that the town had been captured and that Palmer was coming out in force to engage the Confederates. Realizing that he was outnumbered and that his men would be at a serious disadvantage if they engaged the enemy while mounted on mules, Duke decided to avoid a fight. Believing that a countermarch might have an adverse impact on his men's morale, Duke decided that his only alternative was to take an obscure side road and hope that it connected with the Charlotte Road on the other side of Lincolnton. Prior experience had taught him that the federal cavalry seldom ventured off the main roads without a reliable local guide. The brigade followed the path for fifteen miles, using local guides when possible, and later that night found the Charlotte Road on the other side of Lincolnton.[12]

Colonel Napier and the horses were long gone when Stoneman's cavalry entered Lincolnton. Although outmaneuvered by Duke, Stoneman had no intention of ending his pursuit and continued the chase. Winning the race to the Catawba River, Duke's rear guard destroyed the bottom of the bridge, making it virtually impossible for Stoneman to continue the pursuit in a timely manner. Duke moved on to Charlotte, where he found two more cavalry brigades and hundreds of paroled infantrymen waiting to receive direction from someone. The next day, Davis and his cabinet arrived in Charlotte, escorted by George Dibrell's and Willie Breckinridge's cavalries.[13]

Before Davis left Greensboro on April 13, 1865, he had reluctantly agreed that Joseph Johnston would begin surrender negotiations with Sherman. Two days later, Davis and his cabinet left Greensboro and continued traveling south. For two days, Johnston, with the help of John C. Breckinridge, negotiated the surrender of Johnston's army. Finally, on April 18, 1865, the day Duke arrived in Charlotte, an agreement was reached the terms of which were favorable to the Confederates. The agreement was signed and sent on to Washington for review and approval. Breckinridge left Johnston and boarded a train for Charlotte, bringing with him a copy of the agreement to be presented to Davis and the cabinet for their approval. The only Confederate army to remain in the field was Kirby Smith's in the Trans-Mississippi.[14]

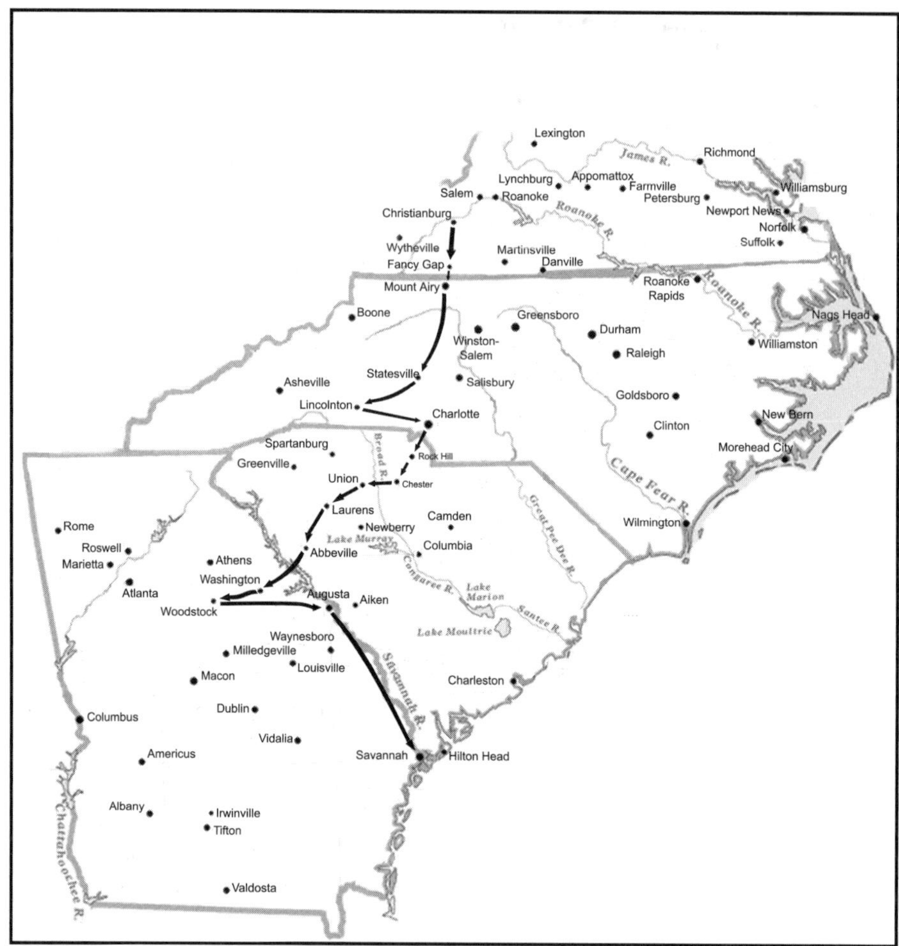

Duke's route through the Carolinas and Georgia, April–May 1865.

Lewis Bates, a local resident, offered Jefferson Davis the use of his home when he arrived in Charlotte. While Davis was making himself comfortable, a large crowd, which included Duke and many of his men, gathered outside Bates's house, waving their regimental banners and calling for a speech. Duke, who was growing restless, was anxious to know the president's thoughts. Davis did eventually emerge and speak, but he disappointed Duke by making no substantive comments, confining himself to thanking the men for their continued loyalty. He did, however, pass on some unexpected news. Having been handed as he was speaking a message informing him that Abraham Lincoln had been assassinated, he read the message to the assembled crowd, giving no indication of his reaction to it other than to note that he doubted its accuracy. While Davis continued to attend to his administrative responsibilities—for example, attempting to procure saddles for Duke's mule cavalry—he spent the next several days, until Breckinridge arrived with the proposed surrender terms, mainly biding his time.[15]

The railroads in North Carolina were in deplorable condition, making the trip from Greensboro extremely difficult and time-consuming. Finally, on April 22, 1865, after two days of traveling, Breckinridge arrived in Charlotte. That night, Davis called a cabinet meeting to review the terms of Johnston's surrender agreement. During the meeting, Davis asked each cabinet secretary to tender his written opinion of the surrender agreement. The next day, each memorandum advised Davis that the terms should be accepted. The cabinet may have been influenced by a telegram that Davis had received from Robert E. Lee urging him not to continue the war. Breckinridge particularly took umbrage at the suggestion that the fighting be continued and lobbied Zebulon Vance, the governor of North Carolina, to support the surrender terms when he discussed the matter with Davis later that day. The secretary of war carried the same message to Duke and his men when he visited their camp that very afternoon. The men in Duke's brigade had plenty of time during the lull in Charlotte to consider the consequences of recent events and were anxious to hear what Breckinridge had to say. After he was done speaking, the secretary sat under a tree and began to talk with the soldiers. After a few minutes, a young soldier, no more than twenty, who had not been present during Breckinridge's speech, rode up on his mule and asked the secretary whether Johnston was about to surrender:

> "It is true," was the response, "and I think the terms are such as all should accept."
>
> "Do you really think, General that any terms of surrender are honorable and should be accepted?"
>
> "I do, or I certainly should not have asserted to them."
>
> "Well I should not be bound by them," the young soldier responded and then drawing himself up more stiffly; with the fire of the tameless spirit flashed from his gray eyes and gleamed in every lineament. At the same time the mule, as if to endorse his master, struck out his fore feet, threw up his head and snorted defiance. Mortal eyes never gazed on a more independent irrepressible looking couple than the mule and his rider.
>
> "I regret that," said General Breckinridge; "and your comrades here, who are all true soldiers, do not agree with you."
>
> "I can't help that," he retorted. "They can do as they please, but the sun shines as bright and the air is as pure on the far side of the Rio Grande as here, and I'll go there rather than give up to the Yankees."[16]

There were some general officers, such as Wade Hampton, who disliked the surrender plan. Hampton, who had seen the proposed surrender terms, had written Davis on April 19, 1865, urging him to continue the war west of the Mississippi. If significant elements of the eastern cavalry could reach Texas, Hampton argued, they could hold that state. And, as soon as these forces were reorganized in Texas, they could start to raid federal territory. Davis, who could not bring himself to accept defeat, found the idea of regrouping in Texas appealing. However, despite the loyalty of Duke's and Breckinridge's brigades, he bowed to pressure from his advisers and, on Monday, April 24, 1865, reluctantly sent Johnston a telegram instructing him to accept Sherman's surrender terms.[17]

Later that day, Davis and his cabinet learned that Washington had rejected Sherman's terms. The only terms that Sherman was now authorized to offer Johnston were those that Grant had given Lee at Appomattox. When Johnston learned of Washington's rejection, he immediately wired Breckinridge, advising him that he had no intention of continuing the fight, and hinting that he was preparing to make a unilateral decision concerning the surrender of his troops. On April 25, Johnston again wired Breckinridge, this time advising him that, in his opinion, the army would no longer fight and that he intended to have another meeting with Sherman to finalize the surrender terms. When Davis realized that Johnston's army was finished, he became adamant about attempting to reach Kirby Smith and Taylor's forces in the Trans-Mississippi and carry on the war. Postmaster General John Reagan later summarized the plan as follows: "It was now our hope to reach General Kirby Smith . . . and with his troops and such others as we could take with us . . . get across the Mississippi . . . and hold out until we could get better terms than unconditional surrender."[18]

The day Johnston's intent to surrender became evident, Hampton and General Joseph Wheeler visited Davis in Charlotte. Wheeler and Hampton asked for permission to pull their cavalry detachments out of Johnston's army before he surrendered. Davis granted the request, and the two generals boarded a train back to Greensboro, where they learned that Johnston had already surrendered. Hampton tried to argue with Johnston that his troops were not part of the surrender, but Johnston made it plain to Hampton that any troops that had remained in camp during the surrender had already been paroled and mustered out of the service. The only troops that Hampton had left to command were his staff and a small escort. He did try to reach Davis but was unable to catch up with him and his entourage. Hampton begrudgingly, but finally, accepted the inevitable.[19]

The last cabinet meeting in Charlotte was held sometime on April 26, 1865, at the William Pfifer house with Braxton Bragg in attendance. The only decision of consequence made was to leave Charlotte as soon as possible. Johnston completed the surrender of his army to Sherman as Davis and his cabinet left Charlotte escorted by some three thousand cavalry, including Duke and his brigade. More than any other event, Johnston's unilateral surrender "altered the status of the man leading the procession." It was a clear indication that Davis no longer had any influence on events and that, but for the loyalty of men such as Breckinridge, Duke, and the others that now followed him into South Carolina, he had no command of the military.[20]

Although Duke remained loyal to Davis, Johnston's surrender had significantly affected him, weakening his resolve to fight. He realized that the soldiers riding with Davis were the only significant Confederate force left in existence and that any hope for successful resistance had passed. Nevertheless, Davis was his commander in chief, and Duke would protect him to the best of his ability. But there appeared to be no sense of urgency or concern on Davis's part as the column slowly moved south. Duke remembered that the pace was no greater than twelve to fifteen miles a day, something inconceivable to a man who during the Ohio Raid had routinely spent twenty hours a day in the saddle. Worried that his own troops were becoming demoralized, and thinking that perhaps Davis and his cabinet no longer had the resolve necessary to effect an escape, Duke became increasingly frustrated. The problem became even more acute when Stoneman's cavalry began to shadow the column fifteen miles to the west. Although the situation was tense, Duke's Kentuckians retained a sense of humor, and, when one old lady in South Carolina chastised them for taking forage, calling them "a gang of thieving, rascally Kentuckians, afraid to go home while our boys are surrendering decently," they responded: "Madame South Carolina had a good deal to say in getting up this war, but we Kentuckians have contracted to close it out."[21]

At Unionville, South Carolina, Duke finally caught up with Colonel Napier and the horses. Napier and his detachment increased Duke's brigade strength to 751 effective troops. The men were understandably ecstatic to receive their horses. Duke mounted as many of his troops as possible on the horses, with the remainder relegated to mule duty. He also requested and received permission to promote several officers, including Major Steele to colonel and William Davis to major. There were many others who Duke felt deserved to be promoted, but he was told that it was not possible to grant so many promotions at one time. Clearly, someone was attempting to retain the decorum of meaningful military administration even as the pall of defeat spread throughout the South.[22]

If the pace of the column annoyed Duke's troops, Davis's and his advisers' congenial attitudes toward them alleviated things somewhat. Davis, Breckinridge, and the rest of the cabinet mixed freely with the enlisted men, allowing them to see their leaders as individuals. And the open discussion that was carried on enabled them to understand what it would take to effect the escape of the Confederate leadership. Most of the escort felt that Davis could escape if he tried, and as a group they were determined to make "extraordinary efforts to prevent him from falling into the hands of the enemy." Breckinridge and Reagan too, they thought, would be able to escape, even if they were forced to do so on their own. But Judah Benjamin, a favorite with the troops, "was sure to be caught," they felt, because of his

It was not until the conference with Duke and the other cavalry brigade commanders at Abbeville, South Carolina, that Jefferson Davis accepted the defeat of the Confederacy. (Courtesy the Filson Historical Society, Louisville.)

weight and seeming lack of wilderness survival skills. Much to everyone's surprise, however, Benjamin did eventually escape on his own, taking an adventurous route through Florida and the Virgin Islands to England.[23]

The column finally reached Abbeville, South Carolina, on May 2, 1865. Breckinridge had become concerned about the men's willingness to fight and, shortly after their arrival, convinced Davis that it was time to call a council of war. It was Duke's impression that, despite their frustration, the troops were willing to fight to protect Davis and the others but that they were unwilling to fight simply to prolong the war. Duke too was convinced that any further fighting was a senseless waste of human lives. He and the other brigade commanders believed that "the best we could hope and do was to get Mr. Davis safely out of the country, and then obtain such terms as had been given General Johnston's army, or failing in that, make the best of our way to the Trans-Mississippi." It must have been emotionally trying for Duke to yield to this inevitable conclusion. He had been a staunch secessionist and truly loved the South and its people, but now, after four years of fighting, he saw no honor in sacrificing his own life or the lives of his troops to help perpetuate a lost cause. It was now his duty to convince Jefferson Davis that he must accept the same conclusion.[24]

That afternoon's council of war was the last held by the Confederate government east of the Mississippi River. Those present for the meeting were Davis, Breckinridge, Bragg, Duke, Ferguson, Vaughn, W. C. P. Breckinridge, and Dibrell. Breckinridge was the only cabinet member present, and, according to Duke, "none of the other members knew what was going on or what to do and therefore there was no reason for them to be there." When the men assembled, Davis appeared to be in a good mood as he joined in the usual small talk that generally preceded such meetings. When the talk died down, Davis opened the meeting: "It is time we adopt some definite plan upon which the further prosecution of our struggle shall be conducted." He then asked each of the brigade commanders to give a report on the condition of the troops and equipment in their commands. Each commander made his report, and, when they had all finished, Davis resumed speaking on the topic of prolonging the war, comparing the Confederacy's present situation with that of the American colonies during the darkest days of the American Revolution: "If the troops now with me be all that I can for the present rely on, three thousand brave men are enough for a nucleus around which the whole people will rally when the panic which now afflicts them has passed away." He then asked each of the commanders to give his opinion on how the war should thereafter be prosecuted.[25]

All in the room were stunned by Davis's comments, and several minutes of embarrassing silence ensued. When the officers were, finally, able to speak, they gave it as their collective opinion that they could neither continue the war nor ask or expect their men to continue to fight. They felt that "an attempt to continue the war, after all means of supporting warfare were gone, would be a cruel injustice to the people of the South." If they continued to fight, they argued, their men would be treated as outlaws, losing any opportunity to return home to their families and friends. W. C. P. Breckinridge added that "the munitions of war were in the hands of the enemy, and there remained no resources; and no people." Davis was clearly taken aback. It took him a few moments to gather his thoughts before he asked why they remained in the field if that was the way they felt. Duke responded that they were there to protect him, that they were concerned what might happen to him if he were captured, and that, disinclined as the men were to fight, they would do so to protect him. Finally, after a few more minutes of embarrassing silence, Davis conceded that "all was indeed lost."[26]

Whether it was due to the emotional strain of accepting the inevitable or just the physical labor of the last month, Davis staggered after he was done speaking. Breckinridge came immediately to his aid, helping him from the room to another part of the house where he could rest. When Breckinridge returned, the conversation was resumed among the officers. During the exchange with Davis, both Breckinridge and Bragg had remained silent, believing that it was best for the president to hear the men's concerns directly from their commanders. The two now spoke, saying that they agreed with what they had heard, and instructing the officers to go back to their commands and poll their men to determine how many were willing to continue. Before dismissing them, Breckinridge revealed his plan to reduce the president's escort to a minimum so that he could move with all possible speed. The balance of the troops would be deployed as diversions, in the hope of giving Davis a better chance at escape. The march was to be resumed that night in the direction of Washington, Georgia.[27]

The council of war at Abbeville stirred up a significant amount of controversy in later years. Davis was working on a history of the Confederate government and had solicited comments from several of the Abbeville participants. Apparently, he no longer recalled the specifics of the meeting, but Duke, Dibrell, and W. C. P. Breckinridge all forwarded to him their recollections of the event. Several years later, Duke wrote an article for the *Southern Bivouac* entitled "After the Fall of Richmond" that was later incorporated into the now-famous *Battles and Leaders of the Civil War* series as "Last Days of the Confederacy" and has since become the accepted account of the Abbeville meeting.[28]

In the years following the Civil War, much has been written about Generals Lee, Johnston, and Kirby Smith's wisdom in laying down their arms and ending the conflict. Arguably, the army could have carried on an effective guerrilla war, hoping to wear down the North's resolve to continue a bloody and protracted contest. However, Lincoln's assassination might have been a sufficient catalyst for the North to find the necessary resolve. Moreover, a guerrilla war would only have intensified the difficulties associated with a postwar reconciliation between the North and the South. Duke and the four other brigade commanders, who were partisans and certainly capable of prosecuting such an action, were, however, also men of integrity and foresight who looked beyond the horizon to recognize the tragedy of such a course of action.

At ten o'clock that evening, Duke received a summons from Breckinridge, prefacing another series of events that created their own share of postwar controversy. When Duke reported, Breckinridge told him that a train containing the Confederate treasure and the funds from several Richmond banks was parked at the Abbeville depot. The secretary trusted Duke and wanted him to take charge of unloading the money from the train and then guard the treasure until it was safe from the roaming Yankee cavalry. The older Kentuckian was able neither to tell Duke the exact amount of money on the train nor to give him the necessary time to count it and establish the extent of his responsibility. This caused Duke some apprehension, and he bluntly told Breckinridge that, without an initial accounting, it would be easy for someone to claim later that some of the money was missing. While he acknowledged Duke's concern, Breckinridge had no other option but to order Duke to proceed to the depot.[29]

Duke handpicked fifty of his most trusted men to guard the treasure and placed them under the command of the recently promoted Colonel Steele and four of his best lieutenants. Six wagons along with fifteen employees from the Treasury Department accompanied Duke and his men to the train. Duke was now concerned that, with so many men roaming around the train, it would be easy for someone to pilfer part of the treasure. To help alleviate his concerns, he posted guards at both doors on each boxcar.[30]

The treasure was stored in every conceivable type of container, from money belts to small iron lockboxes. It took approximately an hour to unload the train, and, when the job was done, Duke himself took a small candle and inspected the dark interiors of each boxcar until he was satisfied that everything had been removed. One of Duke's lieutenants remained behind to examine the boxcars one last time. The wagons had gone only about a half mile when the lieutenant rode up and showed Duke a small strongbox containing approximately $3,000 in gold that he had found covered with a brown sack in a dark corner.[31]

Shortly after Duke collected the treasure, he reported to Breckinridge, and the presidential caravan began its journey to Washington, Georgia. Earlier in the day, about half the men had opted not to continue and had left to surrender to the nearest federal authority. Breckinridge arranged the remaining men in a column and joined Davis at the front. During their ride together, Breckinridge reiterated to Davis the need for him to escape. Later, he dropped back to ride with Duke, never to see Davis again.[32]

During the night, the men became more and more discontent with their situation and began to make covetous comments about the gold in the wagons. Finally, they surrounded the wagon train and told the nervous guards that it would be better for them to take the gold than for it to fall into the hands of the Yankee cavalry. When Breckinridge discovered what had happened, he and Duke rode back to the wagon train and lectured the men, claiming that they were still Confederate soldiers and should comport themselves accordingly. Although controlled to some extent by Breckinridge's presence, the men remained concerned that the money would fall into federal hands. They also demanded their back pay, a point well taken by Breckinridge, who agreed to dispense the money once the wagons crossed the Savannah River. When the men accepted Breckinridge's proposal, he ordered Duke to increase his guard to two hundred men and personally take command. Duke decided to pick men from all the brigades for guard duty in order to avoid charges of favoritism and stirring up jealousies.[33]

The quartermasters devoted most of the day to counting out the money and paying the men. Each man, including Duke, received $26.00 in silver. The total amount that Duke dispersed to the men was $108,322.90, an amount that Duke made sure was accurately reflected on the rolls of each brigade. After all the men had been paid, Breckinridge ordered the wagon train to move on to Washington,

Georgia. Vaughn and Dibrell, along with their respective brigades, had decided not to go any farther unless they were ordered to do so by either Breckinridge or Davis. The other three brigade commanders made it clear to Breckinridge that they would follow him to Mexico if he wished. Bidding farewell to the Tennesseans, Duke prepared for his journey into Georgia.[34]

The remainder of the money was loaded back onto the wagons, and, as dawn broke on May 4, 1865, the column started for Washington. On arrival, Duke parked the wagons and set up camp about a mile outside town. He soon learned that Davis had already left Washington, accompanied by a small escort from the Ninth Kentucky Cavalry under the command of Given Campbell, and was riding deeper into Georgia. Prior to leaving, Davis had appointed Micajah Clark acting treasurer of the Confederate states. When Clark learned of Duke's arrival, he immediately rode out to his camp to take command of the treasure. Much to Duke's relief, Clark audited the remaining funds in his presence. Clark was aware that the treasury had contained $327,022.90 in gold and silver when it left Danville, Virginia. After subtracting the $108,322.90 in silver that Duke had paid out to the troops, Clark satisfactorily accounted for the balance of funds. At Duke's request, Clark endorsed his payments to the cavalry and relieved him of any further responsibility for the treasure. The funds from the Richmond banks were deposited in the local banks. Many years later, there were questions concerning the amount of Confederate funds actually taken from Richmond and dispersed by Duke and Clark. The mild controversy was resolved in a series of articles published by the Southern Historical Society, with Clark's computation being accepted.[35]

The departure of Davis was a signal that few troops were now needed, and most were given their discharge. Duke reflected many years later that Davis "quitted the main body of the troops that they might have an opportunity to surrender before it was too late for surrender upon terms, and that he was resolved that the small escort sent with him should encounter no risk on his behalf." He also never believed "that Mr. Davis really meant or desired to escape after he became convinced that all was lost." He argued that Davis knew that he had to move rapidly to escape and was well mounted for this purpose. Therefore, his hesitation when his whereabouts were well known made his capture by the Union cavalry a foregone conclusion. Whether Duke's assessment is correct will, of course, always be a matter of conjecture. What is certain is that, on May 10, 1865, units of General James Wilson's cavalry captured Jefferson Davis and his escort near Irwinville, Georgia.[36]

Around midday on May 4, Breckinridge toyed with the idea of taking what was left of the three remaining brigades and going west to assist Richard Taylor in negotiating the surrender of his troops. John Reagan did not like the idea and probably convinced Breckinridge that it was time to try to escape himself. A Texan and former ranger, Reagan was well versed in evading pursuers and recommended that Breckinridge head for Florida with a small escort. Breckinridge decided to take this advice, but, before he implemented his escape plan, there was one last duty that he and Duke were to perform for Jefferson Davis.[37]

Early the next day, after Breckinridge discharged most of Ferguson's command, he asked Duke and his cousin Colonel W. C. P. "Willie" Breckinridge if they could hold their commands together for two or three days more, long enough to create a diversion and distract attention from Davis. Of course, both Duke and Breckinridge readily accepted this assignment. General Breckinridge decided that it would be best to head in the direction of Woodstock, Georgia. Realizing that there were two roads leading to Woodstock, he suggested that Duke take one and that he and Willie and about fifty volunteers from Willie's command take the other.[38]

When Duke and Breckinridge parted, the plan was to meet later on in Woodstock. Duke had no difficulty reaching Woodstock, where he camped and waited for Breckinridge. Attempting to draw the Yankee patrols in his direction and away from Davis, Breckinridge moved much more slowly than Duke, and, less than ten miles outside Washington, he ran into a Union cavalry detachment. Colonel Breckinridge began to negotiate with the federal commander, giving the general and several of his staff time to escape. Before departing, however, Breckinridge advised Willie to surrender and get word to Duke to do likewise and forget about "holding out longer." The colonel was given a flag of truce by the union commander and rode to Woodstock to advise Duke of the situation.[39]

As the hours passed without any sign of Breckinridge, Duke became increasingly concerned. That afternoon, he discovered a strong federal force to the west. A Union staff officer rode over to Duke's camp under a flag of truce, requesting permission to talk to the officer in charge. The staff officer told Duke that his commander did not want any unnecessary bloodshed but that, if Duke tried to go to the west, he would be compelled to attack. Duke responded that he would travel in any direction but west. Satisfied, the staff officer returned to his unit, and Duke continued to wait for Breckinridge. Finally, Willie Breckinridge arrived with the general's message instructing Duke and his men to surrender "and to go to Kentucky—to your homes and kindred." With this advice, Duke disbanded his brigade and instructed his men to return to Washington, Georgia, to surrender and accept the parole. He and his staff mounted their horses and rode cross-country to Augusta. For Duke, who had begun his martial odyssey with the Minute Men in early 1861, the war was over.[40]

14

To Perpetuate His Fame

THE WAR AND THE RESULTING vicissitudes for the South affected the remainder of Duke's life. When the war started, Duke was young, only twenty-three years old, with no prior military experience and very little experience with life in general. When it was over, he was a general who commanded respect and admiration from friend and foe alike. During the intervening four years, he had witnessed the destruction of a way of life and a land that he loved and cherished. Duke, more than most men his age, recognized the historical significance of these experiences. Now he had to deal not only with the military aspect of defeat but also with the economic and political consequences. And he would do so in ways that were usually pragmatic and very often unique.

As Duke rode through eastern Georgia, much must have passed through his mind. Of course, he thought of Tommie and the children, but he also wondered of the homecoming that a returning Confederate soldier could expect, particularly one who had repeatedly destroyed military and civilian property in his home state during the war. He certainly had some idea of how tumultuous the political atmosphere was in Kentucky that spring, of how relations between Governor Bramlette and the military government had deteriorated to such an extent that, immediately after the 1864 election, General Burbridge issued an order that several prominent Kentuckians be arrested and banished for what he summarily determined to be traitorous conduct. Lincoln finally replaced Burbridge with Major General John M. Palmer of Illinois. The appointment was initially viewed as a positive move, but, in time, this attitude changed as Kentuckians learned that Palmer's policies were little different from Burbridge's.[1]

From without Kentucky, the heavy hand of the military was recognized as creating dissent and turmoil even within the ranks of the state's loyal elements. The relation between the military and the state government had become so estranged that, in November 1864, a rumor was reported in a Cincinnati newspaper that there was a movement within the state to break away from the Union, not to join the Confederacy, but to create an independent state. Finally, a report made to the secretary of war in late 1864 sanctioned Governor Bramlette's actions and warned that the vast majority of Kentuckians were disloyal to the Union.[2]

The collapse of the Confederacy did not bring political peace to the commonwealth. The military occupation continued, and many of the significant issues, most important, the status of slavery, continued to polarize the people of the state. By the spring of 1865, most Kentuckians realized that slavery, although still legal in the state, was a dead institution. Indicative of the state's position was the general assembly's overwhelming defeat of a bill to approve the Thirteenth Amendment during the winter of 1865.[3]

Men like Duke were more concerned about the state's policy concerning Confederate soldiers returning home after the war than about its attitude toward slavery. Attorney General James Speed, a radical Kentucky Republican, was adamantly opposed to the return of the Confederates and refused to accept their parole. Governor Bramlette was far more pragmatic and announced that ex-Confederates would be permitted back in the state if "they made a personal surrender, giving up their arms and horses and duly registering their names." It would be weeks before Duke would have to confront these issues; in the meantime, he had to complete some unfinished business.[4]

Augusta, Georgia, was bristling with activity when Duke and his staff arrived to surrender and accept their paroles. The Confederates went through the formalities of taking the oath of allegiance without any complications or humiliations. It is difficult to determine which of the group came up with the idea, but Duke and several others concluded that the fastest way for them to return to Kentucky would be by steamship through New York City. They naively rationalized that, in civilian clothes, there was very little chance that anyone in New York, other than their friends and acquaintances, would discover that they had been Confederate officers. On the other hand, traveling home through Georgia and Tennessee could be dangerous, with a far greater chance of being detained by Union troops or even possibly running into bushwhackers.[5]

With their plan set in motion, Duke and his friends booked passage on a riverboat to Savannah. In Savannah, the group, despite their paroles, was detained for several hours by the federal authorities and placed under guard. Once released, Duke discovered that it was not going to be an easy task to obtain permission from the authorities to go to New York. This did not discourage Duke, who resurrected his negotiating skills and, eventually, did obtain permission. Permission, however, did not solve the problem of how the group was actually going to get to New York. Low on federal greenbacks, the men found that it was no easy task to locate and then book passage on a boat they could afford. One such steamship, the *Arago,* was, Duke learned, at Hilton Head and planning a return to New York in the next few days. Passage was secured, which incidentally included meals but, owing to the ship's overcrowded conditions, not sleeping accommodations. Biding time until the *Arago* steamed, Duke and his staff obtained accommodations at the Point Royal House, a hotel on the island. Also staying as a guest at the hotel was John Snider Cooper, an officer in the Union army, who noted Duke's presence at the hotel in his diary on May 16, 1865: "Duke looks like a very sharp man but I would not vouch for his appearance as to principle and honesty."[6]

The lack of sleeping accommodations aboard the *Arago* did not concern Duke, who was used to far worse conditions, and, of course, his fare had been reduced accordingly. Initially, the Northern passengers avoided conversation with Duke and his group. It appeared to him that the civilians, at least, were suspicious of the ex-Confederates and of their intentions in going to New York. The Southerners soon, however, fell into friendly conversation with some of the more affable Northerners and actually enjoyed the balance of their trip. Colonel Steele, whom Duke described as quite a gambler, was anxious to join some federal officers in the then-popular card game of vingt et un. Finally, after asking Duke and the others to stake him by pooling their meager funds, Steele was given his opportunity. He was very lucky and, over the next several days, much to everyone's delight and relief, enlarged the group's bankroll.[7]

The first thought that entered Duke's mind when he reached New York was that he had forgotten the size of the city and the energy of the urban atmosphere, which made everything seem "incredibly large." The whole image of the city was only magnified by Duke's recent experiences in the small towns of the rural South. He detected no evidence that the city had experienced any wartime inconvenience. Years later, Duke cynically wrote that, after being in New York a short while, it was his impression "that the people living there had only known that a war had been raging in one part of their own country by the fluctuations of the Gold Board." It appeared to Duke that even the "most loyal New Yorker" had little concern about his politics. In fact, his friends in the city did everything they could to make his stay as pleasant as possible.[8]

Soon it was time for Duke to return home to his family, who had safely returned to Lexington. Despite being uncertain how he as an ex-Confederate would be treated by the government, Duke returned to his native state at the end of May. When he arrived in Lexington, he was probably not surprised by the political disaffection among those who had supported the Confederacy, but the attitude of the wartime Unionists may have given him reason to chortle. However, political considerations took a back seat to the more pressing problem of making a living. By this time, possibly owing to family pressure or the political environment in St. Louis, he had decided not to return to Missouri. Although not appealing for several reasons, the most obvious choice was to start a law practice in Lexington.

Between 1950 and 1965, the Old Crow Bourbon Whiskey Distillery national advertising program included illustrations of famous historical figures enjoying Old Crow. This ca. 1960 magazine advertisement shows Basil Duke and friends on his arrival in New York harbor in May 1865.

Duke had moved to St. Louis in 1858 because Lexington had had more than its share of lawyers, and things certainly had not changed by 1865. The war may also have tempered his desire to practice law. For four years, Duke had lived an exciting life, surviving by finding quick solutions in adverse situations. The prospect of exchanging a saddle for a seat behind a lawyer's desk—however comfortable—could not have been an attractive one for him.[9]

Like most of the returning soldiers, Duke was discouraged by the economic situation in the state and the opportunities offered for making a living. The war had caused property values to depreciate, and, of course, slave values were down to nothing by the summer of 1865. The hardest-hit section of the state's economy was agriculture. The inability of farmers to maintain their crops owing to the constant interference of the two armies was a contributing factor, but the most obvious reason for the decline in production was the "demoralization of the labor force." As Duke quickly discovered, the Bluegrass, which had always been driven by agriculture, had not escaped the general economic downturn. He decided that he needed money and that he needed it quick, something a lawyer with no client base could not hope to achieve through the practice of law.[10]

During the summer of 1865, cash was in short supply, and those who were fortunate enough to have access to specie certainly had an opportunity to turn adversity into profit. The value of almost everything in the postwar South was depreciated, including cotton, a fact that was not lost on Duke when he traveled through Georgia and South Carolina at the end of the war. The old economic maxim of buy low and sell high was an argument that Duke presented to his cousin James K. Duke. It was Duke's plan to return to the Deep South, purchase cotton, and sell it in the North for what he anticipated would be a tidy profit. The two cousins formed a partnership, with Basil contributing his services and traveling south to purchase the cotton and his cousin advancing the cash and contacting his commercial connections in the North to sell the cotton when Basil returned. With the formation of the partnership, and much to the dismay of Tommie, in early August Duke once again left home and headed south.[11]

When Duke returned to Augusta, he began to purchase as much cotton as the partnership could afford. Then, several days later, while traveling down the Savannah River, he discovered a sunken barge loaded with cotton ten miles south of Augusta. He went back to Augusta and made arrangements to acquire the contract to raise the barge. Once the contract was secure, he hired twenty ex-slaves to help him with the work. For the next two weeks, Duke supervised the work in the hot, humid, and mosquito-infested Savannah River. As a result of sleeping in these conditions each night on the ground near the shoreline of the river, Duke contracted a fever common to the area. With the work done, he returned to Augusta, where the fever forced him to remain in bed for two weeks. Although not fully recovered, Duke wrapped up his affairs in Augusta and started for home by way of St. Louis.[12]

The most direct route between Augusta and St. Louis was by railroad. The trip was not very pleasant for Duke, who was still suffering from his fever. Except for the Louisville and Nashville, the railroads in the South were in a horrible state, a situation that was not to change for many years. It took Duke several days to reach Memphis, sometimes traveling with the freight in boxcars. One morning as he waited on a station platform for the next train, he noticed a half-starved, dirty-looking ex-Confederate soldier next to a bale of cotton. Nearby were some federal soldiers eating their breakfast. The soldiers apparently caught sight of the down-and-out rebel the same time as Duke. When the soldiers yelled at the rebel, he, as did Duke, assumed that they were going to arrest him. However, when the gray-clad veteran went over to see what the soldiers wanted, they fed him breakfast and then filled his haversack with food and sent him on his way. This act of benevolence may have been a very small one, but it served to reinforce Duke's budding conviction that reconciliation was in the best interests of the country.[13]

Once he had wrapped up his prewar affairs in St. Louis, Duke returned to Lexington in September. He and his cousin reviewed the accounting of their cotton venture and were apparently satisfied with the profit. They decided to continue their partnership, fashioning themselves as produce and commission merchants, and opening a new office on West Second Street in Cincinnati. For the immediate future at least, Duke had no intention of practicing law.[14]

The August election, conducted during Duke's absence, had brought certain political issues to a head. The state's Republicans, who reasonably considered themselves the rightful heirs to Kentucky's political throne owing to the federal military victory, became incensed when the ex-Confederates and exiled sympathizers returned to the state and were welcomed as heroes. Through the summer of 1865, men like Duke discovered that being a Confederate veteran was, not a liability, but, in fact, fast becoming a political asset. Duke and his friends quickly found a home within the Conservative Party, which also included prewar Democrats and lukewarm Unionists. The influx of Confederates into the Conservative Party troubled the Republicans, who were preparing for the August election.[15]

Concerned that the disenfranchised Confederates would attempt to vote in the election, Governor Bramlette issued a proclamation warning the veterans not to violate the voting prohibitions. The list of names of those who were precluded from voting, which included Duke, was circulated to the individual precinct officers prior to the election. General Palmer, however, expanded the voting exclusions to anyone who directly or indirectly "gave aid and comfort or encouragement to persons in the rebellion."[16]

The election was held on August 7, 1865, and, although the Confederates stayed away from the polls, the Conservatives achieved a narrow victory, which gave them control of the state legislature and five of the nine congressional seats. As expected, the voters elected a general assembly that eventually rejected the Thirteenth Amendment. The Conservatives were elected simply because they had resisted unpopular federal policies and had supported the Confederates during the war. As E. Merton Coulter concluded in his detailed account of this period in Kentucky history: "The war after the war had now started."[17]

The rapid rise of Confederate political influence in postwar Kentucky convinced Duke that he would maintain his status as a popular general even after having returned to civilian life. Other members of Morgan's cavalry, such as D. H. Smith and James McCreary, were fast establishing a presence on the political scene, something that Duke himself would do slowly but surely over the next several years. There was also a natural tendency for the men from his command to look to Duke for continued leadership and, when there was no one else to whom they could turn, for help resolving their problems. The Morgan family too looked to him for leadership, particularly concerning the resolution of the questions surrounding John Hunt Morgan's death. And, of course, there were Tommie and the children, a responsibility that he thoroughly enjoyed, particularly with the addition of their second son, John Morgan, known affectionately as Johnnie Reb.[18]

The responsibilities that consumed much of Duke's time were not so burdensome as to interfere with the maintenance of his wartime friendships, such as that with John C. Breckinridge. Breckinridge, who was in self-imposed exile in Canada, maintained a regular correspondence with Duke. Their letters clearly reveal that Breckinridge was using Duke to gauge the political climate, not just in Kentucky, but in the South generally. Many different subjects were touched on, but, in December 1865, Breckinridge was most concerned about a rumor, which had apparently started in Georgia, concerning the disposition of the Confederate treasury. Knowing the rumor to be false, Breckinridge naturally wanted to set the record straight. He advised Duke that he "and others who know the facts should prepare and publish a statement to meet any possible absurd and wicked interpretation on our characters." This may have been the catalyst that Duke needed to take up the pen and write *A History of Morgan's Cavalry.*[19]

Most likely, Duke started working on the book in late 1865, and it seems to have taken him roughly a year to complete it. Although the *History* was based largely on Duke's personal experience, at times he had to rely on others, such as William Preston Johnston, Thomas H. Hines, D. H. Smith, and Morgan's widow Mattie, to provide information regarding events that had occurred when he was not with the command. The tone that the book would take was revealed in an April 1866 letter to Hines in which Duke wrote that, while he admired Jeb Stuart, there were no grounds for crediting him with originality and that the results of Morgan's raids were far more significant.[20]

The year 1866 began with bright hopes for Duke and his family. The war had been over for almost nine months, and Duke and his fellow Confederates were far from being ostracized in Kentucky, most having regained or achieved a certain prominence in their communities. Duke and his cousin James were busy with their business, and Duke planned to work on his book when time permitted. Shortly after the start of the new year, Duke wrote Mattie, Morgan's widow, an enthusiastic letter about his prospects and included a note about his young son: "Johnnie Reb had smartened some since you saw him, but poor little fellow he is still awkward to show off well—he rolls about like a young bear." Within a month of Duke's letter, however, tragedy entered his and Tommie's lives. In the middle of February, little Johnnie Reb died. The Dukes mourned their son deeply, but even then Tommie was several months pregnant, and life went on.[21]

With so many veterans from both armies attempting to make their way in the civilian world once again, life in postwar Kentucky could be hazardous at times. The war had left many veterans bitter, and that bitterness at times escalated into violence. During a visit in Cynthiana with fellow veteran Joseph Desha, Duke found reason to draw his pistol. Desha spotted an old prewar nemesis and Union veteran, Alexander Kimbrough, in the lobby of a local hotel. Desha, who wanted to bury the hatchet, approached Kimbrough, his hand extended, anticipating a friendly reception. Instead, Kimbrough rebuffed him, calling him a scoundrel and hitting him with a chair. Several bystanders tried to stop the fight, but Duke drew his pistol and told the crowd to back off, saying: "They are equally matched and let them have it out." Desha got the better of Kimbrough, and a challenge was forthcoming, resulting in a duel at Richland. Evidently, it was only the illness of Tommie, whose bedside he could not leave, that prevented Duke from seconding Desha. Kimbrough was wounded in the duel, and afterward Desha and his second fled to Canada, where he remained until receiving a pardon from Governor McCreary in the mid-1870s. Duke most likely used Tommie's illness as an excuse to extricate himself from the duel, which was illegal, and its consequences, a practice he was soon to repeat.[22]

The spring of 1866 found Duke hard at work on his book. It also found his business arrangements proceeding satisfactorily, so satisfactorily, in fact, that he even wrote Thomas Hines, who was studying law in Memphis with General Albert Pike, that he and James "would have been gratified to welcome you as another colonist here. . . . Our business has opened in a manner which has greatly encouraged us, and we expect to do well." Despite these time-consuming activities, Duke was beginning to keep his eye on state and national politics. Andrew Johnson's lenient postwar attitude toward the South impressed Duke and won Johnson his favor. In fact, Duke was so impressed with Johnson that he wrote W. C. P. Breckinridge in April 1866: "If anybody should want to impose on Andy Johnson it would be a good thing to be able to help him." Most Kentucky Confederates shared Duke's opinion of Johnson, and, when they took control of the Conservative Party later that spring, support for Johnson was formally adopted as part of the party's platform.[23]

The Conservative Party leadership recognized the Confederate challenge. Confederates, such as D. H. Smith, were increasingly becoming candidates for public office, an obvious indication of a shift in party power. In a desperate move to regain control, the Conservatives called for a party convention, which never materialized. The Confederates now began to question the viability of their alliance with the Conservatives. Although Duke was hesitant to attack the alliance, he emphasized the need for new leadership within the party, stressing that the old, prewar leaders had seen their day.[24]

The Confederates called for a convention to be held in Louisville on May 1, 1866, an event that the Conservative Party leadership purposely avoided, planning its own convention later that month. Distancing themselves from the Confederates was a serious miscalculation on the part of the Conservatives, whose absence from the May 1 convention only accelerated the Confederate takeover of the party. The end result of the convention was a party platform that embodied Kentucky's postwar struggle with Washington. Andrew Johnson himself was praised but the government censured for its usurpation of power and infringement on states' rights. The convention accepted the emancipation of Kentucky's slaves but demanded control of their political status. Finally, there was a general sense of sympathy for the Southern states and their continued postwar trauma. However, the boldest move was the nomination of Alvin Duvall as a candidate for the clerkship of the court of appeals, the only office to be decided in the August election. Duvall, an outspoken Confederate, had been forced to flee the state in 1863 under threat of arrest by the federal government.[25]

Although only one office was at stake, the election was a test of strength between Union and Confederate voters. The Confederates won a stunning victory, inaugurating the Democratic Party and voter support that would continue into the twentieth century. The voters of Kentucky had, within sixteen months of Appomattox, repudiated the federal government's postwar policies in favor of the Confederates'. The state was to continue a political struggle with the federal government and, during Reconstruction, championed the rights of the disenfranchised Southern states. Duke, who was an integral part of this political metamorphosis, concluded:

> The emancipation of the slaves and the horrible atrocities perpetrated by two Federal generals—Burbridge and Paine, the former a native Kentuckian—who, under the guise

of military execution, murdered nearly two hundred citizens and Confederate prisoners, had caused a great revulsion of feeling in that element of the population which had originally staunchly adhered to the Union. Reinforced by these recruits, those who have always entertained Southern proclivities suddenly found themselves overwhelmingly in control, and the post-bellum democracy of Kentucky began its career with a majority that could scarcely be counted.[26]

The business venture into which Duke had entered with his cousin soon became a problem. James Duke had decided to quit the firm and move to Montana with his brother-in-law, Green Clay Smith, who had been appointed Montana's territorial governor. The sudden loss of his business partner caused an abrupt change in Duke's plans. He was now forced to spend considerable amounts of time in Cincinnati dealing with the firm's transactions, thus slowing progress on his book. However, with the arrival of summer and hot weather, business activity slowed down, permitting Duke to remain in Lexington. Duke had recruited Dick Morgan to spend the summer in Cincinnati and oversee the firm's business. With his brother-in-law minding the store, Duke made considerable progress on the *History* and soon began to hope for a fall publication date.[27]

On July 29, 1866, Tommie gave birth to a second daughter, who was named Mary Currie in honor of Duke's mother. Dick Morgan, who was extremely bored and possibly a bit aggravated with Duke for making him spend the summer in Cincinnati, referred to the new baby as the "ugliest thing he ever saw." Morgan upset Duke and his sister with his unkind comment and most likely reevaluated Cincinnati, which would at least prove a safe haven until family sensitivities returned to normal. Aside from her uncle's remarks, life was kind to Mary Currie. She, like her father, loved to play the violin and became a popular virtuoso before she married and had two children of her own.[28]

For the remainder of the summer and into the early fall, Duke spent most of his time working on his book. Finally, by November, *A History of Morgan's Cavalry* was completed, and Duke began to search for a reputable printing company that would publish his book for a reasonable charge. There were several printers in Louisville and Cincinnati from whom Duke solicited estimates. In the end, he chose a Cincinnati company, and the book appeared in early 1867. The first edition contained numerous spelling and other errors, revealing that it had not been well edited. Nevertheless, the *History* was destined to become the most respected and most quoted work on the Morgan-Duke command that has been written to date.[29]

Duke, like most Confederate veterans, had been struggling with the pathos of the recent defeat. Having been raised in a society that, according to Gaines M. Foster, "celebrated personal bravery and martial skills," Duke sensed that others had been questioning whether he, Morgan, and the rest of the command had acted honorably during the war. By taking up the pen, Duke wanted, as he put it, not only to "perpetuate . . . Morgan's fame" but also to establish the true character "of the men who served under him." This was an easy task for Duke, who worshiped Morgan, almost to a fault.[30]

A History of Morgan's Cavalry was written in what was to become Duke's typical, selfless style. Duke had a flair for making history read like an adventure novel. Not only did he not hesitate to demonstrate his command of the English language, but he also had the ability to describe complex battles and other events in an easily understood manner. Although it lacks the attention to detail that we have come to expect of works of history, is devoid of any serious criticism of Morgan, and is largely unenlightening as to Duke's own contribution to the command, the *History* has, nevertheless, met the test of time and continues to be the primary source for its subject. Through it, Duke became a literary partisan for Morgan and one of the first proponents of the Lost Cause. More important, by fashioning Morgan's story as a heroic struggle against all odds, he helped his and future generations of Southerners cope with the stigma of defeat. Duke's own words are the best evidence of his intent:

> In undertaking to write the History of General Morgan's services, and of the command which he created, it is but fair that I shall acknowledge myself influenced in great measure, by the feelings of the friend and follower; that I desire, if I can do so by relating facts, of most which I am personally cognizant, to perpetuate his fame. . . . A Southern man, once a Confederate soldier—always thoroughly Southern in sentiments and feeling, I can, of course, write only a Southern account of what I saw in the late war and as such what is herein written must be received.[31]

Duke was not the first Kentuckian to write of Morgan and his men. During the war, Sallie Rochester Ford wrote a lively novel entitled *Raids and Romances of Morgan and His Men* (1863) that contained, according to William Ward, an "inordinately idealized conception of the Confederacy." Although *A History of Morgan's Cavalry* is historically reliable, Duke's eulogistic treatment of his subject certainly contributed to the almost-mythic status accorded Morgan by future novelists. Approximately half the sixty or more Civil War novels written by Kentucky authors feature Morgan.[32]

Shortly after the *History* was made available to the public, Duke received some constructive criticism from D. H. Smith concerning the all-too-obvious lack of proofreading plus several points at which Duke's interpretation was questionable. Smith's primary criticism was that Duke had minimized the significance of the Battle of Buffington, treating it as a "very short and small affair," and failed to give the Fifth and Sixth Kentucky proper recognition for their role in the engagement. The point is very well taken. Buffington was probably the most critical engagement during the entire Indiana-Ohio Raid, yet Duke devoted barely three pages to it. Perhaps he felt that an in-depth discussion might elevate his own accomplishments to the detriment of Morgan's, or perhaps even cast Morgan's actions in a poor light, and chose instead to write a brief synopsis of the battle so as not to compromise the integrity of his book.[33]

Other members of Morgan's command also had significant criticisms of the *History,* criticisms of which Duke may not have been aware. For example, in a letter to Thomas Hines, John Castleman openly expressed his feelings concerning Duke's treatment of Morgan: "It is quickly told. The book is thoroughly ex-parte! It recounts most of the better, with few of the worst features of the command. It pictures Morgan as a hero of fact & out of romance. It accords him all of noble & soldierly elements & endorses him with none of the faults, which were most glaring in his character as an officer! It makes heroes of anything & it makes nothing of heroes!"[34]

Whereas Smith's criticisms are substantive, Castleman's are more related to the general tone and theme of the book. And Castleman's criticisms may be valid. They miss the point, however, that, had Duke presented a critical analysis of Morgan, the *History* would have been anathema in the postwar South. Southerners for generations would be preoccupied with the past, and only the most incautious of writers dared approach Confederate war heroes with anything other than reverence.[35]

With his book completed, Duke began to work at establishing a law practice in Lexington with his fellow brigade commander Willie Breckinridge. Throughout the rest of his life, Duke tended to use the legal profession as catalyst for other pursuits and ways to make a living. Law was always the fulcrum on which his livelihood rested, but he soon discovered that he was not going to get rich selling his time, particularly in a cash-poor economy. From time to time, Duke pursued various business ventures, none of which were very successful. He was, however, a very political person and sensed the opportunities associated with a strong Democratic Party affiliation. During 1867, Duke, whose political opinions were seen as perceptive and whose influence with the Democratic leadership was well known, was consulted by Kentuckians as well as by national Democratic Party figures on a regular basis. By the end of the year, he had developed a significant network of connections at the national party level, including the presidential candidate George H. Pendleton. He would continue such political networking throughout his life.[36]

The Democrats easily elected John Larue Helm governor in August 1867. Helm's election completed the Democratic Party's sweep of state and federal political offices in Kentucky. Helm, however, was in poor health and died only five days after taking the oath of office. A special gubernatorial election was, therefore, called for 1868. The Democrats held their convention in Frankfort on February 22, 1868. In the meantime, Lieutenant Governor John W. Stevenson succeeded Helm.

Stevenson was the Republicans' worst nightmare come true; less than two years after the war, a true secessionist was governor.[37]

In association with men such as James Cantrill, Duke was able to influence much of the thought process behind the forthcoming party platform. He was working hard to obtain the delegates' endorsement of George H. Pendleton as the Democrats' nominee for president. The convention—much to Duke's delight—called for an across-the-board amnesty for all Confederate soldiers in response to the newly enacted Fourteenth Amendment, which the Republicans interpreted as disqualifying many, if not all, secessionists from holding public office.[38]

Even with the resurgence of the Bourbon Democrats, there was a sense that the times were changing, particularly in the fast-growing industrial and commercial metropolis of Louisville. A good portion of the city's population had witnessed the rapid industrial growth of the states just north of the Ohio River and appreciated the advantages that similar growth could have for Louisville. There was a cadre of Democrats, led by Henry Watterson, the editor of the *Louisville Courier-Journal*, who were more liberal and progressive than most Kentuckians. These New Departure Democrats also believed that reconciliation with the North would benefit the South economically. The conservatives, or so-called Bourbons, however, were far more numerous and controlled the party machine. It would take time before they became receptive to the New Departure philosophy and grasped the benefits of sectional reconciliation. At this point in his political career, Duke, like most Bluegrass Democrats, was firmly ensconced in the Bourbon camp, but events would soon enable him to incorporate a more progressive political philosophy, including a strong belief in reconciliation and Watterson's New Departure, into his own moderate political philosophy.[39]

15

My Prospects in That Line Were Not Brilliant

A FACTOR CONTRIBUTING TO Louisville's emergence as a major postwar commercial trade center was the virtual monopoly that the Louisville and Nashville (L&N) Railroad had on north–south rail traffic, a monopoly that permitted Louisville to dominate the Southern markets. Duke had this dominance brought forcefully home to him in the course of managing his Cincinnati brokerage firm, and, by mid-1867, it had become clear that Louisville offered far more opportunities than Lexington. Also, the city's prosperity, unusual in the postwar South, was a drawing card for ex-Confederates, many of whom Duke already knew, either through the war, or politics, or business dealings. Louisville had always had interests in common with its Southern sisters, but the migration of ex-Confederates was transforming it into a truly Southern city. For all these reasons, in March 1868 Duke moved his family to Louisville, where he intended to practice law.[1]

The year 1868 was one of transition, not just for Duke, but for Kentucky itself. The main transformation was in the state's politics. The rise of the Democratic Party had simultaneously destroyed the Conservative Party's political power base and weakened the Republican Party to such an extent that it captured only 18 percent of the vote in the August election.[2] Some Republicans sought to achieve through legal maneuvering what they could not achieve politically—hence their support of the Fourteenth Amendment. The Republicans claimed not only that the Fourteenth Amendment granted suffrage to African Americans but also that it granted Congress the authority to disenfranchise from public office elected or appointed officials who had supported the recent rebellion. If this view was correct, then being an ex-Confederate would certainly be a "disability." This development caused some Democratic state officials more than a little concern. D. H. Smith, for example, wrote his wife: "This matter of disabilities under the Fourteenth Constitutional amendment has given me a great deal of uneasiness and trouble for the last two months. It has made me exceedingly unhappy. If I would be thrown out of office it would ruin me. Hence my anxiety and trouble." In 1871, Congress did remove the disabilities for some sixty Kentucky ex-Confederates, including D. H. Smith, but not Duke.[3]

The more astute Republicans felt that their chances of winning back political control were dependent on the African American voters who had recently been granted the franchise by the Fifteenth Amendment. However, as of the winter of 1868–69, the Kentucky General Assembly had not ratified the amendment. The subsequent steps taken by Washington to secure the ratification of the Fourteenth and Fifteenth Amendments, to enforce the Civil Rights Act of 1866 in the federal courts, and to establish the Freedman's Bureau were strongly opposed by the Kentucky Democrats, including a very hostile Duke, who viewed them as nothing more than attempts to subject the Southern people to the "baser" whims of Northern politicians.[4]

To the south of Kentucky, federal agents and the military were enforcing the Civil Rights Act with impunity, causing some white males to organize into reactionary groups, such as the Ku Klux Klan. The Klan became notorious for its night rides and the terror tactics that it directed at the African American community. In Kentucky, several organized bands of white males operating under names like the Regulators or Skagg's Men used similar tactics.[5] Other Kentuckians expressed their disenchantment with the policies of the federal government in a more conventional manner. For example, ex-governor Bramlette and a host of lawyers filed a petition with Governor Stevenson expressing their indignation with the Civil Rights Act, which they called "unconstitutional and the most dangerous attack ever made upon our republican form of government."[6]

Duke was concerned about the legal consequences of the constitutional amendments pushed through by the radical Republicans. In 1868, he became active in the Soldiers of the Red Cross, a secret organization formed in opposition to the Fourteenth and Fifteenth Amendments as well as any other perceived radical Republican threat to ex-Confederate soldiers and the citizenry of the state of Kentucky. An undated printed broadside describes in detail not only the primary concerns of the organization and its objectives but also its reasons for operating under a cloak of secrecy. Its author acknowledges Americans' distaste for secrecy but argues that public disclosure of the identities of the organization's members would result in the government employing all its power to break it up. In terms of the tone of its polemic and its embrace of secrecy, the Soldiers of the Red Cross was similar to the other militant organizations that had been springing up throughout the South. Still, although there are racial overtones to the message conveyed by the broadside, there is no evidence that the organization was itself responsible for any acts of violence. In fact, there is no evidence that it did anything of substance at all.[7]

Duke wrote several letters to Thomas Hines concerning the organization during 1868, including one in which he appointed Hines a colonel in the Soldiers of the Red Cross. Duke, in his capacity as "the Director," signed all the letters sent to Hines. Whether "the Director" was the leader of the organization is not evident from its constitution. However, a general order issued on August 12, 1868, from its headquarters appears to support the argument that "the Director" was the man in charge. There is no question that Duke was involved in this organization at a high level. With the demise of the radical element of the Republican Party in Kentucky and the federal government's inability to impose Reconstruction on the state, organizations such as the Soldiers of the Red Cross began to fade from the scene, and, by 1875, even the Ku Klux Klan had gone into hibernation, not just in Kentucky, but throughout the South.[8]

During the summer of 1868, Duke attended the national Democratic convention in New York City. With him on the train to New York were other Kentuckians as well as several Tennessee Democrats, including Nathan Bedford Forrest. It was most likely that his discussions with Forrest and other Southern reactionaries during the trip motivated him to conceptualize the Soldiers of the Red Cross. Forrest had been involved in the formation of the Ku Klux Klan the previous year in Tennessee. However, as Klan violence grew, Forrest and many more responsible members quit the organization in protest. Forrest disbanded the organization in 1869, but, by then, it was under the control of its worst elements, which continued the violence under other banners.[9]

At one point during the trip, when the train stopped to take on water, the conductor came up to Duke and told him that the town bully was outside on the platform proclaiming that he wanted to fight Forrest. The conductor was hopeful that Duke could restrain Forrest and avoid a brawl. Duke spoke to Forrest, who readily agreed to remain in the coach. When the train reached the depot, the bully jumped from the platform onto the train and burst into Duke's coach, yelling: "Where is that damn butcher Forrest? I want him." Duke had never seen such an "instantaneous and marvelous transformation" in a man as he saw in Forrest that day. Forrest stood up and walked over to the bully with the demeanor of a man who demanded respect and, in a commanding voice, said: "What do you want?" Completely taken aback by Forrest's overpowering presence, the man turned and ran from the coach, with Forrest, Duke, and several others hot on his heels. Forrest shouted for the man to stop, but, to the amusement of a gathering crowd, he kept on running. When Forrest returned to the coach, he remained on the outside platform, waving to a cheering crowd as the train pulled away from the station.[10]

Several months later, Duke became involved in a nationally publicized quarrel between Forrest and General Judson Kilpatrick. The quarrel began when Forrest received a letter from another Union officer, General James Shackelford, advising him that Kilpatrick had made a speech in Connecticut stating that Forrest had "nailed Negroes to the fences, set fires to the fences, and burned the Negroes to death." All this had supposedly taken place at Fort Pillow, Tennessee, during the war. In response to these allegations, Forrest wrote a letter to Kilpatrick that was published on the front page of the *New York Times* on November 3 and, in pertinent part, stated: "I think the public would justify me in denouncing, as I now do, Gen. Judson Kilpatrick as a blackguard, a liar, a scoundrel, and poltroon. If he is the heroic figure he would have northern people believe him, my friend, Gen. Basil W. Duke, at Louisville, Ky.; is authorized to receive on my behalf, any communication he may choose to make."[11]

The first time Duke became aware of this challenge was when he read the published letter in the *Louisville Courier-Journal* several days after its publication in the *New York Times.* Duke was surprised at Forrest's indignation because he had assumed that he "had become much accustomed to such attacks as to regard them with indifference." Of a more serious nature were the possible implications for Duke if he acted as Forrest's second in any forthcoming duel. The laws of Kentucky were quite explicit and provided that, if any attorney did take part in a duel within the state's borders, he could lose his law license for a minimum of five years. In his *Reminiscences,* Duke was very candid about his financial and professional situation at that time: "I had come out of the war with a ready-made family and no visible means of support and had begun the practice of law in Louisville. My prospects in that line were not brilliant, it is true, but were all that I had, and I was exceedingly loath to relinquish even a very small chance of making a living." The challenge created another quandary for Duke, who believed that Kentucky was the only state where Forrest could be assured that the duel would be a fair fight. A duel in a state north of the Ohio River was literally impossible and one in a Southern state occupied by federal troops was not in Forrest's best interests. The same day Duke learned of the challenge, he received a letter from Forrest stating that, as Duke put it, "he Forrest thought it would be highly appropriate to fight mounted with sabers."[12]

Still wanting to help Forrest, just not to the extent of actual involvement in a duel, Duke sought out an expert in code duello who would be an acceptable second for Forrest. He wired Dr. James Keller of St. Louis, an old acquaintance, who agreed to come to Louisville and discuss matters with Duke. Fortunately for Duke, Kilpatrick never responded to Forrest's *New York Times* challenge. Instead, he published a statement claiming that a congressional committee had found Forrest guilty of the atrocities committed at Fort Pillow and that he could not, therefore, regard him as a gentleman. The implication was, of course, that it would be beneath Kilpatrick, a gentleman, to fight someone like Forrest, who was, in his opinion, not a gentleman. General Shackelford responded to Kilpatrick's published letter by indicating that the committee had drawn no conclusions as to Forrest's status as a gentleman and that Kilpatrick should fight him. Shackelford's letter—which was,

A. E. Richards became Duke's law partner in 1868. A successful guerrilla fighter under John Mosby, Richards is shown here as he appeared in 1865. (Courtesy the Kentucky Historical Society.)

according to Duke, published—evidently constituted the last shot fired in this verbal duel.[13]

No matter how committed to his political activity he might have been, Duke still needed to make a living. In order to improve his chances of success at his chosen profession, he decided to take on a partner and, by the fall of 1868, was practicing with one A. E. Richards. Adolphus (Dolly) Edward Richards had been admitted to the Kentucky bar only in the spring of 1868. He was seven years younger than Duke and had lived in Louisville for little more than a year. On meeting shortly after Duke moved to Louisville, the two young lawyers bonded immediately, their relationship finding a solid footing in the similarity of their Civil War exploits.

Richards had been born in Loudoun County, Virginia, and attended Randolph Macon College until the beginning of the war, when he enlisted as a private with Turner Ashby's cavalry. After Ashby's death in the spring of 1862, Richards joined the staff of General William "Grumble" Jones and stayed in the Valley of Virginia for the next eighteen months. In September 1863, he resigned from Jones's staff and once again enlisted as a private, this time with the Forty-third Battalion of Virginia cavalry commanded by John Singleton Mosby. For the rest of the war, Richards became so adept at Mosby's style of guerrilla warfare that, at times, enemy commanders reported that they had engaged Mosby when, in fact, it was Richards. There was no lack of audacity in Mosby's command, and, during one night raid in August 1864, Richards took a small group of men and infiltrated the camp of General Phillip Sheridan with the intention of capturing him. Except for the scream of a captured Union soldier that alerted the camp of the group's presence, the action might have been successful. In December 1864, Richards was promoted to major and given his own battalion. After the war, he remained in Virginia for two years to complete his education. During his second year of study, he focused on law and, eventually, moved to Louisville, where he attended the University of Louisville Law School.[14]

Richards was optimistic about the partnership's potential and believed that he and Duke could "build up a fine practice." Duke immediately immersed himself in his work, concentrating mostly on commercial litigation. It was during these early years of the practice that Duke wrote amusingly to W. H. Mackoy, a Cincinnati lawyer, regarding his intuitive abilities to select a jury. He and Mackoy were in the process of selecting the proper venue for a trial, and Duke indicated a preference for Cincinnati over Louisville because he would rather "risk a commercial jury on a point like this, than a set of agricultural, whiskey making Kentuckians anyhow." Over the years, Richards and Duke had some success, but the practice never lived up to their original expectations.[15]

With his law practice started, Duke turned his attention to creating a political base, with an eye to the August 1869 state election. During the winter of 1868–69, the primary political issue was the ratification of the Fifteenth Amendment. It was, of course, no surprise that the Kentucky legislature voted against ratification. The deeply rooted prejudice of most of the legislators, coupled with their resentment of federal interference, would never allow them willingly to enfranchise African Americans. The legislature's stand was merely symbolic, however; by the end of the year, enough states had voted for ratification to make the Fifteenth Amendment the law of the land.[16]

Duke's political philosophy during these early postwar years never ventured far from that of the prototypical Southern Democrat. He was antagonistic toward Washington's authority and adamant in the belief that the recently emancipated African American was nothing more than a puppet of the Freedman's Bureau, which was, he felt, waging a vendetta against the "rebel trash." Defending his opinions years later in his *Reminiscences,* Duke argued that Northerners condemned "the conduct of the Southern people toward the black race simply because they have not understood it." More likely, what Northerners didn't understand was that, because Duke and his contemporaries were the products of a society that saw slavery as natural and white supremacy as incontestable, the notion of an enfranchised black man was anathema to them.[17]

Duke's political career began when he was nominated to run as the Democratic Party's candidate for the state House of Representatives from the Sixth District of Louisville, a bid that was successful. Even before Duke took his seat, it was decided that he would take the lead in the upcoming battle against the proposed Cincinnati Southern Railroad, a project that had grown out of the recent contestation of Louisville's commercial supremacy by Cincinnati. Even in the late 1860s Louisville continued to be the only Ohio River city with direct rail links to Tennessee and points farther south. Although Cincinnati had a rail route to Lexington, there was no railroad constructed south beyond that point. Then, in 1869, the Louisville, Cincinnati and Lexington Railroad, commonly known as the Louisville Short Line, completed its line from Cincinnati to a few miles outside Louisville at La Grange, Kentucky. However, the railroad's connection with the L&N at this point was made contingent on its changing its gauge width to four feet, eight and a half inches. All railroads in the South were five-feet gauge. The gauge distinction would force southbound trains traveling on the Louisville, Cincinnati and Lexington Railroad to break bulk in Louisville before being transferred to the L&N for the remainder of the trip. Breaking bulk was cost prohibitive, forcing Cincinnati to seek a rail route south that it could control. Cincinnati had tried for years to raise funds to extend the Cincinnati–Lexington line farther south, always unsuccessfully. Finally, on May 4, 1869, the governor of Ohio signed into law a bill authorizing Cincinnati to participate in the construction of a railroad south of Lexington to be known as the Cincinnati Southern. Cincinnati, with the avid support of the Bluegrass, was now prepared to introduce a bill in the next Kentucky legislative session authorizing the project.[18]

Duke's first political skirmish was set in motion when he learned that Cincinnati would also have to obtain permission from the general assembly in Tennessee, which met a month earlier than the Kentucky legislature, in order to construct its railroad in that state. On November 13, 1869, the trustees of the Cincinnati Southern were notified that Basil Duke and others from Louisville were in Nashville, lobbying in opposition to the bill. They immediately caught a train for Nashville and were ultimately successful in overcoming Duke's opposition to the bill.[19]

The Kentucky legislature was scheduled to convene on December 6, 1869. During the train ride from Louisville to the state capital, Frankfort, Duke must have recognized the irony in the position that he was about to take. His defense before the legislature of Louisville's commercial interests would directly benefit the L&N, the railroad that he repeatedly tried to destroy during the war.[20]

The day before the session began, the *Cincinnati Commercial* quoted Duke as stating: "As soon as it was seen that Louisville is earnestly and actively prosecuting it [i.e., contesting the Cincinnati Southern bill], Cincinnati will back down." But that proved to be wishful thinking. Cincinnati was not to back down regardless of the intensity of Duke's opposition. The real battle over the railroad bill was to begin in January after the Christmas break. First the legislature intended to devote itself to the introduction of bills and the determination of the composition of the House committees. On December 14, Duke was appointed to the important position of chairman of the committee on railroads, which was responsible for reviewing and working on the bill introduced for the Cincinnati Southern.[21]

The Cincinnati reporters covering the session assessed the bill's opponents, and, on December 10, the *Cincinnati Enquirer* wrote of Duke: "He is a genius. Such an embodiment of zeal, energy and indomitable will I never saw, and I can assure you his opposition to the Southern Railway will be a serious one. He is, in a physical sense, one of the smaller men of the House, but intellectually, he is a giant—one of those restless, sleepless, Giants, who, if they do not overcome you by the profundity of their reasoning, are certain to undermine you by their zeal and earnestness."[22]

Concerned about the opposition to the bill, the trustees of the Cincinnati Southern intelligently retained John C. Breckinridge to represent them. Although Breckinridge was not a member of the general assembly, he would be permitted to argue Cincinnati's case in front of Duke and his committee during the public hearings. Breckinridge brought a progressive view to Frankfort and, as Duke intently listened, argued that Louisville had done absolutely nothing to extend rail lines into eastern Tennessee. Cincinnati, on the other hand, was willing to expend funds for such a railroad, a project with direct benefits to central and southeastern Kentucky.[23]

Breckinridge had not planned to make a set speech; rather, he had expected an open discussion with both the House and the Senate committees concerning the bill. On finding out that a general address was required, he rose to the occasion and made an outstanding speech, pointing out in pertinent part the benefits that the railroad would bring to the state generally, and pleading that the issue not be viewed as a partisan one. The debates continued on into February 1870, with funds from both Cincinnati and Louisville fueling the fires of tension.[24]

Finally, on February 9, 1870, Duke reported the bill from his committee to the House without any attached recommendation for passage. The vote on the bill was then scheduled for February 15. On February 15, it was referred to the Committee of the Whole House, where it stayed for several more weeks.[25]

The *Cincinnati Commercial* reported that Duke had argued that the Cincinnati Southern could never pay for itself and that its real purpose was to divert as much trade as possible from Louisville. This and similar legislative tactics continued to tie up the bill in the House. On March 1, however, the Senate forced a vote on its bill, which was easily defeated 22 to 13. As the House bill languished in Duke's committee, the proponents of the Cincinnati Southern tried to force the bill onto the floor for a vote. Recognizing that he could not stall things much longer, Duke introduced so many substantive changes to the bill that the mutilated version that did reach the floor resembled the original only in title. After some postponement, the bill was finally tabled by a vote of 49 to 43. Duke's actions effectively destroyed any hope for passage that session. The Cincinnati newspapers decried the Louisville lobbyists, claiming that they bought the votes that defeated the bill. Even more outraged were the people of central Kentucky, who threatened to no longer purchase goods from or conduct any other commercial activity with the city of Louisville.[26]

During the debate on the Cincinnati Southern, the project's Louisville opponents introduced their own bill proposing the construction of a trunk line through the same part of central and southeastern Kentucky. This railroad was to be called the Louisville and Chattanooga Grand Trunk, and its obvious purpose was to undermine the Cincinnati proposal. Hoping to add some appeal to the proposal, the bill's authors mentioned both Robert E. Lee and Basil Duke as possible presidents of the new line. However, when the Cincinnati Southern bill was defeated, the trunk line proposal was shelved.[27]

By the end of March 1870, as the legislative session was beginning to wind down, Duke became aware of an opening in Louisville for the position of chief of police. He wrote the mayor, John Baxter, that he had been advised by many influential citizens that Baxter was ready to appoint him chief of police, but only on the assurance that he would accept. Duke was, of course, more than willing to give such an assurance, candidly stating that he had been persuaded by his friends to accept "the proffered honor." With a growing family and the attendant expenses, Duke obviously wanted a secure source of income, something that his law practice had failed to provide. The appointment went to one W. Jenkins.[28]

Within three months of his letter to Mayor Baxter, Duke had tendered to Governor Stevenson his letter of resignation from the House of Representatives. Although that letter is perfunctory, giving no indication of his reasons, it has been traditionally accepted that Duke resigned in protest over the Fourteenth Amendment and its potential application of civil disabilities to ex-Confederates. This interpretation is, however, doubtful. It is much more likely that, as a legislator, Duke found himself in a very uncomfortable position. To take a stand—as he did in the Cincinnati Southern battle—against the interests of central Kentucky would undoubtedly make him a pariah in both his family and his wife's. Moreover, the conflict of interest presented by his lobbying efforts in Nashville and resulting remuneration, if any, must also have been obvious to him. Still, his resignation did not prevent him from returning to the 1870–71 legislative session to lobby on behalf of Louisville in the continuing Cincinnati Southern odyssey. During the legislative session Duke and several other prominent people from Louisville held an open house in a Frankfort hotel where they lavishly entertained and lobbied legislators. Apparently, Duke's lobbying efforts were successful, for, once again, the Cincinnati Southern bill failed to collect the necessary votes. However, with the August 1871 election, a new group of legislators was elected, and, in 1872, the Cincinnati Southern bill finally passed. However, it would not be until 1880 that the Cincinnati Southern would reach Chattanooga.[29]

Duke returned to his law practice with A. E. Richards. He was, however, never far from the political arena and remained interested in political developments at both the state and the federal levels, taking care to stay informed. Over a period of time, he became an accepted behind-the-scenes strategist for the Democratic Party, using his influence and political awareness to structure the party's program for years to come. For many years, he was a member of the Kentucky Central Committee of the Democratic Party. The role that Duke played in the party was similar to that which he played in Morgan's command—not necessarily a kingmaker, but definitely one of the brains behind the operation.

Since Duke had been raised among the landed gentry of central Kentucky, his initial political inclinations had been to champion the position of the Bourbon conservatives. It was not long after his move to Louisville, however, that he came in contact with the more progressive Democrats. During the legislative struggle over the Cincinnati Southern, he became acquainted with Henry Watterson and learned to respect his power as the editor of Kentucky's largest newspaper, the *Courier-Journal.* Watterson, a visionary ex-Confederate, appreciated the industrial achievements of the North. He visualized a "new departure" from the old sectional antagonism, which was to be replaced by a political-economic reconciliation that would allow the South, and Kentucky in particular, to reap the benefits of Northern industrialization. Its strong commercial base had already made Louisville anxious to industrialize, and Duke quickly subscribed to Watterson's ideas. The perceptive editor understood that Northern participation would be required if industrialization were to succeed and that that meant that Kentuckians would have to be brought round to a more liberal attitude concerning the Fourteenth and Fifteenth Amendments. Of course, unlike Duke, conservative Democrats were resistant to this idea, as Watterson soon discovered. Correctly identifying the party's Confederate roots as the source of this resistance, Watterson called for a burying of the hatchet and a recognition that the war was over.[30]

In the meantime, on the national level, a liberal Republican movement had developed to counteract the Grant administration. Watterson realized that the Democrats had little chance of defeating Grant but that a coalition between the Democrats and a strong liberal element within the Republican Party might possibly influence or temper the administration's harsh Reconstruction policies.[31] However, the liberals bolted the Republican Party and called their own convention, to meet in May 1872 in Cincinnati. Although skeptical of the liberals' ability to form a viable party, Watterson was too interested not to attend. He assessed the situation, particularly the intellectual attributes of the delegates, and described the delegates from the South as a "motley array of Southerners of every sort who were ready to clutch at any straw that promised relief to intolerable conditions." Horace Greeley, a noted eccentric and the liberal with the least chance of winning, was nominated to run for president. Watterson, nonetheless, published editorial after editorial in the *Courier-Journal* attempting to convince the state Democrats to abandon the national party's ticket and support the liberal Republicans. On May 17, 1872, employing language that even the staunchest Bourbon could appreciate, he wrote: "The triumph of Greeley over Grant would be an emphatic recognition of the principle that the power of the federal Government is limited by the constitution and that the proper guarantee of local interests is found in state legislation." Duke, who was initially suspicious and reluctant to form a coalition with the liberal Republicans, began to appreciate Watterson's arguments and, by the time of the Democratic state convention, was his staunchest ally within the party.[32]

The Kentucky Democrats met as scheduled on June 20, 1872, in Frankfort. On the convention's agenda was the issue of whether the party would support the liberal Republican platform. As the convention progressed, Duke rose to speak and introduced a resolution to require the Kentucky delegation to vote for Greeley at the national convention. Duke's support of Greeley and the liberal platform created quite a commotion. Fearing the dissension that his resolution would cause, the Democratic leadership did not permit it to come to a vote. One Kentucky newspaper believed that, had it been voted on, it would have passed, causing a split in the party. However, Duke did manage to influence the convention managers so that most of the delegates chosen by the convention supported Greeley. Even with Watterson's and Duke's support, Greeley was unable to capture the imagination of Kentucky voters. He did carry Kentucky, but by only twelve thousand votes, and was soundly defeated nationally, carrying only six states.[33]

By 1873, Duke and his family were well established in Louisville, and two more children had been added to the fast-growing family. Both were boys, Calvin, born in 1869, and Henry, born two years to the month later. Duke continued to practice law with A. E. Richards and work within the Democratic Party. When the city of Louisville prepared and issued an immigration pamphlet entitled "Kentucky and Louisville, Material Interests of State and City," Duke authored the first fifty pages. It was also during this period that he cultivated lifelong associations with some very interesting and talented men. Several of these men—for example, Horatio Bruce, who was to become chief counsel of the L&N Railroad,[34] and the future

Reuben Durrett, a Louisville lawyer and noted historian of the Ohio Valley, was a motivating factor in regenerating Duke's interest in writing Civil War history. (Courtesy the Filson Historical Society, Louisville.)

U.S. senator William Lindsay[35]—were to have a significant impact on the balance of Duke's professional life, while others, such as Reuben T. Durrett, helped him develop his other interests, particularly those in the literary field.

A particularly fruitful friendship developed between Duke and Colonel Reuben T. Durrett through their mutual love of history. Durrett, a lawyer and noted published historian, had perhaps the finest private library in Louisville, with over fifty thousand books, manuscripts, and pamphlets. Duke was to spend countless hours in the colonel's library discussing with him and others all facets of history and contemporary issues of interest. With Duke and Durrett in the vanguard, these meetings would evolve into what became known as the Filson Club, which survives today as the Filson Historical Society. Many of Duke's political philosophies were brought to maturity through his interactions with these gentlemen-scholars. And the relationships that he cultivated with them would lead to many important later connections.[36]

Duke, of course, made many other friends during the 1870s, all of whom could only have encouraged him to keep his hat in the political ring. His resignation from the state legislature hurt him politically, however, in the sense that others, such as James McCreary, had gained much more momentum and statewide political exposure during the years Duke struggled practicing law in Louisville. Duke was, however, a regular delegate to the state Democratic convention and continued to be active in party affairs at both the state and the local levels. With the Panic of 1873 and the resulting economic downturn, he found it was even more difficult to make a comfortable living for himself and his growing family. In 1875, he decided to run for commonwealth attorney of Jefferson County. If elected, he would receive a guaranteed salary and still be able to maintain his partnership with A. E. Richards.

16

Salmagundi

THE PANIC OF 1873 caused a significant amount of personal financial stress throughout Kentucky, with the farmers in the western part of the state suffering the most from the economic downturn. When the Panic struck, tobacco prices fell to an all-time low, resulting in the devaluation of farmland and hundreds of mortgage foreclosures. The severe economic consequences soon spread to the industrial and business sectors of Louisville, with the iron industry being particularly hard-hit. The layoffs that followed resulted in high levels of unemployment that continued for years, affecting other businesses, including Duke's struggling law practice.[1]

The Democratic Party, under the leadership of Governor Leslie, pledged to support the farmer. Before the Panic hit, Leslie had invested the state treasury in federal gold-bearing bonds, a move that had the unintended but fortuitous effect of stimulating the national economy and, at the same time, strengthening Kentucky's economic base during these hard times. Leslie, however, was soon to leave office, and Duke's wartime and legislative associate James McCreary of Madison County was nominated as the Democrats' candidate for governor, running on a platform that called for, among other things, internal economic development.[2]

In the spring of 1875, looking for a way to supplement the income derived from his law practice, Duke entered the race for commonwealth attorney of Jefferson County. Two other candidates, George William Caruth and Nat Robertson, were running against him. Duke received considerable support from the *Louisville Courier-Journal,* which ran articles linking his conduct during the war to the integrity expected of the office to which he aspired. The congenial Duke—who was so well liked by Bluegrass horse breeders that one winning racehorse had been named "Gen'l Duke" in his honor—was also asked by the *Courier-Journal* to attend and report on a stake race organized to inaugurate a new racetrack. Meriwether Lewis Clark Jr., grandson of the famed William Clark, had leased a tract of land on the south side of Louisville from his uncles John and Henry Churchill and, with the help of other investors, had built the racetrack, hoping to lure the Bluegrass breeders and their wallets to town. It is unlikely that Duke or anyone else realized the significance of that particular race—which would become known as the first Kentucky Derby—but the exposure certainly did no harm to his election chances.[3]

In August 1875, both Duke and McCreary won their respective elections. Duke was to serve as commonwealth attorney for five years. During his tenure in office, the discontent of the state's agrarian sector continued to grow. The farmers directed their anger mostly at the railroads' unregulated freight rates, which they viewed as onerous. But they were also critical of the Democratic Party. The tobacco farmers of western Kentucky, for example, had come to see party leaders as having sold out to the railroads and the former governor, Leslie, in particular as a "special interest man."[4]

Setting aside the discontent of the Kentucky farmers, the Democratic Party faithful were very confident during the summer of 1876 and sensed victory in the upcoming presidential election. The Panic of 1873 and the Horace Greeley fiasco were believed to have substantially weakened the Republican Party and hurt its chances in November.[5] And Green Clay Smith, the Prohibition Party's nominee for president—and, coincidentally, Duke's brother-in-law—would clearly have little, if any, impact on the race.

Samuel Tilden, the Democrats' presidential candidate, easily bested his opponent, Rutherford B. Hayes, in Kentucky and appeared to have won the national election. The Republicans immediately contested the results, embittering partisan Democrats such as Watterson and Duke. Watterson began writing irate editorials, alleging fraud on the part of the Republicans, and threatening to raise a force of 100,000 men to march on Washington and claim the White House for Tilden. This type of writing easily stoked the fires of agitation in a state where old animosities against the radical Republicans still smoldered.[6]

After the election, Watterson agreed to finish out E. Y. Parsons's term in the U.S. House of Representatives, Parsons having died on July 8, 1876. Now perfectly situated in the middle of the controversy, he wrote even more inflammatory editorials, which he wired back to Louisville for publication in the *Courier-Journal.* Watterson was, however, largely preaching to the choir, Kentucky Democrats, at least, being thoroughly convinced that the Republicans were trying to steal the election. It seems likely, therefore, that his editorials—which, while dramatic, generally counseled peace—were directed at the twenty-five hundred delegates planning to attend the state Democratic convention scheduled for January 18–19, 1877, in Louisville.[7]

At the start of the convention, an unmistakable atmosphere of anger and hostility toward the Republicans permeated the hall. Responding to calls from the floor, Duke rose and gave a short but incendiary speech, according to the *Louisville*

Henry Watterson's New Departure philosophy fit well with Duke's belief in sectional reconciliation and the use of Northern capital to help resuscitate the Southern economy. (Courtesy the Filson Historical Society, Louisville.)

Commercial stating: "[That] the convention had met for action and not for talk; that its purpose was to show the oppressor of the people that hands, which grasped the olive branch of peace could raise the gauntlet and wield the sword. That even war was preferable to peace and, when that peace must be gained by submission, that our love of liberty was deeper than our love for peace, and that the time, had come when the people must protect against the conduct of a drunken and disorderly president." Following up on this harsh statement, according to the *Courier-Journal,* he called for Governor McCreary to place the state militia on a war footing. After Duke had finished, the Louisville newspapers reported, the chairman of the Committee on Resolutions came forward and read several resolutions confirming the party's belief that Samuel Tilden should be placed "in the office to which the voice of the people has called him." The delegates also reiterated the cornerstone of their political beliefs, resolving: "We reaffirm our ancient faith in republican institutions, our devotion to the Union of the States, the doctrine that the federal government is strictly one of delegated powers and that each state has the right to regulate its own domestic concerns."[8]

When the political feuding ended and the dust finally settled, both parties bargained for an acceptable solution. The Democrats ended up casting the necessary votes in the Electoral College to confirm Hayes's election, and the Republicans agreed to withdraw all remaining federal troops stationed in the South by

April 1877. This compromise signaled the end of Reconstruction and the beginning of a century of Democratic political hegemony in the South.[9]

The end of Reconstruction, however, did little, if anything, to alleviate the economic hard times in the South, hard times that were afflicting all Americans. Southerners, of course, found it easy to blame their troubles on either Reconstruction or, as Henry Watterson had been doing for years, Republican policies in general and high tariffs in particular. Whatever the cause, it was the workers and farmers who inevitably bore the brunt of the downturn and suffered more than any other segment of society.[10]

The year 1877 marked the beginning of significant unrest among the rank and file of America's workforce, and the country began to witness organized labor strikes, particularly in the coalfields and the textile mills of the Northeast. These strikes were, however, not nearly as dangerous to the economy as the railroad strikes, which began on the Baltimore and Ohio in July 1877. The railroad strikes moved west through the country and, by the end of the month, had reached Louisville. For months prior to the strikes, economic woes had intensified in Louisville. It was estimated that 20 percent of the labor force was unemployed and that another 40 percent worked only part-time. In order to reduce expenses, railroad management decided to cut back by either reducing employees' wages or merely laying off workers until the economy improved. All the railroads, including the Louisville and Nashville (L&N), instituted these cuts.[11]

The *Courier-Journal,* a staunch supporter and advocate of the economic policies of the L&N, ran a series of articles attempting to placate the workers. According to Allan Pinkerton, the founder of the famous detective agency, beginning with its July 23 issue, the newspaper "eloquently and earnestly exhorted to the workers of Louisville to remain quiet" during the eastern labor disturbances.[12] A committee of railworkers from the financially troubled Louisville Short Line was formed and met in court with Duke's close friend Judge H. W. Bruce, who rescinded their wage reduction. At least that is what the committee alleged. However, on July 24, the *Louisville Commercial* reported that Bruce denied knowing anything about the rescission order and objected to implications that he had issued it. The Short Line workers' action fueled the interest of the L&N employees, who called a meeting themselves for the same day.[12]

The next day, the *Commercial* reported that a committee of approximately forty men marched to the main offices of the L&N and presented their resolutions in what Allan Pinkerton called "a very respectful plea." The L&N gave the resolutions serious consideration, and a compromise was reached that was, apparently, acceptable to both management and labor. In another part of the city, a group of idle workmen led by an organizer from Cincinnati called "Buffalo Bill" began to make the rounds of various sewage plant projects to talk with the workers. It did not take long before most of the sewer construction workers, the majority of whom were African American, were convinced to strike for higher wages.[14]

Around noon on July 24, 1877, Mayor Jacob issued a proclamation blaming the trouble on outside agitators and asking the workmen to remain calm and not pay attention to these "worthless creatures who were unwilling to work themselves." He also pointed out that vagrants and tramps generally caused disturbances in other cities but that the poor workingman had to bear "the odium of the outbreak." That afternoon, a group of citizens, including Duke, met at the request of the mayor and the chief of police to help organize a defense against any possible uprising by the workers. Almost immediately, it was decided that Duke was the obvious candidate to command the "militia." Not only was he a respected veteran, but his position as county attorney also lent the appearance of legality to the expected police action.[15]

The mayor sent a dispatch to the governor requesting arms and ammunition for Duke's hastily assembled city militia. Duke had as his aides Sheriff Able and Neil S. Field, and among his captains were A. E. Richards, Duke's law partner, Bennett Young, W. O. Harris, Thomas Bullitt, Gabriel Wharton, and Thomas Speed. One of Duke's first orders was to send several hundred men to a small town outside Louisville to pick up the weapons and ammunition that Frankfort had sent. In the meantime, city hall was converted into an arsenal, and the chief of police ordered his policemen to rendezvous at both the central and the First Street stations. Duke and his cohorts had organized two regiments of infantry and one squadron of cavalry. As Allan Pinkerton noted: "General Duke and his staff of able officers, under the direction of the mayor made all needed arrangements to meet any emergency."[16]

Duke worked on organizing the city militia the entire day. Toward evening, a crowd, estimated at approximately two thousand people, gathered in front of the courthouse. Several agitators made inflammatory speeches, forcing the mayor, along with Duke and the chief of police, to make an appearance that was intended to temper the crowd's anger. However, there was so much commotion and noise that it was impossible for the mayor to make a coherent speech. Nevertheless, he stood his ground and pleaded with the crowd to disperse without causing any trouble and go to their homes. Few, if any, paid him any heed, and the more vocal elements of the crowd continually shouted him down.[17]

When the mayor finished, the principal agitators worked up the crowd with additional inflammatory comments and speeches. Approximately five hundred people decided to march to the L&N depot. The crowd liked the idea of heading for a symbolic target, but, as the marchers headed in the direction of the depot, their collective mentality degenerated, and they devolved into a mob. As the mob snaked its way down Jefferson Street, someone threw a rock through the window of the Home Sewing Machine Company. The breaking glass was a catalyst, and the crowd began to break streetlamps and windows all along the route.[18]

On reaching the L&N depot, the rioters used a pile of rocks and debris that they found across the street from the station to break every window in the structure. Just as the last windows were being broken, a contingent of police and Duke's armed citizens arrived. The police immediately arrested three men who they claimed were the mob's leaders. Some of the rioters were then convinced to go home, but the more militant elements stayed in the streets and turned up Broadway, breaking more windows as they moved along.[19]

As the night wore on, the mob grew smaller and smaller as the police and Duke's armed militia captured or dispersed the troublemakers. It was down to approximately twenty-five diehards when a belligerent-looking line of police and Duke's militia brought its progress to an abrupt halt. Sensing indecision, the militia, employing Duke's aggressive tactics, charged. The crowd dispersed, individuals and small groups running in every direction down alleys and streets trying to avoid arrest.[20]

Duke and his militia continued to patrol the streets of Louisville for the next week. Pinkerton noted that the coming together of old rebels and Yankees as part of Duke's militia provided "a vast amount of amusement to the citizens of the city," but he also prophesied that the swift response of the citizen militia "will remain a perpetual warning to the turbulent lawless elements of Louisville." Pinkerton noted that Louisville seemed not to have received the full force of worker discontent and that the disturbances could have been worse had the city "not been so little affected by the increasing stringency of the times."[21]

The riots may have had little immediate effect, but, because they forcefully demonstrated the power of collective action, they weakened the railroads' position in the long run. The point that the potential for violence still existed was not lost on Duke, who wrote McCreary several days after the disturbance, proposing that the state equip a special police force under the control of the mayor and capable of responding rapidly to such emergencies. In his lengthy reply, McCreary advised his old commander that the law of Kentucky did not authorize him to arm an independent military organization. However, McCreary believed that an organization of soldiers or a citizen militia under state control was within the purview of the state constitution. Eventually, the city of Louisville formed a militia unit within the framework of the state constitution.[22]

As life in Louisville returned to normal, Duke continued to serve out his term as commonwealth attorney without complication or controversy. When time permitted, he participated in various veterans' activities, but he admitted that, for many years, he had not kept up as closely with the various war-related publications "as an ex-confederate perhaps ought to." Then, in 1878, Jefferson Davis began to gather the information he would need to write his memoirs. W. T. Walthall, who was assisting Davis in this endeavor, wrote Duke in March 1878 to solicit the Kentuckian's comments concerning the historical accuracy of a draft of an article that he, Walthall, had written, but not yet published, describing the events leading up to the capture of Davis by federal troops in 1865. Walthall's article was in response and generally took exception to an essay discussing the same events written by the commander of the Union cavalry that had captured Davis, Major General James H. Wilson. Duke's answer took immediate exception to representations made by Walthall that a council of war had not been held in Abbeville, South Carolina, and that the distribution of part of the Confederate treasury to the troops at the Savannah River had been a "bounty or an inducement" for them to continue the march with Davis. Duke defended the integrity of the cavalry and argued convincingly that the men were never demoralized. He also emphasized that it was his belief that Davis did not comprehend the tactical or strategic military situation until days later. The effect of Duke's response was to support the accuracy of several important points made by Wilson.[23]

Davis himself then wrote Duke, informing him that he had no recollection of the conference at Abbeville. After taking time to reconsider Walthall's draft, Duke responded with a carefully worded follow-up letter to Walthall. He began by advising Walthall that he had asked Major William Davis, who served on Breckinridge's staff at the time in question, to address the question as to whether the troops escorting Davis were demoralized when they learned the result of the Abbeville conference. Duke then addressed the real purpose behind his letter, advising Walthall that Davis had written him concerning the Abbeville conference. Duke felt it necessary that he explain to Walthall what he meant when he said that "Mr. Davis did not seem to realize the situation." It was his impression that Davis was so determined to continue the struggle that the opinions of those who disagreed with him were dismissed. Further: "I think the very ardor of his resolution prevented him from properly estimating the resources of his command." Finally, Duke warned Walthall: "I am very much opposed to any publication upon this subject by any other person, and prefer that you should, if you deem it proper, make any corrections, required." Obviously, Duke believed that his account of the events at Abbeville was the accurate one and that it was now up to either Walthall or Davis to use his information as their better judgment dictated. Ultimately, Davis's memoirs, which were published three years later, made no reference to Abbeville whatsoever. And, in 1886, Duke published "After the Fall of Richmond," which offered his own account of Abbeville.[24]

Perhaps the exchange with Walthall and Davis rekindled Duke's interest in the war and his enthusiasm for literary pursuits in general. Certainly, it was not long afterward that Duke published "The Confederate Career of Albert Sidney Johnston" in the *Papers* of the Southern Historical Society. Under the leadership of

Jubal A. Early, the Southern Historical Society had become the foremost proponent of the Lost Cause. Early was determined to create a written record of the war favorable to the South. This was Duke's first significant publication since *A History of Morgan's Cavalry.* The article, which by any standards must be seen as an entirely uncritical account of Johnston's military performance, was written to further glorify yet another Confederate icon. It also furthered the notion that, but for Johnston's death, the Confederacy would have been victorious at Shiloh:

Under Johnston's admirable tactical arrangement and supremely energetic conduct, the confusion into which the Federal army was thrown by the first onset was propagated and continued until he fell. . . . Johnston's death at the moment of victory had declared itself for him, the consequent suspension of the attack and partial withdrawal of the Confederate lines before Beauregard could "gather the reins of the battle," and the timely arrival of Buell that saved the army they commanded from destruction.

The article was replete with laurels, even for a Yankee general. Don Carlos Buell was described as "the only federal general in the west whom the Confederates feared when at the head of a comparatively small army." More intriguing, however, is Duke's writing style. Much as he does in the *History,* Duke romanticizes both the war and Southern honor. For example, the last paragraph of the article reads more like the epitaph for a medieval knight than a Confederate general: "The young knighthood of the South—sometimes mutinous under authority founded upon hollow and pretentious claims, but instinctively obedient to true leadership—admired him living and revere him dead."[25]

It is impossible to deny that Duke was well read, as so aptly pointed out by Isaac Handy. Duke's affinity for the classics and the romantic is made more than apparent in his writings. Such a florid style was not, of course, unusual for the time, and it helped bring home to Southern readers the honor and romance inherent in the notion of losing a war waged against impossible odds. In some respects, however, Duke's treatment of his subject is a bit heavy-handed even by the standards of the day. Nonetheless, Duke was clearly a talented writer, and many of his contemporaries felt that, had he focused on a literary career, he could have become an accomplished writer.[26]

Duke's interest in literature and writing inevitably led him to associate with those of similar interests. In January 1879, Duke and several friends, including William Davis, formed the Salmagundi Club. The word *salmagundi,* which means "a mixture, an assortment, or a potpourri," had been used by Washington Irving as the name of a periodical that he published in 1807–8. It made the perfect name for a club whose members were imbued with the literary and historical spirit for debate and discussion within the framework of a social atmosphere. The club eventually attracted other like-minded men such as John Castleman, Henry Watterson, and Richard W. Knott. It provided Duke the opportunity to extend his literary and political connections. Certainly, whether coincidentally or not, after the formation of the club, his literary and professional career became much more active.[27]

Of course, these literary and social pursuits took second place to Duke's political interests, which became more and more important to him as the years passed. By 1879, Duke was in the fourth year of his five-year term as commonwealth attorney. The forty-two-year-old Duke seems not to have been motivated at this time to seek a higher elected political office. His and Tommie's family had grown to seven children with the addition of Julia in 1875 and Frances Key in 1881, and, in the absence of a substantial independent source of income, he could not afford to abandon his professional career in search of a political office. Duke had also firmly established himself within the Democratic Party as somewhat of a moderate. He was no longer looked on as a traditional Bourbon Democrat, the element that continued to dominate state party politics. These were also the days of machine politics, and seldom were incumbent party candidates challenged within the party. This did not mean that Duke had no power or influence within the party. His position as an ex-Confederate general still carried immense clout, and he was a very popular figure within the state and throughout the South. His intellectual ability and his popularity made him a force to be reckoned with for quite a number of years.[28]

Because the Democrats dominated state politics, the intraparty struggle for the governorship was of vital importance. By the spring of 1879, the memories and effects of the Panic of 1873 and the Louisville labor unrest of 1877 were beginning to fade. Within this environment, a unique political figure began to rise to prominence outside the traditional framework of the Democratic Party. Dr. Luke Blackburn, a native Kentuckian and close friend of Duke's, announced his candidacy for the governorship.[29]

Duke recalled that many of Blackburn's close friends were amused by his leap into politics. Then, in the middle of the Democratic canvass, a yellow fever epidemic struck Hickman, a small town in southern Kentucky. Few, if any, were willing to risk their lives to assist the stricken community. Blackburn had, over the course of his career, including time spent as a surgeon in the Confederate army, risked his own life many times fighting for the lives of others. Characteristically, he abandoned his canvass to work among the sick in Hickman for two weeks. When he returned to the campaign, he had become known as the "Hero of Hickman," and opposition to his candidacy had all but disappeared.[30]

The Democratic convention opened in Louisville on May 1, 1879. When it was time for the delegates to elect the slate of candidates for the upcoming election, Duke walked to center stage and eloquently nominated Blackburn as the party's candidate for governor. The Democratic old guard was well aware that any Republican candidate stood little or no chance against the Hero of Hickman and supported Blackburn's nomination overwhelmingly. With a supporting cast of veteran candidates to rely on, all of whom had solid Confederate credentials, Blackburn spent most of the campaign at a resort in Crab Orchard Springs. The Democratic slate carried the state.[31]

The Blackburn administration undertook the first attempt at reform that Kentucky had seen in many years. The new governor was quick to point out that he intended to retire from political office after his term in Frankfort and that, consequently, it was his hope that he could count on the general assembly to pass significant reform legislation over the course of the next four years. With the advent of Blackburn's administration, Duke gained additional political clout, a factor that, when combined with a series of other political appointments and a major change in the corporate management of the L&N, was to position him to make a career change, leaving the law for something for which he was much better suited.[32]

The L&N was in 1880 in the seminal stages of a development and expansion period that would by 1884 place the railroad in a precarious financial position. Because, prior to 1879, the corporation's capital stock was owned largely by the city of Louisville itself as well as wealthy and prominent members of the community, the railroad had been basically a hometown industry that enjoyed local control. However, in 1879, the city of Louisville sold exactly half its L&N stock to outside parties, and the election that year of a new board of directors resulted in the adoption of an acquisition program that eventually doubled the mileage operated by the railroad. Such rapid expansion made it difficult to integrate the newly acquired companies within the system. In order for them to become functional and, more important, profitable, substantial capital expenditures on infrastructure would, the financial experts quickly determined, be required.[33]

An almost immediate result of the L&N expansion was the initiation of a rate war in the South. This might not have been a major problem for the L&N except that, owing to the lack of continuity in management—the railroad had had four different presidents between 1880 and 1884—it had no coherent business plan. Alarmed that it might be heading into serious financial trouble, the railroad in 1882 hired Milton Smith as third vice president and traffic manager; Smith became the L&N's president two years later. He had previously been employed by the railroad as general freight agent and, in that position, had developed a reputation for possessing a keen awareness of the L&N's operating characteristics. He therefore recognized that the cure for the railroad's financial malady was a strong management team, to take charge of the programs that he planned on introducing; a multitalented legal staff, to deal with evolving government regulatory practices; and a cabal of capable lobbyists, to control or at least curb the growth of regulatory legislation.[34]

Milton Smith, president of the Louisville and Nashville Railroad, effectively employed Duke's talents in controlling legislation that could overregulate his railroad. (Courtesy the Kentucky Historical Society.)

Prior to Smith's return to the L&N, the company's management had employed Horatio W. Bruce as its chief counsel, primarily to assist with the myriad of legal issues that accompanied the acquisition of the smaller railroads. The same year, 1880, that Bruce was employed by the L&N, Duke's tenure as commonwealth attorney for Jefferson County ended. With no further desire to run for political office, Duke had no real option left after leaving office but to continue the practice of law with A. E. Richards. Little did he realize, however, the impact that Governor Luke Blackburn's judicial reforms would have on his legal career. The general assembly enacted legislation creating the superior court, an intermediate court, consisting of a panel of three judges, among whom was included A. E. Richards. Richards's elevation meant the end of his partnership with Duke. Also that same year, Blackburn appointed D. H. Smith chairman of the state railroad commission.[35]

The contacts that Duke had with state government and particularly with the railroad commission were not lost on either Horatio Bruce or Milton Smith. It was fairly obvious to the politically astute railroad management that Basil Duke's ability to present an argument in a coherent, clear, and convincing manner would make him an impressive addition to the company's legal staff. However, even more important to the railroad was his potential to be a powerful and influential lobbyist. Also attractive was his background as a popular Confederate general. The railroad could best take advantage of its expansion into the heart of Dixie if it could identify itself with the Confederate tradition, which was still flourishing there, and having Duke on board would go a long way toward achieving that end. For all these reasons, Duke was offered in 1882 a position with the L&N, and he readily accepted. At the age of forty-five, Duke was entering, if not the most exciting, then certainly the most interesting part of his postwar career. Until the early years of the twentieth century, he and the L&N would be inseparable in the minds of many in government, industry, and, particularly, journalistic circles.[36]

The political atmosphere in Louisville was changing dramatically in the early 1880s, and, as a result, so was the position of the old "hometown" railroad. Since the city had disposed of half of its shares of L&N stock, it had become much more interested in attracting the competition to Louisville. Although the L&N's relative monopoly on the Southern markets had been broken by the construction of the Cincinnati Southern to Chattanooga in 1880, the railroad had still been able to control the freight coming into Louisville and the rates for taking it farther south. But Northern rail lines were now attempting to circumvent L&N control by acquiring track rights into the city. In fact, in 1882, the Chesapeake and Ohio, the L&N's main competitor, succeeded, acquiring the Short Line from Louisville investors. To complicate matters further, Paul Booker Reed was elected mayor of Louisville.[37]

Paul Booker Reed's mayoral campaign strategy focused on the city's large debt and the need to make Louisville solvent. Running without significant opposition, Reed won over most of the city's newspapers, which touted him as a reformer and a man who would run the city like a business. When he became mayor, Reed worked very closely with the city council, making significant strides in cutting fiscal expenses. The first hint that the new mayor intended to tackle what he visualized as significant impediments to competition erected by the L&N came when he vetoed an ordinance permitting the Jeffersonville, Madison and Indianapolis (JM&I) Railroad to re-lay its tracks between Thirteenth and Fourteenth Streets. The JM&I was a lessee of the strong Pennsylvania Railroad, which had made Louisville its southern terminus. Reed perceived the relocation of the tracks as an attempt by the L&N to control all north–south rail traffic through the city. The effect of the JM&I track relocation, Reed argued, would be to connect the L&N with the Pennsylvania. This hookup would allow the JM&I to control all rail traffic going north and the L&N to control all rail traffic going south. The city council ultimately sustained the mayor's veto.[38]

The following October, Reed took another step forward in his battle with the L&N when he sold the city's remaining ten thousand shares of the railroad's stock. The mayor had traveled to New York to negotiate the sale of the stock and, according to the newspapers, to search for a new stock investment, one that would generate more income for the city. The sale of the L&N stock had netted the city approximately $1 million, and Reed intended to use the money to purchase stock in the Louisville Southern. The president of the Louisville Southern was Bennett Young, a former Confederate soldier and one of Morgan's Raiders.[39]

Young had been with Duke on the Ohio Raid and, along with Morgan, had escaped the trap at Buffington only to be captured near Lisbon, Ohio. He spent the last year of the war participating in clandestine military operations, including the raid on St. Albans, Vermont, in 1864. Like Duke a lawyer, Young returned to Louisville after the war to practice law. At the same time that Young became involved with the Louisville Southern, he was also involved in the building of a railroad bridge over the Ohio River on the west side of Louisville. The bridge was scheduled for completion in 1886, and its use by the Louisville Southern was a direct challenge to the L&N's tight grip on access to Nashville and points south.[40]

When Reed returned to Louisville, he soon discovered that Duke and the L&N were prepared to prevent him from acquiring the stock of the Louisville Southern. The L&N had acquired a newspaper, the *Louisville Evening Post,* and made Duke the railroad editor. Although the move was fairly transparent, Duke's pen became an effective advocate for the L&N's position on political and economic issues. Duke did not directly attack the Louisville Southern but instead argued that Reed was attempting to manipulate the city council's ordinance procedure to gain approval for the acquisition of Louisville Southern stock. Typically, an ordinance was introduced at a meeting of the city council, and then, after a two-week waiting period, the council voted on its acceptance or rejection. Duke argued that Reed planned to circumvent the procedure and pass the ordinance the evening it was introduced. In tandem with Duke's newspaper editorials, the L&N was able to persuade a group of its supporters to file an action requesting the court to enjoin the city from expending the funds to honor its Louisville Southern stock subscription. On November 2, 1885, the local court granted a permanent injunction prohibiting the city from expending said funds. Bennett Young was forced to seek his funding elsewhere.[41]

One of Duke's responsibilities in his new position with the L&N was to draft position papers addressing topics such as government and rate regulation. He would then present the papers to politically helpful audiences or at conferences. This assignment combined Duke's best talents as a writer and speaker. The railroad realized that Duke was an exceptional writer, always presenting his argument in a clear and persuasive manner. His first practical experience came with a paper on government regulation of railroads that he presented at Central Kentucky University in Richmond on December 16, 1884. The paper presented a coherent, understandable, and well-reasoned thesis arguing for deregulation and stressed, convincingly, that the railroads were far more effective when government intervention was at a minimum. His next major paper addressed the L&N's position on transportation tariffs, with emphasis on distinguishing the factors that determined short- and long-haul rates.[42]

In 1887, at the state industrial and commercial conference, Duke presented a paper entitled "The Commercial and the Railroad Development of Kentucky." This paper was almost entirely historical in nature and far less politically charged than the earlier two. However, Duke could not refrain from addressing the state's general legislative policy regarding railroad construction and regulation. He praised the state for not providing funding for railroad construction. State funding for construction would, of course, have significantly benefited smaller railroads, any of which could have set itself up as a competitor of the L&N. Duke also summarized the railroad legislation in Kentucky "as conservative, and not unfriendly to the interest and growth of the corporations." Duke made every effort during these years to emphasize the state's historic reluctance to regulate business interests.[43]

To some observers, Duke's papers and pamphlets may appear to be tedious and mundane, but they were essential to the railroad in that they encouraged favorable public opinion, which was often badly needed. They were also helpful in the effort to persuade the government that the railroads were capable of managing their own affairs. Of the three discussed here, the last reflected Duke's ability to present a historical argument, in this case one that shrewdly stressed state government's friendly attitude toward railroad regulation. Yet the first and second are far more creative, being similar to papers and briefs that modern lawyers and government officials prepare in support of their oral arguments. In the end, Duke's arguments were always finely tuned and carefully grounded by the citation of respected authorities, both European and American.[44]

17

A Distinctively Southern Magazine

ALMOST CONTEMPORANEOUS WITH the beginning of Duke's new career with the railroad was the beginning of his involvement with a new magazine called the *Southern Bivouac.* The *Southern Bivouac*'s antecedents can be traced back to the evening of February 7, 1879, when Duke and forty-seven other ex-Confederates formed the Kentucky chapter of the Southern Historical Society. The chapter elected Duke its first president and began to hold regular meetings on the third Tuesday of each month. It soon became customary to solicit guest speakers for the monthly meetings, but, by 1882, so many people wanted to present a paper or a speech to the chapter that it was impossible for all to be heard at the monthly meetings. This abundance of material prompted the idea that the chapter publish a journal in order to accommodate all proffered papers. The magazine was launched in August 1882, with the first issue scheduled for the following month. The *Southern Bivouac* soon expanded its range to include all kinds of articles of interest to the Confederate veteran. During the first year of the magazine's existence, almost 80 percent of its articles concerned the western theater of the Civil War, with an emphasis on the common soldier.[1]

The magazine saw subscriptions start to increase with regularity soon after its inaugural issue. Its initial success may be attributable to its ability to attract readers north of the Ohio River, which the editors did by purposefully presenting a more conciliatory tone and engaging in less Yankee bashing than did other Southern publications. This did not mean that the magazine intended to abandon its Southern and Confederate roots. The editors continuously supported the Confederate soldier in his attempts to maintain the Southern tradition and even urged their readers not to sacrifice their regional identity for Yankee dollars. By the 1880s, Southern historians had embraced the notion of the Lost Cause with an almost religious fervor, and the *Southern Bivouac,* much like the *Southern Historical Society Papers,* contributed to this molding of the Confederate image. The notion of the Lost Cause resonates throughout the very first issue of the *Southern Bivouac,* where we find articles about Vicksburg and Appomattox stressing the overwhelming and growing strength of the federal army against which the hopelessly outmatched Confederates nonetheless continued to fight until there was no recourse but surrender.[2]

During the first thirty-four months of the magazine's existence, Duke limited his involvement, serving only as a contributing writer. His debut in the *Southern Bivouac* came with "The Battle of Hartsville," which appeared in the October 1883 second issue. The article is written in the same style as *A History of Morgan's Cavalry* and grants Morgan similar accolades. However, in the form of a preamble to his depiction of the battle, Duke wrote of the Confederate retreat from Kentucky in the fall of 1862 in the best tradition of the Lost Cause, identifying it as the real turning point in the war:

> The war then became simply a comparison of national resources. The Northern people then learned their real strength. They found that bounties and the draft, and the black freedman, and importations from all the recruiting markets of the world would keep their armies full; and finding that success was but a matter of time, nothing could have made them again dependent. I have always believed that from this retreat, and not from Gettysburg, dates our death-stroke. All subsequent effort was but the dying agony of a grand cause and gallant people.[3]

It was not until over a year later that Duke followed the Hartsville article with a two-part series on the Battle of Shiloh. Measured by contemporary historiographic standards, "The Battle of Shiloh" can be easily criticized for its lack of detail. It must be remembered, however, that Duke was writing just as *The War of the Rebellion,* a compilation of the official records of both sides, had begun to appear. Duke's sketch of the battle had originally been published, as Duke wrote, some time before in the *Cincinnati Gazette* and had also been sent to Confederate General Marcus Wright, who was collecting information to be used in compiling the official records. Included with Duke's transmittal letter to Wright was a hand-drawn map of the battle. The two parts of the article appeared in December 1883 and January 1884 and, consistent with Duke's 1878 article on Albert Sidney Johnston, were highly complimentary of the general's role in the battle. In fact, Duke once again concluded: "Had General Johnston lived long enough to gather his army together again for one more vigorous and sustained assault . . . that gallant federal array must have surrendered, or have been driven into the river surging in their rear."[4]

At the end of the magazine's first year, the society's editorial committee abdicated its responsibility in favor of William M. Marriner and William N. McDonald. Marriner withdrew as editor after only two months and was replaced by Edward McDonald. Within a year, the McDonalds had increased the number of subscribers to approximately three thousand. However, by January 1885, the magazine be-

Richard W. Knott introduced Basil Duke to the editorial side of publishing. Their coeditorship of the *Southern Bivouac* sparked Duke's interest in literary magazines. (Courtesy the Filson Historical Society, Louisville.)

gan to experience financial difficulties, and, in order to make ends meet, the editors resorted to increasing the subscription rate, a move that they justified by touting the magazine as "the only Confederate soldier's magazine published in United States." Considering the existence of the *Southern Historical Society Papers,* this statement may not have been thoroughly thought through before it was published. In May 1885, B. F. Avery and Sons, publishers of *Home and Farm,* bought the magazine and its unresolved problems. They, in turn, passed on the management and editorial responsibilities to Richard W. Knott and Duke.[5] The thirty-seven-year-old Knott, the manager of *Home and Farm,* had been in the publishing and newspaper business in Louisville his entire adult life.[6]

With the hope of appealing to a more diverse audience, Duke and Knott immediately changed the direction of the *Southern Bivouac* by altering its contents to reflect a literary style exemplifying Southern culture. The name of the publication was also changed, and the magazine officially became *The Southern Bivouac: A Monthly Literary and Historical Magazine.* This title was intended to announce the cultural turn taken by the magazine. The new regime's first issue appeared in June 1885. In it, Duke and Knott explained to their readers that, although special attention would still be given to papers written about the Civil War, their goal was to make their publication "a distinctively Southern magazine." It was their intention to "appeal to the lovers of good literature everywhere" and to present the various "aspects of Southern life, thought, action, with Southern History and scenery, with Southern traditions and prejudices, in accordance with the accepted rules of art."[7]

The changes made to the magazine were impressive, and critics have concluded that, as a result of the new format, the *Southern Bivouac* improved considerably. Perhaps the Civil War veteran or the military history enthusiast was disappointed in the reduction of war-related material. But, overall, the change in direction must have appealed to the magazine's readers because the number of subscriptions rose dramatically, to approximately seventy-five hundred by the end of 1885.[8]

As part of the change, the *Bivouac*'s editorials took a more political tack, most likely at the instigation of Knott, who was fundamentally a newspaperman. But there is no question that Duke participated in their writing. The magazine's editorials touched on a variety of relevant topics, including reconciliation with the North, which it supported. Duke and Knott tempered the magazine's New Departure philosophy, however, in order not to alienate their Southern readers, who had a strong bias against improving the African American's political position in the "New South." An editorial discussing "the status of the Negro in the South" is a good example of the racism prevailing in the Upper South at the time, a piece that was by no means viewed as expressing improper sentiments when first published. It argued that the North misunderstood the societal relationship that existed in the South between "whites and Negroes." In support of this thesis, the editors took great pains to disparage the character of the "Southern Negro." They candidly concluded that what was really at stake was the question of "white rule or Negro rule." Although the Fifteenth Amendment had already answered this question in the most democratic fashion possible, we see here a demonstration of just how flagrantly it was disregarded and how, according to C. Vann Woodward, "the old doubts and skepticism of the North returned, the doubts that had kept the Negro disfranchised in the North after freedman's suffrage had been imposed upon the South."[9]

The *Southern Bivouac*'s support of reconciliation ran afoul of the unreconstructed old rebels and, most particularly, Jubal Early. Early was critical of the magazine and wrote Duke, complaining about some of its articles. The last thing Duke wanted to do was argue with Early. In an obvious attempt to handle the situation with tact, Duke maintained a congenial attitude, writing back in a friendly manner defending his magazine's articles and even asking Early to contribute something himself. Early never wrote an article for the magazine, but, evidently, Duke's letter satisfied the general, ending the controversy.[10]

Duke wrote several more articles for the *Southern Bivouac,* including "Bragg's Campaign in Kentucky, 1862" and "After the Fall of Richmond." The latter was later incorporated in *Battles and Leaders of the Civil War* under the title "Last Days of the Confederacy." Perhaps the most interesting and controversial article involving Duke was one, not by him, but rather by Thomas H. Hines. In 1882, Hines began to consider writing on the Northwest Conspiracy. The Northwest Conspiracy was the name given to a covert plan to free hundreds of Confederate prisoners of war being held in several of the states located in the old Northwest Territory. After his escape from the Ohio State Penitentiary, Hines returned to Richmond and was detailed for special service in Canada coordinating the escape plan. He met with several war-weary Northern leaders there who were members of a pro-Southern movement located in the Midwest. These people made remarkable claims to Hines of there being literally thousands of followers who, under the proper circumstances, were willing to rally and support any plan to free Confederate prisoners. Although skeptical, Hines enlisted their aid for his venture.[11]

Hines also met up with several escaped and unemployed Confederates who were alumni of Morgan's cavalry. Many of these Confederates, as well as others living in Canada, were bored and looking for some action, making it very easy for Hines to enlist their services. He planned to assemble his forces and lead simultaneous attacks against Camp Douglas, Rock Island, Camp Morton, and Camp Chase. When the time approached and Hines and his men were completing their preparations, the Copperheads (usually antiwar Northern Democrats) pleaded for more time to prepare. The Northerners wanted to delay the attack until the last week of August 1864, when the Democratic Party was scheduled to have its national convention in Chicago. They argued that at least fifty thousand Copperheads would be flocking to the convention and that these people could be recruited to help overthrow the state governments of Illinois and Indiana. Hines, once again, was very skeptical of these claims but did agree to the delay.[12]

As Hines waited, John Castleman joined him, and the two decided to share responsibility for the command of the operation. They had approximately seventy-five of their own men available for the attack on Camp Douglas. They ordered these men to travel to Chicago in pairs, and, by August 27, all had arrived. The escape was planned for August 29, but that date passed without any action taken. As Hines had suspected, the Copperheads equivocated once more and were unable to deliver the promised assistance. Finally, after Hines kept demanding a firm commitment, the Copperheads promised an uprising, but this time it was contingent on a Confederate invasion of Missouri and Kentucky, at this stage of the war a highly unlikely event. Hines now realized that his Northern allies completely lacked credibility, leaving him no option but to abort the operation.[13]

The Northwest operation was an extraordinary adventure for its time. And many of the participants were still alive in the early 1880s, including the principal Copperhead activists. Concerned about the potential political implications for the Northern participants, Hines sent his papers and notes to John Castleman, seeking his opinion as to whether the article should be written. Castleman was in favor of going ahead but felt that it might be prudent to get the approval of Jefferson Davis before the article was actually published. As far as most ex-Confederates were concerned, Davis was still the president of the Confederacy, and Hines and Castleman did not want to reveal any politically sensitive material without his approval. In 1884, Hines wrote Davis at his home in Mississippi, requesting his approval. Davis never responded, a fact that Hines interpreted as tacit approval.[14]

Hines discussed his plans with Duke, who immediately recognized that the article would be something out of the ordinary and became anxious that it be submitted for publication as soon as possible. Hines agreed and, shortly thereafter, submitted a manuscript for Duke's review. In the meantime, Duke began to promote the forthcoming article, releasing an Associated Press dispatch as well as printing an enthusiastic announcement in the *Southern Bivouac.* When Manly Tello, an editor for the *Cleveland Catholic Adviser* who had been in Canada with Hines and had intimate knowledge of his covert activities, read the Associated Press dispatch, he took umbrage and immediately wrote Jefferson Davis: "I take it for granted you have noticed . . . the Louisville Southern Bivouac, conducted by Gen. Basil W. Duke, announcing the immediate publication of the Confederate affairs in Canada. . . . I not only fail to see the benefit derived from these disclosures to which the authors, Hines and Castleman, apparently seek to give quasi-official Confederate stamp, but I believe them to be a breach of Confederate faith."[15]

Davis had been aware of the *Southern Bivouac* for quite some time and had even received a letter from Duke soliciting an article from him concerning the "political status and temper of the South just previous to the war." Tello's letter, however, gained Davis's attention, and he immediately responded, concurring with the Ohio editor's opinion: "In taking the hazards they encountered, they, of course relied upon the good faith of the Confederates with whom they held intercourse, and I do not think there is any higher obligation upon our people than to shield those gallant sympathizers as best they may from harm." The same day Davis wrote Tello, he also wrote a strong letter to Duke, marking it as strictly personal, attempting to dissuade him from publishing the Hines-Castleman article. Unwilling to forgo such a sensational publishing opportunity, Duke responded to Davis, defending Hines and Castleman, and emphasizing that it was not their intention to release the names of any individual "not now known or accused of participation in the conspiracy." He further assured Davis that it was their intention to write a very general, but historically accurate, summary of the events so as to implicate no one. Then, in an effort to convince Davis that the strictest confidentiality would be observed, Duke somewhat self-servingly stressed that Hines was convinced that the *Southern Bivouac* was the best venue for the article "because he could supervise the work" and prevent any unauthorized leaks. Finally, Duke pragmatically pointed out that his failure to publish the article after the magazine's announcement might be interpreted as an acknowledgment that it "was too horrible to see the light."

Two weeks later, Duke again wrote Davis, this time enclosing a clipping from an Ohio newspaper that had printed Davis's letter to Tello. It was obviously Duke's intention to appeal to Davis's sense of honor by implying, not only that Tello's intervention was little more than a clever attempt to create a controversy of which his newspaper could take advantage, but also that the publication by Tello of his and Davis's private correspondence was a breach of confidentiality.[16]

Not wanting to lose his advantage, Duke continued to discuss the matter with Hines and finally counseled him to write Davis himself, explaining that he had written previously requesting a meeting with the president to discuss this matter but had never received a reply. The rest of Hines's letter to Davis was very similar in content and tone to what Duke had written, with an emphasis on removing any aura of "bad faith on his part": "I would not consent to any publication that could injure the living or asperse the memory of the dead, nor would I give my sanction to any publication that could be construed as in 'bad faith' to such person as gave to the undertaking their sympathy and aid. When the papers bearing upon these matters were submitted by me to the editor of the Bivouac it was with the injunction and upon the condition that the publication should be brought within the limits indicated. It was left to the discretion of the editor to determine what came within the limits and I am satisfied that it safely conforms to the judgment of General Duke who will supervise the matter."[17]

Varina Davis responded almost immediately on behalf of her husband. She wrote Hines that both she and Davis were shocked that his request for a meeting had not been answered by a hearty invitation, that they did not recall his letter but that it could have been lost in the mass of mail received by Davis, and that they would be happy to welcome Hines in their home at any time. No mention was made of the controversial article. And the letter ended the correspondence.[18]

It is fairly obvious that Duke, Hines, and Castleman discussed their dilemma and, ultimately, acquiesced to Davis's request that none of the names of the Northern conspirators be revealed. In December 1886, the first of four prosaic articles concerning the Northwest Conspiracy was published in the *Southern Bivouac.* The authors were immediately taken to task by Emmett G. Logan in an editorial in the *Louisville Times* for presenting a sanitized version of the events. Logan pleaded with Hines and Castleman to tell the whole truth. The articles raised the interest of other Southerners as well, who similarly petitioned Hines and Castleman to tell all, but they never did. Hines became so disillusioned with the whole episode that he never again attempted to write about the conspiracy. In 1890, Castleman delivered a speech on the topic at a meeting of the Kentucky Confederate Veterans. Two days later, a petition, signed by thirty Confederates, with Duke's name heading the list, urged Castleman once more to write the complete story. Castleman ignored the petition, and, when he did write his memoirs many years later, the discussion of his and Hines's Chicago escapade was discreet.[19]

One interesting side note to the Hines-Davis episode is that, when Hines rode with Morgan, he was repeatedly sent on missions that were apparently kept secret from the other officers, including, some have speculated, even Duke. Because of this, or because of Hines's intimacy with Morgan, a postwar legend developed that he and Duke disliked each other. This legend, however, is easily dispelled by the friendly postwar correspondence and associations that the two men kept up.[20]

The *Southern Bivouac*'s popularity continued to grow, and, by 1887, the magazine's circulation had climbed to approximately fifteen thousand. However, Knott felt that the magazine needed to attract another ten thousand subscribers before it could be considered profitable. Consequently, readers of the May 1887 issue were informed that the magazine had been purchased by the Century Company and that this would be its final issue. The Century Company would eventually mine the *Southern Bivouac* for material to include in its four-volume *Battles and Leaders of the Civil War,* a military history of the war edited by Robert Underwood Johnson and Clarence Clough Buel that made its debut in the fall of 1887. But what of the grand designs so eloquently presented by Duke and Knott two years before? It was the editors' opinion that the "work of making a distinct literature of the South . . . [would] not cease" with the *Bivouac* and that Southern literature "[would] find its own channel of expression as surely as the rivers find their way to the sea." They wanted to consider their final editorial, not an epitaph, but rather "a prediction of continued advancement."[21]

During the *Southern Bivouac*'s five-year run, several other of Duke's close friends besides Thomas H. Hines, including A. E. Richards, Thomas W. Bullitt, George M. Davie, and William Davis, contributed articles to the magazine, as did the authors John Esten Cooke and Robert Burns Wilson. Alfred, Lord Tennyson's "Locksley Hall Sixty Years After" was published with the author's permission. Colonel Reuben T. Durrett, another of Duke's close friends and one of the most knowledgeable men in the country when it came to the history of the Ohio Valley, also wrote for the magazine. More important, however, Durrett had, as we have seen, perhaps the finest private library in Louisville, which he made available to researchers from all over the country, including Duke. But for that library, Duke might never have met Theodore Roosevelt and developed the lifelong friendship that was to have major political significance in the years to come.[22]

Roosevelt had returned from the West so impressed with that region of the country that he was inspired to write *The Winning of the West* (1889–96). While working on the book, he learned of Reuben Durrett's library and came to Louisville, eager to use its resources. Roosevelt worked for weeks in the colonel's library,

Reuben Durrett's library, where Theodore Roosevelt conducted research for *The Winning of the West,* was the focal point of historical meetings in Louisville. These meetings evolved into the Filson Club (now the Filson Historical Society), of which Duke was one of the ten original members. (Courtesy the Filson Historical Society, Louisville.)

during which time he and Durrett had many conversations. It was during one of these conversations that Durrett learned that Roosevelt had an interest in Morgan's Ohio Raid and in his career in general. When Roosevelt learned that Duke was a friend of Durrett's, he asked if an interview could be arranged. It was then decided that Roosevelt would be the speaker at the next Filson Club meeting, where he would have the opportunity to meet Duke. The meeting most likely took place during the winter or early spring of 1888. In those days, the Filson Club met on the first Monday of the month in Durrett's library. Women generally attended the meetings but sat separately from the men on the south side of the library. When the meeting began, Durrett introduced Roosevelt and announced that his intention was to interview General Duke, who was prepared to answer questions. Roosevelt stood up and began to tell the club about his book, speaking unabated for over an hour. He never did interview Duke, despite the fact that Duke rose several times in anticipation of the promised exchange. At nine o'clock in the evening, the club, as usual, voted on whether to permit the speaker to continue and use time normally set aside for cigars and cider. That night, the cider had been poured, and the members had no intention of letting it go stale.[23]

Roosevelt and Duke never did engage in a public exchange. But they did begin a private correspondence, which was initiated when Roosevelt sent Duke a copy of his *Life of Thomas Hart Benton* (1887). Duke took his time reading the book before writing back to Roosevelt. The letter that he eventually sent is quite interesting, particularly the comments on Roosevelt's characterization of Southern and Western men as good fighters. Having commanded such men during the war, Duke was able to offer the opinion that it was, not just an outdoor life per se that made them good soldiers, as Roosevelt had suggested, but the early and constant exposure to violence and bloodshed that went along with that outdoor life. Duke was also of the opinion that "the 'nonresistance' idea" put forth by Roosevelt in his book "may be carried too far": "While a citizen shouldn't be a bully or desperado, it is well that he lets it be known that he's a bad man to project with."[24]

The remarks made and the conclusions drawn by Duke in his letter to Roosevelt were indicative of his own fearless character. Even at the age of fifty-one, Duke was not a man to be trifled with, nor was he easily frightened. One instance of his bravery is legendary. (Whether it is true is another question.) One night Duke awoke to find a burglar in his bedroom, pistol drawn. After a few tense moments, he was able to sit the man down on the edge of the bed and argue with him about the error of his ways. Duke soon won him over and convinced him to leave the room. As soon as the man went into the next room, Duke jumped up and locked the door, forgetting that his wife slept in that room. Tommie in turn confronted the burglar, who then became so totally demoralized that he jumped out the window, never to be seen by the Dukes again.[25]

Duke's experience with Knott and the *Southern Bivouac* had, unfortunately, engendered in him a fondness for the magazine business. When, in 1893, the *Southern Magazine* approached him about becoming its editor, Duke sensed the opportunity to fully realize his earlier literary objectives for the *Southern Bivouac.* The *Southern Magazine* appeared to be positioned to realize Duke and Knott's prediction that Southern literature would "find its own channel of expression."

The poet George Griffin Fetter had founded *Fetter's Southern Magazine* in the summer of 1892. In less than a year, Fetter had sold the periodical to Sam Stone Bush, who infused enough capital into the enterprise to make the publication an attractive one. When Duke took over the editorship of the *Southern Magazine,* it was an illustrated monthly that targeted Southern readers. Its content was not, however, restricted to matters of Southern interest. The magazine, which had developed a reputation as a high-quality publication, touted itself as a popular journal of literature, romance, and art, and a typical issue contained articles on current events (with foreign affairs a specialty), travelogues, fiction, and poetry, many with illustrations or photographs. As the magazine's editor, Duke was responsible for writing one or more editorials for each issue.[26]

A review of Duke's editorials, which articulately and intelligently addressed a variety of political and economic issues then current, provides insight into his evolving social, political, and even literary philosophy. Duke's worldview was, essentially, a Southern one, rooted in the antebellum past, and molded by the experience of war and its aftermath. There is every reason to believe that, in writing his editorials, Duke consciously catered to the interests, politics, and philosophical beliefs of his Southern audience. For alongside elements of Henry Watterson's New Departure economics, Luke Blackburn's reforms, and racial Southern conservatism can also be found original thought.

In the 1890s, political activists such as Eugene V. Debs were beginning to play an increasingly prominent role in American national politics. Whether those activists were Populists, Socialists, or labor organizers, they were disturbing to men like Duke. Immigrants and the urban poor were, Duke believed, generally more susceptible to their rhetoric than any other segment of society. Conservatives like Duke considered activists dangerous men who threatened the social and economic framework of the country.[27] Duke summarized his concerns in an untitled editorial that appeared in March 1894: "We naturally distrust the sincerity and disinterestedness of an apostle who goes about preaching the 'rights of labor' when we hear him counsel as a necessary feature of the system he wishes to establish, the violent seizure of the other people's property and a wholesale castigation of all who may accept employment and attempt to work without his permission."[28]

Duke distinguished the riot from the strike, tolerating the latter because it had been sanctioned by law. His tolerance was qualified, however, when the destruction of private property was involved; then a strike must be crushed without delay. To protect against such eventualities, Duke suggested: "Ample legislative provision must be made to restrain [strikers] from every feature of trespass and violence and to punish every act done in connection with them which inflicts public or private injury." The preservation of private property was of the utmost importance, not just to Duke, but to most middle- and upper-class Americans. In an August 1894 editorial, Duke stressed that a moderate amount of security could be achieved, and certainly Mr. Debs would be much less of a threat, if the army were increased by twenty-five thousand men.[29]

In September 1894, Duke addressed the unrest among the economically distressed and the unemployed, which he viewed as being fueled by a school of "writers who persistently represent all the poverty which is scourging mankind, and all the dire distress and degradation poverty entails, as more the fault than the misfortune of society." What concerned Duke was that these writers were suggesting "schemes for social amelioration to be enforced by legislation." The schemes "to have government furnish employment for the unemployed," the "propositions for compulsory arbitration and statutory provision for compulsory insurance of employees," disturbed Duke, just as they did most middle-class Americans. The solution to "questions of a very difficult and perplexing character," Duke argued, was, not government intervention, but education. "A sound practical system of education" to enable the "masses to discern what is, and what is not the fit subject of legislative experiment"—this is what Duke envisioned. Of course, in a general sense Duke was right; education was the key. But he had misjudged the root causc of unemployment, which was due, not to "industry and speculative enterprises," but to the radical transformation in American society then under way. As labor unrest subsided, so did the public debate—at least until the 1896 election, in which Duke played a prominent role.[30]

Despite his social conservatism, Duke recognized and understood the need for political reform. In this he was probably influenced both by his association with Luke Blackburn and by his experience as a lobbyist. By the mid-1890s, political bossism was firmly in control of local politics in both Louisville and Lexington. Disgusted, Duke, in a progressive outburst, addressed municipal reform, candidly pointing out that the "desire to pervert government functions to private ends and individual betterment is the bottom fact and ruling factor in this [local] as in the larger field of national politics." Advocating the eradication of bossism, Duke was sensible enough to concede that society was likely to do little at the present time to change matters.[31]

When it came to matters literary, Duke was equally unafraid to speak his mind. In the editorial "Hungry Little Greeks," for example, he was critical of Southern writers who overemphasized Southern dialect or based their characters on negative Southern stereotypes. In particular, he was angered by the image that had developed over the years of the "cracker," that is, the Southern male as violent, whiskey drinking, tobacco chewing, and illiterate, an image unfortunately reinforced by the notoriety of the violent Hatfield and McCoy feud. The perpetuation of such stereotypes was, he felt, a true disservice to Southerners.[32]

In "Hungry Little Greeks," Duke specifically attacked the novelist George Washington Cable. In the 1870s, Cable, a native of Louisiana, had taken a progressive literary position about the recently emancipated slaves, infuriating most Southerners. Soon finding himself ostracized in the South, Cable moved to New York, where he continued his writing career. In the novel *John March, Southerner* (1894), he tackled Southerners' narrow view of emancipation and their attempts to thwart Reconstruction, exposing his contempt for the "brummagem of pseudo chivalry" exhibited by "sincere and brave men who nearly wrecked a nation to preserve a shabby barbaric institution."[33]

Outraged by what he viewed as a personal affront to all Confederate veterans, Duke reacted viscerally. He took particular offense at the manner in which Cable described the treatment of slaves. He argued, with some validity, that Cable's earlier works and "the exaggerated horrors of slavery" that they depicted provided Northern radicals with a constant source of ammunition for the continued prosecution of Reconstruction. While going on to admit that slavery had been a "sin," Duke held that "it was a sin of mankind and the South only bore the consequences because it maintained the last vestige of the institution." He strongly denied that the South should assume the entire responsibility because equally to blame were those Northerners who became wealthy trafficking in slaves.[34]

The mythology of the Lost Cause had become for Duke historical truth. He was, therefore, unable to recognize Cable's truer sense of history. Duke was not alone in this shortsightedness. Not many Southern historians of his day could see past the "truth" of the Lost Cause. In fact, as Woodward has argued: "The historian of the South should join the social novelist who accepts the values of the age and section which he writes." Proponents of the Lost Cause were attaching their own values to history, an intellectual transgression of the first order. But an argument can be made that it was a transgression that allowed the South to deal with the psychological consequences of defeat.[35]

Philosophical shortsightedness aside, however, the politically astute Duke recognized that, from the Southerner's point of view at least, there was no need to continually remind the North that it had won the war but lost the peace. And that was precisely what Cable was doing. Considered from this angle, his attack on Cable was consistent with his support of reconciliation. Certainly, he clearly understood the significance of the Confederate defeat and the need for the South to be rebuilt both emotionally and physically. He readily admitted in "Hungry Little Greeks" that "in light of all that has occurred . . . the triumph of God's purpose is to be seen in the preservation of the union." And he concluded the editorial with the following thoughtful and prophetic statement:

> If the people of the two sections are to live together as one people, in a union which was worth preserving and must never again be threatened, they must cultivate mutual esteem and respect. Neither should the motives of the past be impugned, nor the sentiment of the present be lightly suspected. It is better that each people listen reluctantly and give little heed, to the evil that is spoken of the other; and both should visit contempt and substantial punishment on the man who attempts to keep alive or reawaken any thrill of sectional animosity or distrust.[36]

The *Southern Magazine* went into bankruptcy in December 1894—one of the many victims of the 1893 stock market crash (see chapter 18)—and was ultimately sold and then published under the title of *Mid Continent Magazine.* Duke's involvement with the *Southern Magazine* lasted for a shorter period of time than his involvement with the *Southern Bivouac* but, because the magazine was very close to the literary prototype to which Duke and Knott had aspired, was probably more consequential to him. Sadly, this was Duke's last fling with magazine publishing. More pressing matters, including financial burdens, intervened. As for the *Mid Continent,* despite promising its readers that it would be "less sectional and less bitter and behind"—an obvious reference to Duke's editorials—it ceased publication in August 1895.[37]

During Duke's tenure at the helm of the *Southern Magazine,* he was able to convince such literary personalities as James Lane Allen, F. Hopkins Smith, Maurice Thompson, and a struggling young author named John Fox Jr., among others, to contribute regularly to the magazine. Duke was well acquainted with John Fox Jr., not only as a writer, but also as a suitor of his beautiful daughter Mary Currie. Perhaps owing to Tommie's reputation for "possessing high matrimonial ambitions for her children," Mary Currie and Mr. Fox would never marry. They would, however, maintain a friendship that lasted beyond her marriage to Wilbur Knox Mathews in 1898.[38]

18

Politics and Panic

When Milton Smith became the president of the Louisville and Nashville (L&N) Railroad, he was pessimistic about the future of railroads, believing that government was "ultimately going to suck out the lifeblood of the industry through regulation." Nonetheless, he had no intention of giving in without a fight. He decided, therefore, that it was essential for the railroads to enter the political arena in order "to protect their property from injurious, destructive and confiscatory legislation." Certainly this was a philosophy that, as the L&N's chief lobbyist, the socially conservative Duke found congenial.[1]

Certain aspects of Henry Watterson's New Departure democracy were still in evidence nearly twenty-five years after the war. Democrats continued to court the favor of business, including the railroads, and particularly the L&N. The playing field was, for Duke the lobbyist, vast. During the regular and special sessions of the general assembly, Duke traveled from Louisville to Frankfort, often working with legislators for days to ensure that the L&N received favorable treatment. In order to gain influence with the legislators, Duke did not rely solely on his own powers of persuasion. He employed the power of the press as well. And he also distributed free rail passes. The railroads' practice of issuing free passes in return for favor or influence was notorious. The high-minded saw it as little more than bribery. And the situation was little helped by the fact that politicians at all levels of government had come to see the free passes as their due. The practice could also be counterproductive, railroad officials being constantly hounded, not just by politicians, but by family, friends, friends of friends, and so on looking to be so honored.[2]

Every evening during the legislative session, politicians, lobbyists, businessmen, and reporters came together at the Capitol Hotel in Frankfort, where the best and the worst of behind-the-scenes, smoke-filled-room Kentucky politics took place. Tensions could run high. During one particularly troubled period, for example, a suitcase popped open as a party from Lexington was checking in, and twenty-five loaded revolvers fell out. Most of the time, however, the hotel was a congenial meeting place where Duke conducted a good deal of his work for the railroad.

During the 1890s, Basil Duke was at the apex of his professional, political, and literary careers. (Courtesy the Filson Historical Society, Louisville.)

Whether working with small groups or one-on-one with legislators or other lobbyists, he was able to bring into play his legendary powers of persuasion. His interpersonal skills were so well known that a popular book of the time stated that he controlled men "with the same ease and grace as a lady might show in wielding a fine ivory fan upon a state occasion."[3]

Each night, after supper and before the more serious business was attended to, Duke and such other personalities as Judge Thomas H. Hines, Senator William Lindsay, Stoddard Johnston, and Polk Johnson gathered in the lobby of the Capitol Hotel to smoke and talk. Although the faces might change from night to night, there was always someone who began to tell a story or a joke, and, in minutes, as the cigar smoke permeated the room, a crowd would gather to enjoy the wit and humor of the men sitting in the leather chairs. Most of these men, with Duke and J. Proctor Knott at the forefront, were well known for their ability to tell entertaining stories, the veracity of which was seldom, if ever, questioned. After all, as the old Southern saying goes, a good story is always better than the truth. These nightly gatherings were so much fun that, fifty years afterward, M. B. Morton, himself a legendary Southern reporter and editor, remembered them as the most enjoyable he had ever had the good fortune to be present at.[4]

Ever since the Panic of 1873, the L&N had, because of its size and power, become a visible target, many special-interest groups blaming it for their financial problems. For example, it was not difficult for farmers to trace their problems to high local freight rates, an argument Duke had tried to counter in the 1884 pamphlet "Transportation Tariffs." What no one realized at the time was that farmers' problems were, in fact, the result of the then-ongoing shift from an economy based largely on agriculture to one based largely on industrial production, a shift that would not be complete until the end of World War I. The railroad was simply a convenient target or, as Maury Klein, a historian of the L&N, put it, "more of a product than a cause of the complex interplay of forces spawned by the industrial revolution." Still, the railroad was also taken by some to be a sign of American strength and to represent the progress of the country as a whole. Many Americans had begun to see the country's economic and political institutions as one and the same. This led inevitably to the conclusion that what was bad for the economy was bad for the country. In Duke's particular case, regulation was bad for the L&N and must, therefore, be bad for the country as well.[5] And it was this alignment with the interests of business over those of agriculture that would bring to an end Duke's full support of the state Democratic Party.

Throughout the 1880s, American farmers believed that economic relief could be brought about by increasing the amount of currency in circulation. More currency tended to have an inflationary effect, permitting the farmers to pay off their fixed mortgages with cheaper money. Most of the western Kentucky farmers were debt ridden, their burden one that could be traced to the economic hard times of the mid-1870s. It was only a matter of time before they began to listen to politicians offering Populist reforms.[6]

The Populist reform that ultimately captured the farmers' attention was the remonetization of silver. In 1873, the Grant administration had demonetized silver, leaving gold as the sole standard of the nation's currency. Silver had been restored as legal tender in 1878, but government notes were still backed by gold alone. And the economic hard times of the late 1880s brought renewed demands to reinstitute the coinage of silver at the old ratio of 16:1, thus encouraging inflation. This type of reform could be legislated only in Washington, but the battle lines would first be drawn at the state level. In Kentucky, it all came down to whether the Democrats would support the free silver position. If they did not, there was a very good chance that the farmers would bolt the party.[7]

When the Kentucky Democrats met for their 1887 state convention, the Bourbons still appeared to be in control. For years, the party's platform adhered to the sound money, or gold standard, position, supported by such prominent party members as Duke and Watterson. Duke was also a strong supporter of Grover Cleveland, who believed the concept of free silver to be an unsound idea. As a staunch advocate of the gold standard as well as of the deregulation of the railroads, Duke found himself diametrically opposed to the position taken by the farmers in general and the developing Populist political philosophy rapidly emerging as a force to be reckoned with in Kentucky.[8]

The convention predictably nominated a slate of well-known and well-connected popular Bourbon candidates headed by ex-Confederate general Simon Bolivar Buckner, who was running for the governorship. Also predictably, the platform that it adopted supported Grover Cleveland and the gold standard while shying away from addressing matters of local concern. However, the Democratic Party was not the unified body that it had been in the past. For the first time since the Civil War, ex-Confederate status was not enough to secure a nomination, and, in some cases, it actually worked against candidates. The Republicans, on the other hand, had become a united and cohesive party. They nominated as their candidate for governor W. O. Bradley, who ran on a platform that addressed state issues and, in particular, criticized the financial condition of the Treasury. Although Bradley lost, Buckner's margin of victory was less than seventeen thousand votes, the smallest in years in the race for the governorship. The state election of 1887 was the beginning of the end for Duke and his unqualified support of the Democratic Party. It was becoming clear that the needs of agriculture were at odds with those of business. This conflict resulted in an emerging fusion within the Democratic Party of Populist ideas with the economics of free silver Democrats. The election of nontraditional candidates like William Goebel, who advanced a hard line against the railroads, only put more distance between Duke and the direction of the party. It was not long before Goebel personalized his attacks on the railroads by identifying Duke and Milton Smith as the primary targets of his verbal ire.[9]

The first legislative session during Buckner's administration has been described by George Lee Willis, a historian of the Kentucky Democratic Party, as a "colorless affair," one that "in large part was devoted to bills sponsored by big business and political promoters." However, to the L&N and Duke, the session was anything but colorless. Problems began early for the railroad when the usually conservative Railroad Commission unilaterally initiated an increase of $3 million in the tax-assessed value of the L&N's property. Taken aback by such high-handed treatment, Smith and Duke ratcheted up the pressure on the legislature. Duke had built such a powerful railroad lobby that he was able to lobby successfully for the introduction of a bill to abolish the Railroad Commission and overturn the L&N's tax assessment. Although the bill narrowly passed the House, it met with strong opposition in the Senate, particularly from Goebel.[10]

The bill's opponents in the Senate—among whom was found Goebel, now thoroughly convinced that the railroad wielded undue influence on the legislative process—responded by entering a resolution calling for the establishment of a joint committee to investigate the L&N's lobbying activities. Such a committee was, in fact, established, and Goebel was assigned a seat on it. The report that the committee eventually issued commented critically on the lavish entertainment to which the L&N treated legislators as well as its free hand with passes and concluded by unanimously recommending a grand jury investigation of the lobbyists it had investigated. Although the general assembly never acted on the committee's recommendations, the Senate did defeat Duke's bill, signaling that the L&N and its lobbyists were in for a rough ride.[11]

During the legislative session of 1887–88, Goebel learned that the L&N and Duke were more than capable opponents. It was only through his use of the joint committee's critical report that Goebel was able to derail Duke's plan to abolish the Railroad Commission—but not necessarily permanently. The problem was that, as a creation of the legislature, it could too easily be voted out of existence. However, a constitutional convention had been called for 1890. (The state was operating under the prewar, 1847 proslavery constitution, which was not only out of date but also in violation of the federal Constitution.) Seeing his chance to strengthen the position of the commission, Goebel proposed that it be specifically provided for in the new constitution, meaning that only a constitutional amendment could abolish it. Speaking during the convention, Goebel reminded the delegates of Duke's earlier efforts to legislatively circumvent a tax assessment: "When the railroads failed in their assaults upon that system in the courts they came to the General Assembly and undertook to abolish the system and the Railroad Commission also by repealing the law establishing them. The largest and most aggressive lobby that Frankfort has seen within a quarter of the century was brought here to accomplish that end." The convention endorsed Goebel's idea and included the Railroad Commission in the new constitution, which was approved in 1891 by a substantial majority of Kentucky voters.[12]

Duke continued his lobbying activities and became even more powerful when his friend William Lindsay was elected to the U.S. Senate in 1893. There was a history of political cooperation between Duke and Lindsay that went back to Lindsay's years as a state senator, when he was perhaps Duke's most trusted ally in the general assembly. Typically, when a bill adverse to the L&N was introduced in the legislature, Duke could depend on Lindsay to organize the necessary opposition. Lindsay, who, like Duke, had served in the Confederate army, was a conservative adhering to the New Departure political philosophy and always friendly to Kentucky business. He was adamantly against free silver, a position that was soon to place him in a precarious political situation.[13]

Between 1887 and 1893, the free silver and agrarian Populist movement gathered momentum in Kentucky. Kentucky farmers had over the years formed a number of Populist societies. In recognition of the need for a coordinated effort, however, those societies were in February 1889 merged, creating the Farmers' Alliance. Although eventually the Alliance grew into a formidable political bloc, wielding farmers'

Senator William Lindsay was a trusted political ally and the primary proponent of legislation inspired by Duke and Milton Smith. (Courtesy the Kentucky Historical Society.)

collective political clout in the fight to reduce taxes and regulate the railroads, during the 1891 Democratic convention the farm vote split, resulting in another staunch pro-Southern Bourbon gubernatorial candidate, John Y. Brown. Brown, a conservative and classmate of Duke's at Centre College, had not, however, said or done anything to alienate the Alliance. He was also from western Kentucky, and, for some of the delegates, that fact alone led to the conclusion that there would be a power shift to the agrarian west.[14] Even though the party platform included no free silver clause—on the grounds that the protective tariff issue needed to be addressed first—many observers, including the *Louisville Courier-Journal*'s reporters, concluded that the farmers had left the convention contented.[15]

When the election was over, the Democrats had won once again but, their power base continuing to erode, had captured less than 50 percent of the statewide vote while the Republicans had managed a respectable 40.2 percent and the Populist Party the remaining 8.9 percent. Nevertheless, Duke still found himself positioned well enough in the general assembly to influence the legislative process. Brown had recognized the strength of the Farmers' Alliance and, during the campaign, done his best to win its support. However, the legislative record of his administration after the election did not live up to his campaign rhetoric. For example, Duke successfully blocked legislation harmful to the L&N's interests, and, but for a court-ordered injunction, the railroad would have acquired its longtime competitor, the Chesapeake and Ohio, forming one of the most powerful corporations in the country.[16]

Duke was, however, on the verge of difficult times. As we have seen, he was to become involved with the *Southern Magazine* in 1893. Also in that year he became the president and general manager of the newly formed Columbia Finance Building and Loan Association (whether he was an investor or simply an employee is not clear). Of course, any publishing venture is risky at the best of times. Still, most building-and-loan association ventures are safe enough. But what Duke had not counted on was the worst of times. The failure of the National Cordage Company in May 1893 triggered the collapse of the stock market, and, for the next six months, one business after another failed, including several railroads and over three hundred banks. Unemployment reached an all-time high, and, within a year, many of the nation's unemployed were wandering the country searching for jobs.[17]

Henry Adams wrote of the Panic of 1893: "While the country braced itself up to an effort such as no one had thought within its powers, the individual crawled as best he could, through the wreck, and found many values of life upset." Duke was one such individual. His was a classic case of poor timing. The attempt to keep both ventures afloat and at the same time fulfill his obligations to the L&N proved a terrible drain, not just on his time, but also on his limited financial resources. It is not certain whether Duke was an equity participant in the magazine or the building-and-loan association, but, at a minimum, their failures would have substantially curtailed or terminated any remuneration he was receiving from either enterprise.[18]

Beyond Duke's bad timing in embarking on a new financial venture on the eve of the crash, there is also to be considered the seeming anomaly of his embarking on a financial venture at all. Prior to 1893, all his business ventures had been literary or political in nature. It turns out, however, that the Columbia Finance Building and Loan Association was affiliated with the Columbia Finance and Trust Company—the two were even conveniently located in the same building—and that his old business associate Richard W. Knott was on the board of directors of the trust company. Presumably, Knott and his fellow board members decided to finance the building-and-loan association in order to capitalize on a market unavailable to them otherwise and hired Duke in order to capitalize on his name recognition. Of course, the crash and the depression that followed doomed the venture, and, by 1897, the Columbia Finance Building and Loan Association was in liquidation, a process that was not completed until around 1902.[19]

Another seeming anomaly is Duke's decision to write *The History of the Bank of Kentucky.* Published in 1895, this full-length book traces the history of the bank from its formation in the early 1800s through the mid-1890s. While the book is well written, it can have been of interest to only a limited number of readers, the research on which it is based being limited to the bank's internal records and particularly the minutes of the board of directors and the shareholder meetings. One therefore wonders whether Duke was, in fact, commissioned to write the *History* by the bank itself in an attempt to assure current and prospective customers and investors alike that, despite the depression, the Bank of Kentucky remained a viable financial institution. Certainly, the book ends with the assertion that the bank was as strong and healthy at the present as it had ever been in its past.

Duke's difficult times were not, however, to be limited to his business ventures. Tensions within the state Democratic Party continued to mount as reformers increasingly gained power and influence. And, again, things came to a head over the issue of free silver. After the stock market crash, crop prices became depressed, and interest rates climbed steadily higher, making it impossible for farmers to obtain fresh credit or to pay off existing loans. The newly resurrected Populists blamed the depressed economic conditions on the shortage of money, and the farmers almost to a man made free silver agriculture's primary cause and, by 1895, the only real issue in Kentucky politics. The Democratic Party hierarchy, Duke included, continued firmly in support of the gold standard.[20]

As the 1895 gubernatorial election approached, Duke and the L&N were also finding themselves at odds with Governor John Y. Brown, fed up with his erratic support of the railroad's interests. Still, despite his blockage of the Chesapeake and Ohio merger, Brown retained a strong conservative philosophy and did veto a railroad regulation bill sponsored by William Goebel that prohibited unreasonable passenger and freight rates, attempted to cure the long-/short-haul rate controversy, and granted the Railroad Commission additional investigation powers. The general assembly overrode Brown's veto, and the bill was passed and made into law. However, it was now evident to Duke not only that Brown had become an annoyance but also that he had clearly outlived his usefulness. When, in 1896, he ran for the U.S. Senate, Duke and the L&N refused to support him, and, as we will see in chapter 19, in 1899 he bolted the party.[21]

The disharmony within the party soon became public as Democrats began blasting each other in the newspapers, and some in Kentucky's "Grand Old Party" were already beginning to scent victory in the upcoming election. Setting aside their own partisan squabbles, the Republicans nominated a gubernatorial candidate the entire party could enthusiastically support, William Bradley.[22]

The Democratic disharmony became even more evident in the spring of 1895 when J. C. S. Blackburn, speaking primarily in western Kentucky before friendly audiences, began to argue that it was time for the party to reset its priorities and address the currency issue. By summer, Blackburn became the leading spokesman of the free silver movement within the party.[23] John Carlisle, Grover Cleveland's secretary of the Treasury, also traveled through his native Kentucky delivering his sound money counterarguments. Carlisle emphasized the danger of political radicalism, a concern that had been expressed by Duke from time to time in the *Southern Magazine.* Duke was impressed with Carlisle's intellectualism and convinced that the secretary "presented his arguments in a lucid and comprehensive fashion, impossible for his opponents to contradict." Notwithstanding Duke's opinion, Carlisle's rhetoric failed to sway the western Kentucky farmer and only stoked the fires of discontent within the party ranks.[24]

On the afternoon of April 11, 1895, in the midst of the Democratic debates over the currency standard, John Sanford and William Goebel met on the steps of a bank in Covington, Kentucky. Sanford was an ex-Confederate soldier who cared little for the Northern-born Goebel and was arrogant enough to publicize his contempt.[25] Goebel, who was accompanied by W. J. Hendricks, the state attorney general, and Frank B. Helm, apparently wanted to cash a check in the bank. Sanford and Goebel exchanged some heated words, and then, according to Hendricks and Helm, each man drew a pistol and fired. Events transpired so quickly that neither Hendricks nor Helm was sure who fired first, but, when the smoke cleared, Sanford lay dying on the sidewalk. Five hours later he was dead. Several days later, a hearing held in Covington concluded that the evidence established sufficient reasonable doubt as to Goebel's guilt, and no further action was taken against him. Duke and other ex-Confederates would, however, ever after consider Goebel an "assassin."[26]

One month before the state convention, many Kentucky Democrats attended the district conventions called to nominate candidates for the state Railroad Commission. The Democrats of the First District used their convention, held in Owensboro, to voice their support for a free silver resolution. Immediately following this convention, P. Watt Hardin, a candidate for governor, made a speech endorsing the Owensboro resolution and free silver in general. The Second District railroad convention followed about a month later and was held in Louisville only days before the scheduled state party convention. Two candidates were vying for the nomination. William C. McChord, the incumbent, was a disciple of Goebel's and a proponent of government regulation of the railroads. George Alexander, the challenger, was a railroad man who also happened to be against free silver, and he therefore had the wholehearted support of Duke and the L&N. With Duke diligently working his magic on the delegates, Alexander won the nomination.[27]

When the state convention convened in Louisville, the delegates were seriously split on the currency issue. However, after several indecisive votes, the delegates adopted a statement supporting President Cleveland's open-door policy on the currency issue. The Kentucky conservatives were now convinced that the platform solidly favored sound money and set out to select their candidate for governor.[28] Hardin's earlier endorsement of free silver and his association with reform-minded Democrats, particularly Goebel, made Duke and the L&N uneasy.

W. J. Stone's position on gold probably fell on receptive ears, but Duke already knew that Stone did not have enough support statewide to gather in the nomination. When the delegate votes were finally tabulated, Hardin had won the nomination. Then, to Duke's utter consternation, he opened his campaign by announcing that he had interpreted the party's platform as one "allowing for the calling for Free Silver."[29]

Duke was now in a quandary. He had been a lifelong Democrat, supporting the party in every election since the Civil War. The party, however, was rapidly changing, its younger, reform-minded members, such as William Goebel, taking control of its direction. The "new guard" had begun to court and exploit the support of the agriculture-labor wing of the party. It was already apparent that the more conservative and business-minded voters in Louisville and Jefferson County were going to defect and vote for the Republican candidate. And, indeed, when the November 1895 election results were final, Bradley was victorious, the traditionally Democratic Louisville and Jefferson County having given the Republicans a 60 percent majority.[30]

Bradley discovered almost immediately that it would be a very difficult task for his administration to work constructively with the general assembly. William Goebel had been elected president pro tem of the Senate and for the next four years would be a militant thorn in Bradley's side. During the first postelection legislative session, partisan politics quickly forced a deadlock on several important issues. The atmosphere became so heated that many of the legislators walked the halls of the state capitol armed with pistols. It was not long before the major national newspapers began to publish articles emphasizing the violent dispositions of the Kentucky lawmakers. Duke realized that the spectacle of armed lawmakers was an embarrassment both to the state and to the democratic process, but he also understood that it would take time for the South to rid itself of its propensity for violence because "most Southerners adhered more strongly to their own misconceptions as well as their convictions than people in other parts of the country."[31]

No sooner had the political commotion in Frankfort begun to die down than the 1896 presidential campaign opened. Duke was concerned that the free silver Democrats had massed enough strength to take control of the party convention, scheduled for June 2 and 3 in Lexington. Anticipating a major split in the party, Duke was convinced that it was in everyone's best interests to minimize preconvention rhetorical posturing, particularly on the parts of John Carlisle and Joseph Blackburn. Duke traveled to Washington in early May with the hopes of speaking to both Blackburn and William Lindsay. Blackburn continued to be the leader of the free silver faction in Kentucky, and Duke hoped to gain his help in his effort to diffuse any further polarization within the party. Duke tried to convince Blackburn to stay away from the state prior to the convention, but Blackburn would agree only if Carlisle would agree to stay away as well. Carlisle, a potential contender for

Blackburn's Senate seat, was still an avid defender of the gold standard. Unable to meet with Lindsay, Duke wrote his friend a letter briefing him on his meeting with Blackburn. Duke was convinced more than ever that the free silver people were going to control the state convention and that it would be best for the conservatives if Blackburn stayed away from Kentucky altogether. Duke also told Lindsay he felt that the free silver people were "going to bitterly condemn" their opposition at the convention and personally attack Carlisle. He ended by voicing the opinion that the Democrats might as well all go to bedlam, or, rather, he felt that "we are also going to hell."[32]

When the Democrats convened in Lexington, Duke's assessment of the strength of the free silver movement proved to be accurate. The free silver people dominated the convention, controlling the crafting of the platform and the selection of those delegates who were to attend the national convention. Joseph Blackburn was even nominated as the state's favorite son presidential candidate.[33]

Sitting through the convention, Lindsay and Duke found themselves in the unaccustomed and uncomfortable position of being in the minority and out of power. The dramatic shift within the party caused some, including a reporter for the *Louisville Courier-Journal,* to speculate that Lindsay was so frustrated by the turn of events that he intended to resign his Senate seat. Duke had always found Lindsay to be an intelligent man who dealt with complicated issues both incisively and logically. And, in that regard, Lindsay did not disappoint, either during the convention or afterward, when the party crisis exploded into a major schism. Instead of resigning his Senate seat, Lindsay attended the national convention as a nondelegate and then, as Leonard Schlup put it, "followed his convictions to a logical conclusion."[34]

The sound money people were completely overwhelmed by William Jennings Bryan and the free silver delegates. Bryan, of course, won the nomination and was supported by a platform that denounced the more conservative economic policies of the Cleveland administration. The nomination of Bryan, a Populist, was more than Duke and his fellow conservatives could swallow. Walter Haldeman of the *Courier-Journal* wrote scathingly of Bryan: "His platform is a mockery of all principles for which this newspaper stands. We must fight him to the last ditch." It soon became public knowledge that old-line Democrats such as W. C. P. Breckinridge, Simon Buckner, John Carlisle, William Lindsay, and Duke, who clearly agreed with Haldeman's assessment, were determined not to give their support to either Bryan or the Democratic Party.[35]

Why had the Democrats repudiated Grover Cleveland, the only president their party had placed in the White House in forty years? The issue of free silver is the most readily apparent answer, but the free silver movement did not develop in isolation from the other social and economic conditions that had caused many

Americans to become disillusioned with government. Free silver had proved its appeal to voters in 1892, and, in the intervening four years, other influences, including the depression, had made Americans focus on the money issue. Economic disillusionment bred political disillusionment, which in turn bred a full-scale revolt against the plutocrats in Washington. Although Duke had sensed the strength of the free silver movement within the state party prior to the convention, the old guard of the Democratic Party remained largely blind to the momentum that movement had gained and was, thus, unprepared to meet the challenge when the time came.[36]

The nomination of William Jennings Bryan convinced Duke that the new Democratic Party hierarchy had betrayed the fundamental political and economic principles to which he and the party had subscribed for so long. It was not long before Duke and the other disillusioned Democrats began to consider whether it was time to bolt the party. When Duke learned that Henry L. Martin, a fellow Democrat and friend, was not going to support the Chicago platform, he wrote him:

> Like yourself, I had been loath to break old associations & separate politically from men whom I've always loved, and have acted with so long; but I am compelled to do so. I was willing to make many sacrifices and almost every effort to remain in the regular Democratic ranks; but when that party labels populism & anarchy with the title of Democracy, I cannot swallow it. The policy announced at Chicago menaces not only the business and property of the country but also the institutions and its peace.[37]

Duke concluded that the only option left the conservatives was to form an independent third party. The conservatives realized, of course, that they had no hope of getting their candidate elected. That was not the purpose of calling a convention. Rather, they called the convention simply to rally their supporters. The third-party bid also allowed them to support the Republican candidate, William McKinley, without actually voting for him. The National Democratic Party convention was held on September 2 in Indianapolis. The delegates nominated as their candidates John M. Palmer, a native-born Kentuckian who now resided in Illinois, for president and Simon B. Buckner, the former Confederate general and ex-governor of Kentucky, as vice president. It was not hard for conservative Democrats like Lindsay or Duke to support two native-born Kentuckians and a platform that endorsed sound money as well as other conservative principles. Although Lindsay, who had been ill, did not attend the convention, George M. Davie, a very close friend of Duke's, wrote Lindsay afterward that the proceedings were on a "high plane of patriotism, dignity and eagerness that impressed everyone there to a sense of their duty."[38]

Energized by the convention, Duke returned to Louisville and enthusiastically supported Palmer and Buckner while denouncing Bryan and the Chicago platform. When Palmer and Buckner came to Louisville in September, he played a prominent role in the parade and rally held in their honor. On November 3, 1896, William McKinley won the state, defeating William Jennings Bryan by a mere 281 votes. Palmer and the National Democratic Party received a little over 5,000 votes, a result clearly showing that the conservative nonvoter was the deciding factor in Kentucky. McKinley won the national election by over 600,000 votes; Kentucky was the only Southern state to vote Republican. However, there were still over 200,000 Kentuckians who had voted for Bryan, indicating that the rank and file of the Kentucky Democratic Party found Bryan's form of populism appealing.[39]

With the election over, many Democrats wondered whether the conservatives had any intention of returning to the party. Writing H. L. Martin, William Lindsay continued to repudiate the free silver Democrats and their coalition with the Populists. He was, however, hopeful that, by the next presidential election, there would be a return to what he termed "old-time democracy." The astute Lindsay recognized that the election results were a clear indication that the time of the old-line conservative, aristocratic ex-Confederate had passed. Henry Watterson, whose paper was nearly bankrupt because of its opposition to the free silver Democrats, threw in the towel and began to support the new power elite of the Democratic Party. Others, including Duke, were not so sure where they stood. Duke would wander through the political wilderness for the next few years, constantly growing closer to the Republican Party and its ideology. To some extent, William Goebel's personalization of his attacks on Duke and the L&N became an added incentive for him to become less and less of a Democratic partisan.[40]

In the midst of all this political turmoil, Duke quietly turned sixty, but, even at this milestone, when many men were slowing down or thinking about retirement, he continued to live life to the fullest. His interests had always been varied, and he continued to pursue them with unabated energy. He still loved to write and always did so when given the opportunity. J. Stoddard Johnston, an old war associate who was now a well-known and respected journalist, was compiling and editing a history of the city of Louisville and assigned Duke the appropriate task of writing a chapter on the city's railroads and their impact in general on Louisville.[41] More interesting than Duke's history of the railroads, however, is Johnston's biography of Duke, which he included in volume 1 of the collection. Johnston reiterated what many others had written or said about Duke's modesty concerning his personal accomplishments. Using *A History of Morgan's Cavalry* as an example, Johnston explained the frustration he felt when, using the work as a research tool, he was unable to determine the dates of Duke's promotions through the ranks of the Confederate army. When he asked Duke why there were no such references in the book, Duke responded: "Why I took rank as General Morgan advanced, I thought anybody would have known that."[42]

For many years, both Duke and his wife, Tommie, had been involved in Confederate veterans' affairs. Tommie was very active in the United Daughters of the Confederacy, ultimately obtaining the office of first vice president in the national organization, and was also an officer in the Kentucky branch of the Children of the Confederacy. During these years, Confederate monuments were being erected in great numbers throughout the Southern states. Kentucky was no exception, and Tommie was instrumental in arranging for the construction of a Confederate monument in Louisville honoring the many soldiers from the city who had fought for the Southern army. She was also appointed the state director of the Jefferson Davis monument. It took many years and a small fortune to build that particular monument, and it was a significant tribute to Tommie to be named the state director.[43]

Many of the Confederate veterans' organizations had been organized almost immediately after the Civil War—as yearly reunions or summer picnics meant to give the veterans a chance both to reminisce and to coalesce politically. The men who rode with Morgan were no exception and soon had their own organization, aptly called Morgan's Men. Their descendants carry on the tradition to this day. Until his death, Duke was the commander of the organization, and, each summer at the annual reunion, he delivered an eloquent and interesting speech, several of which were published in the *Southern Bivouac.* In the best tradition of the Lost Cause, these speeches tended to follow Duke's practice of idealizing Morgan and his exploits. For example, at the October 27, 1883, reunion, Duke began his remarks with the following preamble:

> Were it not that I fear to trespass on your patience, and become engaged with a theme upon which I find it difficult to be brief, I would like to speak of General Morgan's character and genius, and endeavor to define and describe the qualities which gave him such aptitude for the warfare in which he achieved so much success and reputation.... He made war after a fashion which was as original and novel, as it was effective. Totally unlearned in the art of war as taught in the schools, his strategy and technique, while in strictest accordance with the true principles of military science, as the greatest captains have applied them, were illustrated by methods, new and unlike anything ever seen or practiced before.[44]

By the 1890s, the most prominent veteran organization in the South was the Confederate Veteran Association. In 1893, the *Confederate Veteran Magazine* became the official publication of the organization and, for the next forty years, reported reunions, deaths, and other pertinent information concerning the members and their families. The magazine also became a forum for veterans' and nonveterans' recollections of their wartime experiences. Many of these articles concerned Morgan and the Kentucky cavalry. It was not uncommon for readers to comment on previously published pieces. Aware of the close scrutiny given each article, the magazine's editors on several occasions sent Duke manuscripts, asking him to review them for accuracy prior to publication. Duke himself submitted several articles to the magazine over the years, including the "Sketch of John H. Morgan" in 1911 and "General Morgan's Escape from Prison" in 1915.[45]

The Southern veterans in Louisville formed a very active and influential core within the hierarchy of the national organization. Bennett Young, for example, became the national commander of the organization and, once elected, held that position until his death. The Kentucky veterans were also instrumental in promoting Louisville on two separate occasions as the site for the organization's annual convention. Perhaps because of Duke's many other interests, he never really became involved in the organization to the same extent that Bennett Young or some of the other Kentuckians did. Nevertheless, he was a general, and, by the 1890s, the ranks of Confederate officers were thinning out quickly. In deference to his rank and popularity with the veterans, Duke was normally included on the executive committee of the state organization and helped plan the two Louisville national conventions, in both cases being assigned the responsibility of providing transportation for the veterans to the convention.[46]

The veterans' organizations were, for Duke, a diversion from his more serious literary and political pursuits. By the late 1890s, his time was occupied with politics and defending the L&N from the constant attacks of William Goebel. As Bradley's administration entered its third year, it appeared that the Republican governor was fated to leave no legislative legacy. The third legislative session of the Bradley administration began on January 4, 1898. Once again, Duke's nemesis William Goebel was elected president pro tem of the Senate. Bradley tried, no more successfully than previously, to persuade the general assembly to enact into law some of his proposed reforms. Instead, the legislature continued to focus on intraparty political squabbles and Goebel's agenda.[47]

The star of the 1898 general assembly was William Goebel, and his legislative activities overshadowed those of all the other legislators. Almost everyone realized that Goebel was a very ambitious man who wanted to be governor. He immediately started the 1898 session with an attack on corporate power and independence, as usual focusing his attack on the L&N. This type of populist position ingratiated Goebel with the voters, which almost guaranteed his legislation's passage. However, it was Charles C. McChord and not Goebel who introduced the major piece of antirailroad legislation. There was probably no legislator more capable than McChord when it came to drafting a complicated railroad regulation bill. McChord had, after all, been on the Railroad Commission and, with Goebel's strong support, was intent on gaining a legislative mandate for regulating railroad rates.[48]

The McChord Bill granted the Railroad Commission the power to call an evidentiary hearing on any written complaint filed with it as long as the pertinent parties were given ten days' notice. The bill further provided that, once each party received the appropriate notice, an evidentiary hearing would be held, at which time both parties were to be given the opportunity to present the merits of their cases. After the evidence was presented, the commission was given the power to adjudicate the validity of the complaint. If the commission so desired, it had the power to unilaterally adjust the rates in question to reflect its final adjudication of the complaint. The public's and, more particularly, the newspaper's immediate response to the McChord Bill was negative. W. C. P. Breckinridge wrote a series of editorials in the *Lexington Herald* denouncing both Goebel and McChord. Duke, with the financial support of the L&N, fought Goebel and McChord tenaciously as the bill made its way through the general assembly.[49]

The tension between Goebel and Duke, already bad, began to mount as Goebel took every opportunity to try to intimidate Duke. Goebel went out of his way to browbeat Duke, including standing and glaring at him while he ate in the hotel or one of the Frankfort restaurants. Although much older than Goebel, Duke was not one to be trifled with. It is very unlikely that Goebel's stares had their desired effect, but, as a result of the Sanford shooting, Duke was concerned about Goebel's propensity for violence. Prudently, Duke began to carry a derringer in his vest pocket for protection.[50]

Despite Duke's opposition and the general unpopularity of McChord's Bill, Goebel and McChord were able to successfully maneuver the bill through the general assembly. However, Governor Bradley quickly vetoed the bill and sent it back to the legislature, where it remained for the rest of the session.[51]

More important to Goebel than the McChord Bill was the election bill, which he himself initiated. The bill was touted as reform legislation and targeted the governor's ability to appoint the members of the state Election Commission as well as the statewide practice of granting the power to counties and local municipalities to appoint local election officers. There is no question that the existing law was abused and that the appointment process was controlled by highly partisan individuals. Goebel was convinced that such abuse had placed sound money Democrats in control of the county election process, permitting them to manipulate the 1896 presidential results to the detriment of his candidate, William Jennings Bryan. The bill proposed that the general assembly would elect the three state election commissioners, who, in turn, would have the power to appoint the county election officers. The bill was immediately recognized as more partisan legislation, only this time dressed in reform clothing. The most obvious weakness of the bill was its failure to make any provision for bipartisan representation on the county election boards. The effect of such an omission guaranteed that whichever party controlled the general assembly controlled the election boards. Many people speculated that Goebel introduced the bill to ensure his own election as governor in the event of a close race. In any event, the bill passed, and Bradley vetoed it, but, voting along strictly partisan lines, the general assembly overrode the veto. The Republicans challenged the bill in the state courts on the grounds that it was unconstitutional, but they were unsuccessful.[52]

In the spring of 1898, bickering between the Democrats and the Republicans was momentarily set aside when the explosion of the battleship *Maine* in Havana Harbor set in motion what would become the Spanish-American War. Most Americans immediately called for war with Spain and the liberation of Cuba. When President McKinley finally did declare war, the country was solidly behind him. The people in Kentucky were no exception and enthusiastically supported the call to arms. Although Duke was now sixty years old, there were some who still rated his combat experience as extremely valuable and placed him in the forefront of America's military talent. James H. Wilson had petitioned and was commissioned by President McKinley a major general early in the war. Prior to his appointment, Wilson had been invited by McKinley to Washington to meet with him and Henry C. Corbin, the adjutant general of the U.S. Army. During the conference, Wilson was handed a list of civilians whom the president and the adjutant general were considering as possible candidates to be commissioned as major generals in charge of volunteers. Wilson was asked to review the list and provide his comments and/or recommendations. On completing his review, Wilson offered the names of several other men, including Duke, who he believed had the ability to command troops effectively in a wartime situation. Duke never did receive a commission, but it does not appear that he was seeking one either.[53]

The state of Kentucky supplied the U.S. Army with four full regiments for the war. The Louisville Legion, a state militia unit commanded by Duke's old friend John Castleman, was designated the First Kentucky regiment. The other three regiments, the Second, Third, and Fourth Kentucky, came from central, western, and eastern Kentucky, respectively. What impressed Duke so much about the Spanish-American War was the manner in which Southerners and Northerners fought together as Americans against a common enemy. Always a proponent of sectional reconciliation, Duke summed up his feelings as follows:

> The spectacle so gratifying and so often commented on, of the Northern and Southern boys in the Spanish American War, marching to battle under the same flag and with a common sentiment of patriotism was merely evidence, a demonstration of the change of feeling that had already taken place. The youth of the South, the men of middle age, all who had grown to manhood since the close of the Civil War, felt full fellowship in the existing civic order and were above all else American.[54]

19

At the Turn of the Century

By 1900, ALL BUT THE MOST recalcitrant of conservatives were coming back to the Democratic Party, a return that can be attributed largely to the strength of William Jennings Bryan as a candidate. Although he had lost the 1896 election, Bryan had come so close to victory, particularly in Kentucky, that he could not, the party realized, be denied a second opportunity. The advent of prosperity and the rise of imperialism following the Spanish-American War also helped lure the conservatives back into the ranks of the party faithful. Many of the sound money conservatives, who had bolted the party in 1896, were very skeptical about the wisdom of McKinley's policy of imperialism. However, to reunite the party philosophically at the national level, a compromise on free silver had to be reached before the national convention. Many Democrats believed that Bryan did not have to abandon free silver entirely but felt that the issue did need to take a subordinate position to others in the upcoming campaign.[1]

During the late summer of 1898, the newspapers began to speculate on whether Bryan's candidacy would receive any opposition from within the party. On September 8, 1898, the *Louisville Dispatch* published an editorial claiming that Senator William Lindsay had expressed his preference for Nelson A. Miles over Bryan. Miles, a Union veteran, was noted in the North mostly for his postwar career as an Indian fighter. He was noted in the South, however, as the jailer of Jefferson Davis. The end of the war found Miles in command of Fort Monroe, Virginia, where, after his capture, Davis was interned for two years. Miles had no intention of permitting Davis to escape and, the day after his arrival, placed him in leg irons. When Edwin Stanton learned of Davis's treatment, he immediately ordered the leg irons removed. For the next two years, Davis languished in his prison cell, until the publication in 1866 of John J. Craven's *Prison Life of Jefferson Davis,* which became an immediate success. Craven skillfully presented a picture of Davis as a tragic hero being cruelly treated by Miles. The book greatly enhanced Davis's symbolic value to the South and also created a significant amount of sympathy for him in the

North, which ultimately led to his release. Forever after, rightly or wrongly, Miles was the blackest of villains in the eyes of most Southerners.[2]

The same day the *Dispatch* article appeared, Duke, certain that the senator was being misrepresented, wrote Lindsay, recalling an earlier article in which, as Duke put it, Lindsay's opinion was reported as being that "if Miles was brought before a Court Martial it might make a sort of martyr of him in the eyes of the public & probably therefore a formidable Presidential possibility." "But," Duke continued, "it did not strike me as anything in the shape of an expression of preference for him." Duke advised that it would be in his best interests for Lindsay to write the *Dispatch* and clarify his position. Just as he had made certain that Morgan was safely distanced from the likes of Champ Ferguson, Duke did not want the senator publicly associated with Miles or identified as his "apologist and advocate." Because Miles was so unpopular in the South, in the "present disposition to fraternize" the Davis episode had the potential to make him unpopular in the North as well. The former commander of Fort Monroe was a political liability, and Duke was of the opinion that he should not be seriously considered as a candidate. Even in 1898, the war cast a long shadow over the country's political process.[3]

Several weeks later, Duke again wrote Lindsay, this time concerning Henry Watterson's shift in support to Bryan and the National Democratic Party machine. During the 1896 campaign, Watterson's editorials in the *Louisville Courier-Journal* had denounced not only Bryan and the Chicago platform but also the National Democratic Party platform. In an act of self-defense, the free silver Democrats started the *Louisville Dispatch* for the sole purpose of retaliating. The *Dispatch* became very popular with its readers, most of whom were Bryan supporters, and its success almost forced the *Courier-Journal* out of business. Some embittered Democrats even burned copies of the *Courier-Journal* left for distribution at depots along the Louisville and Nashville (L&N) line. Watterson, acting out of political self-interest, quickly returned to the party fold. Still objecting to Bryan's candidacy, and unwilling to capitulate, Duke wrote Lindsay: "The trouble is Watterson has written recently so much wild-eyed rot, that no one pays any attention to him now even when he writes rationally." Duke began to reason that the Republican philosophy was more in line with his own than the Democratic philosophy was, offering conservatives like himself a more viable option, particularly at the state level:

I am convinced that any proper policy in Kentucky is to let the Republican candidates win this year, if they can, especially I should like to see Jones beat Hobson the unnecessary aggressive position the latter has taken—and beat Goebel for the gubernatorial nomination and commit the party to a repeal of his bill. If that be done, may have to get a legislature comparatively free from Silver cranks, and which may be controlled by conservative Republicans and the small percentage of sound money Democrats who may get in.[4]

William Goebel's thirteen-year career as a Kentucky state legislator was often fueled by his disdain for the Louisville and Nashville Railroad and Basil Duke. (Courtesy the Kentucky Historical Society.)

It was obvious to Duke that the Republican platform was the more attentive to his own political and economic needs. What he envisioned was a coalition of Republicans and conservative Democrats working together as a large block of independent voters for the common good and abolishing "partisan passion" in favor of a more "patriotic and fraternal spirit." Duke was, however, too well versed in the ways of politics to believe that this would happen any time soon. In some ways the reality of politics had made him bitter. He wrote that politics had become little more than an industry "from which the multitude derives amusement, and substantial benefit accrues to the professionals of high and low degree that deal the cards and run the game." There was also a personal downside to the political game that disturbed Duke. For years, the cohesiveness of the Democratic Party had bred countless friendships, many of which had been destroyed by the 1896 party schism. This development troubled Duke deeply, as did the character of many of the men then involved in politics. He was quite sure that he had known "men to whom it would afford greater satisfaction to think that those they disliked were going to hell, than that they, themselves, were going to heaven."[5]

In the early spring of 1899, three Democratic gubernatorial candidates, William Goebel, P. Watt Hardin, and William J. Stone, toured the state, drumming up support from the delegates for their nomination. All three candidates supported Bryan, but Goebel was not doing well and knew it. He had several hurdles to overcome. For one thing, he had limited name recognition outside his own district.

More important, however, the Sanford affair was a liability among ex-Confederates, as was his status as a "Yankee" among Kentuckians generally. Goebel's intense personality, in tandem with his determined and ruthless struggle for the leadership of the Democratic Party, ensured that the campaign would be anything but pleasant. So did Duke's and the L&N's determined efforts to defeat him. The railroad and its supporters had established two newspapers, both of which constantly attacked Goebel and praised Hardin. Duke also put as much anti-Goebel pressure on as many delegates as he could possibly corner. Goebel and his supporters retaliated, but, as the convention neared, he found himself running a distant third to Hardin.[6]

By the time the Democrats convened in Louisville on June 20, 1899, Goebel had recognized that his only chance to win was to form some sort of coalition with Stone against Hardin. The coalition was quickly arranged, permitting Goebel and Stone to gain control of the powerful platform committee. The end result of this effort was a set of planks incorporating most of Goebel's reforms and endorsing his election bill and the McChord Bill. When the platform was made public, Hardin realized what was up and, in order to avoid an embarrassing political defeat, astutely withdrew his candidacy. It took twenty-six ballots before Goebel finally won the nomination, and, even then, it was apparent that the party was not solidly behind him. Once again, a cadre of disillusioned Democrats, this time led by ex-governor John Y. Brown, bolted, forming an opposition party called the Honest Election Democrats. To no one's surprise, the movement was funded chiefly by money from the L&N. Brown quickly called a convention, and, to nobody's surprise, he was nominated to run for governor. The Republicans, who met several days later, nominated William Taylor for governor.[7]

Perhaps recognizing the deep animosity that Goebel and the Democratic opposition harbored for one another, Duke also concluded that a third party was the only option for the opposition Democrats during the upcoming campaign. On July 17, 1899, he wrote W. H. Mackoy, a Cincinnati lawyer, disclosing his impressions of Goebel's nomination. He predicted, obviously aware of the L&N's intentions, that a third-party ticket composed of opposition Democrats would quickly organize, presenting a significant obstacle for Goebel to overcome, and most likely ensuring his defeat and that of his "gang." Duke compared this movement to the Palmer-Buckner option of 1896, which provided the Democrats "the opportunity of expressing their opinions and then voting as they please." In the event of a close race, Duke argued, a third-party movement would make it more difficult for Goebel to capitalize on his election bill. It was a position, he explained to Mackoy, that he could support with good conscience.[8]

A third-party movement would greatly enhance the L&N's chances of accomplishing its objectives in the upcoming campaign. The railroad was determined to prevent Goebel from winning and launched what Maury Klein has described as a "well financed counter campaign led by Duke." Shortly after the Democratic convention, Henry Watterson petitioned the L&N to stop its anti-Goebel activities, the cost of which, he argued, was draining the company's treasury in a losing proposition. Although Watterson's credibility with the railroad was at an all-time low, several contradictory corporate resolutions were passed in response. The upshot was the adoption of a corporate policy to refrain from publicly supporting any particular candidate but to continue opposing Goebel. In effect, the railroad had adopted Duke's advice to Lindsay "to let the Republican candidates win this year, if they can."[9]

With Senator Blackburn's support, Goebel kicked off his campaign in Mayfield with a speech to over three thousand people on August 12, 1899. He was interrupted several times by hecklers, but the crowd settled down when it became clear that, by arguing that the real question being presented to Kentucky was, as the *Courier-Journal* quoted him, "whether the L&N railroad is the servant or the master of the people of the Commonwealth," he was revealing his campaign game plan. It was the L&N he was running against, not Brown or Taylor. During the entire campaign, Goebel rarely acknowledged that the other two men were even in the race. His focus was on the railroad and, more particularly, its president, Milton Smith, its chairman of the board, August Belmont, and, of course, Basil Duke.[10]

Before television and radio, a candidate's measure was taken by his speeches, and his effectiveness was gauged by what was reported about him in the newspapers and, in particular, how he was portrayed in political cartoons. Consider, for example, the cartoon entitled "The Brownies Are Coming," which ran in the *Louisville Times* after John Y. Brown's nomination as a third-party candidate. It pictured a railroad locomotive carrying Duke as the engineer, Colonel John Whallen, a local Louisville party boss, as the fireman, and August Belmont and John Y. Brown as passengers. Another *Louisville Times* cartoon, this one captioned "Making a Monkey of Him," pictures Duke as an organ-grinder standing on a street corner with John Y. Brown as his little monkey holding a tin cup. Goebel's campaign evoked even more visceral reactions as both Republicans and Brown supporters took exception to his Unionist background and his "murder" of Sanford. The *Louisville Dispatch* published a political cartoon in October entitled "From Crittenden to Goebel." John Crittenden, an esteemed U.S. senator and Unionist who had died in 1863, was pictured as a man of great stature, with a diminutive, rat-tailed Goebel scurrying about his feet. [11]

As Goebel ratcheted his campaign into high gear, the canvass moved closer to Louisville, and the attacks on Duke and the L&N escalated. In Danville in early September, Goebel blasted both Milton Smith and Duke for their attempt to abolish the state Railroad Commission. In his Louisville speeches, he repeatedly referred to Duke as a "professional corruptionist." Goebel obviously believed that, when a challenger moved onto his opponent's home turf, the more vituperative the attack, the better the chance it had of making the papers, and, hence, the better chance he had of getting his message across. Since Duke was not himself a candidate for office, he had few options when it came to defending himself. Nonetheless, he had no intention of letting such personal attacks go unanswered and published the following card, an example of Duke at his most pugnacious:

I wish to be understood that I do not speak as an attorney, agent or employee of the railroad. This is an entirely personal matter between myself and William Goebel. I speak within due bounds when I say that Goebel has been more frequently suspected of bargaining and using his influence as a legislator than I have been of attempting to so control legislation. What I say in this regard rests only on my word, but it is my word against William Goebel's. I have never, whatever else may have been said of me, been accustomed to lying. He has repeatedly been accused and convicted of lying. It has been proven that he is a willful, flagrant and frequent offender in this regard. I am a citizen of Kentucky, having the rights which every other citizen possesses, and determined to assert and maintain them, and I will not submit to an attack from a liar, slanderer and an assassin because he happens to be a self selected candidate for governor.[12]

The L&N continued to spend significant sums of money—over $500,000, according to Belmont's later admission—financing the opposition to Goebel's election. Nevertheless, Goebel's stand against the railroad and corporations in general as well as his targeting of Duke gained him some support, particularly from the state's Populist voters. Goebel also courted the labor vote, and his support of free silver, along with Blackburn's endorsement, naturally made him attractive as a candidate to the farmers. He also went after the African American vote aggressively—an almost-unheard-of tactic for a Southern Democrat—pledging that, if he was elected governor, he would secure for blacks equal accommodations on the railroad.[13]

The mayor of Louisville was concerned that the intensity of the campaign could lead to riots or violent demonstrations in the city when the voters went to the polls. Prudently, he hired an additional five hundred special police to help stabilize any potentially volatile situation. Governor William O. Bradley, however, interpreted the extra policemen as an attempt to intimidate Republican voters. After conferring with Duke and Richard W. Knott, he activated the militia in Louisville as a countermeasure, an action that would later come back to haunt the Republicans.[14]

Election day came and went with no violent outbursts, but, when the sun had set, the election was too close to call. Finally, after several days of suspense, it was announced that the Republican candidate, Taylor, had won a narrow victory, capturing 193,714 votes to Goebel's 191,331 and John Y. Brown's 12,140. Once again, the disillusioned Democrats determined the outcome of the election. The Democrats, however, contested the election, appealing the results to the election board. The board, handpicked by Goebel, did *not* invalidate the results—much to Duke's surprise.[15]

William S. Taylor was sworn in as Kentucky's second postwar Republican governor on December 12, 1900. One month later, the Democrats filed a written notice that they were contesting the election results on nine counts, several of which actually accused the Republicans and the L&N of being coconspirators in perpetrating election fraud. One charge was that "the Republican leaders entered into a conspiracy with the chief officers of the Louisville and Nashville railroad" and other corporations to furnish campaign funds for the specific purpose of bribing voters. It was also alleged that the use of the state militia in Louisville on the day of the election constituted voter intimidation.[16]

Goebel's challenge was a shrewd political move—and an obvious manipulation of state law. The Democrats clearly understood that the Kentucky constitution authorized the general assembly and not the state courts to review allegations of election fraud. With the Democrats in full control of both the House of Representatives and the Senate, it was a foregone conclusion that the contestation would be settled in Goebel's favor. The threat of violence once again reared its ugly head in the streets of the state capital, as armed partisans from both camps poured into Frankfort, itching for a fight. Not surprisingly, even the violence was politicized, the railroad being accused of sponsoring the rugged Republicans who had ridden in to Louisville on the L&N in support of Taylor. Milton Smith, the railroad's president, years later acknowledged that he had provided a special train for the mountain men—but only after they had paid the railroad $1,000 and had signed a formal written contract for the service.[17]

The mountain men were a rough crowd and only made the atmosphere in Frankfort all the more tense. They purposely lined the sidewalks with their weapons in full view, forcing the legislators to walk between them on their way to the state house. When Goebel appeared, they would try to intimidate him both verbally and physically. Taylor finally barred the general assembly from the state house, forcing it to meet at the Capitol Hotel. Still, tensions continued to grow, and worried Republicans asked Taylor to call off the mountain men. Taylor complied—he later admitted that they were in Frankfort at his request—and most returned home as quickly as they had come. However, several hundred remained, under the pretext of wanting to hear the results of the general assembly's decision.[18]

On the afternoon of January 29, 1900, Urey Woodson, a newspaper man and lifelong Republican from Owensboro, Kentucky, sat down with Goebel in his room at the Capitol Hotel to discuss the pending resolution of the election. It was the general consensus—with which Woodson agreed—that the general assembly was about to declare Goebel the new governor, and Woodson wanted to know the first thing Goebel was planning to do after being sworn in. Without any hesitation, Woodson later recalled, Goebel stated that he would ask the judge in Covington to call a special grand jury to indict Milton Smith, Basil Duke, and Richard Knott for criminal libel and put them in jail for at least two years.[19]

The next morning, Goebel met two friends in the lobby of the hotel, and the three men started to walk toward the Senate chambers. As they approached the capitol office building, a rifle shot was fired from another, distant building. Goebel had been struck in the chest and immediately fell to the ground. As he struggled to get up, four more shots were fired, all of which went astray. His friends then picked him up and carried him back to the Capitol Hotel. That night, aware of the seriousness of Goebel's injury, the general assembly met and declared him the winner of the election. The next day, he was propped up in his hotel bed and sworn in as governor. Although Goebel fought for his life for several days, the wound proved mortal, and he died on February 3, 1900. The shooting, and Goebel's subsequent death, threw the government into turmoil. Taylor refused to accept the general assembly's decision and remained in the governor's mansion, protected by armed troops. In the meantime, John Beckham, Goebel's lieutenant governor, was sworn in as the new governor.[20]

Within days of Goebel's death, a tentative compromise was reached between the Democrats and the Republicans whereby, if Taylor agreed to step down as governor, Republicans implicated in the assassination would be granted immunity from prosecution. In an effort to diffuse the situation in Frankfort, the two sides agreed to a suspension of the general assembly for one week, pending Taylor's acceptance of the proposed agreement. Duke was adamantly opposed to the compromise, and either he or W. C. P. Breckinridge advised Taylor not to accept it. When the legislature reconvened, Taylor did, in fact, refuse to accept the compromise and, for several months, tried to carry on with business as usual, he and his cabinet moving to London, Kentucky, a Republican enclave in the foothills of the eastern part of the state. Finally, in April, the court of appeals upheld the general assembly's decision and certified Goebel's election. This decision was appealed to the Kentucky Supreme Court, which, on May 21, 1900, upheld the lower court's ruling.[21]

On February 7, 1900, Duke's old friend Thomas W. Bullitt sent a letter to his son Scott, who was attending Harvard Law School, responding to an earlier letter expressing curiosity about the political situation back home. The elder Bullitt wrote that recent events were beyond his powers of description and that his own feelings were best summed up by the following story:

> An old farmer down in Henderson was hauling home a wagon load of apples. In going from the bottoms into a higher country he had to pull up a long and very straight hill. Just as he got to the top of it, the hind gate of his wagon gave way, and the apples went,

Thomas W. Bullitt, throughout his life, remained one of Duke's closest friends. Bullitt is shown here as a prosperous older gentleman. (Courtesy the Filson Historical Society, Louisville.)

as apples will go under such circumstances, down the hill. As he stood watching the disaster a friend came along observing the situation, and asked him why he did not swear. His answer was, I can't do justice to the subject.[22]

Within hours of Goebel's death, a criminal investigation was launched. Many Democrats, including Goebel's brother, believed that the attack was the result of a conspiracy involving the L&N and, of course, Duke, harboring such suspicions for years to come. However, Maury Klein, the railroad's most recent historian, points out: "It is hard to imagine that the railroad would resort to such tactics in order to achieve political success." For one thing, after Goebel's death, the general assembly continued to pass regulatory legislation adversely affecting the L&N and other railroads. So, clearly, the L&N and Duke had other opponents, a fact of which they must have been well aware. Ironically, Governor Beckham, facing a special election in November for the remaining three years of Goebel's term, did make some timely overtures to the L&N for a truce, hoping either to gain its support or at least to keep it from opposing his candidacy. His efforts were successful, and the railroad did not hamper his fall campaign, from which he emerged victorious.[23]

On April 8, 1900, a grand jury in Franklin County returned indictments for the assassination of William Goebel. These indictments were not made public until April 17. Eventually, over twenty people were indicted and charged with conspiracy, most prominently Barry Howard, Henry E. Youtsey, James O. Howard, and Richard Combs as principals and W. H. Coulton, F. Wharton Golden, Charles Finley, Caleb Powers, and John Powers as accessories. No one affiliated with the L&N, not even Duke, was named in the indictments.[24]

Caleb Powers was the first of the alleged conspirators to be put on trial. His attorneys were granted a change of venue, and the trial was moved to Georgetown in Scott County. Judge James Cantrill, a captain in Morgan's as well as Duke's cavalry and obviously well known to Duke but also a friend of Goebel's, was assigned to the case. In all, twenty-three lawyers were involved: eleven for the prosecution; twelve, led by John Y. Brown, the former governor, for the defense. After weeks of testimony, the end of the trial finally came in August, with each side using five attorneys to make its closing arguments. The day the summations were to be delivered was hot and humid, but the courthouse was nevertheless jammed with spectators anticipating a display of oratorical prowess. They were not disappointed. Thomas C. Campbell, one of the prosecutors, a bitter opponent of Duke and the L&N for what he believed was their complicity in the assassination, dramatically addressed the jury: "I would give my right arm to get Basil Duke here on the witness stand." At that moment an old gentleman sitting in the front row who had fought under Duke during the war and was apparently ready to do so again looked at Campbell and said: "And give your other arm and both your legs to let him go again, suh." Judge Cantrill rapped his gavel to bring order to the courtroom but said nothing to the old Confederate about his outburst. The jury returned a guilty verdict against Caleb Powers, but he was destined to have his case retried three times over the course of many years before the courts were satisfied that no judicial error had been committed. Despite the guilty verdict in all four trials, the prosecution was really never able to demonstrate convincingly who had actually murdered Goebel. Powers was eventually pardoned.[25]

By 1900, most of the old-guard Democrats had returned to the party, at least at the national level. The sound money Democrats had worked out a compromise with Bryan that required him to focus on the party's stand against imperialism and accord the free silver issue secondary status. Bryan lost, however, to William McKinley and his popular running mate, Theodore Roosevelt. In Kentucky, politics had regained some semblance of normalcy after the election. Duke, along with many of the old conservatives, was still alienated philosophically from the Democratic Party and drawing ever closer to the Republican Party or some form of political progressiveness, particularly after Theodore Roosevelt assumed the presidency after McKinley's assassination in 1901.[26]

One of Roosevelt's appointments during his first administration was of Duke as commissioner of the Shiloh National Battlefield in 1904, a position that he retained for the rest of his life. Roosevelt's appointment of Duke was an astute political move for the young president. Even as vice president, Roosevelt had recognized that Southerners like Duke who had supported the Republican ticket in 1900 should in some way be rewarded, advising McKinley accordingly. He also understood that federal appointments of friendly and capable Southern Democrats could not hurt the Republican Party. In response to complaints that many Southerners were making concerning the political appointments in their region, Roosevelt wrote Clark Howell, the influential editor in chief of the *Atlanta Constitution* and a member of the Democratic national convention, a detailed letter explaining his selection process. The president advised Howell that his appointments were based, not just on political affiliation, but also on character, fitness, and ability. To illustrate his point, Roosevelt reminded Howell that many of his appointments were Democrats and added:

> This is true of your own state, and by applying to Mr. Thomas Nelson Page of Virginia, to General Basil Duke of Kentucky, to Mr. George Crawford of Tennessee, to Mr. John McIlhenny of Louisiana, to Judge Jones of Alabama, and to Mr. Edgar S. Wilson of Mississippi, all of them Democrats and all of them of the highest standing in their respective communities, you will find that what I have done in Georgia stands not as the exception but as the rule for what I have done throughout the South.[27]

Although still nominally a Democrat, Duke was for all practical purposes working harder than most Republicans for the benefit of their party. This was the first time Duke had had a direct line to the White House. The friendship between Duke and Roosevelt was, however, deeper and more meaningful than the political benefits that each received from the other. Roosevelt periodically invited Duke to the White House, and Duke, as well as members of his family, called on the president many times. As is inevitable when colorful personalities are involved, their interactions tended to be memorable. For example, Duke once visited the White House to solicit from the president his support for the appointment of a candidate to the U.S. Circuit Court of Appeals. Roosevelt declined Duke's request, then turned around and offered the position to Duke. Duke in turn declined the president's offer, unable honorably to accept a position that he had sought on behalf of another.[28]

Early in 1903, Duke and Roosevelt began a correspondence concerning the Republican Party and its leadership in Kentucky. Several months into the exchange, Morris B. Belknap, who was running against Beckham for the governship, asked Duke to provide Roosevelt with an assessment of the political situation in Kentucky, with an eye toward obtaining Roosevelt's endorsement. Duke obliged, informing Roosevelt that, initially, he had favored A. E. Willson over Belknap as the stronger candidate, but he continued: "What I have learned since the nomination, has induced me to believe that he will be a stronger candidate than I had hoped or supposed he would be." Duke then stated: "If I should form a judgment of the result [of the election] solely from a survey of the present condition of the Democratic Party, I should conclude that the Republicans would certainly win." The Democrats, Duke believed, were being run by an unfair and "autocratic" machine that had created widespread discontent within the party, and he also felt that the state primary was the

> most flagrant and audacious political swindle ever witnessed in Kentucky. There was no semblance or pretense of fair play. The majority of the Democratic state Central Committee struck hands with the Louisville ring and made a "slate" which was elected by open and undisguised fraud in violation of the statutory provisions governing primary elections. . . . The independent Democrats are more than ever aroused to the necessity of correcting such methods and are disposed to vote the Republican ticket; and many regular Democrats will sulk and not vote at all.[29]

Duke then advised Roosevelt that, in his opinion, the Republicans would win the election "hands down"—but for their weak leadership. While these men were "honest, patriotic and capable," "they dislike to take strong decisive measures and don't know how to deal with dilemmas; that is to say, they temporize, compromise and let things drift. I think this habit of mind has been induced by their having been so long in minority that they accept defeat in state politics as a matter of course. The democratic leaders are brigands, but they are shrewd and resourceful. They have the bandit intelligence of Goebel and no end of nerve."[30]

Duke concluded his analysis by suggesting that the president's unqualified endorsement would go a long way in helping the Republican ticket in Kentucky. Roosevelt's response indicated that the president concurred with Duke's assessment of the Republican leadership in Kentucky. Events were to prove Duke's analysis correct, Beckham defeating Belknap and remaining in the governor's mansion another four years.[31]

Having crossed their political Rubicon, Duke, Richard W. Knott, and other progressive Kentucky Democrats supported Roosevelt in his 1904 bid for reelection. In January of that year, Knott drafted a memorandum for Roosevelt outlining his and Duke's joint efforts to unite Republican support for his reelection. Duke and Knott had met on New Year's Day with some "friends of the President" hoping to resolve any potential problems within the party hierarchy and generally seeking the development of a harmonious campaign atmosphere. The meeting appeared to be fairly successful, and those present, including A. E. Willson and William O. Bradley, allegedly agreed that, among other things, John Yerkes would be a delegate at large for the state convention and there would be no opposition to his appointment as national committeeman.[32]

Although Yerkes was in Washington when the meeting took place, the terms were delivered to him in a timely manner, and he gave them his verbal approval. Three weeks later, when he returned to Kentucky, he reiterated his assent to Knott.

Since it had been three weeks since the meeting with Bradley, both Duke and Knott felt that it would be prudent to meet with the former governor to go over the New Year's Day agreement one more time. Indeed it was, Bradley in the meantime having reversed his position and now objecting to Yerkes's being either a delegate at large or the national committeeman. Bradley's opposition to Yerkes can be traced to the prior year's gubernatorial campaign. During the convention, Yerkes had backed Belknap, while Bradley had favored Willson. A contested delegation forced Willson to withdraw from the race, angering Bradley and causing some poorly timed division within the party. Duke and Knott now realized they had been overly optimistic in thinking that the New Year's Day agreement would dissipate any residual animosities remaining within the party ranks.[33]

When Bradley made it clear that he intended to reject the agreement unless some significant changes were made, Duke decided that he and Willson needed to consult with Knott, who gave it as his opinion that Yerkes should not give in to Bradley, on the grounds that, if he did, Bradley might try to capitalize on his success and make further demands later. The next day, Duke and Knott met with Yerkes and made him aware of Bradley's change of position. Yerkes, cognizant of party dynamics, recognized that there was some validity to Bradley's position. However, he made it clear that he would assent to Bradley's conditions only if he were made chairman of the state convention. Bradley, not surprisingly, initially rejected the compromise, telling Duke and Knott that, if that was Yerkes's final position, he had no intention of taking part in the convention. But Duke then pointed out to Bradley that, if he carried through on his threat, his absence at the convention would serve only to point up party discord, forcing Bradley to reconsider. Bradley deferred making a decision, however, until he was able to confer with Willson. The next morning, Duke and Knott, with Willson in tow, met with Yerkes, who further conceded that, if he were chairman, he would not select any anti-Bradley people for the state committee. Willson advised everyone that he had not had an opportunity to discuss the situation with Bradley but intended to do so that day. Bradley telephoned Knott that afternoon turning down the compromise.[34]

Willson wrote his own memorandum to the president, basically replicating what Knott had already told Roosevelt. Willson, however, went to the heart of the matter, emphasizing that Bradley had the support of the people, Yerkes that of the party machine, and that a fight between those two forces could only be detrimental to the party. Willson felt that Yerkes should be a delegate at large but that, since he was not a representative of the people, he should not be the national committeeman. To avoid any further confusion, he telephoned Knott and transcribed a memorandum of their conversation, a copy of which he sent to Roosevelt. Willson made it clear that Bradley's chief objection to the Duke-Knott compromise was that it was an attempt by Yerkes "to hold by consent practically all the political control of the party in the state, instead of securing by his visit the union of two strong forces for the President and the Republican Party."[35]

The next day, Bradley sent a letter to Roosevelt, summarizing his position on the proposed compromise. Bradley pointed out that "as to whether Yerkes should be a delegate at large was never discussed" at the preliminary meeting and that he never "suggested that Mr. Yerkes should give up his place as Commissioner." Bradley continued: "I merely said as he held office under you and directed the office holders at the last convention with such disastrous results, I thought he should not undertake to repeat that blunder."[36]

That same day, Willson sent another memorandum to Knott (copying Roosevelt) supporting Bradley's position and pleading with Knott and Duke to try to resolve the matter with Yerkes. Willson believed that the situation "is not only hopeless but the matter is so sensible and the way so plain it ought to be settled and I shall send a copy of this memorandum to the president with this suggestion, that nothing should do more hurt than to have such use by the Commissioner of his control over his officers in Kentucky as should promote his election as national committeeman or delegate at large or temporary and permanent chairman of the Convention or as should exclude Governor Bradley from being a delegate or as should exercise any material influence in his own behalf if he and Governor Bradley were rival candidates for National Committeeman or chairman or delegate."[37]

Knott was extremely upset when he reviewed Willson's memorandum. Knott wrote Willson: "I hoped we could agree or disagree about a Kentucky policy without calling the president in, preferring to take to him the fruits of harmony rather than the results of dissension." He continued that neither Bradley's nor Yerkes's political fortune concerned him, for he had not "been trying to distribute political sugar plums in order to keep quiet the disorderly children in the political nursery." Instead, he had given his efforts "to get the fragments of the Republican Party together in order to make it useful in the future." Obviously frustrated, he concluded his letter by acknowledging that there was no longer a chance for compromise and that all that he could envision was a "fight to the finish." Duke had also given up on unifying the Republican Party in Kentucky. He sent a handwritten note to the president apologizing for being unable to bring Bradley and Yerkes to an agreement concerning his and Knott's compromise proposals. Although Duke did not believe that "the Kentucky Republicans could ever unite for their own success that year," he did believe that "they would work together for the President's re-election." Roosevelt thanked Duke for his letter, writing simply: "I wish I could make those men agree."[38]

Duke and Knott had reason to be frustrated with the Republican soap opera of 1904. For nearly ten years, the Democratic Party had been divided, with many of the old conservatives excluded from party political power. Finding their political philosophy closer to that of the Republican Party, Duke and Knott had tried to revive the Republicans' fortunes in Kentucky by taking advantage of divisions within the state Democratic Party. But the Bradley-Yerkes debacle and the fact of a newly unified Democratic Party clearly spelled doom for Kentucky Republicans in the 1904 elections. When Duke visited Roosevelt in Washington on April 23, he was still pessimistic about the Republican leadership in Kentucky. However, by the first week of May, the Republican state convention having proved, as he wrote Roosevelt, "more harmonious than most of us dared to hope," his attitude had picked up once again. Once more he reiterated what he had been telling the president for months: "Extravagant as it may seem to many people and perhaps to yourself, I firmly believe that with an absolutely united Republican Party—which is essential to bring to it the independent and conservative Democrat vote—Kentucky can be carried for you in November."[39]

Roosevelt responded to Duke two days later with what turned out to be a pragmatic appraisal of the Kentucky Republican Party. Roosevelt felt that it was impossible for the Kentucky Republicans to unite, and he confided that, even though there was what appeared to be a harmonious convention, he had personally "reached a deep-rooted skepticism on the subject." John Marshall Harlan, an associate justice of the U.S. Supreme Court from Kentucky and Duke's nemesis at the Rolling Fork River, shared Roosevelt's skepticism about Republican Party politics in Kentucky, as he wrote Willson the next day: "I received, and examined the marked places in, the papers sent by you. The condition of the Republican Party in Kentucky is very curious. I think the refusal to make Bradley chairman of the delegation was an indignity that ought not to have been put upon him. It looks as if the Republicans of Kentucky were managed, and so managed as to keep up party organization for the benefit of a few people who want office and patronage."[40]

Roosevelt was correct in his assessment of Kentucky. Although he was reelected in November, the Democratic candidate carried Kentucky by twelve thousand votes. Voter turnout in Kentucky was significantly higher than the national average, resulting in a meaningful increase in Democratic votes and a corresponding success for the Democrats in capturing federal and state offices. The Republicans had lost ground, winning only two of the state's congressional seats. Some of the Democratic success can, perhaps, be attributed to the party's candidate, Alton B. Parker, a conservative, who brought back into the fold some of the old-line conservatives who had previously voted for William McKinley. But account must also be taken of the party's newfound cohesion and the corresponding division within the Republican ranks, a reversal of the situation that had prevailed for the past decade.[41]

20

The Disappointments of Life Should Seem Trivial

IN APRIL 1904, A CREDITOR obtained a judgment against the sixty-seven-year-old Duke, precipitating a crisis in his financial affairs. The genesis of Duke's money problems may never be known, but certainly the bankruptcy of the *Southern Magazine* and the liquidation of the Columbia Finance Building and Loan Association, of which Duke was president, were contributing factors. Whatever the reason, Duke was in debt. It was at this time that Henry Lewis Martin came forward and extricated him from his difficulties. Martin, who had joined Morgan's cavalry when he was only fourteen years old, had, after being captured in 1864, spent some difficult months in the Rock Island prisoner-of-war camp. After the war, Martin prospered and entered the world of politics. Politically, he was allied with the old guard and, in 1896, made an unsuccessful bid for a seat in the U.S. Senate.[1]

In response to Martin's offer to help, Duke expressed both his frustration and his embarrassment:

> I could not accept your offer to the full extent, for I cannot incur an obligation from even a man like you which I have no reason to believe I cannot certainly discharge. I had been so long in debt and felt too keenly its humiliation to incur again if I can possibly avoid it; especially I do not wish to have my friends bear the burden no matter how willing they may be. If, however, I can do this—that is to say pay you $250 or $300 early in May and the balance within two, three or four months, I will gladly, as well as gratefully, avail myself of your kindness.[2]

True to his word, Duke sent Martin a timely check. Martin had either assumed or satisfied the creditor's judgment, and, although he was willing to give Duke an interest-free loan, Duke could not accept such an offer. In his own way, Duke did try to reciprocate Martin's kindness by attempting to secure for him an annual pass on the L&N Railroad. In prior years, Duke had almost unlimited access to passes, but times had changed. The general assembly had passed a statute prohibiting the use of free passes "for the purpose of intimidating any office or officers in this Commonwealth." This forced the railroad to scrutinize each pass to determine whether its issuance was a violation of the new law. Duke went to Lee Hines, an L&N vice president, to present his case for Martin's pass. Duke considered the meeting a success, notifying Martin that he was confident that the pass would be issued in a few days. However, two days later, Hines wrote Duke: "The present restrictions upon issue of free transportation make it entirely impracticable to comply with Mr. Martin's request." Duke sent Martin a copy of Hines's letter along with a note saying that he felt his arguments for the pass had been justified.[3]

The restraining of the L&N's free hand was not the only sign of changing times. Growing tired of the bossism that had long dominated Louisville politics and the resultant recurrent instances of election fraud, voters began to rally around the banner of progressivism. Progressivism meant different things to different people, but to most of its adherents it meant local and state political reform. To Duke it meant maintaining Louisville's strong business presence in the Upper South, and that meant loosening the stranglehold that machine politics had on the city, which was stifling economic progress.[4]

Still, as he aged, Duke naturally took an increasingly skeptical attitude toward reform. He recognized that, for most people, "it is extremely trying to be obliged to relinquish opinions long tenaciously held or surrender even a cherished prejudice, but circumstances sometimes compel such sacrifices." H. L. Martin held similar views but, as Duke remembered in his *Reminiscences,* predicted that they would see an eventual "change of political sentiment and obliteration of existing prejudices in Kentucky." Duke hoped that Martin's prediction would, ultimately, be "verified," but, in his heart, he was not so optimistic. As he wrote Martin in December 1904: "I sometimes hope it myself but then when I see how slavishly the people adhere to obsolete ideas and mere names and labels my heart sinks and hope dies in me. One thing I should be glad of I want you to keep in mind not only as a possibility but as perhaps a duty; I should be glad before I die to vote for you as an independent and reform candidate for governor."[5]

For years, the dynamics of Louisville's metropolitan government had been dominated by bossism and Democratic Party machine politics. The political machine was under the control of John Whallen, who had gained power with the backing of the labor and immigrant votes. However, after enduring years of Whallen's political dominance, Louisville's Republicans and reform-minded Democrats joined forces and formed the Fusionist movement. The Fusionists were principally a group of well-known reform-minded businessmen, professionals, and religious leaders, some of whom, Duke among them, had been anti-Goebel Democrats. Duke and those Fusionists who were principally interested in curbing the influence of the Whallen machine formed an organization known as the City Club. With the 1905 mayoral election on the horizon, the Fusionists—led by Duke, Thomas Bullitt, and Richard W. Knott, the editor of the *Louisville Evening Post*—backed the Republican candidate, Joseph T. O'Neill. The Democratic candidate, Paul C. Barth, was supported by the Whallen machine and endorsed by Henry Watterson and the *Louisville Courier-Journal.* Duke had finally broken with the Democrats, having officially become a member of the Republican committee.[6]

In early October, as the campaign was heating up, a rumor spread rapidly through Louisville that the Whallen machine proposed to open the voter registration books to nonresidents, people described by the *Louisville Evening Post* as drifters or "denizens" of the saloons, houses of prostitution, and similar disreputable establishments. Were these people in fact registered as voters, their numbers would increase the voting base and possibly force the names of some legitimate voters off the rolls. This type of outright fraud was too much for Duke to take sitting down. On the afternoon of October 3, 1905, while at the Fusion Party headquarters, Duke learned that the Democrats were attempting to register some illegal voters in the Thirteenth Precinct. Without any hesitation, the old warrior decided to go down and investigate the situation for himself. Accompanied by John Bradburn, Duke walked down to the precinct and discovered that there was already a large group of these "denizens" milling around the precinct house, located at the corner of Ninth and Jefferson Streets, waiting to register. He immediately voiced his objection to several policemen standing nearby. His outburst drew the attention of one of the more belligerent men of this unsavory bunch, who stepped forward and knocked the old general to the ground. Undeterred, Duke picked himself up, dusted himself off, and walked boldly to the door of the precinct house, only to find it locked. When he demanded that the door be unlocked, the precinct officers refused to let either him or Bradburn inside. At this point, the crowd outside became ugly and began to push Duke and Bradburn around until Duke was knocked to the ground a second time. Once again, Duke picked himself up and glared at the policemen, who were trying to ignore what had just happened. When Duke asked them if they were going to arrest the man who had just hit him, they laughed and said that they had not seen anything that warranted an arrest. Further, when they learned who Duke was, they quickly left the scene and later reported to their superiors that they had seen nothing.[7]

On November 4, only three days before the election, the City Club staged a rally of several thousand people before the Jefferson County courthouse and city hall in downtown Louisville. The crowd was anxious to hear what the Fusionists had to say. The Democrats, however, were intent on doing whatever was necessary to disrupt the speakers. Strategically placed Democratic Party supporters heckled Duke, who presided over the rally. Then, a symphony of disruptive noises composed of clanging trolley cars and horse-drawn fire engines converged on the rally.

Duke certainly must have looked on with disgust at the antics employed by the Democrats that afternoon. His only hope was that the electorate would show the same disgust by voting the machine out of office.[8]

Despite the efforts of Duke and his fellow Fusionists, the city of Louisville once again witnessed widespread election fraud, with the Democrats actually employing force in some instances to secure votes. The result was a Democratic victory by the very slim margin of five thousand votes. The leaders of the Fusion Party and approximately one hundred other outraged citizens met within a few days of the election and raised a legal fund of $10,000 to challenge the election results. As soon as this challenge was officially initiated, Helm Bruce and William Bullitt began to take depositions from key witnesses that became the basis for forty-five charges of election irregularities that were filed with the Jefferson County circuit court. In December, Judge Shackelford Miller upheld the election results. And the Fusionists raised another $10,000 to fund an appeal. But it was not until April 1907 that their case was finally heard in Frankfort.[9]

The Fusionists had amply documented instances of repeat voting, ballot stealing, voter intimidation, and "alphabetical voting" (a process whereby voters were required to line up and vote in alphabetical order, preventing many from voting before the polls closed) in more than one precinct. Their case was strong. After reviewing it, the Kentucky Court of Appeals, by a vote of 4 to 2, in May 1907 reversed Judge Miller's decision. The election results were immediately voided. With the next scheduled elections still seven months away, Governor Beckham had no choice but to appoint an interim government, led by Robert Worth Bingham as mayor. The Fusionists continued their assault on the displaced Barth administration, attacking the ex-mayor for alleged improprieties while in office. Barth, unable psychologically to deal with the assault on his personal integrity, committed suicide in August. By this time, the Fusion Party had split and all but disappeared, and, when the election was held in November, the Republicans won control of the city government, and James E. Grinstead was sworn in as mayor.[10]

Despite his involvement with the Fusion Party, Duke had in recent years cut back significantly on the amount of time that he devoted to politics. He had also ceased working for the L&N sometime in 1902 or 1903. He thus had much more time to devote to some of his other interests. As we have seen, President Roosevelt had appointed him commissioner of Shiloh National Battlefield in 1904, a position that required his participation in dedications and other ceremonies on behalf of the government. In 1905, for example, he presided at the ceremony dedicating the Confederate monument, eloquently and presciently, pointing out to his audience:

It is intended that this spot, where the bones of heroes rest, shall be regarded as holy ground; that the dead who lie here, Federal and Confederate, all distinctions between them forgot, all enmity buried in the grave, shall be held in equal honor as American Soldiers; so that the youth of this country, from generation to generation, who shall visit it, knowing little perhaps of the issues which divided those who fought and fell here, knowing and feeling nothing of the animosities and resentment of the strife, may be taught to entertain the patriotic fervor which animated Confederate and Federal alike, to emulate their conduct, to serve their country, and, if need be, give their breasts to the battle with the same heroic purpose which impelled these men, whether they wore the blue or the gray.[11]

In 1906, at the dedication of the Wisconsin monument, the once fiery secessionist made an even more remarkable speech. Building on forty years of belief in sectional reconciliation, Duke proclaimed that secession, although constitutionally right, was morally wrong. A Confederate victory, he argued, not only would have divided the Union, but in time would also have been the downfall of the Confederacy as a country, which, as William C. Davis put it, "simply contained too many elements at conflict with each other for them to coalesce." Duke was "glad the two sides were now one." He would regularly recur to the theme of reconciliation throughout his years as battlefield commissioner.[12]

Also in 1906, Duke reissued *A History of Morgan's Cavalry.* There were many good reasons to do so. For example, a vast amount of work had been done on the Civil War in the forty years since the *History* had initially appeared. Also, with the publication of *The War of the Rebellion*—a compilation of the official records of both sides, the last volume of which was issued in 1901—a great deal of previously unavailable primary source material was now at his disposal. However, refining the account seems not to have been Duke's goal. Although several of his friends and wartime associates, particularly Thomas W. Bullitt, would have liked to see him expand on his role in the Morgan command structure, the "revision" that Duke produced turned out to be nothing more than a slight abridgment of the original edition. The idealized picture of Morgan that he had painted in 1867 was left unaltered.[13] That leaves us with a motivation that seems to have been purely financial. Duke had arranged for the Neale Publishing Company of New York to bring out *Morgan's Cavalry,* as the new edition was called. Walter Neale, a close friend of Ambrose Bierce's, took the deepest personal pride in publishing books on the Confederacy and, over a twenty-year period, published some seventy classics of Confederate literature. He also paid royalties that were very generous for the time—typically 20 percent of gross sales.[14]

Duke kept up his personal relationship with Theodore Roosevelt during these years, a relationship that, as we have seen, both men also put to political use. For example, when, in a November 1908 *New York Evening Post* article, William Garrott Brown accused the president of abandoning the Republican Party in the South—by ignoring the state committees and using his own set of Washington referees to

SELECTIONS FROM OUR SOUTHERN BOOKS

[WRITE FOR 100 PAGE ILLUSTRATED CATALOGUE]

MEMOIRS OF JOHN H. REAGAN.

A notable book. As Postmaster-General in the Cabinet of President Davis he was regarded as one of the masters who shaped the fortunes of the Confederacy. Fully illustrated. *8vo, $3.00; postage, 25 cents.*

JEFFERSON, CABELL, AND THE UNIVERSITY OF VIRGINIA. By Prof. John S. Patton, Ph. D.

A complete history of the leading educational institution of the South. Fully illustrated. *8vo, postpaid, $2.00.*

LIFE AND LETTERS OF ROBERT EDWARD LEE, SOLDIER AND MAN. By Rev. J. William Jones, D. D.

Dr. Jones was with the Army of Northern Virginia from Harper's Ferry to Appomattox. He was one of the chaplains of Washington College during the whole of Lee's Presidency, and with the full approval of Mrs. Lee and the Faculty of the College, he was given free access to General Lee's private letters and papers. He knew Lee the man as a man among men, and as few have known him, and in his thoughtful and careful book he has made the great General real and near to us. Fully illustrated. *8vo, postpaid, $2.00.*

MORGAN'S CAVALRY. By Gen. Basil W. Duke.

A history of one of the most remarkable commands in the Confederate Army. Illustrated by portraits and maps. *8vo, postpaid, $2.00.*

A HISTORY OF SOUTHERN LITERATURE. By Prof. Carl Holliday.

It begins with the first American book by Capt. John Smith, and is an exhaustive study by a thorough scholar of the whole of a literature of splendid values. *8vo, postpaid, $2.50.*

RECOLLECTIONS OF A LIFETIME. By John Goode of Virginia.

For three-quarters of a century Judge Goode has led a life of extraordinary usefulness. He was a member of the Virginia Secession Convention, the Confederate Congress, of the Congress of the United States, Solicitor General of the United States, Commissioner of this country to settle claims against the United States and Chile, President of the last Virginia Constitutional Convention, etc. *8vo, postpaid, $2.00.*

RECOLLECTIONS OF A CONFEDERATE STAFF OFFICER. By Gen. G. Moxley Sorrel, Chief of Staff of Longstreet's First Army Corps. Introduction by Senator John W. Daniel.

This book, says Lord Gen. Wolseley of the British Army, is one of the most important that has yet been issued with respect to the great American war. *8vo, postpaid, $2.00.*

THE MECKLENBERG DECLARATION OF INDEPENDENCE, May 20, 1775, AND LIVES OF ITS SIGNERS. By Dr. George W. Graham.

8vo, postpaid, $1.50.

CONFEDERATE OPERATIONS IN CANADA AND NEW YORK. By Capt. John W. Headley.

A volume that will perhaps interest as many readers as any book treating of the Civil War. Illustrated by portraits. *8vo, postpaid, $2.00.*

REPRESENTATIVE POETS OF THE SOUTH. By Prof. Charles H. Hubner.

A critical study of the principal Southern poets, with selections from their works. *8vo, postpaid, $2.50.*

JOHNNY REB AND BILLY YANK. By Alexander Hunter.

Being the experiences and observations of a private in the ranks of the Confederate Army. The author was for two years in Pickett's infantry and two years in the Black Horse Cavalry. Illustrated. *8vo, postpaid, $2.00.*

FOUR YEARS UNDER MARSE ROBERT. By Major Robert Stiles.

A full and consecutive record of the surroundings, aspirations, inspirations, experiences, and daily life of the intelligent soldier of the Army of Northern Virginia. *8vo, postpaid, $2.00.*

The Neale Publishing Company, New York & Washington

Morgan's Cavalry

By GENERAL BASIL W. DUKE

IF history be the staid and solemn march of events, this is not history, this narrative that thrills and rouses like a trumpet call. It is romance, the remarkable doings of a brave man brave men loved and followed and fought for; it is high romance, a succession of rapid pictures in which all is movement and color, peril, dash and courage. If history be the past made living, a narrative through which heart-beats and hoof-beats ring surely and clearly, this is history, interesting and convincing.

General John H. Morgan

No one is so capable of writing the story of General John H. Morgan's command as General Basil W. Duke. He is familiar with every event in its history and all of the incidents of the four years' struggle. As soon as Morgan organized his Lexington company, Duke entered that command, and before the first year of the war was over he married Miss Henrietta Morgan, General Morgan's sister, and upon the death of Morgan in '64, Duke was made brigadier-general. His brigade was one of the five commanded by General Breckinridge which formed the escort of President Davis after the evacuation of Richmond.

The story of the soldier-life of John Hunt Morgan is quite worth telling. Brought up in Kentucky where people learn to fight as they learn to breathe, he is fighting in the Mexican War at nineteen; a trained and accomplished soldier when the Civil War opens, he starts with a single company and in two years, by his own exertions and the power of his extraordinary personality, he has recruited and organized a command of nearly five thousand men; he fights many hot battles, destroys supplies, captures prisoners and ammunition, raids hostile territory, plans and executes dangerous expeditions of all sorts, always dashing about, hither and thither, brilliant, magnetic, agile, irrepressible, hard to catch and harder to shake—it is an exciting story and General Duke has told it well.

General Basil W. Duke

The volume is a large octavo, handsomely bound, and the paper and letter-press are excellent. Illustrated with portraits and maps.

Price, postpaid, $2.00

THE NEALE PUBLISHING COMPANY

NEW YORK — Broadway, Fifth Ave. and 23d St.

WASHINGTON — 431 Eleventh Street N. W.

In 1906, the Neale Publishing Company released this four-page promotional pamphlet touting *Morgan's Cavalry. Top,* Front-back cover spread. *Bottom,* Inside spread.

determine federal appointments in the region—a highly offended Roosevelt felt compelled to respond to the article personally. He did so by writing Richard Watson Gilder, the influential editor of the *Century Magazine,* pointing out that he had always striven to appoint "as high grade of men to office in the South as in the North" and that he had, in fact, both consulted and appointed Southerners (albeit sometimes Democratic Southerners):

Whenever I could not get a Republican or felt the local Republican machine ought not to be trusted, then I should appoint a thoroughly good Democrat. Good Proctor, and Basil Duke and the other men I consulted—including for instance General Buckner, of Kentucky, and ex-Governor Thompson of South Carolina—all said that what they propose [i.e., the appointment of reputable African Americans to federal positions in the South] represented probably an impossible idea, but that if it could be adopted all good Southerners would feel the greatest relief, and even though politically they might continue to differ from a Republican president who acted in such a way, they would heartily uphold him on the basis of their common citizenship. Well, I've acted precisely and exactly this way. I have not deviated by a hair's breadth from the ideal thus set up by these ex-confederates, those high-minded gentlemen, all of them Southern Democrats.[15]

Roosevelt's letter can, in many ways, be viewed as a commentary on Duke's lifelong political journey, a journey that itself emphasizes the adaptability and the astuteness of a man who, in his final years, readily adopted a progressive political philosophy. At the same time, Duke did not abandon his conservative beliefs entirely. It was his ability to recognize when change was for the better and merge the best elements of his conservative heritage with the best elements of the new progressivism that made him so valuable to Roosevelt, Louisville, and Kentucky.

Change entered Duke's life in another way late in the first decade of the twentieth century when his wife of almost fifty years died. Tommie Duke had not been the typical Victorian-era housewife. Over the years she had become well known throughout the South for her work with Confederate veterans' associations and related projects. She was the regent of the Kentucky Room at the Museum of the Confederacy in Richmond, Virginia, to which she had donated a significant collection of Civil War artifacts belonging to her brother, John Hunt Morgan. A founder and president of the Albert Sidney Johnston Chapter of the United Daughters of the Confederacy, Tommie had a tendency to use the organization as a vehicle to help poor and sick veterans. Her activities with the United Daughters of the Confederacy were so well known that she became a vice president of the organization's national division. Then, on October 20, 1909, after returning from a convention in Hopkinsville, Kentucky, and giving no indication that she was feeling ill, Tommie went to bed in her normal fashion—and died in her sleep. The official cause of death was a sudden heart failure.[16]

Duke was devastated. The pain that he experienced was probably expressed best in a letter he wrote the Reverend Edward Owings Guerrant: "Mrs. Duke's loss has been the sorest sorrow for me that has ever come—I did not really know before what sorrow was, although I had often been deeply grieved and had cause to mourn. But I am glad to feel with you, that what we call death here, 'does not end a noble life' and hers was the noblest and purest I ever knew."[17]

Tommie was laid to rest in the Morgan family plot in the Lexington Cemetery next to her infant son "Johnny Reb," who had died in 1866, and her daughter Tommie, who had died in 1905 giving birth to her only child. Soon after, Duke moved from his house in the center of town and went to live with his daughter Julia and her family. Julia had married Samuel Henning and lived in the Cherokee Park district of Louisville. Duke remained with his daughter and her family for the remainder of his life.[18]

The years after Tommie's death saw a gradual retrenchment in Duke's life. Still, old interests were not abandoned. From the late 1890s until approximately 1910, Duke had written a series of articles for *Home and Farm,* an obscure local agricultural journal with a small circulation edited by his old friend Richard W. Knott. The articles drew on the experience of a lifetime and ranged widely, covering such topics as his Civil War exploits, the personalities of famous figures, the vagaries of politics, and the challenges of old age. Preston Davie, the son of Duke's old friend George Davie, collected the articles and took them to New York City to show his old friend and schoolmate Arthur Page, who was affiliated with the New York publishing firm of Doubleday, Page and Company. After reviewing the articles, Page was convinced that they should be reissued in book form. With Page's help, Davie convinced Duke of the value of the project—and to edit his articles so that they could be published in book form. The result was the 1911 *Reminiscences of General Basil W. Duke C.S.A.,* an interesting and varied, if somewhat chronologically disjointed, collection, and an invaluable contribution to Confederate/Southern literature. Disappointingly, but not surprisingly, the always modest Duke wrote very little about his individual accomplishments, in particular downplaying his performance as an officer under Morgan.[19]

Duke also maintained an active interest in politics and, even in retirement, continued to dispense advice to those who for many years had relied on his astute observations. In 1911, he wrote H. L. Martin that, of the two candidates for governor in the upcoming election, he preferred the Democrat, James McCreary, over the Republican, Edward O'Rear. However, his real preference was "to see the Republicans put up a man I could vote for, in the event that I should still think it proper to vote that ticket, and I have expressed, whenever the opportunity offered itself, to all who may possibly have influence on the Republican convention, the opinion that neither party should present a candidate who has taken a position so prejudicial to the peace and best interests of the state."[20] Several weeks later, at the instigation of his friend Leslie Combs, who anticipated U.S. military involvement south of the border in response to the Mexican Revolution, Duke wrote Theodore Roosevelt. Combs had heard that, in the event of war, Roosevelt intended to raise a brigade of cavalry. If this was, in fact, the case, the jingoistic Combs gave it as his opinion that Roosevelt should include a regiment from central Kentucky in the brigade and requested that he, Combs, be authorized to raise said regiment. The former president responded that he had no desire to be personally involved in a war with Mexico and that it was his opinion that any border dispute should be handled by the U.S. Army as a police action.[21]

Despite his stepping back from the limelight, Duke was still a public figure, and the year 1911 saw him presiding over the unveiling of the John Hunt Morgan Memorial in Lexington. The memorial project had been in the works since 1906, when the United Daughters of the Confederacy (UDC) had commissioned the Italian-born sculptor Pompeo Coppini to create an equestrian statue of Morgan. Work on the monument was almost abandoned when the UDC found itself unable to raise more than half the agreed-on $15,000 fee. Then, at the last minute, the Kentucky legislature passed a bill appropriating $7,500 to make up for the shortfall. The statue was completed and the unveiling scheduled for October 18, 1911.[22]

The unveiling of the Morgan monument was a momentous event, not just for the city of Lexington, but also for the surviving members of Morgan's cavalry. Duke, naturally expected to play a prominent role in the unveiling, and Major Otis S. Tenney were named masters of ceremonies. But Tenney fell ill and, when the long-awaited day finally arrived, was unable to leave his bed, so Duke presided alone. A parade had been scheduled for 1:30 in the afternoon, following by the unveiling at 2:00. The crowd began to gather early, and, by the time of the parade, people were filling the windows and even sitting on the roofs of the buildings around the courthouse square in order to get a clear view of the ceremonies. The *Lexington Herald* estimated that there were between fifteen and twenty thousand people present.[23]

There were approximately four hundred veterans in the parade, and, although some marched with a faltering step, they were all very proud to be taking part in the festivities. At the head of the column were two men on horseback, Duke and his lifelong friend John Castleman. Although Castleman had never achieved a rank higher than that of captain in the Confederate army, the U.S. government had commissioned him a brigadier general during the Spanish-American War. The newspaper reported that Duke and Castleman never looked handsomer, and they received many a hand wave, which they acknowledged with a tip of the hat.[24]

It took twenty minutes for the parade to pass, but Duke finally reached the courthouse square, where he found the statue flanked by two ceremonial platforms, one for the dignitaries, another for schoolchildren dressed in red, white, and blue and arranged to form the Stars and Bars. It is hard to imagine the thoughts going through his mind as he dismounted and joined the other dignitaries. For one thing, it was just nine days shy of the fiftieth anniversary of when he and Morgan were sworn into the Confederate army on the steps of the Woodsonville church. And, looking around, he would have seen many familiar faces, including Dick and Charlton Morgan. Of course, there were many other faces he would have wanted to see: Tommie, his young brother-in-law Thomas, Mrs. Henrietta Morgan, Thomas Hines, and Thomas W. Bullitt.[25]

Duke did not deliver a speech but simply introduced the keynote speaker, Dr. Guy Carleton Lee of Johns Hopkins University, a third cousin of Robert E. Lee's who waxed as eloquent and partisan as Duke ever did on the topic of Morgan and the Confederacy. Lee was very well received, and, after several other speeches, two young girls stepped forward. Frances Breckinridge Steele, the granddaughter of John C. Breckinridge, and Henrietta Hunt Henning, Duke's granddaughter, pulled back the strings, unveiling the magnificent statute of John Hunt Morgan that still stands on Main Street in Lexington.[26]

As Duke grew older, he made every attempt to keep in contact with old friends. As one of the few surviving high-ranking Confederate officers, he also received a great many inquiries from younger Southerners seeking to mine his memory. Duke cheerfully responded to all such requests to the best of his ability. For example, he was able to provide a Mrs. Beauregard with information about several Missouri Confederates, including Colton Greene and General Frost, for whom he had obtained weapons (see chapter 3). Even a 1914 cataract operation could not keep him from his correspondence, his daughter Julia taking dictation until he could resume writing on his own.[27]

Duke also spent time with his twelve young grandchildren, the oldest having been born in 1898. Grandchildren, of course, have a tendency to idolize their grandparents, and a grandfather who was a legendary storyteller was bound to be a particular favorite. Currie Mathews Cabot, the daughter of Currie Duke Mathews, who was born in 1900, remembered her grandfather so well that, in 1933, she was able to write a portrait of him for the *New English Weekly*—and in a style uncannily like his own. She recalled his stories of the Civil War, which she heard as a child and which made her feel that "his own life had been rich with a kind of adventurousness that is hardly possible in our day." She and her cousins were proud "of the hot stirring" that the stories engendered in their blood "of a history that was beautiful as legend," and often their dreams "were filled with the sweep and thunder of cavalry." They also recognized, quite poignantly, that those stories were of a "fresh-coloured brilliant young man" they would never know except imaginatively.[28]

Duke remained thus occupied until the summer of 1916, which he spent with his daughter Mary Currie and her children in her summer home in Massachusetts.

Life had not been overly kind to Mary Currie. She had moved to New York shortly after marrying William Mathews in 1899. But Mathews had died in 1910, leaving her a widow with two children and an uncertain financial future. She lost another love, the violin, to arthritis soon thereafter. And she was soon to lose her father. During his stay in Massachusetts, Duke began to have problems with his right leg, the result of arteriosclerosis. By the end of the summer, his condition began to deteriorate, and, after a close examination, his physicians decided that it had become necessary to amputate his right foot. Duke was admitted to the Presbyterian hospital in New York City, where the amputation was performed during the first week of September. After the operation, Duke appeared to be doing well physically. However, after further consultation, the surgeons determined that a second amputation was necessary, this time above the right knee. The second operation was performed on September 11. The doctors were pleased with the results and convinced that no further surgery would be necessary. Duke recovered rapidly over the next few days, and everyone was highly encouraged by his endurance. Then, on September 15, he contracted a fever, and his physical condition deteriorated rapidly. Some of Duke's immediate family members remained with him in the hospital that day, and there is also evidence that Theodore Roosevelt visited with him for an hour. In the early morning hours of September 16, 1916, General Basil Wilson Duke died, his son Dr. Henry Duke of Louisville at his side. The cause of death was most likely kidney failure.[29]

Arrangements were quickly made to bring Duke's body back to Kentucky to be buried with his wife in Lexington. On September 17, Duke's remains were put on a Chesapeake and Ohio Railroad car, arriving in Lexington just before 8:00 A.M. the next day. The body was immediately taken from the railroad depot to Dick Morgan's house on Third Street, where it lay in state in a coffin draped with a Confederate flag as hundreds of people viewed the body. The funeral was set for that afternoon at Christ Church Cathedral on Market Street, where the services were conducted by Dean Robert K. Massie assisted by Louis W. Burton and Dean C. E. Cralk of Louisville. Many of Duke's friends, including John Castleman and William Jonathan Davis, were in attendance. It was a very hot day, and at least two of the old veterans passed out, overcome by the heat. Finally, late in the day, Duke reached his final resting place, Lexington Cemetery, where he joined Tommie and John Hunt Morgan.[30]

If Basil Wilson Duke is remembered at all today, it is as the author of several definitive works of Confederate military history. But his life was as important to the shape of American history as it was interesting. He was a militarily astute commander who was largely responsible for the success of Morgan's cavalry. He was a clear-sighted counselor who at Abbeville helped convince Jefferson Davis of the futility of further resistance. After the war he was among the first to recognize the

Basil Duke was imbued with the "intellectuality of the Old South, its spirit, its fire, and he had a breadth and quality of mind that was timeless" (Henning, "Basil Wilson Duke," 63–64). (Courtesy the Filson Historical Society, Louisville.)

necessity of reconciliation with the North. He was also among the first to recognize the importance of business to the country as a whole and of the Louisville and Nashville Railroad to Kentucky in particular. And toward both those ends he was a tireless behind-the-scenes worker, helping determine the shape of both Kentucky and national politics for fifty years.

Duke was, as Currie Mathews Cabot wrote, a "representative, a Southerner before the War, with the intellectuality of the old South."[31] But he was also a product of the Civil War, both burdened and inspired by its legacy. And over the course of an almost eighty-year life span—one that saw the emergence of the United States as an industrial nation and, ultimately, a world power—he remained open to change. His is an understudied life that still has much to tell us about who we are as a nation today and where we might be going. It is my hope that these pages have been a useful first step in that direction.

Notes

The following acronyms have been employed in the notes:

AEWP	Augustus Everett Willson Papers, Filson Historical Society
BFP/FHS	Bullitt Family Papers, Filson Historical Society
CFP	Coburn Family Papers, Kentucky Historical Society
CWC/MHS	Civil War Collection, Missouri Historical Society
CWC/TSLA	Civil War Collection, Tennessee State Library and Archives
DDJC	Don D. John Collection, Kentucky Historical Society
DHSP	D. H. Smith Papers, Filson Historical Society
HFP	Hathaway Family Papers, University of Kentucky
HLMP	H. L. Martin Papers, Kentucky Historical Society
HMFP	Hunt-Morgan Family Papers, University of Kentucky
JHMP	John Hunt Morgan Papers, University of North Carolina, Southern Historical Collection
JWSP	John W. Stevenson Papers, Kentucky State Archives
KSP	Kirby Smith Papers, University of North Carolina, Southern Historical Collection
MDFP	Morgan-Duke Family Papers, Filson Historical Society
THHP	Thomas H. Hines Papers, Filson Historical Society
TRP	Theodore Roosevelt Papers, Library of Congress, Manuscript Division
WHMP	W. H. Mackoy Papers, University of Kentucky
WLP	William Lindsay Papers, University of Kentucky
OR	U.S. War Department, *The War of the Rebellion: A Compilation of the Official Records of the Union and Confederate Armies*

Foreword

1. James A. Ramage, *Rebel Raider: The Life of General John Hunt Morgan,* 278n.36.

2. Ulysses S. Grant, *Personal Memoirs of U. S. Grant,* ed. E. B. Long (1952; repr., New York: Da Capo Press, 1982), p. 563.

3. Theodore Roosevelt, *Ranch Life and the Hunting Trail* (1888; memorial edition), IV, 431–32.

1. The Right Man in the Right Place

1. Leeland Hathaway Memoirs, 59, Hathaway Family Papers, University of Kentucky (hereafter HFP).

2. Davie, "Founders of the Filson Club," 133.

2. The Bluegrass

1. Apple, Johnson, and Bevins, eds., *History of Scott County,* 125; Bevins, *History of Scott County,* 113; Peters and Perrin, eds., *History of Fayette County,* 143–44; Paxton, *The Marshall Family,* 77.

2. Peters and Perrin, eds., *History of Fayette County,* 144.

3. Paxton, *Marshall Family,* 180, 282–89; Stanton, *Henning and Duke Families,* 20–21.

4. Davenport, *Ante-Bellum Kentucky,* 22–36; Paxton, *Marshall Family,* 282–89. There appears to be some confusion as to whether Duke was born in 1837 or 1838. The authors of most nineteenth-century biographical sketches, who would have consulted Duke when they were writing, indicate 1837 as his birth date. This date is also the one used in the 1850 census and Duke's Georgetown College entrance records. See *United States Census, 1850, Kentucky, Scott County, District 1, East Fork* and Georgetown College Archives, Georgetown College.

5. MacKenzie, *Colonial Families,* 197–99.

6. Chinn, *Kentucky Settlement and Statehood,* 294–96.

7. Davenport, *Ante-Bellum Kentucky,* 24–25; Wharton and Barbour, *Bluegrass Land and Life,* 43.

8. Clark, *History of Kentucky,* 161–65. Kentucky also enjoyed extensive overland trade with the antebellum South, shipping out great "droves of cattle, hogs or sheep and wagon loads of bacon, salt or gunpowder." Parr, "Kentucky's Overland Trade," 71 (see also 71–81).

9. MacKenzie, *Colonial Families,* 197–99.

10. Paxton, *Marshall Family,* 76–77; Staples, *Pioneer Lexington,* 319.

11. Railey, *History of Woodford County,* 179.

12. Paxton, *Marshall Family,* 76.

13. Ibid., 77; Staples, *Pioneer Lexington,* 126, 319; Clift, *History of Maysville,* 122–25; Thomas, *Brown County, Ohio,* 121.

14. Railey, *History of Woodford County,* 179.

15. Jillison, *Kentucky Land Grants,* 83–84; Clift, *History of Maysville,* 356–62; Paxton, *Marshall Family,* 178–82.

16. Paxton, *Marshall Family,* 180 (quotation); Duke, *Reminiscences,* 154.

17. Paxton, *Marshall Family,* 181; Stanton, *Henning and Duke Families,* 21.

18. Stanton, *Henning and Duke Families,* 21.

19. Schmant, "Two Letters," 118.

20. Ibid.; Swinford and Swinford, *Great Elm Tree,* 203.

21. Duke, *Reminiscences,* 46–49; Cook, *Old Kentucky,* 116–19.

22. Duke, *Reminiscences,* 46–49; Wharton and Barbour, *Bluegrass Land and Life,* 49.

23. Paxton, *Marshall Family,* 180.

24. Wyatt-Brown, *Southern Honor,* 22–34; Coleman, *Slavery Times,* 25.

25. Coleman, *Famous Kentucky Duels,* 88–96, 127–28; Nevins, *Ordeal of the Union,* 1:65–68.

26. Castleman, *Active Service,* 82.

27. Wilson and Bodley, *History of Kentucky,* 418–24; Johnson, *History of Kentuckians,* 639.

28. Wilson and Bodley, *History of Kentucky,* 418–24; Johnson, *History of Kentuckians,* 639.

29. Davenport, *Ante-Bellum Kentucky,* 52–54; Snyder, *History of Georgetown College,* 34–40.

30. Snyder, *History of Georgetown College,* 34–40.

31. Georgetown College, *Catalogue of the Officers and Students,* and Georgetown College Grade Book, first and second semesters, 1853–54, both in Georgetown College Archives, Georgetown College.

32. Georgetown College, *Catalogue of the Officers and Students,* Georgetown College Archives, Georgetown College; Craven, *Growth of Southern Nationalism,* 171–92.

33. Apple, Johnson, and Bevins, eds., *History of Scott County,* 111; Coulter, *Civil War and Readjustment,* 4–5; Craven, *Growth of Southern Nationalism,* 358.

34. Coulter, *Civil War and Readjustment,* 8–15; Craven, *Growth of Southern Nationalism,* 7–13; Nevins, *Ordeal of the Union,* 2:537–54.

35. Clark, *History of Kentucky,* 315; Coleman, *Slavery Times,* 206–11; Craven, *Growth of Southern Nationalism,* 358–59 (quotation).

36. Tocqueville, *Democracy in America,* 342.

37. Apple, Johnson, and Bevins, eds., *History of Scott County,* 125–27; Harrison, *Antislavery Movement,* 3; *United States Census, Scott County;* Coleman, *Slavery Times,* 45.

38. Duke, *Reminiscences,* 281–86; Coleman, "Lexington's Slave Dealers," 10–11; Coleman, *Slavery Times,* 54; Duke, "Hungry Little Greeks," 205–9; Johnson, *Soul by Soul,* 218. See also Lucas, *Blacks in Kentucky,* 1:45–50.

39. Centre College, *1890 General Catalogue,* and *Thirty-first Annual Catalogue of the Officers and Students,* 5, 9, Centre College Archives, Centre College.

40. Centre College, *1890 General Catalogue,* and *Thirty-first Annual Catalogue of the Officers and Students,* Centre College Archives, Centre College.

41. Bullitt, "Recollections of the War," Bullitt Family Papers, Filson Historical Society (hereafter BFP/FHS).

42. Green, *Historic Families of Kentucky,* 102–3.

43. Paxton, *Marshall Family,* 283.

44. Wright, *Transylvania,* 175; Nevins, *Emergence of Lincoln,* 1:114–15.

45. Leeland Hathaway Memoirs, 33–34, 50, HFP. See also Johnston, ed., *Memorial History of Louisville,* 1:608–11.

46. Ramage, *Rebel Raider,* 11, 16.

47. Ibid., 14; Henning, "Basil Wilson Duke," 60.

48. Hier, "Legend Made Vivid," 45; Coulter, *Civil War and Readjustment,* 13.

3. Missouri

1. *Annual Review,* 8–9, 20–23, 36–37.

2. Duke, *Reminiscences,* 54–56; Meyer, *Missouri,* 316–17, 343; Nevins, *Emergence of Lincoln,* 2:149–51.

3. *United States Biographical Dictionary,* 129–30.

4. Hier, "Legend Made Vivid," 45–47.

5. Ibid.; Meyer, *Missouri,* 333–41; Tucker, *Bowen,* 53–54.

6. Ramage, *Rebel Raider,* 41; Tucker, *Bowen,* 53–54.

7. Meyer, *Missouri,* 341–45; Kirkpatrick, "Missouri on the Eve of Civil War," 99–108.

8. Hummel, *Emancipating Slaves,* 130–32.

9. Phillips, *Claiborne Fox Jackson,* 99–108; Hier, "Legend Made Vivid," 45; Snead, *Fight for Missouri,* 108–9; Gerteis, *Civil War St. Louis,* 79.

10. Fellman, *Inside War,* 5–8; Wallace, "Political Campaign of 1860," 98–102; Phillips, *Claiborne Fox Jackson,* 231–32.

11. Snead, *Fight for Missouri,* 108–9; Duke, *Reminiscences,* 60; Meyer, *Missouri,* 349; Gerteis, *Civil War St. Louis,* 79.

12. Anderson, *Border City,* 72; Snead, *Fight for Missouri,* 108–9.

13. Davis, *Government of Our Own,* 9–15; Meyer, *Missouri,* 349–50; Harrison, *Lincoln of Kentucky,* 130; Basler, ed., *Collected Works of Abraham Lincoln,* 4:263.

14. Duke, *Reminiscences,* 61; Sprague, *Freedom under Lincoln,* 61.

15. Hinze and Farnham, *Battle of Carthage,* 15–16; Snead, "First Year of the War," 263–64; McPherson, *Battle Cry of Freedom,* 290.

16. Meyer, *Missouri,* 350–51; Randall, *Lincoln and the South,* 55.

17. Duke, *Reminiscences,* 61–62; Gerteis, *Civil War St. Louis,* 87 (quotation); Moore, "Missouri," 24–25.

18. Winter, *Civil War in St. Louis,* 32; Basil W. Duke to Stella M. Drum, April 21, 1914, Civil War Collection, Missouri Historical Society (hereafter CWC/MHS); Duke, *Reminiscences,* 66.

19. Snead, "First Year of the War," 264.

20. Snead, *Fight for Missouri,* 137; Duke, *Reminiscences,* 66.

21. Snead, "First Year of the War," 264; Duke, *Reminiscences,* 67–68; Snead, *Fight for Missouri,* 147; Heir, "Legend Made Vivid," 46.

22. Snead, *Fight for Missouri,* 147; Meyer, *Missouri,* 351 (quotation).

23. Duke, *Reminiscences,* 68–69; Kirkpatrick, "Early Months of the Civil War," 254.

24. Duke, *Reminiscences,* 68–69.

25. Ibid., 70.

26. Ibid., 71–74.

27. Snead, "First Year of the War," 264–65.

28. Tucker, *Bowen,* 68.

29. Ibid., 71–74.

30. Duke, *Reminiscences,* 76; Snead, "First Year of the War," 265.

31. Sprague, *Freedom under Lincoln,* 60–63; Winter, *Civil War in St. Louis,* 53; Snead, "First Year of the War," 265.

32. Sprague, *Freedom under Lincoln,* 63; Anderson, *Border City,* 101–5; Sherman, *Memoirs,* 200. Sherman at this point in the war had not received a commission, an event that would occur three days after the Camp Jackson fiasco. Sherman did, however, know Nathaniel Lyon and described him on May 9 as "running about with his hair in the wind, his pockets full of papers, odd and irregular, but I knew him to be a man of vehement purpose and determined action." Sherman, *Memoirs,* 200.

33. Duke, *Reminiscences,* 76–77; Sprague, *Freedom under Lincoln,* 67; Meyer, *Missouri,* 354–55.

34. Thompson, *Civil War Reminiscences,* 59; Peckham, *Lyon and Missouri,* 354–55.

35. Duke, *Reminiscences,* 83–84.

36. Coulter, *Civil War and Readjustment,* 24; John Hunt Morgan to Thomas Morgan, November 9, 17, 1860, Hunt-Morgan Family Papers, University of Kentucky (hereafter HMFP). Morgan first wrote his brother (November 9): "I expect he [Lincoln] will make a good president. South Carolina convened her legislature, but I expect it will end in nothing." He later commented (November 17): "I hope Kentucky will not secede and Lincoln should be given a fair chance."

37. Coulter, *Civil War and Readjustment,* 25–30; Davis, *Government of Our Own,* 19; Harrison, *Lincoln of Kentucky,* 126.

38. Coulter, *Civil War and Readjustment,* 36–37; Randall, *Lincoln and the South,* 56–57; Speed, *Union Cause in Kentucky,* 40–55. Speed's chapter dealing with Kentucky's attempt to maintain neutrality contains a wealth of information, including an analysis of the distinction between mediatorial and armed neutrality.

39. Henning, "Basil Wilson Duke," 60.

40. Thomas Morgan to John Hunt Morgan, July 5, 1861, HMFP. This letter from young Thomas enthusiastically describes the Kentucky Confederates and the number of volunteers arriving each day at Camp Boone.

41. Ramage, *Rebel Raider,* 40, 43.

42. Hinze and Farnham, *Battle of Carthage,* 106–62.

43. Hughes, *Hardee,* 78; Snead, "First Year of the War," 270.

44. Duke, *Reminiscences,* 85–86.

45. Hughes, *Hardee,* 79; Duke, *Reminiscences,* 87; Snead, "First Year of the War," 272–73.

46. Hughes, *Hardee,* 79; Duke, *Reminiscences,* 99.

47. Duke, *Reminiscences,* 110–12.

48. Ibid., 91–95.

49. Simon, "Lincoln, Grant and Kentucky," 10–16; Hughes, *Battle of Belmont,* 4.

50. Hughes, *Hardee,* 81; Roland, "Confederate Defense," 27.

51. John Porter Memoirs (typed copy, n.d.), 6, Civil War Collection, Tennessee State Library and Archives (hereafter CWC/TSLA).

52. Duke, *Reminiscences,* 99–100.

4. On the Green River

1. Randall, *Lincoln and the South,* 61–65; Speed, *Union Cause in Kentucky,* 122–39.

2. Ramage, *Rebel Raider,* 44–45.

3. Brown, *Bold Cavaliers,* 16–29.

4. Duke, *Reminiscences,* 100–101.

5. Tilford, "Delicate Track," 215–16. On September 18, 1861, Simon Buckner seized the L&N track and all its equipment between the Tennessee line and Lebanon Junction, Kentucky. Two days later, William T. Sherman captured the entire track south from Louisville to Elizabethtown, Kentucky. Duke, *Reminiscences,* 139.

6. Duke, *Reminiscences,* 101.

7. Ibid., 102–4.

8. Ibid., 105; Sherman, *Memoirs,* 198–99.

9. Duke, *Reminiscences,* 106–7; Farrell, "John Marshall Harlan," 17–18; Beth, *John Marshall Harlan,* 54.

10. Brown, *Bold Cavaliers,* 31; muster roll of Captain John Hunt Morgan Squadron of Kentucky Volunteer Cavalry, John Hunt Morgan Papers, University of North Carolina, Southern Historical Collection (hereafter JHMP).

11. Duke, *Morgan's Cavalry* (1867), 105–15; Ramage, *Rebel Raider,* 47–49.

12. Ramage, *Rebel Raider,* 47–49.

13. Ibid.; Sherman, *Memoirs,* 365–66.

14. Harrison, "Basil W. Duke," 9; Starr, *Colonel Grenfell's Wars,* 46–48.

15. "Coffee-Boiler Rangers," 442–43.

16. Duke, *Reminiscences,* 128–33.

17. J. M. Hawes to Captain John Hunt Morgan, October 11, 1861, JHMP.

18. Brown, *Bold Cavaliers,* 31; muster roll of Company C, Second Regiment, Morgan's Kentucky Volunteers, CSA, Don D. John Collection, Kentucky Historical Society (hereafter DDJC).

19. Roland, "Confederate Defense," 23–30.

20. Ibid., 31; Cooling, *Forts Henry and Donelson,* 66–67.

21. Duke, *Morgan's Cavalry* (1867), 119–20.

22. U.S. War Department, *War of the Rebellion* (hereafter *OR*), ser. 1, vol. 7, p. 856.

23. Nichols, "Mill Springs," 72–73; Cooling, *Forts Henry and Donelson,* 122–28.

24. Roland, "Confederate Defense," 231.

25. Cooling, *Forts Henry and Donelson,* 205, 231.

26. Theodore S. Dumont to Mrs. Basil W. Duke, February 6, 1862, HMFP.

27. Tilford, "Delicate Track," 215.

28. Roland, "Confederate Defense," 39–41.

29. Duke, *Morgan's Cavalry* (1867), 138.

30. Cooling, *Forts Henry and Donelson,* 235; Duke, *Morgan's Cavalry* (1867), 134.

31. Wulsin, *Fourth Regiment Ohio Volunteer Cavalry,* 28; Duke, *Morgan's Cavalry* (1867), 138.

32. Duke, *Morgan's Cavalry* (1867), 144–45; Berry, *Four Years,* 48–49.

33. Duke, *Morgan's Cavalry* (1867), 45.

34. Ibid., 146; Berry, *Four Years,* 50–52.

35. Brown, *Bold Cavaliers,* 39; Ramage, *Rebel Raider,* 60; Holland, *Morgan and His Raiders,* 89 (quotation).

5. Shiloh, the End of Innocence

1. Daniel, *Shiloh,* 49–50.

2. Johnston, "Albert Sidney Johnston," 550.

3. Hughes, *Hardee,* 99; Johnston, "Albert Sidney Johnston," 550; Duke, "The Battle of Shiloh, Part 1," 160.

4. Duke, *Morgan's Cavalry* (1867), 155–56; Brown, *Bold Cavaliers,* 42.

5. Daniel, *Shiloh,* 124–28; Duke, *Morgan's Cavalry* (1867), 158.

6. Johnston, "Albert Sidney Johnston," 558.

7. Hughes, *Hardee,* 104–6; Daniel, *Shiloh,* 143–52; Duke, "Battle of Shiloh, Part 2," 209.

8. Hughes, *Hardee,* 106; Daniel, *Shiloh,* 143–52.

9. Duke, "Personal Recollections of Shiloh," 6.

10. Ibid., 7; Brown, *Bold Cavaliers,* 47–48.

11. Duke, *Morgan's Cavalry* (1867), 163–64.

12. Duke, "Personal Recollections of Shiloh," 8–9.

13. Brown, *Bold Cavaliers,* 47.

14. Duke, *Morgan's Cavalry* (1906), 84.

15. Ibid.

16. Duke, *Morgan's Cavalry* (1867), 166.

17. Ibid., 166–67; Duke, "Personal Recollections of Shiloh," 10.

18. Duke, *Morgan's Cavalry* (1867), 166, and "Personal Recollections of Shiloh," 10; Daniel, *Shiloh,* 191.

19. Duke, *Morgan's Cavalry* (1906), 85; Castleman, *Active Service,* 96–97.

20. Duke, *Morgan's Cavalry* (1906), 85, and "Personal Recollections of Shiloh," 12–13 (quotation); Daniel, *Shiloh,* 191.

21. Duke, *Morgan's Cavalry* (1906), 86.

22. Johnston, "Albert Sidney Johnston," 564–65; Daniel, *Shiloh,* 226–30.

23. Buell, "Shiloh Reviewed," 505–6; Beauregard, "Campaign of Shiloh," 590–91.

24. Duke, "Battle of Shiloh, Part 2," 215; Brown, *Bold Cavaliers,* 53. According to Johnny Green, who was with the Ninth Kentucky Infantry (Confederate), Morgan's squadron charged the Union line during Grant's counterattack, gaining no advantage, but sustaining significant casualties. Green described the attack as follows: "Morgan's Squadron formed on our left & charged the enemies guns & when thirty yards of them found a fence between them & the battery & therefore they could not capture it & they were forced to wheel to the left & retreat. As they came back to us many an empty saddle we saw. Some of the men were seen to fall in the charge but the horses, when not killed also, kept on the charge as though spurred on by the spirit of the gallant rider just lost." Kirwan, ed., *Johnny Green,* 30. However, this description is not supported by any other contemporary record, and Green may have the charge confused with action that the squadron saw on the first day of battle.

25. Daniel, *Shiloh,* 305.

26. Davis, *Orphan Brigade,* 90, 98.

27. Smith and Cooper, eds., *Diary of Frances Peter,* 14; Thomas Morgan to Henrietta Morgan, May 18, 1862, HMFP.

28. Thomas Morgan to Tommie Duke, May 24, 1862, HMFP.
29. Smith and Cooper, eds., *Diary of Frances Peter,* 11.
30. Tilford, "Delicate Track," 215–18.
31. Duke, *Morgan's Cavalry* (1906), 120; Starr, *Colonel Grenfell's Wars,* 49.
32. Ramage, *Rebel Raider,* 84.
33. Ibid., 64–65; Troutman, ed., *Diaries of George Richard Browder,* 107–8; Estvan, *War Pictures,* 208–13.
34. Duke, *Morgan's Cavalry* (1867), 175.
35. Ibid., 176; Charlton Morgan to Mrs. Henrietta Morgan, May 16, 1862, HMFP; Ramage, *Rebel Raider,* 84.
36. Brown, *Bold Cavaliers,* 59–61; Vale, *Minty,* 54–56.
37. *OR,* ser. 1, vol. 10, pt. 1, pp. 884–86; Vale, *Minty,* 57–60.
38. Vale, *Minty,* 60–61; Duke, *Morgan's Cavalry* (1867), 180–83; Nosworthy, *Bloody Crucible of Courage,* 319–22. Morgan's horse, Black Bess, was captured and, on being put up for sale, was purchased by a Union officer who subsequently sold it to John Prentice of Brooklyn, New York. Mr. Prentice sold the horse for $1,500 to a New York sculptor named Henry K. Brown, who used it as the model for the horse in his equestrian statute of General Winfield Scott in Washington, D.C. H. K. Rush-Brown to Lucas Broadhead, January 31, 1902, Alexander Collection, Kentucky Historical Society.
39. Vale, *Minty,* 60–61; Duke, *Morgan's Cavalry* (1867), 180–83.
40. Duke, *Morgan's Cavalry* (1867), 183.
41. Cooling, *Fort Donelson's Legacy,* 55; Brown, *Bold Cavaliers,* 64.
42. Tilford, "Delicate Track," 218; Ramage, *Rebel Raider,* 85.
43. *OR,* ser. 1, vol. 10, pt. 1, p. 891; Duke, *Morgan's Cavalry* (1867), 85.
44. Ibid., 186.
45. Brown, *Bold Cavaliers,* 68–69.
46. Starr, *Colonel Grenfell's Wars,* 49; Duke, *Morgan's Cavalry* (1867), 190.
47. Duke, *Morgan's Cavalry* (1906), 114.
48. Duke, *Reminiscences,* 160–61.
49. Starr, *Colonel Grenfell's Wars,* 15–37, 44.
50. Ibid., 57–58.
51. Johnston, ed., *Memorial History of Louisville,* 1:611; Sipes, *Seventh Pennsylvania Volunteer Cavalry,* 20; Starr, *Colonel Grenfell's Wars,* 49–50 n. 26.
52. Starr, *Colonel Grenfell's Wars,* 50.
53. Ramage, *Rebel Raider,* 91.

6. Partners in Command

1. Coulter, *Civil War and Readjustment,* 145–54; Sprague, *Freedom under Lincoln,* 263–80. In addition to the arrests, several pro-Southern newspapers, including the *Louisville Courier,* were prohibited from using the mail to circulate their newspapers.
2. Duke, *Morgan's Cavalry* (1906), 136.
3. Duke, *Morgan's Cavalry* (1867), 204–6; *OR,* ser. 1, vol. 16, pt. 1, pp. 754–56.
4. Plum, *Military Telegraph,* 193–96; Duke, *Reminiscences,* 164–65.
5. Duke, *Reminiscences,* 165–66.
6. Ibid., 164–65; Ramage, *Rebel Raider,* 95.
7. *New York Tribune,* August 6, 7, 1862; Basler, ed., *Collected Works of Abraham Lincoln,* 5:313; Smith and Cooper, eds., *Diary of Frances Peter,* 20; Duke, *Morgan's Cavalry* (1867), 208.
8. Ramage, "General John Hunt Morgan," 247; Harrison, "Basil W. Duke," 12.

9. Smith and Cooper, eds., *Diary of Frances Peter,* 21; Brown, *Bold Cavaliers,* 82–85.

10. Duke, *Morgan's Cavalry* (1867), 216.

11. Ibid., 216–19; Harrison, "Basil W. Duke," 12; Tapp, ed., "Dr. John A. Lewis," 122.

12. John Porter Memoirs (typed copy, n.d.), CWC/TSLA.

13. Duke, *Morgan's Cavalry* (1867), 220–21.

14. Brown, *Bold Cavaliers,* 88–89.

15. *OR,* ser. 1, vol. 16, pt. 1, p. 783; Penn, *Rattling Spurs,* 72–73.

16. *OR,* ser. 1, vol. 16, pt. 1, pp. 756–57, 783; Starr, *Colonel Grenfell's Wars,* 69–70; Tapp, ed., "Dr. John A. Lewis," 122–23.

17. *OR,* ser. 1, vol. 16, pt. 1, pp. 769, 771–74, 781–83; Brown, *Bold Cavaliers,* 92; Penn, *Rattling Spurs,* 83.

18. Duke, *Morgan's Cavalry* (1867), 227; *OR,* ser. 1, vol. 16, pt. 1, pp. 760–61.

19. Mattie Wheeler Journal, HFP.

20. Duke, *Morgan's Cavalry* (1867), 227; Lucy Jennings to Tommie Duke, August 3, 1862, Morgan-Duke Family Papers, Filson Historical Society (hereafter MDFP).

21. Lucy Jennings to Tommie Duke, August 3, 1862, MDFP.

22. *OR,* ser. 1, vol. 16, pt. 1, pp. 749–51; Brown, *Bold Cavaliers,* 94.

23. Duke, *Reminiscences,* 166.

24. Duke, *Morgan's Cavalry* (1867), 230; Starr, *Colonel Grenfell*'s *Wars,* 72.

25. *OR,* ser. 1, vol. 16, pt. 1, pp. 767–70; Ramage, *Rebel Raider,* 105–6.

26. Starr, *Colonel Grenfell's Wars,* 72.

27. Ramage, *Rebel Raider,* 107–8.

28. Duke, *Reminiscences,* 309–11; Bullitt, "Recollections of the War," 58, BFP/FHS.

29. Duke, *Reminiscences,* 311–12; Bullitt, "Recollections of the War," 58, BFP/FHS.

30. Duke, *Reminiscences,* 312–14; Bullitt, "Recollections of the War," 58, BFP/FHS.

31. Duke, *Reminiscences,* 314; Bullitt, "Recollections of the War," 59, BFP/FHS.

32. John Porter Memoirs (typed copy, n.d.), CWC/TSLA.

33. McWhiney, *Braxton Bragg,* 266–71.

34. Ibid., 273; General Kirby Smith to Jefferson Davis, August 11, 1862, and General Kirby Smith to General Braxton Bragg, August 9, 1862, *OR,* ser. 1, vol. 16, pt. 2, pp. 752–53, 748. Before sending Duke's letter to Davis, Kirby Smith sent it to Bragg, who returned it to Kirby Smith on August 10, 1862. *OR,* ser. 1, vol. 16, pt. 2, pp. 748–49; Crist, Dix, and Williams, eds., *Papers of Jefferson Davis,* 334. Duke's letter has not been discovered.

35. Cooling, *Fort Donelson's Legacy,* 78; Ramage, *Rebel Raider,* 119–20.

36. General Kirby Smith to Jefferson Davis, August 11, 1862, *OR,* ser. 1, vol. 16, pt. 2, pp. 752–53; McDonough, *War in Kentucky,* 77–78. In a letter delivered by J. Stoddard Johnston, another Kentuckian, Braxton Bragg did, in fact, write Breckinridge: "Your influence in Kentucky would be equal to an extra division in my army." But Bragg wanted Breckinridge to leave the Orphan Brigade behind in Baton Rouge and come to Kentucky himself, a condition that Breckinridge found unacceptable. Davis, *Orphan Brigade,* 121.

37. Tilford, "Delicate Track," 216–17.

38. Duke, *Morgan's Cavalry* (1867), 238; Cooling, *Fort Donelson's Legacy,* 93; Daniel, *Days of Glory,* 106.

39. Ramage, *Rebel Raider,* 111–12.

40. Duke, *Reminiscences,* 205–9.

41. *The Vidette,* August 16, 1862.

42. Brown, *Bold Cavaliers,* 109–10; Duke, *Morgan's Cavalry* (1867), 239–40, and *Reminiscences,* 317–18; Bullitt, "Recollections of the War," 63–64, BFP/FHS.

43. Harrison, "Basil W. Duke," 14; Ramage, *Rebel Raider,* 116; Duke, *Morgan's Cavalry* (1867), 240.

44. Lucy Jennings to Tommie Duke, August 3, 1862, MDFP; Bullitt, "Recollections of the War," 61–64, BFP/FHS.

45. Starr, *War in the West,* 81–82. Another report sets the number of Johnson's force at 767. *OR,* ser. 1, vol. 16, pt. 1, p. 877.

46. Duke, *Morgan's Cavalry* (1906), 146; Hafendorfer, *Twos and Tens,* 197–98.

47. Hafendorfer, *Twos and Tens,* 198.

48. Starr, *War in the West,* 82–83.

49. *OR,* ser. 1, vol. 16, pt. 1, p. 875; Starr, *War in the West,* 83; Duke, *Morgan's Cavalry* (1867), 244.

50. Hafendorfer, *Twos and Tens,* 204.

51. *OR,* ser. 1, vol. 16, pt. 1, p. 875; Duke, *Morgan's Cavalry* (1867), 246.

52. Duke, *Morgan's Cavalry* (1867), 247; Hafendorfer, *Twos and Tens,* 210–11; Vale, *Minty,* 91.

53. *OR,* ser. 1, vol. 16, pt. 1, pp. 880–81; Starr, *War in the West,* 84; Duke, *Morgan's Cavalry* (1867), 248.

54. Bullitt, "Recollections of the War," 70–71, BFP/FHS.

7. All the Kentuckians Wanted to Ride

1. Coulter, *Civil War and Readjustment,* 166; McWhiney, *Braxton Bragg,* 272–73; *OR,* ser. 1, vol. 16, pt. 2, p. 748; McDonough, *War in Kentucky,* 80–82. J. Stoddard Johnston, an officer on Bragg's staff, noted in his diary that he believed the plan to be a bold one, one that seemed worth the risk involved. J. Stoddard Johnston Diary, entry, August 14, 1862, J. Stoddard Johnston Papers, Filson Historical Society.

2. John Hunt Morgan to Basil Duke, order, August 24, 1862, JHMP; Duke, *Morgan's Cavalry* (1867), 254; *OR,* ser. 1, vol. 16, pt. 2, p. 766.

3. Hafendorfer, *Twos and Tens,* 220–21; *OR,* ser. 1, vol. 16, pt. 2, pp. 385–86; Peters and Perrin, eds., *History of Fayette County,* 456.

4. Harrison, *Lincoln of Kentucky,* 168–70; Corporal William Steele, Seventy-ninth Indiana, to Olive Steele, September 11, 1862, William Steele Correspondence Collection, Indiana Historical Society.

5. Lambert, *When the Ripe Pears Fell,* 19–20.

6. Ramage, *Rebel Raider,* 120.

7. *OR,* ser. 1, vol. 16, pt. 1, p. 908; Lambert, *When the Ripe Pears Fell,* 13–23; McDonough, *War in Kentucky,* 117–18.

8. Lambert, *When the Ripe Pears Fell,* 57–59; McDonough, *War in Kentucky,* 117–18.

9. Hafendorfer, *Twos and Tens,* 301–3; Lambert, *When the Ripe Pears Fell,* 138–49. The Mount Zion Christian Church became a federal hospital during the battle, serving the wounded of both sides. It is said that there was a pile of amputated arms and legs window high in the church. Ford, ed., *Sesquicentennial History,* 15–16.

10. Lambert, *When the Ripe Pears Fell,* 223; Mattie Wheeler Journal, HFP. General Nelson was captured but escaped during the confusion that prevailed as the Confederates rounded up the Union prisoners after dark. *OR,* ser. 1, vol. 16, pt. 2, p. 467.

11. Duke, *Morgan's Cavalry* (1867), 254–55.

12. General Kirby Smith to Mrs. Kirby Smith, September 4, 1862, Kirby Smith Papers, University of North Carolina, Southern Historical Collection (hereafter KSP).

13. Duke, *Morgan's Cavalry* (1867), 258; Brown, *Bold Cavaliers,* 122.

14. Smith and Cooper, eds., *Diary of Frances Peter,* 30; Mattie Wheeler Journal, HFP.

15. Duke, *Morgan's Cavalry* (1867), 260, 263.

16. Hammond, "Kirby Smith in Kentucky," 292. On July 16, 1862, Morgan had sent a dispatch from Georgetown, Kentucky, to Kirby Smith, claiming: "I am here with a force sufficient

to hold all the country outside of Lexington and Frankfort. These places are garrisoned chiefly with Home Guards. The bridges between Cincinnati and Lexington have been destroyed. The whole country can be secured and 25,000 or 30,000 men will join you at once." *OR,* ser. 1, vol. 16, pt. 2, pp. 733–34.

17. *Lexington Observer and Reporter,* November 22, 1862; Ranck, *History of Lexington,* 237; Tapp, "Dr. John A. Lewis," 126; Peters and Perrin, eds., *History of Fayette County,* 461–62.

18. Brown, *Bold Cavaliers,* 124; Ramage, *Rebel Raider,* 121.

19. *OR,* ser. 1, vol. 52, pt. 2, pp. 353–54, and vol. 16, pt. 2, p. 551.

20. Auer, "Duke's Raid on Augusta," 28.

21. Duke, *Morgan's Cavalry* (1867), 274; Rankins, "Home Guard at Augusta," 311.

22. Rankins, "Home Guard at Augusta," 311.

23. Duke, *Morgan's Cavalry* (1867), 274–75.

24. Rankins, "Home Guard at Augusta," 312–13; Duke, *Morgan's Cavalry* (1867), 276.

25. Bullitt, "Recollections of the War," 85, BFP/FHS; Duke, *Morgan's Cavalry* (1867), 276.

26. Auer, "Duke's Raid on Augusta," 31; Mary H. Coburn to Mary E. Walton, October 5, 1862, Coburn Family Papers, Kentucky Historical Society (hereafter CFP).

27. Bullitt, "Recollections of the War," 87, BFP/FHS; Duke, *Morgan's Cavalry* (1867), 276–78.

28. Duke, *Morgan's Cavalry* (1867), 280.

29. Ibid.; Mary H. Coburn to Mary E. Walton, October 5, 1862, CFP.

30. Auer, "Duke's Raid on Augusta," 32; Rankins, "Home Guard at Augusta," 315–16; Mary H. Coburn to Mary E. Walton, October 5, 1862, CFP; Mathias, ed., *Incidents and Experiences,* 104–5; *OR,* ser. 1, vol. 16, pt. 1, pp. 1014–15.

31. *OR,* ser. 1, vol. 16, pt. 2, p. 906; Cooling, *Fort Donelson's Legacy,* 142.

32. Parks, *General Edmund Kirby Smith,* 221–22 (Kirby Smith to Bragg); General Kirby Smith to Mrs. Kirby Smith, September 16, 1862, KSP; Shaler, "Border State Men," 256.

33. Horn, *Army of the Tennessee,* 170–71; McWhiney, *Braxton Bragg,* 272–92. It appears that Stanley Horn's analysis of Bragg's indecision was based on the article that Duke wrote for the *Southern Bivouac.* Duke, "Bragg's Campaign in Kentucky," 235.

34. McDonough, *War in Kentucky,* 158–72; Duke, "Bragg's Campaign in Kentucky," 235.

35. Duke, *Morgan's Cavalry* (1867), 288; McWhiney, *Braxton Bragg,* 287–88; McDonough, *War in Kentucky,* 309; *OR,* ser. 1, vol. 16, pt. 1, p. 1090.

36. *OR,* ser. 1, vol. 16, pt. 2, p. 915, and pt. 1, p. 1091; Noe, *Perryville,* 334.

37. *OR,* ser. 1, vol. 16, pt. 1, p. 1093; McWhiney, *Braxton Bragg,* 309–21; Duke, "Bragg's Campaign in Kentucky," 239.

38. Duke, "Bragg's Campaign in Kentucky," 239–40, and *Morgan's Cavalry* (1867), 290; *OR,* ser. 1, vol. 16, pt. 2, p. 936. Duke's comments concerning the concentration of Bragg's and Kirby Smith's armies arguably may be based on self-perpetuated myth. Noe, *Perryville,* 441 n. 12.

39. Braxton Bragg to John Hunt Morgan, order, October 13, 1862, JHMP; Duke, *Morgan's Cavalry* (1867), 310.

40. Duke, *Morgan's Cavalry* (1867), 312–15.

41. Ibid.; Pape-Findley, *The Invincibles,* 103–7.

42. Ramage, *Rebel Raider,* 125.

43. Duke, *Morgan's Cavalry* (1867), 317.

44. Brown, *Bold Cavaliers,* 135.

45. John Porter Memoirs (typed copy, n.d.), CWC/TSLA.

46. *Cincinnati Commercial,* November 7, 1862.

47. Lindsley, ed., *Military Annals of Tennessee,* 681–82; Duke, *Morgan's Cavalry* (1867), 325.

48. Duke, *Morgan's Cavalry* (1867), 327–28.

49. Ibid., 329–31.

50. Duke, *Reminiscences,* 422.

8. December Battles

1. Duke, *Morgan's Cavalry* (1867), 340.

2. Young, *Confederate Wizards,* 225; *OR,* ser. 1, vol. 20, pt. 1, pp. 63–64.

3. McWhiney, *Braxton Bragg,* 341 n. 71.

4. Lamers, *Edge of Glory,* 182–87; *OR,* ser. 1, vol. 16, pt. 2, p. 655.

5. Young, *Confederate Wizards,* 226; Duke, "Battle of Hartsville," 45.

6. Duke, "Battle of Hartsville," 46; Ramage, *Rebel Raider,* 129.

7. Duke, "Battle of Hartsville," 47; Starr, *Colonel Grenfell's Wars,* 84; Davis, *Orphan Brigade,* 143.

8. Young, *Confederate Wizards,* 229–32; Davis, *Orphan Brigade,* 143.

9. Duke, "Battle of Hartsville," 47.

10. McCreary, "Journal, Part 1," 108; Duke, *Morgan's Cavalry* (1867), 342.

11. Bean, "Hartsville" (n.d.); Leeland Hathaway Memoirs, 17, HFP; Duke, "Battle of Hartsville," 48.

12. *OR,* ser. 1, vol. 20, pt. 1, pp. 55, 72; Duke, "Battle of Hartsville," 48. The six thousand additional troops to which Morgan referred were Harlan's at Castalian Springs.

13. Duke, *Morgan's Cavalry* (1867), 344; *OR,* ser. 1, vol. 20, pt. 1, p. 72; Bean, "Hartsville" (n.d.).

14. Duke, "Battle of Hartsville," 48–49.

15. *OR,* ser. 1, vol. 20, pt. 1, pp. 55–56; Duke, *Morgan's Cavalry* (1867), 344–45.

16. Duke, "Battle of Hartsville," 49–50.

17. Duke, *Morgan's Cavalry* (1867), 345–47; Duke, "Battle of Hartsville," 50–51; *OR,* ser. 1, vol. 20, pt. 1, pp. 55, 66, 72.

18. *OR,* ser. 1, vol. 20, pt. 1, p. 56; Bean, "Hartsville" (n.d.); Leeland Hathaway Memoirs, 18, HFP.

19. *OR,* ser. 1, vol. 20, pt. 1, p. 67.

20. *Southern Illustrated News,* December 20, 1862; Cooling, *Fort Donelson's Legacy,* 162; Ramage, *Rebel Raider,* 133; *OR,* ser. 1, vol. 20, pt. 1, p. 67.

21. Ridley, *Army of the Tennessee,* 149; Ramage, *Rebel Raider,* 154–55.

22. Duke, *Morgan's Cavalry* (1867), 356–58. Adam Johnson later wrote that he refused the appointment because he wanted "to get back to his own military province of southwestern Kentucky." Johnson, *Partisan Rangers,* 139.

23. Grenfell had been adverse to Morgan's marriage, a point that Morgan may have taken into consideration in choosing Breckinridge over Grenfell. Starr, *Colonel Grenfell's Wars,* 87–89; Duke, *Morgan's Cavalry* (1867), 358–59.

24. Starr, *War in the West,* 99.

25. Curry, *Rail Routes South,* 20–21; Clark, *Railroads of the Civil War,* 37; Tilford, "Delicate Track," 218–19.

26. Duke, *Morgan's Cavalry* (1867), 361–64; McCreary, "Journal, Part 1," 108–9.

27. *OR,* ser. 1, vol. 20, pt. 2, pp. 191, 210, 214.

28. Brown, *Bold Cavaliers,* 146; Tarrant, *First Kentucky Cavalry,* 130–31.

29. McCreary, "Journal, Part 1," 110; Young, *Confederate Wizards,* 428–29; *OR,* ser. 1, vol. 20, pt. 1, p. 148.

30. Bearss, "Morgan's Second Kentucky Raid, Part 1," 214–17.

31. Duke, *Morgan's Cavalry* (1867), 366; Young, *Confederate Wizards,* 430–31.

32. Duke, *Morgan's Cavalry* (1867), 366–67; Bearss, "Morgan's Second Kentucky Raid, Part 2," 177–78; *OR,* ser. 1, vol. 20, pt. 1, pp. 155–56.

33. Duke, *Morgan's Cavalry* (1867), 368–69.

34. McCreary, "Journal, Part 1," 111; *Louisville Journal,* December 31, 1862.

35. *OR,* ser. 1, vol. 20, pt. 1, p. 153.

36. Ibid., pt. 2, pp. 218–19.

37. Ibid., pt. 1, p. 138.

38. Bearss, "Morgan's Second Kentucky Raid, Part 3," 428; *OR,* ser. 1, vol. 20, pt. 1, p. 139.

39. Duke, *Morgan's Cavalry* (1867), 370–71.

40. Ibid., 371–72; Bearss, "Morgan's Second Kentucky Raid, Part 3," 429.

41. Duke, *Morgan's Cavalry* (1867), 372–74; Brewer, *Raiders of 1862,* 167; Bearss, "Morgan's Second Kentucky Raid, Part 3," 432–33; *OR,* ser. 1, vol. 20, pt. 1, p. 139.

42. Young, *Confederate Wizards,* 437–38; Wyeth, *With Saber and Scalpel,* 186–87.

43. *OR,* ser. 1, vol. 20, pt. 1, pp. 139–40; Beth, *John Marshall Harlan,* 65–67; Brewer, *Raiders of 1862,* 173.

44. James Bullitt to Mrs. Bullitt, December 30, 1862, BFP/FHS; Cunningham, "Memories of Morgan's Christmas Raid," 79–80.

45. Ramage, *Rebel Raider,* 142–43.

46. Duke, *Morgan's Cavalry* (1867), 375–76.

47. Duke, *Reminiscences,* 163.

48. John Hunt Morgan to Mattie Morgan, January 2, 1863, JHMP; Troutman, ed., *Diaries of George Richard Browder,* 145.

49. Cooling, *Fort Donelson's Legacy,* 163.

50. Lamers, *Edge of Glory,* 209–16.

51. On the Battle of Murfreesboro generally, see Cozzens, *No Better Place to Die.*

9. We Found Pies Hot from the Oven

1. Morgan apparently was able to locate his sister for Duke. Basil Duke to Tommie Duke, January 8, 1863, HMFP; Smith and Cooper, eds., *Diary of Frances Peter,* 89.

2. Duke, *Morgan's Cavalry* (1867), 381; Leeland Hathaway Memoirs, 22, HFP.

3. Leeland Hathaway Memoirs, 22, HFP; Brown, *Bold Cavaliers,* 167–68; Duke, *Morgan's Cavalry* (1867), 411–15.

4. Duke, *Morgan's Cavalry* (1867), 395–96; Johnson, *Partisan Rangers,* 140.

5. *OR,* ser. 1, vol. 23, pt. 1, pp. 151, 155–58; Ramage, *Rebel Raider,* 152.

6. *OR,* ser. 1, vol. 23, pt. 1, pp. 209–12; Duke, *Morgan's Cavalry* (1867), 423–25; Logan, *Kelion Franklin Peddicord,* 99.

7. Basil Duke to John Hunt Morgan, two letters, both dated April 1863, JHMP; Duke, *Morgan's Cavalry* (1867), 440–41.

8. Horwitz, *Longest Raid,* 2; Duke, *Morgan's Cavalry* (1867), 450; Ramage, *Rebel Raider,* 158–59.

9. Lamers, *Edge of Glory,* 229, 275; *OR,* ser. 1, vol. 23, pt. 2, pp. 760–61.

10. Duke, *Morgan's Cavalry* (1867), 449–52.

11. *OR,* ser. 1, vol. 23, pt. 2, pp. 817–18.

12. Duke, *Morgan's Cavalry* (1867), 452; Duke, Hines, and Willcox, "Morgan's Rough Riders," 118–19.

13. Brown, *Bold Cavaliers,* 175; Cooling, *Fort Donelson's Legacy,* 280–82.

14. Marvel, *Burnside,* 250–51; Blanton, unpublished manuscript, 24–29, University of Kentucky.

15. Basil W. Duke to Henrietta Morgan, May 12, 1863, MDFP.

16. Duke, *Morgan's Cavalry* (1867), 444; Brown, *Bold Cavaliers,* 176.

17. Brown, *Bold Cavaliers,* 176; S. D. Morgan to John Hunt Morgan, June 11, 1863, JHMP.

18. Duke, *Morgan's Cavalry* (1867), 453–54.

19. Ibid., 451–52; Duke, Hines, and Willcox, "Morgan's Rough Riders," 120–21.

20. Brown, *Bold Cavaliers,* 180; Horwitz, *Longest Raid,* 20.

21. Benedict, "Great Indiana-Ohio Raid," 150; Duke, *Morgan's Cavalry* (1867), 461.

22. *OR,* ser. 1, vol. 23, pt. 1, pp. 645–46; Young, *Confederate Wizards,* 371–72.

23. *OR,* ser. 1, vol. 23, pt. 1, p. 647.

24. Ibid., p. 651.

25. Duke, *Morgan's Cavalry* (1867), 466–67.

26. *OR,* ser. 1, vol. 23, pt. 1, pp. 648–49; Duke, *Morgan's Cavalry* (1867), 467–68; Young, *Confederate Wizards,* 375.

27. *OR,* ser. 1, vol. 23, pt. 1, p. 649; Leeland Hathaway Memoirs, 43, HFP.

28. *OR,* ser. 1, vol. 23, pt. 1, pp. 652–53; Horwitz, *Longest Raid,* 37; Brown, *Bold Cavaliers,* 185–86.

29. Duke, *Morgan's Cavalry* (1867), 470; Duke, Hines, and Willcox, "Morgan's Rough Riders," 130. Davis and forty-seven of his men successfully crossed the Ohio River into Indiana. He and eighteen of his men were later captured as they tried to ride north to catch up with the main body of troops to the east of Salem, Indiana.

30. Tarrant, *First Kentucky Cavalry,* 176.

31. Benedict, "Great Indiana-Ohio Raid," 151; Duke, Hines, and Willcox, "Morgan's Rough Riders," 130.

32. Horwitz, *Longest Raid,* 47.

33. Duke, *Reminiscences,* 340–41.

34. Duke, *Morgan's Cavalry* (1867), 475; McCreary, "Journal, Part 2," 198; Bennett, ed., "Burke's Civil War Journal," 303–5.

35. Duke, *Morgan's Cavalry* (1867), 477; *OR,* ser. 1, vol. 23, pt. 1, p. 659; Taylor, *With Bowie Knives and Pistols,* 44.

36. Duke, *Morgan's Cavalry* (1867), 477; *OR,* ser. 1, vol. 23, pt. 1, p. 659.

37. Duke, *Morgan's Cavalry* (1867), 478; *Corydon Weekly Democrat,* July 14, 1863.

38. *OR,* ser. 1, vol. 23, pt. 1, pp. 716–27; Ramage, *Rebel Raider,* 159; Duke, Hines, and Willcox, "Morgan's Rough Riders," 149.

39. Duke, *Morgan's Cavalry* (1867), 479; Duke, Hines, and Willcox, "Morgan's Rough Riders," 134–35; Bennett, ed., "Burke's Civil War Journal," 309; order (copy), July 10, 1863, DDJC.

40. Duke, *Morgan's Cavalry* (1867), 479; Duke, Hines, and Willcox, "Morgan's Rough Riders," 151.

41. Duke, *Morgan's Cavalry* (1867), 482; Nevins, *War for the Union,* 212–70; Lafferty and Lafferty, *William Lafferty,* n.p.

42. Horwitz, *Longest Raid,* 90–91; Boyer, "Morgan's Raid in Indiana," 159; McCreary, "Journal, Part 2," 199.

43. Leeland Hathaway Memoirs, 49–50, HFP.

44. Duke, Hines, and Willcox, "Morgan's Rough Riders," 133–34; Allen, "Morgan's Raid in Ohio," 51.

45. Johnson, *Partisan Rangers,* 146; Duke, *Morgan's Cavalry* (1867), 484–86; Allen, "Morgan's Raid in Ohio," 52–53.

46. Duke, *Morgan's Cavalry* (1867), 486–87; McCreary, "Journal, Part 2," 199; Allen, "Morgan's Raid in Ohio," 54.

47. Grant, *Memoirs,* 35–36; Williams, *History of Clermont and Brown Counties,* 431.

48. Brown, *Bold Cavaliers,* 210; Bennett, ed., "Burke's Civil War Journal," 319; *Cincinnati Enquirer,* July 17, 1863.

49. Duke, Hines, and Willcox, "Morgan's Rough Riders," 138; McCreary, "Journal, Part 2," 199.

10. The Boys Were Sorry That Duke Was Captured

1. Duke, Hines, and Willcox, "Morgan's Rough Riders," 139; Noe, ed., *Southern Boy in Blue,* 176.

2. *OR,* ser. 1, vol. 23, pt. 1, pp. 760–61; Horwitz, *Longest Raid,* 67, 177–78.

3. Curtis Burke Diary, entry, July 17, 1863, Filson Historical Society.

4. McCreary, "Journal, Part 2," 199–200; *OR,* ser. 1, vol. 23, pt. 1, p. 735; Duke, Hines, and Willcox, "Morgan's Rough Riders," 139.

5. *OR,* ser. 1, vol. 23, pt. 1, p. 770.

6. Curtis Burke Diary, entry, July 18, 1863, Filson Historical Society; Duke, *Morgan's Cavalry* (1867), 489–90; Ramage, *Rebel Raider,* 176; Horwitz, *Longest Raid,* 203; *OR,* ser. 1, vol. 23, pt. 1, pp. 774–75; Duke, Hines, and Willcox, "Morgan's Rough Riders," 139; Johnson, *Partisan Rangers,* 147. The militia's blocking of the roads continued unabated on July 18 as well. Long Bottom, the ford to which the old man referred, was north of Buffington and near the deep ford where Johnson and three hundred of his men crossed the Ohio River, several drowning in the process.

7. Bennett, ed., "Burke's Civil War Journal," 324.

8. Leeland Hathaway Memoirs, 54, HFP.

9. Duke, *Morgan's Cavalry* (1867), 491–92; Smith, *D. Howard Smith,* 73; *OR,* ser. 1, vol. 23, pt. 1, p. 776.

10. Duke, *Morgan's Cavalry* (1867), 493; Smith, *D. Howard Smith,* 74–75; Horwitz, *Longest Raid,* 215.

11. Johnson, *Partisan Rangers,* 148; Duke, *Morgan's Cavalry* (1867), 494.

12. Duke, *Morgan's Cavalry* (1867), 495; Johnson, *Partisan Rangers,* 148–49; Horwitz, *Longest Raid,* 237.

13. Duke, *Morgan's Cavalry* (1867), 496; Horwitz, *Longest Raid,* 222.

14. Curtis Burke Diary, entry, July 19, 1863, Filson Historical Society; Leeland Hathaway Memoirs, 58, HFP; *OR,* ser. 1, vol. 23, pt. 1, p. 657 (quotation).

15. Ramage, *Rebel Raider,* 181; Duke, Hines, and Willcox, "Morgan's Rough Riders," 142–43; Nevins, *War for the Union,* 159.

16. *OR,* ser. 1, vol. 23, pt. 1, pp. 635, 781; Abbott, "Heroic Deeds of Heroic Men," 290.

17. James D. Harbeson to Cousin Nanette, July 25, 1863, Marshall Family Papers, Filson Historical Society; Leeland Hathaway Memoirs, 102–13, HFP.

18. Curtis Burke Diary, entry, July 19, 1863, Filson Historical Society; Leeland Hathaway Memoirs, 58–59, HFP.

19. Curtis Burke Diary, entry, July 19, 1863, Filson Historical Society.

20. Metzler, *Morgan,* 64; Duke, *Morgan's Cavalry* (1867), 508; Berry, *Four Years,* 225–27.

21. Duke, *Morgan's Cavalry* (1867), 508–9; Horwitz, *Longest Raid,* 248–49.

22. Metzler, *Morgan,* 67; Leeland Hathaway Memoirs, 59, HFP.

23. Duke, *Morgan's Cavalry* (1867), 509–10; Brown, *Bold Cavaliers,* 227.

24. Simmons, *Morgan Raid,* 64–67.

25. Metzler, *Morgan,* 67; Duke, *Morgan's Cavalry* (1867), 510.

26. Marvel, *Burnside,* 261; *OR,* ser. 1, vol. 23, pt. 2, p. 545.

27. Ramage, *Rebel Raider,* 123; *OR,* ser. 2, vol. 6, p. 160.

28. *OR,* ser. 2, vol. 6, pp. 156–57; Ramage, *Rebel Raider,* 185; *Blackwell's Edinburgh Magazine,* February 1865, 164.

29. Duke, *Morgan's Cavalry* (1867), 510–12.

30. Ibid., 513–14.

31. Handy, *Journal,* 304; *OR,* ser. 2, vol. 6, p. 174.

32. Charlton Morgan Prison Journal (typed copy), entry, August 1, 1863, HMFP; Ramage, *Rebel Raider,* 186; Metzler, *Morgan,* 69; *OR,* ser. 1, vol. 23, pt. 1, p. 815.

33. Metzler, *Morgan,* 69; Ramage, *Rebel Raider,* 186–87.

34. *OR,* ser. 2, vol. 6, pp. 158–59, 448, 461; Benedict, "Great Indiana-Ohio Raid," 162–63.

35. Basil W. Duke to Mrs. Henrietta Morgan, August 11, 1863, JHMP; Duke, *Morgan's Cavalry* (1867), 524–26.

36. Duke, *Morgan's Cavalry* (1867), 520; Metzler, *Morgan,* 70.

37. Duke, *Morgan's Cavalry* (1867), 520–21.

38. Ibid.; Charlton Morgan Prison Journal (typed copy), entry, December 6, 1863, HMFP.

39. Duke, *Morgan's Cavalry* (1867), 521–23; *OR,* ser. 2, vol. 6, pp. 408–9.

40. Thomas W. Bullitt Prison Journal, Bullitt Family Papers, University of North Carolina, Southern Historical Collection; Willis Jones to Tommie Duke, October 28, 1863, JHMP.

41. Basil W. Duke to Mrs. Henrietta Morgan, August 11, 1863, JHMP; Charlton Morgan Prison Journal, entry, September 1, 1863, HMFP.

42. Willis Jones to Tommie Duke, October 28, 1863, JHMP.

43. Mary Buford Jones Diary, entries, August 27, September 9, 1863, Jones Family Papers, Filson Historial Society; Dick Morgan to Tommie Duke, September, 16, 1863, and Willis Jones to Tommie Duke, October 28, 1863, JHMP.

44. Charlton Morgan Prison Journal, entries, September 21, October 24, 1863, HMFP; Handy, *Journal,* 322–23 (quotation from poem).

45. Ramage, *Rebel Raider,* 190; Duke, *Morgan's Cavalry* (1867), 526.

46. Duke, Hines, and Willcox, "Morgan's Rough Riders," 160.

47. Ibid., 161.

48. Ramage, *Rebel Raider,* 191.

49. Duke, Hines, and Willcox, "Morgan's Rough Riders," 163–64.

50. Duke, *Morgan's Cavalry* (1867), 532–33.

51. Ibid., 538–42; Charlton Morgan Prison Journal, entries, November 29, December 6, 1863, HMFP; McCreary, "Journal, Part 2," 202; Ohio State Penitentiary broadside, MDFP.

52. *OR,* ser. 2, vol. 6, pp. 684–86.

53. Charlton Morgan Prison Journal, entry, December 13, 1863, HMFP; McCreary, "Journal, Part 2," 203.

11. A Convivial Evening in Philadelphia

1. D. H. Llewellyn to John Hunt Morgan, December 29, 1863, JHMP; Ramage, *Rebel Raider,* 199–207.

2. D. H. Llewellyn to John Hunt Morgan, December 29, 1863, and Willis Jones to Tommie Duke, December 28, 1863, JHMP; Calvin Morgan to Mrs. Henrietta Morgan, December 30, 1863, MDFP.

3. Duke, *Morgan's Cavalry* (1867), 543; *OR,* ser. 2, vol. 6, p. 888.

4. Absalom Johnson Diary, entry, February 4, 1864, Filson Historical Society.

5. Basil W. Duke to Mrs. Henrietta Morgan, February 18, 25, 1864, JHMP; *OR,* ser. 2, vol. 6, p. 953.

6. Mrs. Henrietta Morgan to Basil W. Duke, February 25, 1864, JHMP; *OR,* ser. 2, vol. 6, p. 1037.

7. Duke, *Morgan's Cavalry* (1867), 543–46.

8. Absalom Johnson Diary, entry, March 1, 1864, Filson Historical Society; Duke, *Reminiscences,* 446.

9. Duke, *Reminiscences,* 447–48.

10. Ibid., 448–49.

11. Ibid.

12. Ibid., 450.

13. Ibid., 450–51.

14. Ibid.

15. Speer, *Military Prisons of the Civil War,* 100–105, 162–63, 183.

16. Duke, *Morgan's Cavalry* (1867), 546–48; Thompson, *Civil War Reminiscences,* 223–24; Basil W. Duke to Mrs. Henrietta Morgan, March 18, 1864, JHMP. Colonel W. W. Ward of the Ninth Tennessee Cavalry kept a journal during his sojourn at Fort Delaware and only once commented on an incident of prisoner abuse. Ward shared the same experience as Duke, writing favorably of his treatment, and actually gaining several pounds over a period of several weeks. Rosenberg, ed., "Diary of Col. W. W. Ward," 29, 33.

17. Basil W. Duke to Mrs. Henrietta Morgan, March 18, 1864, JHMP; Speer, *Military Prisons of the Civil War,* 147; Hesseltine, ed., *Civil War Prisons,* 6; Leeland Hathaway Memoirs, 102, 103 (quotation), HFP.

18. Handy, *Journal,* 304–5, 316.

19. Ibid., 305; Davis, ed., *Confederate General,* 6:207–9; Thompson, *Civil War Reminiscences,* 223–24.

20. *OR,* ser. 2, vol. 6, pp. 1036, 1094.

21. Handy, *Journal,* 305, 318–19.

22. Ibid.

23. Schmant, "Two Letters," 121; Basil W. Duke to Mrs. Henrietta Morgan, March 18, 1864, JHMP.

24. Handy, *Journal,* 338–39.

25. *OR,* ser. 2, vol. 6, p. 1076; Rosenberg, ed., "Diary of Col. W. W. Ward," 25, 27; Handy, *Journal,* 355.

26. Duke, *Morgan's Cavalry* (1867), 544–45; Thomas W. Bullitt to Mrs. W. C. Bullitt, April 6, 1864, BFP/FHS.

27. *OR,* ser. 2, vol. 6, p. 1082; Handy, *Journal,* 364.

28. Basil W. Duke to Mrs. Henrietta Morgan, April 13, 1864, MDFP.

29. Rosenberg, ed., "Diary of Col. W. W. Ward," 40, 47; Handy, *Journal,* 366, 416.

30. W. C. P. Breckinridge to John Hunt Morgan, April 26, 1864, and Hart Gibson to John Hunt Morgan, May 4, 1864, JHMP.

31. Ramage, *Rebel Raider,* 210–11. Captain Edward O. Guerrant noted in his diary on May 9, 1864: "Genl. Morgan's H'd Q'rs under a cedar tree on opposite bank of Laurel. Genl. very clever indeed. Think he misses Duke very much." Davis and Swentor, eds., *Civil War Diary of Edward O. Guerrant,* 430.

32. Rosenberg, ed., "Diary of Col. W. W. Ward," 40.

33. *OR,* ser. 2, vol. 7, pp. 185, 216, 371, 381, 388.

34. Duke, *Reminiscences,* 455–56, and *Morgan's Cavalry* (1867), 550.

35. *OR,* ser. 2, vol. 7, p. 410. For Jones to Foster with regard to the confinement under fire of both Union and Confederate officers as a retaliatory measure, see *OR,* ser. 1, vol. 53, p. 104. For Jones to Foster with regard to a prisoner exchange, see ibid., vol. 35, pt. 2, p. 161.

36. Duke, *Morgan's Cavalry* (1867), 550.

37. Ibid., 550–51.

38. Ibid., 552; Basil W. Duke to Tommie Duke, July 7, 1864, HMFP.

39. Duke, *Reminiscences,* 457–59; Rosenberg, ed., "Diary of Col. W. W. Ward," 69.

40. Tommie Duke to Basil W. Duke, July 24, 1864, MDFP; General Sam Jones to Tommie Duke, July 30, 1864, JHMP.

41. Duke, *Morgan's Cavalry* (1867), 552–53, and *Reminiscences,* 460.

42. Duke, *Reminiscences,* 460.

43. Ibid., 460–61.

44. Ramage, *Rebel Raider,* 212–25; Davis, *Breckinridge,* 439.

45. Brown, *Bold Cavaliers,* 255–56; Ramage, *Rebel Raider,* 230.

46. Duke, *Morgan's Cavalry* (1867), 582–83; Rosenberg, ed., "Diary of Col. W. W. Ward," 89.

47. Ramage, *Rebel Raider,* 232–35; Basil W. Duke to Richard C. Morgan, April 16, 1905, James L. Norris Papers, University of North Carolina, Southern Historical Collection.

48. Duke, *Morgan's Cavalry* (1867), 590; Basil W. Duke to Major D. Llewellyn, telegram, September 5, 1864, JHMP; Ramage, *Rebel Raider,* 246.

12. The Glory and Chivalry Seemed Gone

1. Davis, *Lost Cause,* 127–47.

2. Coulter, *Civil War and Readjustment,* 179–87, 202, 206–7; *OR,* ser. 2, vol. 4, pp. 688–90.

3. Duke, *Morgan's Cavalry* (1867), 590.

4. Davis, *Breckinridge,* 456–57; Wells and Prichard, *10th Kentucky Cavalry,* 75–76 (quotation).

5. Rosenberg, ed., "Diary of Col. W. W. Ward," 91–92; *OR,* ser. 1, vol. 39, pt. 2, p. 816, and vol. 43, pt. 2, p. 861; Davis, *Breckinridge,* 461.

6. Duke, *Morgan's Cavalry* (1867), 592–93 (quotations); Harrison, "Basil W. Duke," 28–29; Davis and Swentor, eds., *Civil War Diary of Edward O. Guerrant,* 522.

7. *Richmond* (Va.) *Dispatch,* September 14, 1864; Rosenberg, ed., "Diary of Col. W. W. Ward," 91–92.

8. *OR,* ser. 1, vol. 39, pt. 3, p. 907; Brown, *Bold Cavaliers,* 297.

9. *OR,* ser. 1, vol. 39, pt. 3, p. 778.

10. Duke, *Morgan's Cavalry* (1867), 593–600; Davis, *Breckinridge,* 458.

11. Davis, *Breckinridge,* 458; Mosgrove, *Kentucky Cavaliers,* 206–7.

12. Mosgrove, *Kentucky Cavaliers,* 207.

13. Davis, *Breckinridge,* 459–61.

14. Wells and Prichard, *10th Kentucky Cavalry,* 80–81; *OR,* ser. 1, vol. 49, pt. 1, p. 765. This Tenth Kentucky Cavalry was not the regiment commanded by Adam Johnson. There were three different regiments designated the Tenth Kentucky, a situation that created confusion both during and after the war: the Tenth Kentucky Cavalry (Mays-Trimble-Diamond); the Tenth Kentucky Partisan Rangers (Johnson); and the Tenth Kentucky Mounted Rifles (Caudill). A recent study has suggested that the newspapers inflated the number of African Americans murdered after the battle and that the death toll may not have exceeded twelve. Trudeau, *Black Troops in the Civil War,* 274.

15. Mosgrove, *Kentucky Cavaliers,* 208–9.

16. Duke, *Morgan's Cavalry* (1867), 600.

17. Ibid., 600–601; Davis, *Breckinridge,* 461; *OR,* ser. 1, vol. 39, pt. 1, p. 820.

18. *OR,* ser. 1, vol. 43, pt. 2, pp. 907–8, and vol. 39, pt. 1, p. 907; Duke, *Morgan's Cavalry* (1867), 601.

19. Davis, *Breckinridge,* 464; Duke, *Morgan's Cavalry* (1867), 603–4.

20. *OR,* ser. 1, vol. 39, pt. 1, pp. 892, 897; Duke, *Reminiscences,* 236.

21. Duke, *Morgan's Cavalry* (1867), 605–6; *OR,* ser. 1, vol. 39, pt. 1, p. 893.

22. Davis, *Breckinridge,* 466; *OR,* ser. 1, vol. 39, pt. 1, p. 893.

23. *OR,* ser. 1, vol. 39, pt. 1, p. 889.

24. Duke, *Reminiscences,* 239; *OR,* ser. 1, vol. 39, pt. 1, p. 890.

25. *OR,* ser. 1, vol. 39, pt. 1, pp. 890–93; Duke, *Reminiscences,* 239–40.

26. *OR,* ser. 1, vol. 39, pt. 1, pp. 890–93.
27. *OR,* ser. 1, vol. 39, pt. 1, p. 893.
28. Duke, *Reminiscences,* 306–8.
29. Davis, *Breckinridge,* 470; Duke, *Morgan's Cavalry* (1867), 610; *OR,* ser. 1, vol. 45, pt. 1, p. 1164.
30. Duke, *Morgan's Cavalry* (1867), 610; *OR,* ser. 1, vol. 45, pt. 1, pp. 807, 835–38.
31. *OR,* ser. 1, vol. 45, pt. 1, pp. 827–28.
32. Duke, *Morgan's Cavalry* (1867), 612; Davis, *Breckinridge,* 472.
33. *St. Louis Dispatch,* August 18, 1875; Davis and Swentor, eds., *Civil War Diary of Edward O. Guerrant,* 604.
34. *OR,* ser. 1, vol. 45, pt. 1, p. 825; Davis, "Winter Raid," 31.
35. Davis, "Winter Raid," 31; Duke, *Morgan's Cavalry* (1867), 614; Davis, *Breckinridge,* 474.
36. Davis, "Winter Raid," 32; Mosgrove, *Kentucky Cavaliers,* 238; Harrison, "Basil W. Duke," 32.
37. Duke, *Morgan's Cavalry* (1867), 615–16; Davis, *Breckinridge,* 476; *OR,* ser. 1, vol. 45, pt. 1, p. 813.
38. Davis, "Winter Raid," 33; *OR,* ser. 1, vol. 45, pt. 1, p. 838.
39. Davis, "Winter Raid," 33; Brown, *Bold Cavaliers,* 298.
40. Duke, *Morgan's Cavalry* (1867), 617; Davis, "Winter Raid," 34.
41. Duke, *Morgan's Cavalry* (1867), 617; Davis, *Breckinridge,* 476–77.
42. *OR,* ser. 1, vol. 45, pt. 2, pp. 750–51.
43. Brown, *Bold Cavaliers,* 299.
44. Ralph Mann, "Count's Sand Lick Company"; *OR,* ser. 1, vol. 49, pt. 1, pp. 999–1001.
45. William Davis to Frances "Frank" Cunningham, February 22, 1865, William Davis Papers, Filson Historical Society; *OR,* ser. 1, vol. 49, pt. 1, p. 982; Duke, *Morgan's Cavalry* (1867), 617; Rosenberg, ed., "Diary of Col. W. W. Ward," 137–38.
46. H. L. Giltner to Basil W. Duke, January 31, 1865, JHMP.
47. *OR,* ser. 1, vol. 49, pt. 1, p. 817.
48. Basil W. Duke to Major Stoddard Johnston, January 21, 1865, JHMP.
49. Basil W. Duke to Mrs. Henrietta Morgan, January 8, 1865, and Basil W. Duke to Charlton Morgan, February 2, 1865, HMFP.
50. Brown, *Bold Cavaliers,* 299; Duke, *Morgan's Cavalry* (1867), 617.

13. We Looked at Each Other in Amazement

1. Davis, ed., *Confederate General,* 2:93; Mosgrove, *Kentucky Cavaliers,* 262.
2. Duke, *Morgan's Cavalry* (1867), 619, and "After the Fall of Richmond," 156–57.
3. Duke, "After the Fall of Richmond," 158; Mosgrove, *Kentucky Cavaliers,* 262.
4. Duke, "After the Fall of Richmond," 158.
5. Duke, *Morgan's Cavalry* (1867), 619, and *Reminiscences,* 463.
6. Mosgrove, *Kentucky Cavaliers,* 263; Duke, "After the Fall of Richmond," 159.
7. Duke, "After the Fall of Richmond," 159, and *Morgan's Cavalry* (1867), 624 (quotation).
8. Ballard, *Long Shadow,* 57, 65–66.
9. Duke, *Reminiscences,* 463–64.
10. Ibid., 465; Johnston, "Kentucky," 191.
11. Duke, *Reminiscences,* 465.
12. Barret, *Civil War in North Carolina,* 361; Duke, "After the Fall of Richmond," 160–61.
13. Duke, *Reminiscences,* 465, and "After the Fall of Richmond," 161.
14. Ballard, *Long Shadow,* 93–98.
15. Davis, *Honorable Defeat,* 172–74; Duke, "After the Fall of Richmond," 161; *OR,* ser. 1, vol. 47, pt. 3, p. 816.

16. Hanna, *Flight into Oblivion,* 50–52; Davis, *Breckinridge,* 515; Ballard, *Long Shadow,* 104–5; Duke, "After the Fall of Richmond," 161–62.

17. Wellman, *Giant in Gray,* 182–83; Davis, *Honorable Defeat,* 184.

18. Ballard, *Long Shadow,* 105–9; Reagan, *Memoirs,* 212.

19. Wheeler, "Effort to Rescue Jefferson Davis," 86; Wellman, *Giant in Gray,* 185–89.

20. Ballard, *Long Shadow,* 109–13.

21. Duke, "After the Fall of Richmond," 162, and *Morgan's Cavalry* (1867), 626 (quotation).

22. Duke, *Morgan's Cavalry* (1867), 626.

23. Duke, "After the Fall of Richmond," 162 (quotation); "Taps," 393; McDonald and McDonald, "Peace," 481. Benjamin died on May 8, 1884, in Great Britain. Hanna, *Flight into Oblivion,* 194–208; Meade, *Judah P. Benjamin,* 317–25.

24. Ballard, *Long Shadow,* 121–22; Duke, "After the Fall of Richmond," 163.

25. Duke, "After the Fall of Richmond," 163.

26. Ibid.

27. Ibid., 164; Rowland, ed., *Jefferson Davis Letters, Papers and Speeches,* 8:151–54, 158–59.

28. Rowland, ed., *Jefferson Davis Letters, Papers and Speeches,* 8:148, 151–54, 158–59; Davis, *Honorable Defeat,* 226 n. 57.

29. Duke, "After the Fall of Richmond," 164; Davis, *Breckinridge,* 520.

30. Duke, "After the Fall of Richmond," 164.

31. Ibid.

32. Davis, *Jefferson Davis,* 632.

33. Davis, *Breckinridge,* 521; Duke, "After the Fall of Richmond," 164; *OR,* ser. 1, vol. 49, pt. 2, p. 1277.

34. Davis, *Honorable Defeat,* 252; *OR,* ser. 1, vol. 49, pt. 2, p. 1278.

35. Clark, "Last Days of the Confederate Treasury," 542.

36. Duke, "After the Fall of Richmond," 165.

37. Davis, *Breckinridge,* 523; *OR,* ser. 1, vol. 49, pt. 2, p. 1267.

38. Duke, "After the Fall of Richmond," 165. At this time, Duke had about 350 men left in his brigade.

39. Davis, *Breckinridge,* 524.

40. Duke, *Reminiscences,* 469–70.

14. To Perpetuate His Fame

1. *OR,* ser. 1, vol. 39, pt. 3, p. 724; Coulter, *Civil War and Readjustment,* 207–14.

2. *Cincinnati Gazette,* November 16, 1864; *OR,* ser. 1, vol. 45, pt. 2, pp. 93–94.

3. Coulter, *Civil War and Readjustment,* 262; Harrison, *Antislavery Movement,* 107–11.

4. Coulter, *Civil War and Readjustment,* 273–74.

5. Duke, *Reminiscences,* 417.

6. Ibid., 478; John S. Cooper Diary, entry, May 16, 1865, John Snider Cooper Papers, Duke University.

7. Duke, *Reminiscences,* 480–81.

8. Ibid., 482.

9. On June 4, 1865, Duke wrote John Castleman: "We do not know what policy will be inaugurated toward the paroled Confederates." Castleman, *Active Service,* 179; Otken, *Ills of the South,* 1–32.

10. Tapp and Klotter, *Decades of Discord,* 1–10; Goodloe, "Resources and Industrial Condition," 102–36.

11. Duke, *Reminiscences,* 482; Tommie Duke to Basil W. Duke, August 21, 1865, and ac-

counting sheet of transactions between Basil W. Duke and James K. Duke, October 12, 1865, HMFP.

12. Duke, *Reminiscences,* 483.

13. Ibid.

14. Accounting sheet of transactions between Basil W. Duke and James K. Duke, October 12, 1865, HMFP.

15. Coulter, *Civil War and Readjustment,* 274, 282.

16. Ibid., 280; *OR,* ser. 1, vol. 49, pt. 2, p. 1092.

17. Coulter, *Civil War and Readjustment,* 285–86.

18. James H. Mill to Basil W. Duke, October 25, 1865, HMFP; Basil W. Duke to Mattie Morgan, July 25, 1866, JHMP.

19. John C. Breckinridge to Basil W. Duke, December 9, 1865, HMFP.

20. Basil W. Duke to William Preston Johnston, May 9, 1866, Johnston Family Papers, Filson Historical Society; Basil W. Duke to Martha Ready Morgan, January 15, 1866, JHMP; Basil W. Duke to Thomas H. Hines, April 3, 1866, Thomas H. Hines Papers, Filson Historical Society (hereafter THHP).

21. Basil W. Duke to Mattie Ready Morgan, January 15, 1866, JHMP; funeral notice, February 19, 1866, HMFP.

22. Coleman, *Famous Kentucky Duels,* 123–34 (quotation); Gaines, *History of Scott County,* 20; *Frankfort Tri-Weekly Yeoman,* March 27, 1866; Castleman, *Active Service,* 19.

23. Basil W. Duke to Thomas H. Hines, April 3, 1866, THHP; Basil W. Duke to W. C. P. Breckinridge, April 3, 1866, Breckinridge Family Manuscript Collection, Library of Congress, Manuscript Division.

24. *Lexington Observer and Reporter,* February 3, 1866.

25. Coulter, *Civil War and Readjustment,* 303–4; Tapp and Klotter, *Decades of Discord,* 15.

26. Coulter, *Civil War and Readjustment,* 309–11; Duke, *Reminiscences,* 577.

27. Basil W. Duke to D. H. Smith, July 28, 1866, D. H. Smith Papers, Filson Historical Society (hereafter DHSP); Dick Morgan to Martha Ready Morgan, August 9, 1866, JHMP.

28. Dick Morgan to Martha Ready Morgan, August 9, 1866, JHMP.

29. John P. Morton & Co. to Basil W. Duke, November 12, 1866, JHMP.

30. Foster, *Ghosts of the Confederacy,* 25; Duke, *Morgan's Cavalry* (1867), 16. For in-depth discussions concerning how the Confederates came to terms with defeat, see also Wilson, *Baptized in Blood,* and Gallagher, *Confederate War.*

31. Duke, *Morgan's Cavalry* (1867), 17, 24.

32. Ward, *Literary History of Kentucky,* 67–68.

33. D. H. Smith to Basil W. Duke (typed copy), February 6, 1867, DHSP.

34. John Castleman to Thomas H. Hines, February 7, 1867, THHP.

35. Gallagher, *Confederate War,* 171–72.

36. W. C. P. Breckinridge to Thomas W. Bullitt, February 7, 1866, BFP/FHS; George H. Pendleton to Basil W. Duke, December 3, 1867, HMFP.

37. Tapp and Klotter, *Decades of Discord,* 21–23.

38. James Cantrill to Basil W. Duke, February 11, 1868, HMFP; Webb, *Kentucky in the Reconstruction Era,* 30–31.

39. Webb, *Kentucky in the Reconstruction Era,* 33–34; Clark, *History of Kentucky,* 249.

15. My Prospects in That Line Were Not Brilliant

1. Curry, *Rail Routes South,* 22–36; Duke, *Reminiscences,* 589. The population of Louisville grew significantly in the 1860s, from approximately 68,000 in 1860 to over 100,000 in 1870.

Johnston, ed., *Memorial History of Louisville,* 1:105. Not only did growth remain constant in Lexington, but the city was also much smaller than Louisville, with a population of only 17,500 in 1870. Ranck, *History of Lexington,* 404.

2. Coulter, *Civil War and Readjustment,* 411–17; Webb, "Kentucky," 123–25.

3. Smith, *History of Kentucky,* 766–67; Webb, "Kentucky," 125; Coulter, *Civil War and Readjustment,* 415–16, 421; D. H. Smith to Josephine Smith, January 24, 1869, DHSP.

4. Webb, "Kentucky," 125; Duke, *Reminiscences,* 492; Clark and Kirwan, *The South since Appomattox,* 36.

5. Coulter, *Civil War and Readjustment,* 360–65.

6. Undated petition to His Excellency John W. Stevenson, Governor of Kentucky, John W. Stevenson Papers, Kentucky State Archives (hereafter JWSP).

7. General order (printed broadside), August 12, 1868, and handwritten constitution of the Soldiers of the Red Cross, THHP.

8. Basil W. Duke to Thomas H. Hines, n.d., October 20, 31, 1868, general order (printed broadside), August 12, 1868, and handwritten constitution of the Soldiers of the Red Cross, THHP.

9. Clark and Kirwan, *The South since Appomattox,* 41–42.

10. Hurst, *Nathan Bedford Forrest,* 300; Duke, *Reminiscences,* 425–26.

11. *New York Times,* November 3, 1868; Duke, *Reminiscences,* 427–28.

12. Duke, *Reminiscences,* 429–30.

13. Ibid., 430–33.

14. Ramage, *Gray Ghost,* 118, 147; Levin, *Lawyers and Law Makers,* 138–39.

15. A. E. Richards to Alexander Scott Bullitt, October 30, 1868, BFP/FHS; Basil W. Duke to W. H. Mackoy, January 11, 1869, W. H. Mackoy Papers, University of Kentucky (hereafter WHMP).

16. Webb, "Kentucky," 125.

17. Knott and Duke, "Editors Table" (April 1887), 711; Duke, *Reminiscences,* 500–503 (quotation).

18. Curry, *Rail Routes South,* 45–72; Tapp and Klotter, *Decades of Discord,* 54–55.

19. Curry, *Rail Routes South,* 73.

20. Tilford, "Delicate Track," 219–20.

21. *Cincinnati Commercial,* December 5, 1869; *Journal of the House of Representatives,* 53, 59, 62, 162; Curry, *Rail Routes South,* 74–75.

22. *Cincinnati Enquirer,* December 10, 1869.

23. Davis, *Breckinridge,* 601.

24. Ibid., 601–3; Klotter, *Breckinridges of Kentucky,* 134.

25. Curry, *Rail Routes South,* 79–83.

26. Ibid., 86–87; *Cincinnati Commercial,* February 25, 1870.

27. *Journal of the House of Representatives,* 194; Curry, *Rail Routes South,* 93.

28. *History of the Ohio Falls Cities,* 583–84; Basil W. Duke to Mayor John Baxter, March 24, 1870, MDFP.

29. Basil W. Duke to Governor Stevenson, resignation, June 28, 1870, JWSP; Curry, *Rail Routes South,* 106–7; Tapp and Klotter, *Decades of Discord,* 55–68.

30. Clark, *History of Kentucky,* 416–19.

31. Marcosson, *Marse Henry,* 85–91.

32. Watterson, *"Marse Henry,"* 1:243, 259; Marcosson, *Marse Henry,* 99–100.

33. Tapp and Klotter, *Decades of Discord,* 122–23; *Louisville Courier-Journal,* June 26, 1872.

34. Johnston, ed., *Memorial History of Louisville,* 2:388–90.

35. Levin, *Lawyers and Law Makers,* 90–93.

36. Johnston, ed., *Memorial History of Louisville,* 1:403–6.

16. Salmagundi

1. Webb, "Kentucky," 141; Basil W. Duke to Calvin Morgan, April 7, 1874, John Hunt Morgan II Collection, Transylvania University.

2. Tapp and Klotter, *Decades of Discord,* 141–48.

3. McAfee, *Kentucky Politicians,* 62–63; Morton, *Kentuckians Are Different,* 153; Fisher, *For All Times,* 92. The Churchills were prominent members of the Louisville community and had amassed a fair amount of property south of Louisville. See Kleber, ed., *Encyclopedia of Louisville,* 198–99.

4. *Louisville Courier-Journal,* August 7, 1875; Tapp and Klotter, *Decades of Discord,* 142.

5. Duke, *Reminiscences,* 277; Willis, *Kentucky Democracy,* 253; Smith, *History of Kentucky,* 775–76.

6. Wall, *Henry Watterson,* 139–49; Morris, *Fraud of the Century,* 164–99.

7. *Louisville Commercial,* January 19, 1877.

8. *Louisville Courier-Journal,* January 19, 1877; *Louisville Commercial,* January 19, 1877; Marcosson, *Marse Henry,* 108–36.

9. Grantham, *Solid South,* 3.

10. Painter, *Standing at Armageddon,* 3–4.

11. Ibid., 15–18.

12. *Louisville Courier-Journal,* July 18, 1877; Weaver, "Louisville Labor Disturbances," 178–79; Pinkerton, *Strikers,* 379.

13. *Louisville Commercial,* July 24, 1877; Pinkerton, *Strikers,* 381.

14. Weaver, "Louisville Labor Disturbances," 180; Wright, *Life behind a Veil,* 85–86.

15. *Louisville Commercial,* July 25, 1877.

16. *Louisville Commercial,* July 26, 1877; Pinkerton, *Strikers,* 386.

17. Weaver, "Louisville Labor Disturbances," 181; *Louisville Courier-Journal,* July 25, 1877; *Louisville Commercial,* July 25, 1877.

18. *Louisville Commercial,* July 25, 1877; Pinkerton, *Strikers,* 382–83.

19. *Louisville Commercial,* July 25, 1877; Weaver, "Louisville Labor Disturbances," 182; Pinkerton, *Strikers,* 383–85.

20. *Louisville Commercial,* July 25, 1877; Weaver, "Louisville Labor Disturbances," 182.

21. Pinkerton, *Strikers,* 379, 386–87; Weaver, "Louisville Labor Disturbances," 185.

22. Governor James B. McCreary to Basil W. Duke, August 9, 1877, James Bennett McCreary Papers, Filson Historical Society.

23. Rowland, ed., *Jefferson Davis Letters, Papers and Speeches,* 8:156–60 (quotation); *Philadelphia Weekly Times,* July 7, 1877.

24. Rowland, ed., *Jefferson Davis Letters, Papers and Speeches,* 8:170–71.

25. Duke, "Albert Sidney Johnston," 133–41.

26. Handy, *Journal,* 319.

27. Salmagundi Club records, January 18, 1879, Belknap Family Papers, Filson Historical Society; Duke, *Reminiscences,* 611–12.

28. Paxton, *Marshall Family,* 376.

29. Willis, *Kentucky Democracy,* 260–61.

30. Duke, *Reminiscences,* 579; Baird, "Blackburn's Campaign for Governor," 308.

31. Baird, "Blackburn's Campaign for Governor," 308–9; *Louisville Courier-Journal,* May 1–4, 1879.

32. Tapp and Klotter, *Decades of Discord,* 173–83.

33. Tachau, "Railroad President," 125–26.

34. Ibid., 140; Klein, *Louisville and Nashville Railroad,* 368–69.

35. Willis, *Kentucky Democracy,* 262–63; Smith, *D. Howard Smith,* 164.

36. Hesseltine, *Confederate Leaders in the South,* 16.

37. Yates and Gray, "Business Conflicts," 295–97.

38. Ibid., 298–301.

39. Ibid., 302–3.

40. Kinchen, *General Bennett Young,* 84–85.

41. Yates and Gray, "Business Conflicts," 304–5; *Louisville Commercial,* October 14, 15, 1885; *Louisville Times,* February 15, 1886.

42. Duke, *Governmental Regulation of Railroads* and *Transportation Tariffs,* 16, 28.

43. Duke, "The Commercial and the Railroad Development of Kentucky," 45–50.

44. Duke, *Transportation Tariffs,* 11–13.

17. A Distinctively Southern Magazine

1. Marriner, ed., "Organization of the Southern Historical Society" and "Confederate History"; Gallagher, introduction, ii–iv.

2. Gallagher, introduction, iii; Dodd, "Recollections," 2–11; McDonald, "Lee's Retreat," 26–34.

3. Duke, "Battle of Hartsville," 42–51.

4. Duke, "Battle of Shiloh, Part 2," 215.

5. Gallagher, introduction, vi–vii; Osborne, *Jubal,* 485; Mott, *American Magazine,* 3:47 n. 85.

6. Johnston, ed., *Memorial History of Louisville,* 1:422–23.

7. Duke and Knott, "Editors Table" (April 1887), 710–12.

8. Gallagher, introduction, ix; Mott, *American Magazine,* 3:47.

9. Duke and Knott, "Editors Table" (April 1887), 710–12; Woodward, *Burdens of Southern History,* 89–107.

10. Basil W. Duke to Jubal Early, September 7, 1886, Jubal Early Papers, Library of Congress, Manuscript Division; Foster, *Ghosts of the Confederacy,* 90.

11. Brown, *Bold Cavaliers,* 274–77; Horan, *Confederate Agent,* 67–83.

12. Horan, *Confederate Agent,* 89–90, 125–30.

13. Ibid., 286.

14. Thomas H. Hines to Jefferson Davis, November 20, 1882, THHP.

15. Rowland, ed., *Jefferson Davis Letters, Papers and Speeches,* 9:501.

16. Ibid., 388–89, 501–11.

17. Thomas H. Hines to Jefferson Davis (copy), November 20, 1886, THHP.

18. Varina Davis to Thomas H. Hines, December 11, 1886, THHP.

19. Horan, *Confederate Agent,* 286–88.

20. Ibid.

21. Duke and Knott, "Editors Table" (May 1887), 773.

22. Davie, "Founders of the Filson Club," 127–29.

23. Weeks, ed., "Teddy Roosevelt," 122–35.

24. Basil W. Duke to Theodore Roosevelt, May 19, 1888, Theodore Roosevelt Papers, Library of Congress, Manuscript Division (hereafter TRP).

25. Davie, "Founders of the Filson Club," 135.

26. Mott, *American Magazine,* 3:47 n. 51.

27. Painter, *Standing at Armageddon,* 263.

28. Duke, "Editors Table" (March 1894), 205.

29. Duke, "Labor Organizations and the Law."

30. Duke, "Editors Table" (September 1894), 208–14; Painter, *Standing at Armageddon,* 120–21, 139–40.

31. Duke, "Municipal Reform," 323.

32. Duke, "Hungry Little Greeks," 206.

33. Ayers, *New South,* 30–31, 345–48; Aaron, *Unwritten War,* 278 (quoting Cable).

34. Duke, "Hungry Little Greeks," 205–9; Ayers, *New South,* 30–31, 345–48; Aaron, *Unwritten War,* 278.

35. Woodward, *Burdens of Southern History,* 37–38.

36. Duke, "Hungry Little Greeks," 205–8; Otken, *Ills of the South,* 209.

37. Mott, *American Magazine,* 4:93 n. 51.

38. York, *John Fox,* 52–53.

18. Politics and Panic

1. Klein, *Louisville and Nashville Railroad,* 372–75.

2. Basil W. Duke to William Lindsay, September 18, 1892, December 24, 1894, William Lindsay Papers, University of Kentucky (hereafter WLP). When these two letters were written, William Lindsay was a U.S. senator and a longtime friend of Duke's. The first was intended to convey a railroad pass to Miss Fannie E. Varnon, the second a pass to Miss Fannie Crittenden. Klein, *Louisville and Nashville Railroad,* 375–80.

3. Morton, *Kentuckians Are Different,* 44–45; McAfee, *Kentucky Politicians,* 64 (quotation).

4. Morton, *Kentuckians Are Different,* 44–45.

5. Klein, *Louisville and Nashville Railroad,* 368–72; Painter, *Standing at Armageddon,* 37–38.

6. Lambert, "Free Silver," 146; Tapp and Klotter, *Decades of Discord,* 228.

7. Clark, *History of Kentucky,* 425–26.

8. Tapp and Klotter, *Decades of Discord,* 222–29; Burckel, "William Goebel," 43–44; Marcosson, *Marse Henry,* 148.

9. Tapp and Klotter, *Decades of Discord,* 231–36; Willis, *Kentucky Democracy,* 299; Burckel, "William Goebel," 44.

10. Willis, *Kentucky Democracy,* 305; Burckel, "William Goebel," 44–45.

11. Klotter, *Politics of Wrath,* 20–21; *Journal of the Senate,* 1751–54.

12. Burckel, "William Goebel," 45–46; *Official Records of the Constitutional Convention,* 5809.

13. Basil W. Duke to J. Blackburn, June 11, 1889, John F. Dahringer Collection, Kentucky Historical Society; Basil W. Duke to William Lindsay, June 5, 1892, WLP.

14. Tapp and Klotter, *Decades of Discord,* 314–17.

15. Lambert, "Free Silver," 148–51.

16. Ibid., 152–55; Clark, *History of Kentucky,* 428–29.

17. Painter, *Standing at Armageddon,* 116–21. Duke took notice of the nation's economic crisis in at least one *Southern Magazine* editorial, writing about the groups of men from all parts of the country who banded together in so-called industrial armies and converged on the nation's capital to protest economic conditions. See Duke, "Editors Table" (September 1894), 208–14.

18. Adams, *Education,* 346; Johnston, ed., *Memorial History of Louisville,* 1:297.

19. Ibid., 2:207.

20. Painter, *Standing at Armageddon,* 121–25; Lambert, "Free Silver," 156.

21. Harrison, ed., *Kentucky's Governors,* 103–6; Burckel, "William Goebel," 46.

22. Wiltz, "1895 Election," 119–20.

23. Lambert, "Free Silver," 156–60; *Louisville Courier-Journal,* May 25, 1895.

24. *Louisville Courier-Journal,* May 28, 1895; Duke, *Reminiscences,* 585.

25. Willis, *Kentucky Democracy,* 371–72. The *Louisville Courier-Journal* reported on April 12, 1895, that the article concerning Sanford appeared in the *Covington* (Ky.) *Ledger* on April 6, 1895. Thomas, ed., "Goebel Affair," 327–29.

26. Willis, *Kentucky Democracy,* 373–74; Tapp and Klotter, *Decades of Discord,* 434.

27. Lambert, "Free Silver," 160–61.

28. Ibid., 153; Wiltz, "1895 Election," 124.

29. Tapp and Klotter, *Decades of Discord,* 348–54; Wiltz, "1895 Election," 128; *Louisville Evening Post,* August 21, 1895.

30. Lambert, "Free Silver," 170–74; Willis, *Kentucky Democracy,* 353–54.

31. Tapp and Klotter, *Decades of Discord,* 355–60; Duke, *Reminiscences,* 573.

32. Basil W. Duke to William Lindsay, May 10, 1896, WLP.

33. Schlup, "William Lindsay," 23–24.

34. Ibid., 24–25; Duke, *Reminiscences,* 585.

35. Willis, *Kentucky Democracy,* 359–60; Bryan, *First Battle,* 214–20; Marcosson, *Marse Henry,* 165.

36. Glad, *Trumpet Soundeth,* 53–57.

37. Basil W. Duke to H. L. Martin, July 16, 1896, H. L. Martin Papers, Kentucky Historical Society (hereafter HLMP).

38. George M. Davie to William Lindsay, September 4, 1896, WLP.

39. *Louisville Courier-Journal,* September 12, 13, 1896; Schlup, "William Lindsay," 32–33; Tapp and Klotter, *Decades of Discord,* 364.

40. William Lindsay to H. L. Martin, November 27, 1897, HLMP; Tapp and Klotter, *Decades of Discord,* 366.

41. Johnston, ed., *Memorial History of Louisville,* 1:318–28.

42. Ibid., 609.

43. *Confederate Veteran Magazine* 3 (October 1895): 4, 9 (May 1901): 227, and 12 (June 1904): 289.

44. Duke, "Address," 105–11.

45. Ridley, "Morgan's War-Horse," 627; Bean, "Battle of Hartsville" (1915), 125; Duke, "Sketch," 568, and "General Morgan's Escape," 499; Foster, *Ghosts of the Confederacy,* 141.

46. *Confederate Veteran Magazine* 5 (May 1897): 210 and 13 (April 1905): 149; Kinchen, *General Bennett Young,* 111.

47. Tapp and Klotter, *Decades of Discord,* 370.

48. Burckel, "William Goebel," 47.

49. Ibid., 47–48.

50. Thomas, ed., "Goebel Affair," 339.

51. Burckel, "William Goebel," 48–49; Willis, *Kentucky Democracy,* 375–77.

52. Burckel, "William Goebel," 49.

53. Longacre, *Union Stars,* 254.

54. Duke, *Reminiscences,* 574.

19. At the Turn of the Century

1. Glad, *Trumpet Soundeth,* 143.

2. *Louisville Dispatch,* September 8, 1898; Davis, *Jefferson Davis,* 644–54.

3. Basil W. Duke to William Lindsay, September 8, 1898, WLP.

4. Basil W. Duke to William Lindsay, October 4, 1898, WLP. Duke is referring to Goebel's election bill. Marcosson, *Marse Henry,* 169; Wall, *Henry Watterson,* 233–36; Willis, *Kentucky Democracy,* 360.

5. Duke, *Reminiscences,* 586–88.

6. Burckel, "William Goebel," 50; Klein, *Louisville and Nashville Railroad,* 383–84.

7. Tapp and Klotter, *Decades of Discord,* 418–20; Burckel, "William Goebel," 51.

8. Basil W. Duke to W. H. Mackoy, July 17, 1899, WHMP.

9. Klein, *Louisville and Nashville Railroad,* 383–84.

10. Tapp and Klotter, *Decades of Discord,* 430; Burckel, "William Goebel," 52–53; *Louisville Courier-Journal,* August 13, 1899.

11. Hughes, Schrader, and Williams, *That Kentucky Campaign,* 61, 65.

12. Ibid., 110.

13. Burckel, "William Goebel," 55–57; Klotter, *Politics of Wrath,* 74–75.

14. Tapp and Klotter, *Decades of Discord,* 440.

15. Klein, *Louisville and Nashville Railroad,* 384; Burckel, "William Goebel," 57–58; Klotter, *Politics of Wrath,* 97–98.

16. Hughes, Schrader, and Williams, *That Kentucky Campaign,* 168; *Louisville Courier-Journal,* January 3, 1900.

17. Burckel, "William Goebel," 58–59; Thomas, ed., "Goebel Affair," 336–37.

18. Klein, *Louisville and Nashville Railroad,* 385; Tapp and Klotter, *Decades of Discord,* 446–47; Woodson, *First New Dealer,* 6–7.

19. Woodson, *First New Dealer,* 9.

20. Klein, *Louisville and Nashville Railroad,* 385; Clark, *History of Kentucky,* 441.

21. Tapp and Klotter, *Decades of Discord,* 453; Klotter, *Politics of Wrath,* 111.

22. Thomas W. Bullitt to Alexander Scott Bullitt, February 7, 1900, BFP/FHS.

23. Thomas, ed., "Goebel Affair," 338–42; Klein, *Louisville and Nashville Railroad,* 386.

24. Bursch, *They Escaped the Hangman,* 28–29.

25. Cobb, *Stickfuls,* 284–88 (quotations); Clark, *History of Kentucky,* 441–42.

26. While Grover Cleveland, the former president, as well as a small cadre of Democrats withheld their support from Bryan, his loss was more likely attributable to the nation's newfound prosperity under the McKinley administration. Glad, *Trumpet Soundeth,* 143–45.

27. Henning, "Basil Wilson Duke," 62; Morrison, ed., *Letters of Theodore Roosevelt,* 3:26–28, 430–32.

28. Henning, "Basil Wilson Duke," 62.

29. Basil W. Duke to Theodore Roosevelt, February 15, July 28, 1903, TRP.

30. Basil W. Duke to Theodore Roosevelt, July 23, 1903, TRP.

31. Ibid.; Theodore Roosevelt to Basil W. Duke, July 31, 1903, TRP. In this letter, the president references a visit from one of Duke's daughters, and this may have been Currie Mathews, who at that time lived in New York.

32. Richard W. Knott, memorandum, January 26, 1904, TRP.

33. Klotter, *Portrait in Paradox,* 206.

34. Richard W. Knott, memorandum, January 26, 1904, TRP.

35. A. E. Willson, memorandum for the president on Kentucky matters, January 26, 1904, and A. E. Willson, telephone memorandum, January 26, 1904, TRP.

36. W. O. Bradley to Theodore Roosevelt, January 27, 1904, TRP.

37. A. E. Willson to Richard W. Knott, memorandum, with a copy to Theodore Roosevelt, January 27, 1904, TRP.

38. Richard W. Knott to A. E. Willson, January 28, 1904, Basil W. Duke to Theodore Roosevelt, January 27, 1904, and Theodore Roosevelt to Basil W. Duke, January 29, 1904, TRP.

39. Basil W. Duke to Theodore Roosevelt, May 6, 1904, TRP.

40. Theodore Roosevelt to Basil W. Duke, May 6, 1904, TRP; John Marshall Harlan to A. E. Willson, May 9, 1904, Augustus Everett Willson Papers, Filson Historical Society (hereafter AEWP).

41. Klotter, *Portrait in Paradox,* 208.

20. The Disappointments of Life Should Seem Trivial

1. Basil W. Duke to H. L. Martin, May 2, 1904, HLMP; Tapp and Klotter, *Decades of Discord,* 365.

2. Basil W. Duke to H. L. Martin, April 18, 1904, HLMP.

3. Basil W. Duke to H. L. Martin, May 2, 1904, May 24, 1904, William D. Hines to Basil W. Duke, May, 26, 1904, and Basil W. Duke to H. L. Martin, May 20, 1904, HLMP; Klotter, *Politics of Wrath,* 129.

4. Ellis, *Robert Worth Bingham,* 27–28.

5. Duke, *Reminiscences,* 515; Basil W. Duke to H. L. Martin, December 10, 1904, HLMP.

6. Clark, *Helm Bruce,* 32; Ellis, *Robert Worth Bingham,* 32; Basil W. Duke to A. E. Willson, September 7, 1905, October 31, 1905, AEWP.

7. Clark, *Helm Bruce,* 32–33.

8. "Fusionist Movement," 325.

9. Ellis, *Robert Worth Bingham,* 32–33.

10. Ibid., 34–36; Klotter, *Portrait in Paradox,* 208–9; Basil W. Duke to Robert Worth Bingham, September 1907, Robert Worth Bingham Papers, Filson Historical Society.

11. *Confederate Veteran Magazine* 13 (October 1905): 441–42.

12. Smith, *This Great Battlefield,* 91; Davis, *Government of Our Own,* 405.

13. Until Ramage's recent *Rebel Raider,* an in-depth study of Morgan's personality, his biographers adhered steadfastly to the image of Morgan that Duke had painted. See, e.g., Holland, *Morgan and His Raiders,* and Thomas, *John Hunt Morgan.*

14. Thomas W. Bullitt to Basil W. Duke, April 11, 1906, BFP/FHS; Theodore Roosevelt to Basil W. Duke, July 9, 1906, TRP; Krick, *Neale Books,* xi–xii.

15. Theodore Roosevelt to Richard Watson Gilder, November 16, 1908, Morrison, ed., *Letters of Theodore Roosevelt,* 6:1356–65.

16. *Confederate Veteran Magazine* 17 (December 1909): 610.

17. Basil W. Duke to Edward Owings Guerrant, November 12, 1909, Edward Owings Guerrant Papers, Filson Historical Society.

18. *Lexington Herald,* September 17, 1916.

19. Davie, "Founders of the Filson Club," 133.

20. Basil W. Duke to H. L. Martin, March 29, 1911, HLMP.

21. Basil W. Duke to Theodore Roosevelt, May 22, 1911, and Theodore Roosevelt to Basil W. Duke, June 2, 1911, TRP.

22. Ramage, *Rebel Raider,* 257.

23. *Lexington Herald,* October 19, 1911.

24. Ibid.

25. Ibid.

26. Ibid. Lee's speech was printed in its entirety in the December issue of the *Confederate Veteran,* as was a biographical sketch of Morgan written by Duke. Considering Duke's past history when writing or speaking about Morgan's exploits, the sketch proved remarkably prosaic, almost as if it had been written by someone else. See Lee, "Tribute," and Duke, "Sketch."

27. Basil W. Duke to Mrs. Beauregard, March 17, 1914, CWC/MHS.

28. Henning, "Basil Wilson Duke," 63–64; *New English Weekly,* June 8, 1933.

29. York, *John Fox,* 272; *Lexington Herald,* September 17, 1916; *Louisville Courier-Journal,* September 17, 1916; Margaret Shaw Grahm to Mrs. Hagedorn, June 4, 1920, Julia D. Henning Letters, Filson Historical Society.

30. *Louisville Courier-Journal,* September 18, 1916; Annie Logan Bullitt to William Marshall Bullitt, September 18, 1916, BFP/FHS.

31. *New English Weekly,* June 8, 1933.

Bibliography

Manuscript Collections

Centre College (Danville, Ky.)

Centre College Archives.

Duke University (Durham, N.C.)

John Snider Cooper Papers.

Filson Historical Society (Louisville)

Belknap Family Papers.
Robert Worth Bingham Papers.
Bullitt Family Papers.
William Davis Papers.
Edward Owings Guerrant Papers.
Thomas H. Hines Papers.
J. Stoddard Johnston Papers.
Johnston Family Papers.
Jones Family Papers.
Marshall Family Papers.
James Bennett McCreary Papers.
Morgan-Duke Family Papers.
D. H. Smith Papers.
Augustus Everett Willson Papers.

Georgetown College (Georgetown, Ky.)

Georgetown College Archives.

Indiana Historical Society (Indianapolis)

William Steele Correspondence Collection.
Williamson D. Ward Diary and Letters Collection.

Kentucky Historical Society (Frankfort)

Alexander Collection.
Barlow Family Civil War Collection.
Coburn Family Papers.
John F. Dahringer Collection.
Don D. John Collection.
H. L. Martin Papers.
D. H. Smith Papers.

Kentucky State Archives (Frankfort)

John W. Stevenson Papers.

Library of Congress, Manuscript Division (Washington, D.C.)

Breckinridge Family Manuscript Collection.
Jubal Early Papers.
Theodore Roosevelt Papers.

Missouri Historical Society (St. Louis)

Civil War Collection.

Tennessee State Library and Archives (Nashville)

Civil War Collection.

Transylvania University (Lexington)

John Hunt Morgan II Collection.

University of Kentucky (Lexington)

Fackler Family Papers.
Hathaway Family Papers.
Thomas H. Hines Papers.
Hunt-Morgan Family Papers.
William Lindsay Papers.
W. H. Mackoy Papers.

University of North Carolina, Southern Historical Collection (Chapel Hill)

Bullitt Family Papers.
Basil Wilson Duke Papers.
John Hunt Morgan Papers.
James L. Norris Papers.
Kirby Smith Papers.

Unpublished Sources

Bean, R. T. "Hartsville." Unpublished manuscript, n.d. Morgan-Duke Family Papers, Filson Historical Society, Louisville.

Blanton, James. Unpublished manuscript (typed copy), n.d. University of Kentucky.

Bullitt, Thomas W. "Recollections of the War." Unpublished manuscript, August 29, 1907. Bullitt Family Papers, Filson Historical Society, Louisville.

Curtis Burke Diary. Filson Historical Society, Louisville.

Duke, Basil W. "Personal Recollections of Shiloh by Gen. Basil W. Duke." Unpublished address presented to the Filson Club, April 6, 1914. Filson Historical Society, Louisville.

Julia D. Henning Letters. Morgan-Duke Family Papers, Filson Historical Society, Louisville.

Absalom Johnson Diary. Filson Historical Society, Louisville.

J. Stoddard Johnston Diary. J. Stoddard Johnston Papers, Filson Historical Society, Louisville.

Mary Buford Jones Diary. Jones Family Papers, Filson Historical Society, Louisville.

John Porter Memoirs (typed copy). N.d. Civil War Collection, Tennessee State Library and Archives, Nashville.

Published Sources

Aaron, Daniel. *The Unwritten War: American Writers and the Civil War.* Madison: University of Wisconsin Press, 1987.

Abbott, John S. C. "Heroic Deeds of Heroic Men: The Pursuit and Capture of Morgan." *Harpers New Monthly Magazine* 31 (August 1865): 287–97.

Adams, Henry. *The Education of Henry Adams.* Edited by Ernest Samuels. Boston: Houghton Mifflin, 1974.

Allen, Theodore Frelinghuysen. "John Morgan's Raid in Ohio." *Ohio Archaeological and Historical Quarterly* 17 (January 1908): 48–59.

Anderson, Galusha. *The Story of a Border City during the Civil War.* Boston: Little, Brown, 1908.

Annual Review, History of St. Louis, Commercial Statistics, Improvements of the Year and Account of Leading Manufactories &c.: From the St. Louis Missouri Republican, January 10, 1854. St. Louis: Chambers & Knapp, 1854.

Apple, Linsey, Fredrick A. Johnson, and Ann Bolten Bevins, eds. *A History of Scott County.* Georgetown, Ky.: Scott County Historical Society, 1993.

Auer, Jeffrey. "The Little Fight: Duke's Raid on Augusta, September 27, 1862." *Register of the Kentucky Historical Society* 49 (January 1951): 28–34.

Ayres, Edward I. *The Promise of the New South: Life after Reconstruction.* New York: Oxford University Press, 1992.

Baird, Nancy D. "Luke Pryor Blackburn's Campaign for Governor." *Register of the Kentucky Historical Society* 74 (October 1976): 300–313.

———. *Luke Pryor Blackburn: Physician, Governor and Reformer.* Lexington: University Press of Kentucky, 1979.

Ballard, Michael D. *A Long Shadow: Jefferson Davis and the Final Days of the Confederacy.* Athens: University of Georgia Press, 1985.

Barret, John G. *The Civil War in North Carolina.* Chapel Hill: University of North Carolina Press, 1963.

Basler, Roy A., ed. *The Collected Works of Abraham Lincoln.* Vols. 4, 5. New Brunswick, N.J.: Rutgers University Press, 1953.

Bean, R. T. "The Battle of Hartsville, Tennessee." *Confederate Veteran Magazine* 23 (March 1915): 125.

Bearss, Edwin. "Morgan's Second Kentucky Raid, December 1862, Part 1." *Register of the Kentucky Historical Society* 70 (July 1972): 200–218.

———. "Morgan's Second Kentucky Raid, December 1862, Part 2." *Register of the Kentucky Historical Society* 71 (April 1973): 177–188.

———. "Morgan's Second Kentucky Raid, December 1862, Part 3." *Register of the Kentucky Historical Society* 71 (October 1973): 426–438.

Beauregard, G. T. "The Campaign of Shiloh." In *Battles and Leaders of the Civil War,* vol. 1, *From Sumter to Shiloh,* ed. Robert Underwood Johnson and Clarence Clough Buel. New York: Century, 1887. Reprint, New York: Thomas Yoseloff, 1956.

Benedict, James Bell, Jr. "General John Hunt Morgan: The Great Indiana-Ohio Raid." *Filson Club History Quarterly* 31 (April 1957): 147–71.

Bennett, Pamela J., ed. "Curtis R. Burke's Civil War Journal." *Indiana Magazine of History* 55 (December 1969): 283–327.

Berry, Mary Clay. *Voices from the Century Before: The Odyssey of a Nineteenth Century Kentucky Family.* New York: Arcade, 1997.

Berry, Thomas F. *Four Years with Morgan and Forrest.* Oklahoma City, Okla.: Harlow Ratliff, 1914.

Beth, Loren P. *John Marshall Harlan: The Last Whig Justice.* Lexington: University Press of Kentucky, 1992.

Betts, Edward C. *Early History of Huntsville, Alabama, 1804–1870.* Montgomery: Brown, 1916.

Bevins, Ann Bolton. *A History of Scott County as Told by Selected Buildings.* Georgetown, Ky.: privately printed, 1981.

Boyd, Lucinda. *Chronicles of Cynthiana and Other Chronicles.* Cincinnati: Robert Clarke, 1894.

Boyer, Margeritte. "Morgan's Raid in Indiana." *Indiana Magazine of History* 8 (December 1912): 149–65.

Brewer, James D. *The Raiders of 1862.* Westport, Conn.: Praeger, 1997.

Brown, Dee Alexander. *The Bold Cavaliers: Morgan's Second Kentucky Cavalry Raiders.* Philadelphia: Lippincott, 1959.

Bruce, Robert V. *1877: Year of Violence.* Indianapolis: Bobbs-Merrill, 1959.

Bryan, William Jennings. *The First Battle: A History of the Campaign of 1896.* Chicago: W. B. Conke, 1896.

Buell, Don Carlos. "Shiloh Reviewed." In *Battles and Leaders of the Civil War,* vol. 1, *From Sumter to Shiloh,* ed. Robert Underwood Johnson and Clarence Clough Buel. New York: Century, 1887. Reprint, New York: Thomas Yoseloff, 1956.

Burckel, Nicholas. "William Goebel and the Campaign for Railroad Regulation in Kentucky, 1888–1900." *Filson Club History Quarterly* 48 (January 1974): 43–60.

Bursch, Frances X. *They Escaped the Hangman: An Account of the Trials of the Caleb Powers Case, the Rice-Patrick Case, the Halls Mello Case, the Hans Haupt Case.* Indianapolis: Bobbs-Merrill, 1953.

Butterfield, Consul Willshire. *History of the Girtys.* Cincinnati: Robert Clarke, 1890.

Cable, George W. *John March, Southerner.* New York: Scribner's, 1894.

Castleman, John D. *Active Service.* Louisville: Courier-Journal Job Printing, 1917.

Chinn, George Morgan. *Kentucky Settlement and Statehood, 1750–1800.* Frankfort: Kentucky Historical Society, 1975.

Clark, James C. *Last Train South: The Flight of the Confederate Government from Richmond.* Jefferson, N.C.: McFarland, 1984.

Clark, John E., Jr. *Railroads of the Civil War: The Impact of Management on Victory and Defeat.* Baton Route: Louisiana State University Press, 2001.

Clark, M. H. "The Last Days of the Confederate Treasury and What Became of Its Specie." *Southern Historical Society Papers* 9 (1881): 542–56.

Clark, Thomas D. *Helm Bruce, Public Defender: Breaking Louisville's Gothic Political Ring, 1905.* Louisville: Filson Club, 1973.

———. *A History of Kentucky.* Ashland, Ky.: Jesse Stuart, 1992.

Clark, Thomas D., and Albert D. Kirwan. *The South since Appomattox: A Century of Regional Change.* New York: Oxford University Press, 1967.

Clift, G. Glenn. *History of Maysville and Mason County.* Vol. 1. Lexington: Transylvania University, 1936.

Cobb, Irvin S. *Stickfuls: Compositions of a Newspaper Minion.* New York: George H. Doran, 1923.

"Coffee-Boiler Rangers." *Southern Bivouac* 1 (July 1883): 442–45.

Coleman, J. Winston, Jr. "Lexington's Slave Dealers and Their Southern Trade." *Filson Club History Quarterly* 12 (January 1938): 1–23.

———. *Slavery Times in Kentucky.* Chapel Hill: University of North Carolina Press, 1940.

———. *Famous Kentucky Duels.* Lexington: Henry Clay, 1969.

Collins, Lewis. *Historical Sketches of Kentucky.* Cincinnati: Lewis Collins & J. A. and U. P. James, 1848.

Connelly, Thomas Lawrence, and Archer Jones. *The Politics of Command: Factions and Ideas in Confederate Strategy.* Baton Rouge: Louisiana State University Press, 1998.

Cook, J. F. *Old Kentucky.* New York, 1908.

Cooling, Benjamin Franklin. *Forts Henry and Donelson: The Key to the Confederate Heartland.* Knoxville: University of Tennessee Press, 1987.

———. *Fort Donelson's Legacy: War and Society in Kentucky and Tennessee, 1862–1863.* Knoxville: University of Tennessee Press, 1997.

Cotterill, R. S. "The Louisville and Nashville Railroad, 1861–1865." *American Historical Review* 29 (July 1924): 700–715.

Coulter, E. Merton. *The Civil War and Readjustment in Kentucky.* Gloucester, Mass.: Peter Smith, 1966.

Cozzens, Peter. *No Better Place to Die: The Battle of Stones River.* Urbana: University of Illinois Press, 1990.

Craven, Avery O. *The Growth of Southern Nationalism, 1848–1861.* Vol. 6 of *A History of the South,* ed. Wendell Holmes Stephenson and E. Merton Coulter. Baton Rouge: Louisiana State University Press, 1953.

Crist, Laswell, Mary Seaton Dix, and Kenneth Williams, eds. *The Papers of Jefferson Davis, 1862.* Vol. 8. Baton Rouge: Louisiana State University Press, 1995.

Crumbaugh, J. W. *Augusta, Kentucky: Old Timer Talks, Recalls the Old Days in Augusta.* Edited by Caroline R. Miller. Brooksville, Ky.: Bracken County Historical Society, 2003.

Cunningham, J. W. "Memories of Morgan's Christmas Raid." *Confederate Veteran Magazine* 18 (February 1909): 79–80.

Curry, Leonard P. *Rail Routes South: Louisville's Fight for the Southern Market, 1865–1872.* Lexington: University Press of Kentucky, 1969.

Daniel, Larry J. *Shiloh: The Battle That Changed the Civil War.* New York: Simon & Schuster, 1997.

———. *Days of Glory: The Army of the Cumberland, 1861–1865.* Baton Rouge: Louisiana State University Press, 2004.

Davenport, E. Gavin. *Ante-Bellum Kentucky: A Social History, 1800–1860.* Oxford, Miss.: Mississippi Valley, 1943.

Davie, Preston. "Personal Reminiscences concerning Some of the Founders of the Filson Club." *Filson Club History Quarterly* 18 (July 1944): 127–40.

Davis, Jefferson. *The Rise and Fall of the Confederate Government.* Vol. 2. New York: D. Appleton, 1881.

Davis, William C., ed. *The Confederate General.* 6 vols. Harrisburg, Pa.: National Historical Society, 1991.

———. *Jefferson Davis, the Man and His Hour: A Biography.* New York: Harper-Collins, 1991.

———. *Breckinridge: Statesman Soldier Symbol.* Baton Rouge: Louisiana State University Press, 1992.

———. *The Orphan Brigade: The Kentucky Confederates Who Couldn't Go Home.* Mechanicsburg, Pa.: Stackpole, 1993.

———. *A Government of Our Own: The Making of the Confederacy.* New York: Free Press, 1994.

———. *The Lost Cause: Myths and Realities of the Confederacy.* Lawrence: University Press of Kansas, 1996.

———. *An Honorable Defeat: The Last Days of the Confederate Government.* New York: Harcourt, 2001.

Davis, William C., and Meredith L. Swentor, eds. *Bluegrass Confederate: The Civil War Diary of Edward O. Guerrant.* Baton Rouge: Louisiana State University Press, 1999.

Davis, William J. "A Winter Raid." *Southern Bivouac* 1 (June 1885): 28–34.

Denison, George T. *A History of Cavalry, from the Earliest Times, with Lessons for the Future.* London: Macmillan, 1913.

Dodd, W. O. "Recollections of Vicksburg during the Siege." *Southern Bivouac* 1 (September 1882): 2–11.

Dorris, Jonathan Truman. *Old Cane Springs: A Story of the War between the States in Madison County, Kentucky.* Louisville: Standard, 1937.

Duke, Basil W. *A History of Morgan's Cavalry.* Cincinnati: Miami, 1867. Reprint, West Jefferson, Ohio: Genesis, 1997.

———. "The Confederate Career of Albert Sidney Johnston." *Southern Historical Society Papers* 6 (September 1878): 133–41.

———. "The Battle of Hartsville." *Southern Bivouac* 1 (October 1882): 41–51.

———. "Address of General Basil W. Duke of Louisville, at a Reunion of Morgan's Men Held at Rich Pond, Warren County, Kentucky, October 27, 1883." *Southern Bivouac* 1 (November 1883): 105–11.

———. "The Battle of Shiloh, Part 1." *Southern Bivouac* 1 (December 1883): 150–62.

———. "The Battle of Shiloh, Part 2." *Southern Bivouac* 2 (January 1884): 201–16.

———. *Governmental Regulation of Railroads.* Louisville: John P. Morton, 1884.

———. "Bragg's Campaign in Kentucky, 1862, Part 2." *Southern Bivouac* 1 (September 1885): 232–40.

———. "After the Fall of Richmond." *Southern Bivouac* 2 (August 1886): 156–66. This article, retitled "Last Days of the Confederacy," was later incorporated in *Battles and Leaders of the Civil War,* vol. 4, *The Way to Appomattox,* ed. Robert Underwood Johnson and Clarence Clough Buel. New York: Century, 1888. Reprint, New York: Thomas Yoseloff, 1956.

———. *Transportation Tariffs: A Discussion of the Proper Relative Rates on Short Hauls as Compared with Long Hauls.* Louisville: J. P. Morton, 1886.

———. "The Commercial and the Railroad Development of Kentucky." In *Kentucky Resources: Transportation Systems Together with a Review of Transportation Problems and Opportunities to Be Developed; Papers Read at the State Industrial and Commercial Conference Held in Louisville, October 4th, 1887.* Frankfort, Ky.: Capital Printing Co., 1887.

———. "The Editors Table." *Southern Magazine Illustrated,* March 1894, 203–5.

———. "Hungry Little Greeks." *Southern Magazine Illustrated,* March 1894, 205–8.

———. "Municipal Reform." *Southern Magazine Illustrated,* April 1894, 322–24.

———. "Immigration and the South." *Southern Magazine Illustrated,* May 1894, 429–31.

———. "Labor Organizations and the Law." *Southern Magazine Illustrated,* August 1894, 103–8.

———. "The Editors Table." *Southern Magazine Illustrated,* September 1894, 208–19.

———. *The History of the Bank of Kentucky, 1792–1895.* Louisville: John P. Morton, 1895.

———. *Morgan's Cavalry.* New York: Neale, 1906.

———. *Reminiscences of General Basil W. Duke, C.S.A.* New York: Doubleday Page, 1911. Reprint, West Jefferson, Ohio: Genesis, 1997.

———. "Sketch of John H. Morgan." *Confederate Veteran Magazine* 20 (December 1911): 568–69.

———. "General Morgan's Escape from Prison." *Confederate Veteran Magazine* 26 (October 1916): 449–53.

Duke, Basil W., Thomas Hines, and Orlando Willcox. "A Romance of Morgan's Rough Riders: The Raid, the Capture, and the Escape." In *Famous Adventures and Prison Escapes of the Civil War.* New York: Century, 1898. This article originally appeared in the January 1891 issue of *Century Magazine.*

Duke, Basil W., and Richard W. Knott. "The Editors Table." *Southern Bivouac* 2 (April 1887): 709–712.

———. "The Editors Table." *Southern Bivouac* 2 (April 1887): 710–12.

———. "The Editors Table." *Southern Bivouac* 2 (May 1887): 773–76.

Eicher, David J. *The Longest Night: A Military History of the Civil War.* New York: Simon & Schuster, 2001.

Ellis, William E. *Robert Worth Bingham and the Southern Mystique: From the Old South to the New South and Beyond.* Kent, Ohio: Kent State University Press, 1997.

Engle, Stephen D. *Don Carlos Buell: Most Promising of All.* Chapel Hill: University of North Carolina Press, 1999.

Estvan, B. *War Pictures from the South.* New York: D. Appleton, 1863.

Farrell, David C. "John Marshall Harlan and the Union Cause in Kentucky, 1861." *Filson Club History Quarterly* 37 (January 1963): 5–23.

Fellman, Michael. *Inside War: The Guerrilla Conflict in Missouri during the American Civil War.* New York: Oxford University Press, 1989.

Fisher, Jonelle. *For All Times: The Story of Lucas Brodhead.* N.p.: privately printed, 2002.

Ford, C. Edward, ed. *The Sesquicentennial History of Mt. Zion Christian Church, Madison County, Kentucky, 1852–2002.* Richmond, Ky.: Mt. Zion Christian Church, 2002.

Foster, Gaines M. *Ghosts of the Confederacy: Defeat, the Lost Cause, and the Emergence of the New South.* New York: Oxford University Press, 1987.

"Fusionist Movement." In *The Encyclopedia of Louisville,* ed. John E. Kleber. Lexington: University Press of Kentucky, 2001.

Gaines, B. O. *History of Scott County.* Georgetown, Ky.: privately printed, 1905.

Gallagher, Gary W. Introduction to *Southern Bivouac,* vol. 1. Wilmington, N.C.: Broadfoot, 1992.

———. *The Confederate War: How Popular Will, Nationalism, and Military Strategy Could Not Stave off Defeat.* Cambridge, Mass.: Harvard University Press, 1997.

Gerteis, Louis S. *Civil War St. Louis.* Lawrence: University Press of Kansas, 2001.

Glad, Paul W. *The Trumpet Soundeth: William Jennings Bryan and the Democracy, 1896–1912.* Lincoln: University of Nebraska Press, 1960.

Goodloe, Daniel R. "Resources and Industrial Condition of the Southern States." In *Report of the Commission of Agriculture for the Year 1865.* Washington, D.C., 1866.

Grant, U. S. *Personal Memoirs of U. S. Grant.* Vol. 1. New York: Charles L. Webster, 1885.

Grantham, Dewey W. *The Life and Death of the Solid South: A Political History.* Lexington: University Press of Kentucky, 1989.

Green, Thomas Marshall. *Historic Families of Kentucky.* Cincinnati: Robert Clarke, 1899.

Hafendorfer, Kenneth A. *They Died by Twos and Tens: The Confederate Cavalry in the Kentucky Campaign of 1862.* Louisville: KH, 1995.

Hall, B. C., and C. T. Wood. *The South.* New York: Scribner's, 1995.

Hammond, Paul F. "Campaign of General E. Kirby Smith in Kentucky, in 1862." *Southern Historical Society Papers* 9 (1881): 225–33, 246–54, 289–97, 455–62.

Handy, Isaac. *United States Bonds; or, Duress by Federal Authority: A Journal of Current Events during an Imprisonment of Fifteen Months at Fort Delaware.* Baltimore: Turnbull Bros., 1874.

Hanna, A. J. *Flight into Oblivion.* Baton Rouge: Louisiana State University Press, 1999.

Harrison, Lowell H. *The Antislavery Movement in Kentucky.* Lexington: University Press of Kentucky, 1978.

———. "General Basil W. Duke C.S.A." *Filson Club History Quarterly* 54 (January 1980): 5–36.

———, ed. *Kentucky's Governors: 1792–1985.* Lexington: University Press of Kentucky, 1985.

———. *Lincoln of Kentucky.* Lexington: University Press of Kentucky, 2000.

Headley, John W. *Confederate Operations in Canada and New York.* New York: Neale, 1906.

Henning, James W. "Basil Wilson Duke, 1838–1916: One of the Founders of the Filson Club." *Filson Club History Quarterly* 14 (April 1940): 59–64.

Hesseltine, William B. *Confederate Leaders in the South.* Baton Rouge: Louisiana State University Press, 1950.

———, ed. *Civil War Prisons.* Kent, Ohio: Kent State University Press, 1966.

Hier, Marshall D. "Basil W. Duke, Legend Made Vivid." *St. Louis Bar Journal* 43 (Fall 1996): 45–47.

Hinze, David C., and Karen Farnham. *The Battle of Carthage: Border War in Southwest Missouri, July 5, 1861.* Campbell, Calif.: Decapo, 1997.

History of the Ohio Falls Cities, and Their Counties with Illustrations and Biographical Sketches. Vol. 1. Cleveland: L. A. Williams, 1883.

Holland, Cecil Fletcher. *Morgan and His Raiders.* New York: Macmillan Company, 1943.

Horan, James D. *Confederate Agent: A Discovery in History.* New York: Crown, 1954.

Horn, Stanley F. *The Army of the Tennessee.* Norman: University of Oklahoma Press, 1953.

Horwitz, Lester V. *The Longest Raid of the Civil War.* Cincinnati: Farmcourt, 1999.

Hughes, Nathaniel C., Jr. *General William J. Hardee: Old Reliable.* Wilmington, N.C.: Broadfoot, 1987.

———. *The Battle of Belmont: Grant Strikes South.* Chapel Hill: University of North Carolina Press, 1991.

Hughes, R. E., F. W. Schrader, and E. L. Williams. *That Kentucky Campaign; or, The Law, the Ballot and Its People in the Goebel-Taylor Contest.* Cincinnati: Robert Clarke, 1900.

Hummel, Jeffrey Rogers. *Emancipating Slaves, Enslaving Free Men.* Chicago: Open Court, 1996.

Hurst, Jack. *Nathan Bedford Forrest: A Biography.* New York: Knopf, 1993.

Jenkins, Kirk C. *The Battle Rages Higher: The Union Fifteenth Kentucky Infantry.* Lexington: University Press of Kentucky, 2003.

Jillison, Willard Rouse. *The Kentucky Land Grants.* Baltimore: Genealogical, 1994.

Johnson, Adam R. *The Partisan Rangers of the Confederate States Army: Memoirs of General Adam R. Johnson.* Edited by William J. Davis. Austin, Tex.: State House, 1995.

Johnson, E. Polk. *A History of Kentuckians: The Leaders and Representative Men in Commerce, Industry and Modern Activities.* Vol. 2. Chicago: Lewis, 1912.

Johnson, Robert Underwood, and Clarence Clough Buel, eds. *Battles and Leaders of the Civil War.* Vol. 1, *From Sumter to Shiloh.* Vol. 2., *North to Antietam.* Vol. 3, *Retreat from Gettysburg.* Vol. 4, *The Way to Appomattox.* New York: Century, 1887–88.

Johnson, Walter. *Soul by Soul: Life inside the Antebellum Slave Market.* Cambridge, Mass.: Harvard University Press, 1999.

Johnston, J. Stoddard, ed. *Memorial History of Louisville: From Its First Settlement to the Year 1896.* 2 vols. Louisville: American Biographical, 1896.

———. "Kentucky." In *Confederate Military History: A Library of Confederate and States History, Written by Distinguished Men of the South, and Edited by Gen. Clement A. Evans of Georgia,* vol. 9. Atlanta: Confederate, 1899.

Johnston, William Preston. "Albert Sidney Johnston at Shiloh." In *Battles and Leaders of the Civil War,* vol. 1, *From Sumter to Shiloh,* ed. Robert Underwood Johnson and Clarence Clough Buel. New York: Century, 1887. Reprint, New York: Thomas Yoseloff, 1956.

Jones, Archer. *Confederate Strategy from Shiloh to Vicksburg.* Baton Rouge: Louisiana State University Press, 1991.

Journal of the Regular Session of the House of Representatives of the Commonwealth of Kentucky. Frankfort, 1869.

Journal of the Regular Session of the Kentucky Senate. Frankfort, 1887.

Kinchen, Oscar A. *General Bennett Young.* West Hanover, Mass.: Christopher, 1981.

Kirkpatrick, Arthur R. "Missouri on the Eve of Civil War." *Missouri Historical Review* 55 (January 1961): 95–108.

———. "Missouri in the Early Months of the Civil War." *Missouri Historical Review* 55 (April 1961): 235–66.

Kirwan, A. D., ed. *Johnny Green of the Orphan Brigade.* Lexington: University Press of Kentucky, 2002.

Kleber, John E., ed. *The Encyclopedia of Louisville.* Lexington: University Press of Kentucky, 2001.

Klein, Maury. *History of the Louisville and Nashville Railroad.* New York: Macmillan, 1972.

Klotter, James C. *William Goebel: The Politics of Wrath.* Lexington: University Press of Kentucky, 1977.

———. *The Breckinridges of Kentucky, 1760–1981.* Lexington: University Press of Kentucky, 1986.

———. *Kentucky, Portrait in Paradox, 1900–1950.* Frankfort: Kentucky Historical Society, 1996.

Krick, Robert, K. *Neale Books: An Annotated Bibliography.* Dayton, Ohio: Morningside House, 1977.

Lafferty, John A., and Frances Henry Lafferty. *William Lafferty.* Cynthiana, Ky.: privately printed, 1921.

Lambert, D. Warren. *When the Ripe Pears Fell: The Battle of Richmond, Kentucky.* Richmond, Ky.: Madison County Historical Society, 1995.

Lambert, Fletcher T. "Free Silver and the Kentucky Democracy, 1891–1895." *Filson Club History Quarterly* 53 (April 1979): 145–77.

Lamers, William M. *The Edge of Glory: A Biography of General William S. Rosecrans, U.S.A.* New York: Harcourt, Brace & World, 1961.

Lee, Guy Carleton. "Guy Carleton Lee's Tribute to Gen. J. H. Morgan." *Confederate Veteran Magazine* 20 (December 1911): 568–71.

Levin, H. *Lawyers and Law Makers of Kentucky.* Chicago: Lewis, 1897.

Lindsley, John Berrien, ed. *The Military Annals of Tennessee, Confederate, First Series: Embracing a Review of Military Operations, with Regimental Histories and Memorial Rolls, Compiled from Original and Official Sources.* Vol. 2. Nashville: J. M. Lindsley, 1886. Reprint, Wilmington, N.C.: Broadfoot, 1995.

Logan, India. *W. P. Kelion Franklin Peddicord of Quirk's Scouts, Morgan's Cavalry CSA.* New York: Neale, 1908.

Longacre, Edward G. *From Union Stars to Top Hat: A Biography of the Extraordinary James Harrison Wilson.* Harrisburg, Pa.: Stackpole, 1972.

Lucas, Marion B. *A History of Blacks in Kentucky.* Vol. 1, *From Slavery to Segregation, 1760–1891.* Frankfort: Kentucky Historical Society, 1992.

Mackenzie, George Norbury. *Colonial Families of the United States of America.* Vol. 7. Baltimore: Seaforth, 1917.

Mackey, Robert. *The Uncivil War: Irregular Warfare in the Upper South, 1861–1865.* Norman: University of Oklahoma Press, 2004.

Mann, Ralph. "Ezekiel Count's Sand Lick Company: Civil War and Localism in the Mountain South." In *The Civil War in Appalachia: Collected Essays,* ed. Kenneth W. Noe and Shannon H. Wilson. Knoxville: University of Tennessee Press, 1997.

Marcosson, Isaac F. *Marse Henry: A Biography of Henry Watterson.* New York: Dodd, Mead, 1951.

Marriner, William M., ed. "Confederate History." *Southern Bivouac* 1 (October 1882): 79.

———, ed. "Organization of the Southern Historical Society." *Southern Bivouac* 1 (October 1882): 78–79.

Marvel, William. *Burnside.* Chapel Hill: University of North Carolina Press, 1991.

Mathias, Frank Furlong, ed. *Incidents and Experiences in the Life of Thomas W. Parsons, from 1826 to 1900.* Lexington: University Press of Kentucky, 1975.

McAfee, John J. *Kentucky Politicans: Sketches of Representative Corncrackers and Other Miscellany.* Louisville: Press of the Courier-Journal Job Printing, 1886.

McCreary, James Bennett. "The Journal of My Soldier's Life, Part 1." *Registry of the Kentucky State Historical Society* 33 (April 1935): 97–117.

———. "The Journal of My Soldier's Life, Part 2." *Registry of the Kentucky State Historical Society* 33 (July 1935): 192–211.

McDonald, W. N. "Lee's Retreat." *Southern Bivouac* 1 (September 1882): 28–34.

McDonald, W. N., and E. H. McDonald. "Peace." *Southern Bivouac* 2 (June 1884): 478–81.

McDonough, James Lee. *War in Kentucky: From Shiloh to Perryville.* Knoxville: University of Tennessee Press, 1994.

McPherson, James M. *Battle Cry of Freedom: The Civil War Era.* New York: Oxford University Press, 1988.

McWhiney, Grady. *Braxton Bragg and Confederate Defeat.* Vol. 1. Tuscaloosa: University of Alabama Press, 1991.

Meade, Robert Douthat. *Judah P. Benjamin: Confederate Statesman.* Baton Rouge: Louisiana State University Press, 2001.

Metzler, William E. *Morgan and His Dixie Cavaliers: A Biography of the Colorful Confederate General.* N.p.: privately printed, 1976.

Meyer, Duane C. *The Heritage of Missouri.* St. Louis: River City, 1982.

Miller, Caroline R., ed. *Battle of Augusta: Accounts by Colonel Basil Duke, Colonel Dr. Joshua T. Bradford.* Brooksville, Ky.: Bracken County Historical Society, 2003.

Moore, John C. "Missouri." In *Confederate Military History: A Library of Confederate States History, Written by Distinguished Men of the South, and Edited by Gen. Clement A. Evans of Georgia,* vol. 9. Atlanta: Confederate, 1896.

Morris, Roy, Jr. *Fraud of the Century: Rutherford B. Hayes, Samuel Tilden, and the Stolen Election of 1876.* New York: Simon & Schuster, 2003.

Morrison, Elting E., ed. *The Letters of Theodore Roosevelt.* 8 vols. Cambridge, Mass.: Harvard University Press, 1951–54.

Morton, M. B. *Kentuckians Are Different.* Louisville: Standard, 1938.

Mosgrove, George Dallas. *Kentucky Cavaliers in Dixie: Reminiscences of a Confederate Cavalryman.* Lincoln: University of Nebraska Press, 1999.

Mott, Frank Luther. *A History of the American Magazine.* 5 vols. Cambridge, Mass.: Harvard University Press, 1937.

Nevins, Allan. *Ordeal of the Union.* Vol. 1, *Fruits of Manifest Destiny, 1847–1852.* Vol. 2, *A House Dividing, 1852–1857.* New York: Scribner's, 1947.

———. *The Emergence of Lincoln.* Vol. 1, *Douglas, Buchanan, and Party Chaos, 1857–1859.* Vol. 2, *Prologue to Civil War, 1859–1861.* New York: Scribner's, 1950.

———. *The War for the Union.* Vol. 3, *The Organized War, 1863–1864.* New York: Scribner's, 1971.

Nichols, Ron. "Mill Springs: The First Battle of Kentucky." In *The Civil War in Kentucky: Battle for the Bluegrass State,* ed. Kent Masterson Brown. Mason City, Iowa: Savas, 2000.

Noe, Kenneth W., ed. *A Southern Boy in Blue: The Memoir of Marcus Woodcock, 9th Kentucky Infantry (USA).* Knoxville: University of Tennessee Press, 1996.

———. *Perryville: This Grand Havoc of Battle.* Lexington: University Press of Kentucky, 2001.

Nosworthy, Brent. *The Bloody Crucible of Courage: Fighting Methods and Combat Experience in the Civil War.* New York: Carroll & Graf, 2003.

Official Records of the Proceedings and Debates in the Constitutional Convention of Kentucky. Vol. 4. Frankfort, 1890.

Osborne, Charles C. *Jubal: The Life and Times of General Jubal A. Early, C.S.A.* Chapel Hill: University of North Carolina Press, 1992.

Otken, Charles H. *The Ills of the South; or, Related Causes to the General Prosperity of the Southern People.* New York: Putnam's, 1894.

Painter, Nell I. *Standing at Armageddon: The United States, 1877–1919.* New York: Norton, 1987.

———. *Southern History across the Color Line.* Chapel Hill: University of North Carolina Press, 2002.

Pape-Findley, Nancy. *The Invincibles: The Story of the Fourth Ohio Veteran Volunteer Cavalry, 1861–1865.* Tecumseh, Mich.: Blood Road, 2002.

Parks, Joseph Howard. *General Edmund Kirby Smith, C.S.A.* Baton Rouge: Louisiana State University Press, 1954.

Parr, Elizabeth L. "Kentucky's Overland Trade with the Anti-Bellum South." *Filson Club History Quarterly* 2 (October 1927): 71–81.

Paxton, W. M. *The Marshall Family.* Baltimore: Gateway, 1970.

Peckham, Jack. *General Nathaniel Lyon and Missouri in 1861.* New York: New York American News Co., 1866.

Penn, William R. *Rattling Spurs and Broad Rimmed Hats: The Civil War in Cynthiana and Harrison County, Kentucky.* Midway, Ky.: Battle Grove, 1995.

Perry, Robert. *Jack May's War: Colonel Andrew Jackson May and the Civil War in Eastern Kentucky, Eastern Tennessee and Southwest Virginia.* Jackson City, Tenn.: Intermountain, 1998.

Peters, Robert, and William Henry Perrin, eds. *History of Fayette County Kentucky, with an Outline Sketch of the Blue Grass Region.* Chicago: O. L. Baskin, 1882.

Phillips, Christopher. *Missouri's Confederate: Claiborne Fox Jackson and the Creation of Southern Identity in the Border West.* Columbia: University of Missouri Press, 2000.

Pinkerton, Allen. *Strikers, Communists, Tramps and Detectives.* New York: G. W. Carleton, 1880.

Plum, William R. *The Military Telegraph during the Civil War in the United States.* Vol. 1. Chicago: Jansen, McClurg, 1882.

Railey, William Edward. *History of Woodford County by Wm. E. Railey.* Versailles, Ky.: Woodford Improvement League, 1968.

Ramage, James A. *Rebel Raider: The Life of John Hunt Morgan.* Lexington: University Press of Kentucky, 1986.

———. *Gray Ghost: The Life of John Singleton Mosby.* Lexington: University Press of Kentucky, 1999.

———. "General John Hunt Morgan and His Great Raids into Kentucky." In *The Civil War in Kentucky: Battle for the Bluegrass State,* ed. Kent Masterson Brown. Mason City, Iowa: Savas, 2000.

Ranck, George W. *History of Lexington Kentucky: Its Early Annals and Recent Progress.* Cincinnati: Robert Clarke, 1872.

———. *Boonesborough: Its Founding, Pioneer Struggles, Indian Experiences, Transylvania Days, and Revolutionary Annals.* No. 16. Louisville: Filson Club, 1901.

Randall, J. G. *Lincoln and the South.* Baton Rouge: Louisiana State University Press, 1946.

Rankins, Walter. "Morgan's Cavalry and the Home Guard at Augusta, September 27, 1862." *Filson Club History Quarterly* 27 (October 1953): 308–19.

Reagan, John H. *Memoirs of John H. Reagan with Special Reference to Secession and the Civil War.* New York: Neale, 1906.

Reid, Samuel C., Jr. "The Capture and Wonderful Escape of General John Hunt Morgan as Reported by Samuel C. Reid, Jr., of the Atlanta Intelligencer, 1864." *Emory University Publications Series and Reprints, Series IV,* ed. Joseph J. Matthews. Atlanta: Emory University Press, 1947.

Rhea, William L. "Storming Bull's Gap." *Confederate Veteran Magazine* 25 (July 1917): 302.

Ridley, Bromfield L. "General John H. Morgan's War-Horse." *Confederate Veteran Magazine* 5 (December 1897): 627–28.

———. *Battle and Sketches of the Army of the Tennessee.* Mexico, Mo.: Missouri Printing and Publishing Co., 1906.

Roland, Charles. "The Confederate Defense of Kentucky." In *The Civil War in Kentucky: Battle for the Bluegrass State,* ed. Kent Masterson Brown. Mason City, Iowa: Savas, 2000.

Roosevelt, Theodore. "True Americans." In *The Works of Theodore Roosevelt,* vol. 18. New York: Scribner's, 1906.

Rosenberg, R. B., ed. "For the Sake of My Country: The Diary of Col. W. W. Ward, 9th Tennessee Cavalry, Morgan's Brigade C.S.A." *Journal of Confederate History* (Murfreesboro, Tenn.) 7 (1992): 1–164.

Rowland, Dunbar, ed. *Jefferson Davis, Constitutionalist: His Letters, Papers and Speeches.* 10 vols. Jackson: Mississippi Department of Archives and History, 1923.

Schlup, Leonard. "William Lindsay and the 1896 Party Crisis." *Register of the Kentucky Historical Society* 76 (January 1978): 22–33.

Schmant, Raymond H. "Two Letters of Bishop James F. Wood to Colonel Basil W. Duke, C.S.A. at Fort Delaware Prison." *Records of the American Catholic Historical Society of Philadelphia* 89 (March–December 1978): 118–22.

Scott, Robert Garth. *Forgotten Valor: The Memoirs, Journals and Civil War Letters of Orlando B. Willcox.* Kent, Ohio: Kent State University Press, 1999.

Sehlinger, Peter J. *Kentucky's Last Cavalier: General William Preston, 1816–1887.* Frankfort: Kentucky Historical Society, 2004.

Shaler, Nathaniel Southgate. "The Border State Men of the Civil War." *Atlantic Monthly* 69 (February 1892): 245–58.

Sherman, William T. *Memoirs of General W. T. Sherman.* Vol. 1. New York: Charles L. Webster, 1890.

Simmons, Flora E. *Complete Account of the John Hunt Morgan Raid through Kentucky, Indiana and Ohio in July 1863.* N.p.: privately printed, 1863.

Simon, John Y. "Lincoln, Grant and Kentucky in 1861." In *The Civil War in Kentucky: Battle for the Bluegrass State,* ed. Kent Masterson Brown. Mason City, Iowa: Savas, 2000.

Sipes, William B. *The Saber Regimen: The Seventh Pennsylvania Volunteer Cavalry.* Pottsville, Pa.: Miners, 1906.

Smith, John David, and William Cooper Jr., eds. *A Union Woman in Civil War Kentucky: The Diary of Frances Peter.* Lexington: University Press of Kentucky, 2000.

Smith, Sydney K. *Life and Record and Public Service of D. Howard Smith.* Louisville: Bradley & Gilbert, 1890.

Smith, Timothy B. *This Great Battlefield of Shiloh: History, Memory, and the Establishment of a Civil War National Park.* Knoxville: University of Tennessee Press, 2004.

Smith, Z. F. *The History of Kentucky.* 4th ed. Louisville: Prentice, 1901.

Snead, Thomas L. "The First Year of the War in Missouri." In *Battles and Leaders of the Civil War,* vol. 1, *From Sumter to Shiloh,* ed. Robert Underwood Johnson and Clarence Clough Buel. New York: Century, 1887. Reprint, New York: Thomas Yoseloff, 1956.

———. *The Fight for Missouri from the Election of Lincoln to the Death of Lyon.* New York: Scribner's, 1888.

Snyder, Robert. *A History of Georgetown College.* Georgetown, Ky.: Georgetown College, 1979.

Speed, Thomas. *The Union Cause in Kentucky.* New York: Putnam's, 1907.

Speer, Lonnie R. *Portals to Hell: Military Prisons of the Civil War.* Mechanicsburg, Pa.: Stackpole, 1987.

Sprague, Dean. *Freedom under Lincoln: Federal Power and Personal Liberty under the Strain of the Civil War.* Boston: Houghton Mifflin, 1965.

Stanton, Charles P. *The Henning and Duke Families of Louisville, Kentucky.* Louisville: privately printed, 1983.

Staples, Charles R. *The History of Pioneer Lexington, 1779–1800.* Lexington: University Press of Kentucky, 1996.

Starr, Stephen Z. *The War in the West, 1861–1865.* Vol. 3 of *The Union Cavalry in the Civil War.* Baton Rouge: Louisiana State University Press, 1985.

———. *Colonel Grenfell's Wars: The Life of a Soldier of Fortune.* Baton Rouge: Louisiana State University Press, 1995.

Swinford, Frances Keller, and Rebecca Keller Swinford. *The Great Elm Tree, Heritage of the Episcopal Diocese of Lexington.* Lexington: Faith House, 1969.

Tachau, Mary K. "The Making of a Railroad President: Milton Hanibal Smith and the L&N." *Filson Club History Quarterly* 43 (April 1969): 125–50.

Tapp, Hamilton, ed. "A Sketch of the Early Life and Service in the Confederate Army of Dr. John A. Lewis of Georgetown, Kentucky." *Register of the Kentucky Historical Society* 75 (April 1977): 121–31.

Tapp, Hamilton, and James C. Klotter. *Kentucky: Decades of Discord, 1865–1900.* Frankfort: Kentucky Historical Society, 1977.

"Taps." *Southern Bivouac* 1 (June 1883): 393.

Tarrant, Eastham. *The Wild Riders of the First Kentucky Cavalry.* Louisville: R. H. Carothers, 1894.

Taylor, David L. *With Bowie Knives and Pistols: Morgan's Raid in Indiana.* Lexington, Ind.: privately printed, 1993.

Thomas, Edison. *John Hunt Morgan and His Raiders.* Lexington: University Press of Kentucky, 1975.

———, ed. "Milton H. Smith Talks about the Goebel Affair." *Register of the Kentucky Historical Society* 78 (August 1980): 322–42.

Thompson, Carl N., ed. *Historical Collections of Brown County, Ohio.* Piqua, Ohio: Hammer Graphics, 1969.

Thompson, M. Jeff. *The Civil War Reminiscences of General M. Jeff Thompson.* Edited by Donald J. Stanton, Goodwin F. Berquist, and Paul C. Bowers. Dayton, Ohio: Morningside, 1988.

Tilford, John, Jr. "The Delicate Track: The L&N's Role in the Civil War." *Filson Club History Quarterly* 36 (July 1962): 209–21.

Tocqueville, Alexis de. *Democracy in America.* Translated by George Lawrence. Vol. 1. New York: Harper & Row, 1966.

Troutman, Richard L., ed. *The Heavens Are Weeping: The Diaries of George Richard Browder, 1852–1886.* Grand Rapids, Mich.: Zondervan, 1987.

Trudeau, Noah Andre. *Like Men of War: Black Troops in the Civil War, 1862–1865.* Edison, N.J.: Castle, 2002.

Tucker, Phillip Thomas. *The Forgotten Stonewall of the West: Major General John Stevens Bowen.* Macon, Ga.: Mercer University Press, 1997.

The United States Biographical Dictionary. Chicago: American Biographical, 1878.

United States Census, *Scott County, 1850.* Washington, D.C., 1850.

U.S. War Department. *The War of the Rebellion: A Compilation of the Official Records of the Union and Confederate Armies.* 129 vols. Washington, D.C., 1880–1901.

Vale, Joseph G. *Minty and the Cavalry: A History of Cavalry Campaigns in the Western Armies.* Harrisburg, Pa.: Edwin K. Meyers, 1886.

Wall, Joseph Frazier. *Henry Watterson: Reconstructed Rebel.* New York: Oxford University Press, 1956.

Wallace, Doris. "The Political Campaign of 1860 in Missouri." *Missouri Historical Review* 70 (January 1976): 162–83.

Ward, William S. *A Literary History of Kentucky.* Knoxville: University of Tennessee Press, 1988.

Watterson, Henry. *"Marse Henry": An Autobiography.* 2 vols. New York: G. H. Doran, 1919.

Weaver, Bill L. "Louisville Labor Disturbances, July, 1877." *Filson Club History Quarterly* 48 (April 1974): 177–86.

Webb, Ross A. "Kentucky: Pariah among the Elect." In *Radicalism, Racism and Party Realignment: The Border States during Reconstruction,* ed. Richard O. Curry. Baltimore: Johns Hopkins University Press, 1969.

———. *Kentucky in the Reconstruction Era.* Lexington: University Press of Kentucky, 1979.

Weeks, Mabel C., ed. "Teddy Roosevelt Spoke before the Filson Club: As Related by the Late Lewis A. Walker." *Filson Club History Quarterly* 32 (April 1958): 132–35.

Wellman, Manly Wade. *Giant in Gray: A Biography of Wade Hampton of South Carolina.* Dayton, Ohio: Morningside, 1988.

Wells, John Britton, III, and James M. Prichard. *10th Kentucky Cavalry C.S.A., May's Trimble-Diamonds, Yankee Chasers.* Baltimore: Gateway, 1996.

Wharton, Mary E., and Roger W. Barbour. *Bluegrass Land and Life.* Lexington: University Press of Kentucky, 1991.

Wheeler, Joseph. "An Effort to Rescue Jefferson Davis." *Century Magazine,* May 1898, 85–91.

Williams, Bryon. *History of Clermont and Brown Counties Ohio: A Reprint of the 1913 Edition with Index.* Vol. 1. Baltimore: Gateway, 1987.

Willis, George Lee. *Kentucky Democracy: A History of the Party and Its Representative Members, Past and Present.* Vol. 1. Louisville: Democratic Historical Society, 1935.

Wilson, Charles Reagan. *Baptized in Blood: The Religion of the Lost Cause, 1865–1920.* Athens: University of Georgia Press, 1980.

Wilson, Samuel L., and Temple Bodley. *History of Kentucky the Blue Grass State.* Vol. 3. Louisville: S. J. Clarke, 1928.

Wiltz, John Edward. "The 1895 Election: A Watershed in Kentucky Politics." *Filson Club History Quarterly* 37 (April 1963): 117–36.

Winter, William C. *The Civil War in St. Louis: A Guided Tour.* St. Louis: Missouri Historical Society Press, 1994.

Woodson, Urey. *The First New Dealer: William Goebel, His Origin, Ambitions, Achievements, His Assassination, Loss to a Nation, the Story of a Great Crime.* Louisville: Standard, 1939.

Woodward, C. Vann. *The Burdens of Southern History.* Rev. ed. Baton Rouge: Louisiana State University Press, 1991.

Wright, George C. *Life behind a Veil: Blacks in Louisville, Kentucky, 1865–1930.* Baton Rouge: Louisiana State University Press, 1985.

Wright, John D., Jr. *Transylvania, Tutor to the West.* Lexington: Transylvania University, 1975.

Wulsin, Lucien. *The Story of the Fourth Regiment Ohio Volunteer Cavalry.* Cincinnati: Charles H. Thomson, 1912.

Wyatt-Brown, Bertram. *Southern Honor: Ethics and Behavior in the Old South.* New York: Oxford University Press, 1982.

———. *The Shaping of Southern Culture: Honor, Grace, and War, 1760s–1880s.* Chapel Hill: University of North Carolina Press, 2001.

Wyeth, John Allen. *With Saber and Scalpel: The Autobiography of a Soldier and Surgeon.* New York: Harper Bros., 1914.

Yates, Sarah A., and Karen R. Gray. "Business Conflicts in the Mayoralty of Paul Booker Reed, 1885–1887." *Filson Club History Quarterly* 61 (July 1987): 295–314.

York, Bill. *John Fox, Jr.: Appalachian Author.* Jefferson, N.C.: McFarland, 2003.

Young, Bennett. *Confederate Wizards of the Saddle.* Boston: Chapple, 1914.

Newspapers

Blackwell's Edinburgh Magazine.
Century Magazine.
Cincinnati Commercial.
Cincinnati Enquirer.
Cincinnati Gazette.
Corydon Weekly Democrat.
Covington (Ky.) *Ledger.*
Lexington Herald.
Lexington Observer and Reporter.
Frankfort Tri-Weekly Yeoman.
Louisville Commercial.
Louisville Courier.
Louisville Courier-Journal.
Louisville Dispatch.
Louisville Evening Post.
Louisville Journal.
Louisville Times.
New English Weekly.
New York Times.
New York Tribune
Philadelphia Weekly Times.
Richmond (Va.) *Dispatch.*
St. Louis Dispatch.
St. Louis Missouri Republican.
Southern Illustrated News.
The Vidette.

Index